"I just look illegal."

Inscription on the T-shirt worn by San Francisco Giants
closing pitcher Sergio Romo at the team's public celebration
of its 2012 World Series victory

PRAISE FOR *PASSAIC*

"This book uncovers the human tragedy that all too often results from the U.S. immigration system. Superbly written and compellingly told, Kunstler's book should be read by all who care about justice in our nation. Debate about immigration reform must address the detention and deportation practices Kunstler describes. This book inspires a way forward to restore pride in America's image at home and abroad."

—POLLY J. PRICE, Professor of Law, Emory University

"Daniel Kunstler's impeccable depiction of the United State's inhumane and irrational immigration law and detention practices as told through one man's story is exceedingly timely. During the writing of this book, the public gradually awakened to the effects of the immigration enforcement practices described by Kunstler, once a secret known only by the jailers and those dedicated to human rights. Kunstler succeeds in taking a complex legal subject and making it a human story."

—MARIA BLANCO, Vice President, California Community Foundation; former Executive Director of Earl Warren Institute on Law and Social Policy, University of California, Berkeley

"Daniel Kunstler's compelling examination of Hemnauth Mohabir's journey through the byzantine U.S. immigration system is not only an important exposé of systematic injustice, but also a compelling and eminently readable reminder of the real-life consequences of modern immigration enforcement. Kunstler's narrative is a clarion call on behalf of the men, women and children caught up in the clutches of a broken and dehumanizing system."

—VINCE WARREN, Executive Director, Center for Constitutional Rights

Passaic

The True Story of One Man's Journey
Through American Immigration,
Detention and Deportation

Daniel Kunstler

TAMALPAIS
PRESS

Published in the United States by Tamalpais Press, 180 Harbor Drive, Suite 101, Sausalito, California 94965

Cover illustration: Kathryn Jacobi, www.kathrynjacobi.com
Cover design production: David Woods

Publishers Cataloging-in-Publication Data

Kunstler, Daniel.
   Passaic : the true story of one man's journey through American immigration, detention and deportation / Daniel Kunstler.
      p. cm.
   Includes bibliographical references and index.
   ISBN 978-0-9906831-0-0
   1. Mohabir, Hemnauth. 2. Immigrants—United States. 3. United
   States—Emigration and immigration—History. 4. United States—
   Emigration and immigration—Government policy. 5. Emigration
   and immigration law—United States.   I. Title.
   JV6455 .K91 2014
   304.8/73—dc23   2014914046

First Edition
LCCN: 2014914046
ISBN: 978-0-9906831-0-0

Academic and Educational Institutions, Professional Organizations and Corporations: Quantity discounts are available for educational and gift purposes. Book excerpts can also be created to fit specific needs. For information, please contact Tamalpais Press at the above address or the author through www.danielkunstler.com.

For
Bonnie, Joshua and Naomi

In memory of
Mike Kunstler
Josh Rosenthal

CONTENTS

1

DISBELIEF

ON THE EVE OF HEMNAUTH MOHABIR'S RETURN from Georgetown in Guyana to New York on the only aircraft operated by Guyana's short-lived and now-defunct flag carrier, both he and Rawti, his mother, had bad dreams. Rawti saw an apparition of her long-deceased husband. She took it as an omen. An omen of what, she could not explain, but she was certain the vision coincided with Hemnauth being present in her house after ten years away. The ghost stared at both of them in silence for a long spell and then left for whence he came, wherever that was.

In Hemnauth's dream, he is swimming in an ocean, far from any shore. He is fighting a seaborne wooden horse, which is trying to drown him. God, appearing sometimes as Jesus, sometimes as Krishna, arrives in a boat, with one hand raised. He calms the ocean. The horse becomes a raft and Hemnauth's salvation.

The dream is interlaced with a recurring one, the same Hemnauth had while sleeping in a Kmart parking lot on a long drive north along the eastern seaboard from Florida five years earlier, where he saw himself imprisoned for no particular offense. From the time he was a child, Hemnauth has recorded his dreams to memory and tried to interpret each of them. To this day he remains convinced that his dreams are revelatory, this latest one among them. He insists that I listen closely to his narration of them, and I comply.

It is April 2002. Mother and son are sitting in her kitchen on the morning of Hemnauth's departure, and she is giving him her parting admonishments.

Hemnauth's divorce from his wife, Rahoni, had been more bitter than it need have been, but the ex-spouses had gotten past the pain of it and are raising their boy, Kevin, together. Kevin is ten and was born an American.

"Look, son," the mother says. "I want you to go and be a good father to Kevin, and try to go back to Rahoni." Rawti's dogged attachment to matrimonial constancy had not diminished over the years of separation and upheaval that followed Hemnauth's emigration to the United States. Hemnauth may have felt warm to the idea at the time, and no doubt his relationship with Rahoni had emerged from its years in the wilderness and stepped into a brighter clearing. Yet to him that was all the more reason not to press his luck and place his bond with Kevin at risk, a bond many parents would envy. As I was later to observe, Hemnauth and Kevin resonate with one another wholly and unconditionally, and their relationship has survived circumstances that have conspired to crush it.

"Mom," Hemnauth answers, "I will go home, but I dream of shackles and chains, and I'll be a slave. I'll go and face it."

Rawti was not pleased with what she heard, and Hemnauth's dream frightened her all the more for having had one of her own. She tearfully implored her son to never speak of it again.

Hemnauth's airplane ride was uneventful. True, his dream of the previous night would not leave him as he flew north, but he did not read any immediate prediction of trouble into it. The lessons he draws from his dreams rarely flash alerts of imminent hazard, but warn him of dangers in the path of life without specifying the whens and wheres. So although U.S. immigration personnel were on high alert triggered by the still-recent September 11 attacks, Hemnauth did not suspect he would undergo particular scrutiny upon his arrival, nor did any such thought even cross his mind.

There were about half a dozen people in line ahead of him who glided through the immigration procedures without incident and advanced to the baggage claim and customs hall. When beckoned, Hemnauth stepped up to the officer's station and presented his Guyanese travel document and his green card. She took his papers and looked them over. They were unremarkable and her face registered no expression. She was all business. Then she typed his alien registration number into her computer terminal and read the result. Hemnauth could not see it, nor was he concerned that any problematic data might show up to impede his reentry into the country. His residency papers were in order.

Nevertheless, an alert must have popped onto the screen, for the officer told Hemnauth he would have to go to another room. She gave the room a name and pointed, but Hemnauth has forgotten what she called it. By all indications, it was the holding and processing area for travelers and returning residents for whom further clearance was required. The officer called a uniformed security guard to escort Hemnauth, lest he stray, although the escort was presented to him as a courtesy rather than a security precaution. The guard neither touched nor addressed him. Hemnauth's documents were placed in a large brown envelope that he carried himself.

The room was a secondary inspection area operated by U.S. Customs and Border Protection (CBP). It divided into two halves, with airport-style seating: benches secured to the floor and divided into individual spaces. Half of the room's occupants had free limbs, the other half were restrained. Hemnauth recalls chains secured to the benches. CBP has since claimed that they use only ankle bracelets.[1] In any event, Hemnauth was not cuffed when he first entered the room, and he took a seat among the unrestrained, assuming that there was some minor administrative mix-up that would be quickly resolved. For instance, it happens that a visitor may have qualified for multiple visas and that a decision must be made in secondary inspection as to which one applies. The cases requiring the restraints often involve document fraud or other criminal violations directly related to an individual's attempt to enter the country.[2] These can trigger a prosecution by the criminal justice system. Hemnauth had a green card, valid and current, right there in the big brown envelope.

Yet, after about a half an hour, Hemnauth noticed that a group of immigration officers had gathered in conference about his case. They were casting occasional glances toward him. Finally one of the officers approached him and recited his script: "You have violated immigration law. You will need to see an immigration judge." He did not volunteer any further explanation — none was in the script — until Hemnauth asked for one, nor did

---

1 Shea, "CBP Inspections at JFK."
2 Shea, "CBP Inspections at JFK."

he attempt to shield the discussion from onlookers.

An old misdemeanor charge had come back to bite him, for a petty offense that had occurred fully six years earlier. The officer told him that the specifics of the charge, possession of a controlled substance in the seventh degree, made him inadmissible. Period. Hemnauth immediately perceived the double jeopardy. "I already paid a fine," he told the officers, quite truthfully. A New York State jury and a judge had estimated his debt to society at $250, which he had long settled, along with a short suspension of his driver's license, and nothing more. He had been duly acquitted of other, more serious charges — felonies — by the same jury. At trial he had rebuffed all suggestions of a plea bargain, so there was no suggestion that he had gotten off lightly in exchange for testimony against another party.

What Hemnauth did not know was that immigration violations fall within the realm of civil code and redress is extracted separately from any criminal penalty, as a collateral consequence. So, in the eyes of the law, there is no double jeopardy implicit in exiling an individual from U.S. territory and away from his family, any more than there is against a reckless driver who has been fined and subsequently denied auto insurance. This is not to dismiss the reality of the double jeopardy imbedded in the deportation process, far from it: Deportation, particularly in the case of one whose criminal offense, long past, was trivial by the government's own tally, piles on the infinitely more severe penalty of exile, with forced separation from family and livelihood. It is punishment upon punishment regardless of the evasion of that fact in the text of the legal statutes. Hardliners might point to other instances where the collateral consequences of a conviction are deemed legally permissible, such as the eviction of a tenant from public housing pursuant to even a minor criminal offense. Such instances might appear equally troublesome as deportation viewed through a moral lens, since both imply official retribution beyond that imposed by a court of law; however, exile according to recognized norms of civilization we profess to defend stands apart for its severity.

Regardless, compared to the treatment consequent to stages of the process that were to follow later, the double jeopardy Hemnauth imagined at the time was but the tip of the iceberg. In the immediate, the position of his captors was that he should tell it to the judge. The immigration judge, that is.

Hemnauth looked toward the shackled side of the room. He had a lot of questions to which the officer had no answers, at least none they were willing to share spontaneously. Finally, Hemnauth asked, "What are you going to do with me? Are you going to lock me up?"

"We don't know. That's up to the officer." Hemnauth took that for a "yes."

The next officer was among a series of many, between varying stations in the chain of command and shift changes in CBP's holding facility at JFK. Apparently Hemnauth was to be assigned to a specific custody official, at least for the duration of the shift currently on duty. He would determine whether Hemnauth was a candidate for detention, unless there was some further procedural reason to defer a decision and carry it over to the next shift. No one had directly spoken of an arrest, but it seemed clear to Hemnauth that this is what was being arranged. The interminable wait, colorless bureaucracy and lumping amid dejected men, some shackled, were simply a means of softening him up and deflecting any resistance. Hemnauth ended up sitting through three shift changes.

After what seemed like an eternity, another man arrived and took Hemnauth to a separate side room. It was now getting late in the evening. Rahoni and her sister, who had come to the airport to greet him, would have been waiting ever more frantically as the hours passed. That was of no concern to the officer, with whom Hemnauth was now alone. The man interrogated Hemnauth in a cynical tone designed to diminish him. "He was unfriendly in a smiling way." Hemnauth began to feel like a terror suspect and the effect was crushing: "I was suffocating." The officer bombarded him with questions focused on the history of his whereabouts and associations, particularly with organizations.

The line of questioning might have been understandable, perhaps even justified, had there been any debate or ambiguity as to why Hemnauth had been detained in the first place, any suspicion of violent associations or even the most casual encounter with persons or ideology hostile to the country. There was nothing of the sort. Simply an old — very old — drug-related misdemeanor had triggered a provision of immigration law that stipulated that Hemnauth be detained and tagged for removal. Period.

Every detail of the misdemeanor was immediately available to the immigration officers handling Hemnauth's situation. Hemnauth interpreted the stew of indifference, disdain and suspicion being fed to him plainly as a process of repeat criminalization and dehumanization. As we examine the process in retrospect, it is very hard to disagree. And what he went through at Kennedy Airport was but a mild foretaste of what was to come.

With another shift change, after midnight, Hemnauth was assigned to another CBP officer who first put him through the same wringer of questions, but then focused on the misdemeanor charge. Hemnauth explained what had happened, that it was a "really stupid thing." His explanations fell on deaf ears. Deaf ears are exactly what the law prescribed in his case. The questions were perfunctory and did not invite any defense, explanation of the circumstances or, for that matter, any latitude at all in the exchange between Hemnauth and his CBP captors.

Hemnauth asked the officer if someone could find out if this were indeed the case — that he was to be "locked up" — and turn his luggage over to his family. He was told that the rules did not provide for assistance with luggage or concern themselves with anyone who might be worried about a detainee's whereabouts. Still, the officer, of his own volition, did send a subordinate to collect Hemnauth's bags and call Rahoni on her mobile phone for her to retrieve them. However they offered her no further information on where Hemnauth was to be taken once they were through with him at the airport, let alone what was to ultimately become of him.

With the latest set of interrogations completed, Hemnauth was brought back into the larger holding space. He was told to sit on a bench among men in shackles. Eventually they give him a bologna sandwich — which his religion forbids him to eat — and a carton of fruit juice. The atmosphere was "already [that of] a prison."

There was another shift change in the early morning hours and, finally, the charges against Hemnauth were printed from a computer. An officer from the new shift walked over to Hemnauth and handed him a copy of the document with the charges stating a violation of immigration law. At this point, Hemnauth had been officially charged, and it was time to move to the next procedural directive. He had stopped counting the hours since he had stepped up to the booth of the agent clearing incoming passengers. The present officer in the relay sequence summoned a guard who now cuffed Hemnauth and shackled him to the bench. He was to be turned over to an INS officer assigned to accompany Hemnauth to wherever the Immigration and Naturalization Service meant to take him. Meanwhile he would wait, shackled to the bench.

"Am I going to jail?" Hemnauth asked.

"Yes," came the solemn response. "You are a detainee."

Among the immigration and detention personnel Hemnauth would encounter over the course of his two-year ordeal that was just commencing, several would display genuine empathy. Some understood, quickly and at a gut level, that Hemnauth was being subjected to treatment he did not deserve because of the mechanical rigidity of the then- (and still) current immigration statutes and the recipes of their enforcement. The officer who ordered the cuffs and shackles was the first among them. He actually encouraged Hemnauth to fight the charge and thought he could prevail. "Don't worry," he told Hemnauth. "You can win this." He added, "It's a procedure. I'm just doing my job." The interesting phenomenon, and one that would recur, is that over the course of Hemnauth's ordeal, many personnel assigned to apply the immigration statutes and standards deplored their use in this instance. They ranged from the first officer to cuff Hemnauth, to the judge who signed his deportation order, to the transit agent who delivered him to his exile two years later — and actually removed the cuffs earlier than prescribed in order to grant Hemnauth a measure of dignity as he took his last steps on U.S. soil.

Hemnauth sat around for another four hours in his shackles. The bologna sandwiches he could not eat and the juice boxes kept on coming. Hemnauth did not speak to anyone, partly by choice, partly because the people around him, most or all of apparent Middle Eastern origin, were speaking languages he did not understand and could not identify. I asked him if any of the detainees were white. None were.

Finally, two INS transit agents in green uniforms arrived. Hemnauth describes them as stocky "tough cop" types. They were cordial to the extent they were benignly indifferent to the people in their custody and did not care enough about them to be unpleasant. "Like they were picking up a box [they needed] to deliver and take it to a warehouse. They didn't seem to care about what they were doing." One does not bother to harass packaged merchandise or, for that matter, engage it in any way.

U.S. Department of Justice
Immigration and Naturalization Service   Notice to Appear

In removal proceedings under section 240 of the Immigration and Nationality Act

File No: A 44-267-779

In the Matter of:
Respondent: MOHABIR   Hemnauth
A/K/A   MOHABIR   Hemnauth   currently residing at:

     (Number, street, city, state and ZIP code)   (Area code and phone number)

[X]   1. You are an arriving alien.
[ ]   2. You are an alien present in the United States who has not been admitted or paroled.
[ ]   3. You have been admitted to the United States, but are deportable for the reasons stated below.

The Service alleges that you:

    1. You are not a citizen or national of the United States.
    2. You are a native of   Guyana   and a citizen of
    Guyana

SEE ATTACHED I-831 FOR CONTINUED ALLEGATIONS.

On the basis of the foregoing, it is charged that you are subject to removal from the United States pursuant to the following provision(s) of law:

SEE ATTACHED I-831 FOR CHARGES

[ ]   This notice is being issued after an asylum officer has found that the respondent has demonstrated a credible fear of persecution.

[ ]   Section 235(b)(1) order was vacated pursuant to: ___ 8 CFR 208.30(f)(2)   ___ 8 CFR 235.3(b)(5)(iv)

YOU ARE ORDERED to appear before an immigration judge of the United States Department of Justice at:
    The Office of the Immigration Judge   Executive Office for Immigration Review

    (Complete Address of Immigration Court, Including Room Number, if any)
           to show why you should not be removed from the
(Date)   (Time)
United States based on the charge(s) set forth above.

Date: April 21, 2002

                        (Signature and Title of Issuing Officer)
                        II. A. Steinborn
                        NYCJFKIA , NEW YORK. NEW YORK
Form I-862(Rev. 3/22/99)   (City and State)

INS Form I-862, dated April 21, 2002, officially tagging Hemnauth as removable and ordering him to appear before an immigration judge. There is no hearing date set.

Form I-831 Continuation Page (Rev. 4/1, 9/2)

U.S. Department of Justice

Immigration and Naturalization Service Continuation Page for Form NTA

Alien's Name		File Number	Date
	MOHABIR Hemnauth		
AKA	MOHABIR Hemnauth	A 44-267-779	April 21, 2002

CHARGE(S)

Section 212(a)(2)(A)(i)(II)-Controlled Substance

Section 212(a)(2)(A)(i)(II) of the Immigration and Nationality Act, as amended, as any alien who has been convicted of, or admits having committed, or admits committing acts which constitute the essential elements of, a violation (or a conspiracy or attempt to violate any law) or regulation of a State, the United States, or a foreign country relating to a controlled substance (as defined in section 102 of the Controlled Substances Act, 21 U.S.C. 802)) is inadmissible.

U.S. Department of Justice

Immigration and Naturalization Service Continuation Page for Form NTA

Alien's Name		File Number	Date
	MOHABIR Hemnauth		
AKA	MOHABIR Hemnauth	A 44-267-779	April 21, 2002

ALLEGATIONS

3. You applied for admission to enter the United States at or near New York, New York on or about April 20, 2002.

4. At that time you applied for admission as a returning Lawful Permanent Resident presenting I-551 A 44-267-779.

5. You were convicted of the crime of Criminal Possession of a Controled substance in the 7th degree in violation of section 220.03 of the New York State Penal Code, pursuant to a judgement entered on or about September 16, 1997 by the Queens County Supreme court of the State of New York, under indictment number 20423928K, paid a fine of $250.00 and had your license suspended for six months.

Signature		Title	
		IMMIGRATION INSPECTOR	
		PAGE #	

INS Form I-831 specifying allegations and charges against Hemnauth. The invoked section of the immigration statutes, 212(a)(2)(A)(i)(II), would prove to be relentlessly rigid.

One of the agents unclipped Hemnauth from the bench and removed the shackles, but not the handcuffs. The reprieve was short. His escorts took him to a kind of storage room where the restraining irons were kept. The agents then uncuffed him and tossed the manacles and shackles into a box, only to pick out another set of restraints from a different bin. Apparently the INS transit agents have their own gear, which they must keep separate from what belongs to the airport crew and cannot be taken from the airport's premises. Or perhaps the new set was more elaborate. The agents placed the shackles around Hemnauth's ankles, as before, but the handcuffs came prefitted with chains; they wrapped them around his torso, keeping his hands up to and against his chest. They also confiscated the contents of his pockets and his handcrafted beret. The frog-walk they were dressing him for required the proper costume.

In this instance, "costume" truly fits the description. Hemnauth was being detained pursuant to a six-year-old petty misdemeanor, not to a crime of violence or even unruliness. Part of the conceit embedded in immigration enforcement regulations was to magnify his criminal persona by dressing him in the feathers of a hardened miscreant. As we shall later see, the 1996 immigration statutes liberally upgrade small offenses to "aggravated felonies" or crimes "of moral turpitude," terms of art more than legal categories derived from specific state or federal statutes. All the better to conflate trivial misdemeanors with the most heinous of evils. All the better to impose terms of detention disproportionate to the risks to the public in violation of international law, as well as inflated bond requirements beyond the reach of most detainees. All the better to justify uncompromising deportations and harden public attitudes toward deportees.

The agents frog-walked Hemnauth through the crowded airport, provoking a small commotion. It was now well into the following morning, and the usual daytime hordes of arriving and departing passengers crowded the terminal. Everyone stared at the scene. The way Hemnauth was elaborately trussed, his dark complexion, and the short months since 9/11 would have had many suspect he was a dangerous criminal or, worse and more likely, a foiled terrorist. The humiliation was a crushing, unbearable agony. It played out for Hemnauth in slow motion worthy of an R-rated horror movie. He told me that he felt like dropping dead. Even days later into our session in Trinidad — where I had traveled to interview him over five days — after Hemnauth had chronicled for me a glut of numbing accounts of mistreatment, from malnutrition to violent physical abuse and everything in between, he highlights the humiliation of disapproving stares as the source of his worst moments of suffering.

Barring death, Hemnauth suggested to his escort that they simply put him on the next flight back to Guyana. He felt he was sliding into a bottomless canyon from which he would never resurface. The sensations of irreversible doom, of being buried alive, were amplified by the intractable, just-doing-my-job indifference of a series of handlers. True, one man in the chain had suggested he fight his deportation, although the word had not yet been spoken, but even he was just a cog in a process moving inexorably forward and would be quickly displaced by the next one.

"I was begging him to put me back on the plane," he later told me. "I had seen other people being put back on planes." The agent told him that might have been a possibility if Hemnauth had a return ticket, but under the circumstances the decision to purchase return passage fell to an immigration judge as did, by implication, his entire fate. No one else had such authority, certainly not an INS transit officer.

It had now been over twenty-four hours since Hemnauth had landed at Kennedy. The agent sat him in a van, where he waited another hour. He was left unsupervised, but still in his restraints. I asked him if there were bars over the windows. Thankfully, there were not. (I have since observed larger carriers, converted school buses, used by the immigration authorities. They do have bars.) The van finally left Kennedy with Hemnauth as its sole passenger, bound for Middlesex County Jail in central New Jersey, near the small city of New Brunswick, home of Rutgers University. Hemnauth remembers the journey taking several hours, although the distance is fifty-five miles by road, most of it highway, and normally takes about eighty minutes using the most direct itinerary. In any event, night had fallen by the time the van reached its destination.

Hemnauth continued to seek confirmation that he was being taken to prison, although given his restraints any other outcome would have seemed far-fetched. The driver made light of it in order to deflect questions and keep a presumably terrified passenger calm, even "making jokes about the whole thing." He had few comments Hemnauth could remember, except to repeat references to their destination as a detention center, not a jail.

"You'll have a lot of friends there," the driver told him, not facetiously. Getting no useful information, Hemnauth withdrew into himself, and, after a few more miles, the driver asked him what type of music he might enjoy from the radio. "I began to get the impression that, hey, this is the last I'll be able to hear music for a long time." He does not recall his selection.

Daniel Zwerdling is a seasoned and tenacious investigative reporter for National Public Radio. He does not have a particular "beat," as do, say, the White House, Afghanistan or economics correspondents. His segments are not the most frequent on NPR. They often are the product of painstaking research conducted over not days but several months. His delivery on the radio is scrupulously dispassionate, and his choice of words simple and clear, scrubbed of pretense and editorial jabbing.

The facts of his story, in this instance, were straightforward enough.

Hemnauth Mohabir was a commercial refrigeration technician by day and a performing musician by night. Guyana, his homeland, is a small country in South America measured by the size of its population. He had a green card and an American child, a son, born in New York. The government had voided his U.S. residency because of an ancient and petty misdemeanor conviction for simple drug possession. Although he had promptly paid the related and correspondingly piddling penalty — $250, the sentencing judge's assessment of an appropriate sanction, along with a six-month suspension of his driver's license — unbeknownst to him, the conviction, however minor the offense, had automatically tagged him an inadmissible alien and a target for removal. He was arrested, a full five years later, at Kennedy Airport in New York, by the Immigration and Naturalization Service as he reentered the country from a brief absence abroad to visit his mother. In addition to his young son, he had a steady job to return to in Manhattan, keeping the computer control room at Madison Square Garden cool enough to function without unscheduled interruption. Instead, the immigration service jailed him for two years, one of them at the Passaic County Jail in New Jersey. Then the government deported him.

The conditions of this man's detention and of those around him, right here on U.S. soil, were disturbingly reminiscent of Guantánamo Bay,

Bagram, "black sites" and Abu Ghraib: dogs sicced on prisoners ("detainees" in the official phraseology), beatings, guards gone wild, denial of adequate legal representation and protections, degrading strip searches, constant contempt laced with curses invoking a presumed promiscuity of the detainees and their mothers. Unlike "Gitmo," where the Bush administration showily thumbed its nose at *habeas corpus* and other constitutional guarantees from across a body of water, Passaic dodged the attention of the broad public and, until Daniel Zwerdling came along, the national broadcast media. A dehumanizing pit, with mold saturating its walls, neglectful and incompetent medical care, unsanitary plumbing and ventilation, a diet of feedings rather than meals: Even Zwerdling, eminently versed in how to be skeptical of government conduct, later told a public radio interviewer in New York that he "didn't believe it at first . . . I seriously did not believe it."[3]

What Zwerdling learned in his investigation should not have been a secret, neither then nor now. After all, the immigration enforcement service of the U.S. government has jurisdiction over the largest detention system in the country, larger than any state or federal prison system.[4] In fact, it has never been a secret at all, but rather a bleak demonstration of the blindness of those who will not see.

Many who worked in detention centers around the country and who, therefore, were familiar with the immigration detention regimen spoke openly of their misgivings[5] and even joined street demonstrations organized by civil rights or church groups to protest conditions in the detention centers. Newspapers from the *Miami Herald* to the *Dallas Morning News* and the *Los Angeles Times* have reported on detainee abuse and on the stonewalling of prison wardens, sheriffs and immigration authorities. The *New York Times* and the *Washington Post* have featured stories on the breathtaking displays of harshness or malfeasance by an immigration enforcement network comprising federal agencies, deputized state and local authorities, and contract jailers. In 2009, Amnesty International released a full and damning report, "Jailed without Justice," detailing the persistent lack of compliance of the U.S. immigration detention system with accepted norms of human rights and with its own declared standards. Amnesty's findings

3 Zwerdling and Casciato, "Investigating Abuse."
4 "TRAC Immigration: Huge Increase in Transfers of ICE Detainees."
5 Dow, *American Gulag: Inside U.S. Immigration Prisons.*

were largely ignored by broadcast and cable media, save for an allotment of 100 seconds — I counted them — on MSNBC. Finally, in October 2011, the investigative public television journal *Frontline*[6] reported on the aggressive government arrests of aliens under the Immigration and Customs Enforcement's Secure Communities program and — a rare occurrence on broadcast television — emphasized instances of parents forcibly separated by the American government from their American children. Yet the extent of the roundup of immigrants and of the deliberate denial of judicial protection for them remains unknown to many.

A Google search on Passaic County Jail, where Hemnauth Mohabir was held alongside its general prison population, yields a good many accounts of abuse, subterranean standards of hygiene and safety, corruption and violence. For a while, Passaic suffered some local notoriety for the conditions within its walls, although it has since fallen off the radar once trained on it.

And yet, relatively few Americans beyond the initiated — the inmates, their lawyers, their jailers, a cadre of journalists and civil rights activists — knew the full extent of the abuse being perpetrated in their name at Passaic, mere minutes from the bustle of Manhattan, or at similar detention facilities around the country, at the time of NPR's report. Or know now that federal law, judicial doctrine and political expediency conspired to permit it.

Today, as so many continue to struggle astride the tail of the mother of financial meltdowns, the old adage, that what appears too good to be true probably is, has come back into vogue from its years in a wilderness of suspended disbelief and delusion. "Too good to be true" has reclaimed its rightful place in the pantheon of precious pearls of wisdom, as livelihoods we once thought secure are subject to constant jeopardy. But when it comes to threats of embarrassment to our national self-image, like the medieval treatment of immigrants in our custody or the whimsy with which

---

6 Young, "Lost in Detention."

we exile them, the reverse adage might also have embedded our collective psyche. And unlike its mirror maxim, back from an extended furlough as a slogan-length explanation for the ruinous bursting of an economic bubble, it has never left: We are conditioned in our land of the free and the righteous to believe that what is *too bad to be true* probably is as well, despite contrary evidence floating around us like pollen. To our minds, American democracy, and commitment to freedom and virtue, are so superior to those of any other civilization in time or space that any violation of human rights in ours can only be the product of a rogue, not of our nation as a whole or its methods of government. Yes, indeed, Hemnauth Mohabir's story *is* too bad to be true, as are the stories others have told before and since. But true it is.

Even stagecraft can fall short in conveying the full drama of the reality unfolding in the shadows of our immigration and deportation system. *The Visitor* (2007) is an impressive and informative movie, perhaps even daring. It alerted those who saw it — a minority of moviegoers in search of enlightenment — to cruel, but lawful government policies of which they knew little. It does not sugarcoat the faceless intransigence of the INS's post-9/11 successor agency, the Bureau of Immigration and Customs Enforcement, commonly referred to as ICE. In a climactic scene, the main protagonist, a mournful and bland economics professor who has taken an accidental interest in an undocumented Syrian man facing deportation, explodes at the robotic, fluorescent-lit indifference of the man behind the reception desk at a detention center to the implications of what he does for a living, that it implicates him in the machinery of dehumanization. The deliberate anonymity of the detention facility is well conveyed: a windowless, warehouse-like structure with a single metal door in a dour Queens, New York neighborhood dominated by a mass transit rail yard.

With all this, the story unfolding on the screen, for all its drama, still understates the harshness of the system it tries to expose. The detainee portrayed in the movie is removed after ten days or so in captivity, not the months to years that people like the subject of this book have endured. And while the scenes of *The Visitor* shot in the detention center highlight the grimly featureless waiting room and automaton employees who point to a call center number posted on the wall in response to every query, we do not observe what goes on in the detainees' quarters. They are hidden from us. The imprisoned man tells of the despair he faces there. We do not witness it. *The Visitor*'s main protagonist, as heroic as he is, resides on the safe side of our immigration law's robotic lack of compassion and intransigent enforcement. We do not see attack dogs lunging at inmates.

The enforcement apparatus summarily sketched in *The Visitor* has become so entrenched that the Obama administration's desire, muted as it might be, to bring it to acceptable standards of human decency has required substantial commitments of political will in the face of restrictionist opposition to any immigration reform that mitigates the intransigence of the system's enforcement provisions, and to funding immigration policy prerogatives other than militarization of the southern border. And that is even before the most egregious flaws of the body of law regulating detention and deportation — a creation of the U.S. Congress that, ultimately, only it can adequately correct — even begin to get addressed in earnest.

When I first heard Hemnauth's story on the radio, my disbelief yielded quickly to the simple thesis that his substantive rights had been violated, that these rights were entitled to federal protection under the law, and that relief, if not for him at least for others in similar predicaments, would be expeditiously granted. If not immediately as a result of Daniel Zwerdling's reporting, later, once a more principled cadre of American leaders had replaced the then-current one. My faith in basic constitutional safeguards convinced me that Hemnauth's case raised such glaring issues of denial of rights and due process that a remedy would eventually be ordered by a contrite government or the Supreme Court, even one with Antonin Scalia as the Pied Piper of its majority. Hemnauth's imprisonment at Passaic also raised a legitimate concern about the anti-constitutional practice of cruel and unusual punishment by a state-sanctioned prison system. Its practitioners would surely face censure, sooner or later. In other words, Hemnauth's treatment was all a huge mistake, not a systemic practice.

This was all rather wishful thinking on the part of one caught in an idealistic crouch. As I gathered and asked my many questions in order to hone my understanding of how Hemnauth's ordeal could have conceivably been permitted under the rule of law, I confronted a web of legalistic rationale

and administrative guidelines that confirmed that, yes, indeed, the disposition of his case by our immigration enforcement system was permissible under federal rules and statutes, judicial doctrine and Supreme Court
precedent, however dated and misguided. Except maybe for the dogs, but
Passaic had discontinued their use in an effort to deflect further scrutiny.
Even a swaggering county sheriff can bear only so much comparison of
his jurisdiction to Abu Ghraib before altering his behavior. Although, on
second thought, if the more recent actions — and reelection — of Sheriff
Joe Arpaio of Maricopa County in Arizona are any indication, even that
assumption may prove to have been mistaken.

Yet explanations of rationale and procedure are not answers in any fundamental sense. They do not address, indeed they boldly sidestep, the overarching question of why Hemnauth Mohabir was treated as uncivilly as he
was. Of who had an interest in such an unforgiving disposition of his case
and in such blindness to his grievances. Of why international norms of
civilization and our own ideals were brushed aside in favor of government-
sanctioned ruthlessness, indeed were barely even considered. Of how a
system came into being that grafts atop a body of remarkably rigid federal immigration law an enforcement apparatus that has rarely been called
to account.

The exploration of these questions led me to places few Americans
want to go:

To the realization that the history of immigration and deportation in
America is studded with the passage of laws and court decisions that aim
to erect as high a barrier as possible between the rights of citizens and
those of aliens, including legally resident aliens, even though the Constitution makes little to no such distinction beyond the right to vote and be
elected to federal office. (The equal protection and due process language
of the Fourteenth Amendment refers, pointedly, to *persons*.)

That unconstrained executive and legislative power to exclude and
remove noncitizens has been a cornerstone of U.S. federal immigration
policy for over a hundred years.

That the government's sway over immigrants' rights has been reinforced
by the progressive imposition of an extra-Constitutional doctrine barring
scrutiny of immigration law by our federal court system, including the
Supreme Court.

That the same mindset and legal mechanics that enabled the banishment of Native Americans, the seizure of fugitive slaves, the Chinese Exclusion Act, the internment of citizens of Japanese extraction, the McCarran-Walter Act of the McCarthy era and other episodes of the American experience we would sooner forget reappear in our current immigration laws.

That the purpose of these laws, just like their antecedents, has not been merely to protect our borders and our sovereignty, but, through summary deportation of long-established resident aliens, to exert social, political — and, yes, racial — control over many who live among us and to subject them to our whims and bouts of paranoia.

That we deny persons in deportation proceedings access to the judicial system created under Article III of the Constitution, and hence to the comprehensive due process we are taught in grade school is the inalienable right not only of citizens, but of all persons present within our federal and state jurisdictions.

That the government can move detainees from jail to jail at will, without informing anyone, often in places far away from family members legally residing in the country, not to mention from their lawyers if they are fortunate enough to have a competent one.

That Congress and our immigration authorities have circumvented the constitutional proscription of double jeopardy with semantic hat tricks.

That with few exceptions, international law, treaties and conventions — even those our Senate has ratified — have no standing in immigration hearings, despite Americans' hyperventilated championship of human rights.

That the warm embrace of family values by our legislators does not extend to the recognition of a fundamental right to family integrity.

Hemnauth Mohabir's two years of imprisonment and subsequent exile are not even acknowledged as punishment, but rather as stations in an administrative process pursuant to a civil action on the part of the government, *not* a criminal charge. Never mind that one of the parties to the civil case, the INS succeeded by the Bureau of Immigration and Customs Enforcement (ICE), sets the rules of adjudication and controls the machinery of detention and deportation. To call Hemnauth's ordeal a punishment would have triggered pesky constitutional entitlements such as the right to an attorney, a trial before a jury of his peers, protection from double jeopardy and a modicum of proportionality of the penalty imposed to the infraction he may have committed. All were denied him. Instead Hemnauth Mohabir received two years imprisonment; permanent exile from his home; forced separation from his ten-year-old child; public hearings whilst in belly chains, handcuffs and leg irons; loss of employment; forfeiture of benefits he had paid for with his taxes; and threats to his health and his life. These brutal penalties amounted to supplemental retaliation by the government for an underlying misdemeanor, which, five years earlier, a court of justice deemed worth all of a $250 fine.

Hemnauth Mohabir is not a saint, and the pages that follow are not a hagiography. Like the rest of us, Hemnauth is of this earth. He has done a thing or two in his past that he regrets, likely with reason, and not done things he sorely wishes he had. For a time, he drifted and kept mischievous company in New York. He knows from experience that he does not tolerate alcohol and now avoids it.

Hemnauth is not even the worst case of suffering at the hands of ICE's immigrant detention and deportation apparatus. He couldn't be. The worst cases are dead.

Hemnauth Mohabir is simply a modest, soulful and guileless man. He is certainly not the "criminal alien" our immigration law's inflammatory and Orwellian lexicon labels him, not even close. He is more an exemplary than exceptional instance of an immigration enforcement apparatus impervious to history and the human condition, for there are countless other cases that share a like element of unrelenting official callousness, some of it explicitly sanctioned by Federal statutes, some of it not.

This is one good man's life story.

It is a story of law estranged from justice.

2

A Home Until It Wasn't

"WERE YOU HAPPY, AS A CHILD, IN GUYANA?" I asked Hemnauth Mohabir the first evening I spent taking his testimony in Chaguanas, a township in Trinidad to the south of Port of Spain. He lives in a section west of the central area called Felicity. He has left Guyana, perhaps permanently, perhaps not. That was the literal wording of my opening question to him. It sounds trite, but in the context it wasn't.

"At the time, yes," he answers, without hesitation. "But," he adds pensively, "Guyana has changed a lot, since then."

I have a long list of questions, but our discussion quickly becomes freeform and it will remain that way over its course. I tried to start from the beginning, to trace the full trajectory of a life stumbled on injustice, from where he had come to where forces more powerful than he had taken him, on a seeming whim.

He explained that he had a purpose in life, and despite the obstacles he always assumed he could pursue it on his own terms. This sense of purpose was how he thought he could define happiness under the circumstances that were, and are, his life. When he was at the deepest of his despair in immigration detention, the image of his childhood is among those that came the most often to him. Not a carefree time by any stretch of the imagination, but the furthest removed from the watch of a jailer reminding him of the futility of any aspiration of the spirit an inmate might harbor.

We are sitting in his apartment, a compact two-room corrugated shed attached to the larger home of his landlord. It is the first of the four days I will spend at the apartment, talking well into each night. Hemnauth occupies one of the rooms; his roommate, a pleasant thirty-something woman named Sherry, the other. They look after each other. She is not Hemnauth's love interest when I visit, although their relationship has deepened since. The furnishings consist of a bed, a spare cot, one chair, a desk and some shelves. The only closet is in Sherry's room. There is a refrigerator and a propane-fired pair of burners for cooking. There is running water, cold only, but, in the tropical Trinidadian heat, cold water works just fine. Three showers a day is the norm. Hemnauth's sole possessions are his few clothes, some pots and pans, disparate unmatched dishware, a small television set and DVD player, an old and beat-up nylon-string guitar and, hanging from a nail over one of the beds, a water pressure gauge with rubber tubes sprouting from it like the tentacles of an octopus. It is the essential tool of the more prosaic of Hemnauth's two trades, commercial refrigeration.

I have brought him a digital effects processor for electric guitars that he intends to use for performance gigs. Music making is his other trade, his true calling, and he has started to make some inroads as a performer in Trinidad. His stage name is Ravi. For the time being he borrows guitars when he has a live show for lack of a performance-worthy one of his own. Sherry does not possess much more than Hemnauth, save an impressive array of cosmetics.

Hemnauth had met me a few hours earlier on the sidewalk outside the airport terminal. I recognized him from a picture posted on the NPR website, and I had sent him a snapshot of myself. He is a bit slighter a man than I had expected. He looks younger than his forty-seven years, with unblemished nut-brown skin, jet-black hair and a gleaming smile. I had originally intended to book a room at a guesthouse in the capital, Port of Spain, fifteen miles north of Chaguanas by the trunk road, but Hemnauth thought it an unwise idea. By day the road is clogged. Too much time would have gone to transit. By night the road is a launch pad for armed robbery of taxi passengers. Crime has become increasingly abundant on Trinidad.

There are no hotels or inns in Chaguanas, as the town attracts only the most purposeful visitors who, like I did, tend to have private hosts. Hemnauth had originally made arrangements for me to stay at the temple where he worships, but he had had a recent falling out with the pandit and was awaiting an opportunity to patch things up. It turned out that I was the opportunity, but not immediate enough for the option of the guest room at the temple to materialize. Hemnauth is the first to admit that his temper can flare, like a fever left over from the disease that was his imprisonment and severance from his only child. One senses that he is just now beginning to shed the uneasy sensation that Trinidad is his place of exile rather than a new home.

Guyana was home.

Until it wasn't.

It has not been easy being Guyana, an improbable nation-state scooped from colonialism's twilight, and a poster child for its vagaries. Guyana covers an area roughly the size of the United Kingdom, its former ruler, and has a total population approximately equal to that of Austin, Texas. The populated regions are concentrated along the coast and the navigable stretches of the major rivers, near their estuaries. A 140-mile-long set of dikes protects the coastal strip from invasive seawater. Most of the country's territory is uninhabited rainforest, a naturalists' wonderland with hundreds, maybe even thousands, of uncatalogued animal species, along with free-roaming jaguar, tapirs, ocelots and giant otters. One of the largest freshwater fish on earth, the pirarucu, swims Guyana's rivers. The indigenous Amerindian population is miniscule, by most accounts less than 5% of the total. Guyana's people are in their vast majority the descendants of two waves of immigration, the first enslaved, the second indentured.

From the perspective of many outsiders, the seminal event of the country's history was a mass suicide and murder by poison at the hands of the Reverend Jim Jones, who unwittingly bequeathed to the vernacular the now-common expression "to drink the Kool Aid." Few who use the idiom today realize the horror of its genesis. The Jonestown massacre occurred more than thirty years ago, only a dozen later than Guyana's independence from Britain in 1966. Independence was less an achievement than the only possible outcome of the dismantling of Britain's colonial empire for one of its more remote colonies. Remote in every sense of the word.

As nation-states go, Guyana has had its work cut out for it from the start. Its citizens for their larger number are split between two ethnic groups, one of African origin, the other East Indian. The balance is made up of the

small minority of Amerindians, ethnic Chinese, Portuguese and a smatter-
ing of other Europeans. The two main groups have managed a tenuous co-
existence, but suspicion and resentment lie fitfully beneath the surface layer
of sovereign identity. (Trinidad, which has carried colonial baggage similar
to Guyana's, also left me with an impression of manufactured national
unity when I visited Hemnauth there.) Both ethnic groups have a legacy
of injustice, although not toward each other. Both were the tools of European colonialism, neither of them its beneficiaries. Still, when the masters
finally departed, they left behind accidental partners joined in a precarious
national experiment. It has survived thus far, but not always with ease.

Early sightings of the shores of Guyana by would-be conquistadores occurred at the end of the fifteenth century, the first by none other than
Christopher Columbus in 1493, followed in short order by Amerigo Ves-
pucci, Alonso de Ojeda and Vicente Pinzon. Roughly a century later, Sir
Walter Raleigh showed up in the neighborhood in search of El Dorado,
the fabled land of gold rumored to lie secluded up one of the rivers flow-
ing into the Atlantic, off the coast of what are now Guyana, Venezuela
and northeastern Brazil. Sir Walter's exploration failed, as did the overland
expeditions originating to the west, for the rather predictable reason that
El Dorado did not exist, no more than the equally legendary lake on whose
shores it was reputed to have been located. The lake, elusive to reality,
nevertheless figured on period maps.

The Dutch, embodied in their East India Company, appear to have been
peering further into a future that dispensed with the lunatic fantasy of a city
of gold, toward the possibility of settlement and cash crops. The English
and the French caught on quickly, and for two hundred years the threesome — or their privateers — squabbled tit-for-tat over who would plant
their flag where along the stretch of plain at South America's northeastern
corner, much of it below sea level.

Immigration to the "Land of the Three Rivers" (in point of fact, it has
many more) commenced in earnest in the middle of the eighteenth century
under the sponsorship of Holland, whose government offered land grants
and tax exemptions to Dutch settlers. The three rivers were the Essequibo,

Demerara and Berbice. They gave their names to the three colonies that later became British Guiana, and whose territory now makes up Guyana.

The English picked up the pace of colonization after Great Britain recaptured Guyana in 1803, and steered their investments most prominently toward sugar cane plantations fueled by slavery.

It is difficult to overstate the importance of sugar to the English colonial enterprise in the West Indies. Sugar went from being a luxury item in England at the beginning of eighteenth century to an indispensable consumer necessity by 1800 and the country's largest single import until at least 1820. The boom in the consumption of coffee, tea and cocoa produced collateral demand for sugar, in addition to England's outsized fondness for cakes and puddings. Per capita intake of sugar was twenty pounds a year in Britain in the early nineteenth century versus a tenth of that amount in France, the mark of a national addiction. It distorted the Englishman's diet, "distending his belly and rotting his teeth."[7]

Cheap labor was critical to sugar's economic profile and to the immense profitability of the plantations, and labor did not come any cheaper than slaves. The colonists attempted to capture indigenous Amerindian men to work the fields, but they proved inadaptable to slavery, meaning that knowing the bush, they were most adept at escaping into it. The alternative to the taming of the natives was the importation of slaves from Africa to an unfamiliar setting that left them few choices other than submission.

There was, however, a small miscalculation in the sugar planters' business plan. In 1807, Parliament outlawed the international slave trade. While the act did not outlaw slavery in the British colonies — nor the continuation of slaves' status as chattel rather than people, let alone citizens — the abolitionist movement had scored a major victory. It was only a question of time before slavery itself would formally end throughout the British Empire. In the United States, the 1807 decision was greeted with a shrug. For one thing, phobia toward the prospect of too many Africans on American soil had begun to build toward the end of the eighteenth century. More importantly, natural demographic expansion of the American slave population could ensure an ample supply of free farm labor in the slaveholding states, without recourse to the international slave trade.

---

7 Brendon, *Decline and Fall of the British Empire*.

The sugar, tobacco and coffee planters in British Guiana were not so fortunate. To be sure, momentum toward complete abolition slowed in the years following the 1807 abolitionist triumph. Still, after steadily growing from the time the Dutch East India Company first arrived on the scene, the slave population peaked and then dropped by about a third between 1807 and Britain's abolition of colonial slavery proper in 1833. The reasons for the decline were obvious in hindsight. Importation of slaves had ceased. Untreated disease along with other forms of abuse had exacerbated the decline in the number of live births. Accounts of the harsh mistreatment perpetrated by both Dutch and English settlers against their slaves in Guyana fit every stereotype of slave-era brutality.

So, between 1832 and 1833, plantation owners in Guyana were taken off guard by two events, neither of which should have come as a great surprise, but somehow did. First a census confirming the downward trend in the slave population in two of British Guiana's three districts, Demerara and Essequibo, followed by the resolution in the English House of Commons endorsing abolition in all overseas colonies. The planters' response, coordinated with the governor, was to search for loopholes and other ways to circumvent an abrupt depletion of their labor pool. The British governor initially tried to downplay the significance of emancipation, describing it as a general aspiration on the part of the Crown to improve the living conditions of its colonies' slave population with no immediate practical consequence or requirements. That went over like a lead balloon with the designated beneficiaries of emancipation. The slaves, keenly attuned to the radical distinction between bondage and liberty, were long prepared to greet the latter with considerable delight. A second strategy the planters attempted to deploy was to reclassify a number of slaves as apprentices with attendant obligations of service under terms of apprenticeship designed by those who formerly owned them. This plan did not work especially well either.

The plantations' fallback position lay in the hope that many former slaves would agree voluntarily to employment by their erstwhile masters — at bargain wages — rather than face the economic and social uncertainties that weigh upon the free. Again, the owners miscalculated. The emancipated slaves proved capable of organizing themselves into viable, if tenuous, communities, and even of negotiating the purchase of cultivatable land for their own use. In any event, they were disinclined to return to the service of those who had enslaved and brutally oppressed them, except on terms that gave them more bargaining power and freedom of movement. The sour-grapes, after-all-we've-done-for-them version of the period's history was quick to ascribe this reluctance to the defective character of black people and to refute their competency as free agents. One historian wrote, at the end of the nineteenth century, "Yet, with all their efforts to raise the negro and make him honest and industrious, the [British] missionaries could do little. The negroes did not want ruling by any one and would not govern themselves."[8] In the small island colonies of the Caribbean, such as Barbados and Antigua, former slaves indeed tended to stay on the established plantations, whereas the ample availability of arable land in Guyana offered an alternative.

Unless they were to scrap the entire sugar enterprise in British Guiana, the planters needed to devise another system for acquiring cheap — very cheap — manpower, contractually bound to their service and predictably pliant, a lighter version of servitude that would not run afoul of the Slavery Abolition Act. As is often the case, necessity sired invention. "Command of the labor market was the central political purpose of the planting interests, and . . . it rested primarily on a high level of Indian immigration," writes Stephen Spencer, a contemporary historian, describing the "economic supremacy of sugar" in Guyana.[9] And so, indenture came into being, the genesis of an expatriate East Indian social system and legacy in the Caribbean region into which Hemnauth Mohabir was born, a century and a half after its inception.

The first indentured immigrant ship to dock in Guyana arrived from Calcutta early in 1838, the date often given as the dawn of the indenture era in British Guiana and other colonies of the Caribbean region, as well as in South Africa, Mauritius and Fiji. The practice of indentured servitude was to last until 1920. The dominant majority of indentured arrivals in Guyana were recruited in East India and embarked in Calcutta or Madras. A 1911 census of 126,517

8 Rodway, *History of British Guiana.*
9 Spencer, *A Dream Deferred: Guyana, Identities Under the Colonial Shadow.*

Indians residing in British Guiana confirms this.[10] They were often referred to as "Gladstone Coolies," named for John Gladstone, a plantation owner, commodities merchant and the very first to dispatch a ship to Calcutta for the transport of 396 contract laborers from the Subcontinent to Guyana.

A critical — and rather fascinating — feature of the indenture system in the English colonies of the West Indies was its meticulous framework of regulation and record keeping. Thanks to the latter we know, with some accuracy, who came from where, and when.

The intent of drafting explicit rules was obvious. The planters, or whoever imported labor from afar, needed to shield themselves from suggestions that indenture was slavery by another name. The similarities could be disturbing. By spelling out a roster of rights and responsibilities endorsed by the English government, the system could draw a delineation that distinguished it from its ugly forebear, in addition to recruiting manpower rather than abducting it. At the outset, the Colonial Office appears to have been sincere in its desire to prevent reincarnation of slavery in the British West Indies. However, absolute protection of immigrant labor ran into direct conflict with the economic interests of the planters who formed the Caribbean plutocracy. With the help of the local colonial administration, the planters kept the pressure on the Colonial Government, representing the prerogatives of a home government intent on making abolition stick. Their objective was to obtain legal sanction for contracts binding indentured laborers to their employers for a fixed term, the longer the better. The Colonial Office grew gradually more sympathetic to the planters, who argued that the absence of enforceable employment contracts led to chaos in the labor pool. By any objective tally, the Colonial Office and its successor agencies remained sympathetic to the sugar plutocracy for the next 120 years.

The Sugar Duties Act of 1846 was the turning point. The sugar estates in the British West Indies lost their tariff protection, rendering them uncompetitive, particularly versus slaveholding rivals in Brazil and Cuba. The only solution was to work the cost and productivity variables of the sugar business model. Key to the solution was some measure of predictable loyalty and work habits on part of the laborers. The profile that finally emerged in Guyana and in Trinidad was a five-year commitment of the

_____

10 Lai, *Indentured Labor, Caribbean Sugar: Chinese and Indian Migrants to the British West Indies.*

indentured immigrant to his assigned plantation, mitigated by return passage to India at the maturity of the term, if desired, an elaborate code of reciprocal rights and responsibilities, government oversight at the points of departure and arrival, as well as subsidization of the system.

The appeal to the candidates for indenture was relief from grinding poverty, perpetuated by "the hardy weed called untouchability"[11] and from the prospect of early mortality in India. These were sufficient incentive for them to accept a human condition that straddled freedom and bondage and to remain in the West Indies permanently as the pioneers of a small diaspora. From 1838 to 1920, when the system was terminated, 238,909 Indians moved to Guyana as indentured laborers, more than to any other colony under European rule. True, the Indians were not a uniform or homogenous group. The differences resided in specific ethnicity, language and custom. There were periods of rift within the overall Indian population, often along a northern versus southern Indian divide, or one of caste. Still, they all shared an identity as subjects of a particular form of exploitive forced labor. Their descendants, Hemnauth among them, make up the majority of the country today.

In theory, the indenture system was based on the notion of a civil contract between an employer and a willing laborer, assumed to be equal partners in a pact of rights and responsibilities. In practice, of course, the rights accrued disproportionately to the planters, and the responsibilities weighed lopsidedly on the indentured. Transgressions by the indentured of the terms of his contract stood as crimes punishable by fines and imprisonment enforced by the authorities.

The rules were many and all encompassing. Pass laws, or their functional equivalents, severely restricted freedom of movement to a small radius — typically two miles — around the estate to which an indentured laborer was assigned. Absence from work was considered desertion carrying imprisonment and monetary penalties. There were regulations aimed at the quality of a laborer's output. Shortcomings could lead to criminal convictions before a magistrate, and often did. The bosses recruited trustees, known as *sirdars,* from among the Indians as informants and strongmen who regularly extracted bribes from the immigrant population.

---

11 Lelyveld, *Great Soul: Mahatma Gandhi and His Struggle with India.*

About the only offense for which an employer or his agent could theoretically face criminal penalties was physical assault of a worker. True, the indenture ordinances varied over time and came under the scrutiny of antislavery watchdogs in England. There were also provisions for adequate housing, care for the ill and the organization of Indian festivals. Labor strikes were forbidden by law, although they did occur, as did the use of armed force to quell them.

In short, throughout the Guyanese indenture era the sugar interests could call upon penal sanctions imposed by government authority for what amounted to breaches in a civil contract between them and their laborers, although it must be said that in the nineteenth century the practice was certainly not unheard of elsewhere. I cannot help but draw the parallel with our current deportation enforcement by a federal agency, replete with prisons and the use of force, whereas the government has been explicit in positioning immigration statutes as items of civil and not penal law. One normally thinks of a civil suit as resulting in proportional compensation that a responsible party must pay to one harmed by that party's deeds or neglect, with a court of law as arbiter. We do not associate a civil action with loss of liberty or other punishment normally reserved for criminal behavior. Yet our government does send civil immigration offenders to jail, as was typical in British Guyana under indenture.

Indenture was not slavery, with its drumbeat of savage cruelty. Yet indenture was no Garden of Eden, and the system was highly oppressive by any contemporary standard. Adding to the climate of subsistence-level living was a severe dearth of women in the Indian community. The immigration quota for much of the indenture period was forty women per one hundred men. The shortage had a degrading effect on sexual relations. Although the indenture ordinances by 1876 included a Compulsory Education Act, it appears to have been largely ignored by the colony, and the illiteracy rate remained high among East Indians. The Indians' imported rituals were spottily accommodated, with the authorities drawing the line at Hindu and Muslim weddings and cremations at the pyre in accordance with Hindu tradition. (The pyre was finally allowed in 1956, just one decade before independence.)

The indenture system had its overarching impact on wages, as indenture precluded an immigrant from seeking higher pay from a competing employer. Its point was to allow the sugar economy to extract as much labor as possible at as low as possible a cost. Drastically limiting movement beyond the plantation boundaries, through fear of penal sanction, was an effective mechanism for controlling output and pay.

The fear was genuine, and the planters definitely used the pass laws to keep their labor force under a heavy thumb. Passes were not rights, but privileges that could be granted as generously or parsimoniously as the planters and the police desired. Prosecutions were common. In fact, toward the end of the indenture era after the turn of the twentieth century, prosecutions of indentured Indians could number in the thousands in a single year. British Guiana appears from the historical record to have wielded the pass laws more vigorously than other English colonies in the West Indies, particularly Trinidad. In Guyana, indenture was the immediate successor to a brutal regime of slavery with its hardened attitudes toward plantation labor.[12]

Early in my time with Hemnauth, he spoke of the legacy of oppression in Guyana that has informed his life and inspired the songs he has written. That legacy and Hemnauth's interpretation of it have many components besides indenture, particularly the antagonism between the Afro-Caribbean and East Indian heritage groups. Still, indenture provided the historical springboard to his feelings and mindset. Indenture made him Guyanese.

Indeed, notwithstanding the exploitive nature — and purpose — of indenture, its salient feature was that it led to the permanent establishment of an immigrated East Indian majority presence in the overall population, albeit a narrow and diverse one, of the colony and later the country. Indenture led to reindenture, leading, eventually, to permanent settlement in the colony. By the time of the 1911 census, Guyana-born East Indians outnumbered immigrants.

Some of the immigrants began to trickle off the sugar plantations as the indenture era drew to a close. Still, the fizzling of the indenture system did not end the chronic penury of the East Indian population, nor did it necessarily curb the planters' proclivity to subject their labor to hardship. In fact, it appears the sugar industry was quite expert at compressing wages and manipulating work rules in order to extract costless additional work

---

12 Lai, *Indentured Labor.*

product. This situation far outlived indenture, by more than a half a century, and confined much of the Indo-Caribbean population to lives divided between backbreaking labor in the daylight hours and nights in leaking mud huts. Not surprisingly, labor unrest and violent repression intensified in the twilight of British colonialism.

No more surprising than the dissent in the ranks of the dispossessed was the growth of a populist surge that embraced a socialist message. It was embodied in Guyana's first national political party, the People's Progressive Party, or PPP, and in its charismatic leader, Cheddi Jagan. While Guyana remained a British colony until 1966, there was nominal local elected representation in the years prior to independence, including universal suffrage after 1953. It was a pattern repeated throughout the Empire. However, the elected legislative House of Assembly was held in check by a State Council of appointed members. Also, as the PPP organized as a bona fide political movement and emerged as a voice in Guyanese national affairs, English nerves began to fray. Arrangements would have to be made to ensure power was vested in a local government that would operate at the pleasure of the English and under the watchful eye of the United States.

Jagan's support of an assertive labor movement, his willingness to confront the sugar barons, his socialist ideology and, later, his cozying up to Fidel Castro — these were not the makings of endearment to the English or the Americans in their peak hour of anticommunist fervor. The English countered Jagan with little heed to subtlety and less effort to conceal their homage to American interests in the Caribbean. They suspended Guyana's new constitution and imprisoned political and labor activists on ideological grounds immediately after the 1953 revision granting universal suffrage in legislative contests. The day after the passage of a labor relations bill viewed unfavorably by the sugar industry, British troops stormed the colony and dismissed the local government.

The constitution was restored in 1957, but by then the PPP had already begun to fracture along a racial divide between East Indian and black. Three years of strife and intermittent rioting — some of it fomented by the CIA[13] — followed in the early sixties, and back came the English army to quell the violence and arbitrate between the PPP and the split-away black faction, the People's National Congress, or PNC, led by another charismatic figure, Linden Forbes Sampson ("Forbes") Burnham. The British, prodded by Washington, tweaked the electoral system to allow the PNC to thwart the demographic advantage of the East Indian political class by promoting a coalition with a smaller — and suitably conservative — party under a system of proportional representation designed to keep Jagan from power. The coalition took Guyana (the country's new name) through independence in 1966. The English hoped to have left behind a reliably pliant and reputable prospective member of the Commonwealth.

No such luck. Burnham concentrated increasing power into his own hands, virtually merged state with party, and in the process became the very despot and outward firebrand the Americans and the English had feared in Jagan. Burnham also succeeded in sapping the country's economy to the point that he needed to turn to the Soviet Bloc for assistance, which obliged with its usual altruistic motives. As it was, Guyana's fiscal fortunes were vulnerable to the vagaries of world demand for sugar and bauxite. Under Burnham, the hostility of the political elite toward the East Indian community severely undermined the education system and standards of public health, not to mention the tone of political discourse. Walter Rodney, a celebrated Pan-African scholar and political challenger, was but one of many victims of assassination during Burnham's long authoritarian tenure.

It ended in 1985 when Forbes Burnham died, at age sixty-two, while in hospital for throat surgery, leaving behind six children and a vast offshore fortune. His corpse was mummified at the Lenin Mausoleum, presumably as recompense for services rendered. Burnham was succeeded in office by an understudy, Hugh Desmond Hoyte, who split from Burnham's economic policy of wholesale nationalization paired with official corruption. By that point in the late 1980s, Guyana's economy simply could not take the punishment any longer, and Soviet patronage had long run out of steam. Electoral reform followed, and in 1992, Cheddi Jagan finally won his chance at office in a contest deemed generally fair by international standards.

---

13 Brendon, *Decline and Fall of the British Empire*.

Too little, too late. What can only be described as a Guyanese diaspora, rooted in indenture and slavery, had scattered in large numbers. The result is a population that has remained stagnant since independence, hardly a harbinger of lasting national prosperity. A society that has been kept from investing in itself. A tenuous union of two ethnic groups, both heirs of bondage, yet wary of each other.

Hemnauth Mohabir is a member of that diaspora. I did not use the term in speaking with him, simply because I did not think to do so in the days and evenings I spent with him in Trinidad. Since I am myself a product of a much different diaspora, I may have been subconsciously reluctant to paint my own attributes onto the canvas of Hemnauth's contrasting history. Still, the word applies to him. Hemnauth was born to people with shallow roots in a place where others had settled their recent forebears, leaving in the wake of colonialism a mortar of hostility, at times violent, between the groups the rulers had oppressed at the altar of cheap sugar. That a child of that diaspora might seek fulfillment elsewhere is unsurprising, perhaps even defensible. Colonial rule trivialized the attachment of those it indentured to Guyana as a homeland. Why should the colonial era's beneficiaries not reap what they have sown?

For certain, most every story of emigration is personal and circumstantially distinctive. Hemnauth Mohabir's, as we shall see, is no exception. While the theme of displacement by intractable forces emerges from his dreams — Hemnauth records his dreams and is prone to interpreting recurring keynotes — his departure from Guyana, as he describes it, was triggered in practice by events and choices peculiar to him. In a snowfall, every flake is its own crystal. Still, it takes little in the way of rationalization or theorizing to recognize Hemnauth as party to an exodus from a homeland of someone else's invention.

Hemnauth Mohabir was born into the tumult of Guyana's drawn-out transition from British colony to fragile nation-state on July 14, 1961.

Hemnauth is an astrological name given in accordance with East Indian custom. Several members of the extended family preferred he be named for the Bengali poet, polymath, artist and Nobel laureate Rabindranath Tagore,[14] at whose feet "the whole Western world paid homage,"[15] in the hope the child would become a writer. One uncle bolstered the suggestion with the gift of a Parker fountain pen, a singular luxury. Hemnauth's stage name, Ravi, pays tribute to both Rabindranath Tagore and *raga* master Ravi Shankar, and his family gladly adopted it once his musicianship bloomed.

Hemnauth's parents were ethnic East Indians. His father was Christian and his mother, still living as of this writing, is Hindu. Hemnauth paints a portrait of a family that seems to embody the struggle of a generation once removed from indenture to free itself of a legacy of confinement to the whims and estates of others. In the context of Guyana, one might argue that Hemnauth's family was successful — they were off the sugar plantation — but at a price that we, in richer places, would find too steep to even fathom.

Hemnauth describes his father as a barber, gardener, tailor and electrician from the Berbice colony of eastern Guyana. He worked in the laundry room of a public hospital in Georgetown and later as its resident handyman. But his salient avocation was drink. Each January, he would take a one-month leave of absence from his hospital job, tack it onto his December vacation break and devote the combined period to the methodical pursuit of drunkenness. His children were moved to their grandmother's house to provide a wide enough berth for the man and his alcohol. He died, Hemnauth tells me, when a hospital attempted to pump his empty stomach and botched the procedure, triggering some kind of lethal trauma. A doctor or paramedical staff reckoned the patient had poisoned himself, but the hospital coroner registered the cause of death as cirrhosis of the liver. I could not help but remark, wryly, that I did not see the difference. Hemnauth was twelve at his father's passing and his memory of him has dimmed, but not so much as to fail to recognize the symptoms of alienation and cultural displacement.

---

14 Tagore is also credited with having given Gandhi his honorific title *mahatma,* or "great soul." Two of his songs are the national anthems, respectively, of India and Bangladesh.

15 Yogananda, *Autobiography of a Yogi.*

"She's a darling lady," Hemnauth says of his mother, now in her late seventies (when I ask her age, Hemnauth calls her from his mobile phone to inquire) and still residing in Georgetown, Guyana. Out of context, Hemnauth's oath of reverence for his mother may ring like a familiar and universal cliché. However, his gratitude and admiration are not only sincere, but reasoned as well. She provided a model of self-sufficiency that her sons tried to follow with some, if not complete or constant, success. Hemnauth, for all his travails, has rarely, if ever, assumed he was entitled to anything but the most basic fairness. He is more concerned with his debts toward others than with what he might be owed.

He describes his mother as "a business type of woman" whose enterprises have included a farmers' market vegetable stand, stocked in part with produce from her own garden, and a bookstall. (That his mother ran small businesses in Georgetown was placed in evidence before the U.S. immigration courts to counter Hemnauth's claim — a legitimate one it turned out — that he risked persecution if he were returned to Guyana.) Alone she saved enough money after her husband's death to build a three-bedroom house for herself and her sons. Hemnauth singles out this accomplishment as a remarkable feat of strength; as a picture of Guyanese society becomes clearer to me, I easily believe him. She lives in the house she built to this day.

Other than his mother, Hemnauth does not dwell on family or forebears. He speaks of his three brothers with some detachment, and had I not asked he might hardly have mentioned them. Still, he emphasizes that he is close to them.

The eldest of the Mohabir brothers lives in southern Trinidad and works as a mechanic. For a period, he battled alcoholism, but has stopped drinking and escaped addiction.

His middle brother he describes as well educated and "the bright one." After graduating, which in the Guyanese context means passing the O-levels of the old British secondary system, he went into the bush and signed on to work in the gold mines. Malaria dispatched him back to town for a spell, but he has since returned to mining. Until recently he was part owner in a business selling automotive accessories. In 2008 the world food crisis hit Guyana, sending the price of rice and other food commodities into the stratosphere. The government of Guyana responded by restricting exports and distributing seeds to whoever would plant them, be it in the yards of their homes. Hemnauth's brother responded to the crisis by retreating to the hill country from the polder plains to grow his own crops. (Guyana, of course, has had plenty of prior experience with food shortages. After Forbes Burnham about-faced on his erstwhile patrons and nationalized commerce, Guyana suffered a long trade squeeze and few commodities entered the country.)

The youngest brother has two sons and a wife. He owns a bookstore, lives with his family on the lower storey of the house Hemnauth's mother built and looks after her in her elderly years.

But as we talk, Hemnauth seems eager to shift the conversation toward the topic that dominated his childhood, adolescence and beyond. Music still ranks as a motivating element of his life, along with his spiritual quests and his son Kevin.

As I noted earlier, when I asked Hemnauth if he had been happy as a child in Guyana, he unhesitatingly declared that he had been, then immediately qualified his answer. In short, he wishes the Guyana he knew through a young boy's eyes could have been frozen in time. That was never in the cards. "Leaving Guyana, going abroad, living abroad and going back to Guyana now, and finding the changes that have occurred, I cannot cope with it . . . The killing thing" — he means Guyana's deplorably high murder rate — "and then there's no music scene."

The "music scene" is of paramount importance to Hemnauth and always has been. He frames everything, from the narrative of his early years to his insights on race relations in the Caribbean and his spiritual predilections, within the context of the music he has played, and with or for whom he has played it. Indeed, music is the common thread through Hemnauth's life, even if it disappears occasionally into the folds of its fabric.

Like his brother, Hemnauth was drawn to the backcountry five years after leaving high school. He told me he was driven by curiosity. He injected a distinctively mystical ingredient into the experience, tinged with environmentalism, rather than merely surrender to the imperatives of survival, although those imperatives were certainly present in his mind. "As long as

I was livin' in a place that could grow food, I knew I would survive." He also went deeper into the jungle than his brother, and edged closer to the indigenous Amerindians in search of higher meaning within a lifestyle governed by subsistence and rural isolationism, in a place "where people rise and sleep with the sun": a call to primitivism that Hemnauth was willing to answer in full, not only in part.

He stayed for two years — far longer than required to satisfy fleeting curiosity about primitivism — in a mountainous region of the rainforest, along the Mazaruni River, about a hundred miles as the crow flies from Georgetown and the coastal areas, much farther by passable road, trail and waterway. He placed himself under the aegis of a Hindu sage named Narang, who had four acres; as many cows; and a credo that joined vegetarianism to sustainable agriculture, biodiversity and a gentle disdain for book learning. The prerequisite for this practice is, of course, a remote setting such as the rainforest can uniquely provide, beyond the gravitational pull of an interdependent society at large.

Narang had built an *ashram* on the site, a combination of Hindu temple, meditation space and yoga studio typically insulated from urban life. Where it is located within access of a large enough group of people to form a community, the ashram would also serve as a cultural center. On the small scale of a remote, miniature farm, the younger Hemnauth could find fulfillment in subsistence-level agriculture that happily abandoned a share of the crop to the creatures of the forest and had no ambition of bringing its fruits to market. The gist of Narang's Rousseau-esque philosophy was that whatever man planted was to be shared with the surroundings, to the pleasure of God. In the Guyanese rainforest, that meant monkeys by the thousands from deep in the jungle, in addition to worms, bugs and birds. There was no such thing as a parasite. The animals that raided Narang's crop were simply eating their due. What they left on the field was adequate to feed the farmer.

For a young man with an idealistic penchant stronger than the magnetic appeal of materialism, Narang's message was seductive, even if the remote yet real risk of encounter with a tiger was not. Equally appealing was the notion of rubbing shoulders with a native population far disconnected from the latter-day Guyanese majority whose citizenship was rooted in trans-oceanic immigration. The spiritual content was never lost; with Hemnauth it never is. When it comes to his religion, he accumulates, assimilates and synthesizes a wide spectrum of beliefs, from naturalism to the Hindu concept of karma, and even Christian notions of redemption and revelation. Still, life in the hinterland would not, could not hold him forever.

Talk of no music scene.

"I had this love for music, right, ever since I was a kid. I was always beating on things, banging on things." His talent appears to have drawn the attention of his teachers, and by his early teens he was well grounded in music theory, so well that picking up a variety of instruments became a matter of practice making perfect, and still is. At fifteen he was fluent enough in percussion, keyboards and especially guitar that he was playing professionally and being signed for gigs by nearly every performing act in Georgetown. It was a heady opportunity, notwithstanding the limited audience in Guyana.

Given the ethnic divide in Guyana, being solicited across the board was a notable accomplishment. Hemnauth does not boast while he is talking to me, but he was quite conscious of his crashing the racial gates. In a conversation we had on the phone much after my trip to Trinidad, he told me, wistfully, that "breaking barriers" of race was his unspoken — or, shall we say, unsung — objective in gigging with whomever he could. Another truth that went unmentioned at the time is that Hemnauth was attracted to the rhythms and textures of black music more than to the "chutney" genre hugely popular among the Indo-Caribbean public of Guyana, Trinidad and Suriname. Chutney also has a large following in immigrant communities from the West Indies in Canada, the United States and, so I hear, Holland. Chutney also grabbed a large place in Hemnauth's musical life and career, once he was asked to tour and when he lived amid an immigrant crowd himself in New York City. Chutney was also his steppingstone back into musicianship once he settled in Trinidad after his incarceration and deportation by the United States. However, to Hemnauth's developing ear, African music was more "intelligent." And those barriers were worth breaking, if only he could.

Ultimately — no surprise — he could not. Yet, by refusing to be limited to the music of his tribe, even at a very young age, he was able to blossom as a musician and garner recognition among those promoting a broad range of popular styles. It also enabled him to make some money, which he promptly blew, mostly by giving it away. Not big money, just twenty dollars here and there, but more than those around him could hope to have at any one time. He figured that since his mother provided him with the bare necessities of life, and that he did not need much more, he could make his friends happy.

Hemnauth's life as a budding artist, however, did not make his mother particularly happy, since he provided little evidence that the potential for earning a proper living existed in such a quixotic avocation. "She started to get frustrated with me and this band thing. So . . . she was telling me to get a job." In a poor country — and Guyana certainly is one — a son's deviation from a base level of material ambition is frightening, especially for a widowed mother whose husband has drowned in a brew of alcohol and despair.

Mrs. Mohabir brought the issue to a head when Hemnauth came due for his O-levels. The O (for "ordinary") levels of the General Certificate of Education (GCE) were the old British secondary school graduation exams that set the standard for scholastic aptitude. Guyana and several other former colonies continued to adhere to it long after their independence. She asked Hemnauth for which school subjects he intended to "write," the British formula that means to sit for an examination. She had set money aside to pay the fee. It was substantial enough to require the building of a budget reserve.

"I want to be a guitar player," Hemnauth exclaimed.

She hit him, yelling: "You're going to destroy your life."

"Mom, I'm serious about this thing. I want to play this thing. I love this thing."

A day or two later, Mom dragged her son off for a tongue-lashing to be delivered by two of her cousins, who served as surrogate fathers when she thought her sons in need of a dose of discipline administered by a male elder. One was an attorney, the other a magistrate, positions at a high rung of the social ladder in Guyana. She figured they would bring the boy to his senses.

They did not get very far in dissuading Hemnauth from his guitar and his bands. In any event, simply reversing course and declaring renewed fealty to his academic classes was not an option. For one thing, Hemnauth had liberally cut classes to spend most of the day in the school's music room during his fifth form, the last year of high school. It was behavior he could get away with. As long as he stayed on school grounds, no one suspected him of truancy even if he seemed to have a curiously large number of free periods in the school day. Still, it meant he had not completed a large swath of the curriculum. Worse, only one teacher agreed to allow him to sit for an O-level exam, one of four — English, math, history and art — he needed for the GCE. A teacher authorization was required for each examination in order to spare families the expense of the test fees if the student was not deemed likely to pass. In the end, Hemnauth took the one test and cut a deal with the dean for the others. He stayed in high school an additional year to prepare for his remaining O-levels under the dean's supervision. He pacified his mother and continued to study music just as before. The best of both worlds.

While it appeared the school dean was bending over backward to accommodate a wayward student, the special dispensation Hemnauth received was not a disinterested act of tolerance. The school often showcased Hemnauth as its eminent artist in residence, be it to impress whomever needed impressing — such as government officials — or, tellingly, at fundraisers.

As Hemnauth narrates his youth, the chronology can be nebulous, not because he is attempting to hide anything — he isn't — but rather because he tends to rank events, influences and relationships according to his perception of their importance rather than set them along a timeline. The small inconsistencies in his sequencing of milestones from his youth are inconsequential, and I came to appreciate as more valuable than proper dating Hemnauth's particular method of emphasis, despite his proclivity to recount certain important events as occurring sooner than they actually did. Later, as he underwent his ordeals in the United States, I did need to reconcile when Hemnauth situated events — incidents at jailhouses, court hearings, and the like — with dates I gathered independently, and sometimes correct Hemnauth's recollections of timing. Again, this does not reflect at all on the accuracy of his narrative.

Notwithstanding the wobbly chronology, a portrait of Hemnauth as a young man emerges clearly as we talk late into the night of my arrival in Trinidad. Here is a youth who, while not compliant with every rule, is neither a troublemaker nor an arrant goof-off. On the contrary, he has a definite purpose and the will to advocate for it. Behind the happy-go-lucky façade is a boy with enough self-awareness to work hard at a passion for music and look beyond what is immediately familiar to him. And as he grows into adulthood, he quenches his spiritual thirsts not with instant conformity to a text or to preaching, but far from them: in the jungle.

To his mother's infinite pleasure, Hemnauth did get a job when, as he puts it quite literally, he "came out of the jungle." And not just any job. A job in the government, at the Department of Culture within the ministry of the same name. The department was the interventionist branch of the ministry, leaving to question what the other branches did. It endowed artists, operated a national cultural center and ran the national school of dance. Hemnauth's specific function was to host foreign delegations of musicians, in many cases from Africa. Apparently the president's wife had taken on the project of disseminating Guyanese expertise in the musical syntax of steel drum bands and of bringing a steady stream of musical groups to Georgetown. Hemnauth was dispatched to perform with visiting ensembles. He also played the African drums, learned on the job, with the department's dance school and performance troupe. A loose hodgepodge of a profession, but at least it had the advantage of using Hemnauth's musical ability and of offering some job stability. It was bound to evolve, and it did. There was only so much one could accomplish as the official African drummer of a subministerial agency.

Hemnauth found himself in short order working directly for the rebranded Ministry of Mobilization and Culture, so designated as to associate culture with national unity, notwithstanding the stark ethnic divisions, or perhaps because of them. The Burnham-appointed minister — an uneducated individual whose main qualification was his love of calypso — was Hemnauth's immediate boss, and Hemnauth reported for daily duty at the main government office complex. He was assigned as a guitarist to an official government band dubbed the "People's Culture Corps" that played at all government functions and receptions. The band was the brainchild of a presidential advisor who thought that members of the cabinet and the parliament would reach better decisions if government musicians set the right mood before their legislative sessions. If the idea sounds ominously capricious, it is because it was. After Forbes Burnham's death, the new president disbanded The People's Culture Corps on the bizarrely disconnected pretext that it was costing money and not producing revenues. The musicians were summarily fired. "We received a letter and that was it."

By then Hemnauth was well into his twenties and had had a strong whiff of the corruption swirling around Guyana's ruling circle. "The dismantling of the [People's Culture Corps] was a wake-up call," he tells me. He was ready to be freed from officialdom and was sufficiently well established as a musician to be welcomed into other groups with open arms. He was also ready to write songs about what he had learned and sing them. "I'm beginning to see how Parliament operates, how the government operates. I find a lot of what they do is to benefit themselves and not the masses, the population. There was a lot of killing, basically.

"You could get locked up for just talking against the government. So our music couldn't really get played on the radio. We had no recordings. No one would record it. The most we had was [the opportunity] to go perform this music live. Most of the music we would play is the music about our struggle. And we would go play it live. So that was our newspaper, and that aspect I began to support. I am a [song]writer. I'll write a song and perform it. Sing about the oppression we are going through."

Hemnauth is not an ideologue, be it by nature, osmosis or learned reflection. The oppression from the Burnham regime, and only timidly addressed by his successor, was simply so unbearable as to provoke a reaction from anyone outside the circle of Burnham's patronage and not wholly paralyzed by fear. Hemnauth's response was to apply his métier to the cause of justice. The clenched-fist variety of protest — street demonstrations and the like — is not his style, and in the Guyanese context of the day would have landed him in jail, the morgue or both in rapid succession. And brought misery to everyone he knew.

The return to Guyana in 1974 of Walter Rodney, the renowned Pan-African scholar and civil rights activist, and his assassination by way of

a car bomb five years later were flashpoints in the country's history of
political turmoil, stoked by the Burnham government's incompetence, corruption, wanton repression and hypocrisy. Rodney had spent the bulk of
his adult years studying, lecturing and organizing in England, Africa, the
United States and Jamaica, from where he had been banned as subversive.
He had produced a huge body of scholarly writing on the theme of black
liberation. At the time of his return to Guyana, he was the closest thing the
country had to an internationally recognized household name.

Burnham had claim-jumped the title of guiding light of Guyanese so-
cialism — decorated by Fidel Castro himself, no less. To have a genuine intellectual with impeccable socialist credentials call his bluff was particularly
vexing for Burnham. Furthermore, Rodney was a proud black nationalist
and could not be dismissed as a malcontent from the politically disenfran-
chised East Indian side of the ethnic chasm. Rodney had to be stopped,
and Burnham had to make a big show of stopping him. After Burnham
overruled his appointment to a professorship at the University of Guyana,
Rodney focused his efforts on the promotion of a new political party, the
Working People's Alliance, in a direct challenge to Burnham. Subtlety was
absent Burnham's arsenal. He resorted to his prime areas of expertise: arbitrary arrest, police brutality and, when those failed, murder.

Rodney was a hero to his followers. To Hemnauth as well. A telling sign
in that Hemnauth belonged to an East Indian majority in Guyana that
to its chagrin held virtually no political power, and Rodney, while fiercely
opposed to Burnham, advocated in favor of black political emancipation
worldwide. Nor would Hemnauth have been attracted to Rodney out of
fealty to socialist doctrine. He had never studied it, and he was drawn more
to spiritual interpretations of the world around him than to theoretical
models. On the other hand, Rodney's message of liberation hit a resonant
chord.

Hemnauth sheepishly told me that when, by chance, he got to meet
Rodney in the street, he was in such awe of the man that he did not know
what to say other than to ask Rodney for the time. Rodney smiled and
glanced at his wristwatch: "It's ten to six."

Equally impressive were the armored vehicles and squadrons of restless
Burnham thugs who followed Rodney on his neighborhood tours. Impressive and very common. "They beat a lot of people up in the streets," says

Hemnauth. On the day Hemnauth got to shake hands with Rodney, the police charged his parade. Hemnauth saw Rodney escape by jumping onto a donkey cart and, once a fair distance from the cops, into a getaway car.

Hemnauth also found remarkable that so many of Guyana's educated elite would risk their livelihoods and face almost certain bodily harm by supporting Rodney, even to the point of joining street demonstrations. They had secure jobs and relative material privilege under Burnham, yet seemed ready to sacrifice them to support Rodney. It led Hemnauth to thinking of protest as a matter of conscience and integrity, not one of pure ideology, and not of a nature to grab him away from music and into other pursuits. That would require more radical changes in Hemnauth's circumstances. They would come later, but not much so.

"I had a dream one night that Lord Krishna, he came and he told me that he had a job for me. The next day when I woke up, the singer Lionel Abel knocked on my door." From what I gather, Lionel Abel was for all practical purposes the musical director of the People's Culture Corps. (It appears that he remains an active recording artist in Guyana. With a little digging, one can find his CDs for sale on websites, if not on Apple's iTunes site.) The People's Culture Corps lost its bureaucratic identity, along with the steady paychecks for its members, at the stroke of a political pen. Abel resurrected the band under an independent charter and gave it a new name, the "Mischievous Guys." He enlisted Hemnauth, first to fill in for the lead guitarist, then to replace him. Hemnauth's skill at improvisation is uncannily fluid, as I got to observe myself when I watched him audition in Trinidad. The skill made him a key asset for a band with loyal fans, constant bookings and little rehearsal time.

Going from gig to gig with the Mischievous Guys was definitely gratifying to him. The band performed almost every night. Hemnauth was now playing lead guitar for a successful group and earning a living at it, or at least a semblance of one. Hemnauth had nurtured his musical identity in a place where cultural allegiances tended to pull in one or the other specific direction. The People's Culture Corps and the Mischievous Guys recognized his versatility and carried him across the barriers he was born behind — and disliked. They did not, however, deflect his lingering affinity for Indian rhythm and melody, even less their potent spiritual underpinnings.

Hemnauth met his wife Rahoni while working in an Indian band, the "Merry Tones." Rahoni was a stage dancer for the group, originally the brainchild of a Hindu priest, or pandit, and domiciled in his temple. The dancing itself was not specifically religious, but rather of a semiclassical concert style featured in Indian movies and that had mutated into a form of entertainment popular at Indian weddings, parties and cultural events. Rahoni sang when the band performed at temple services. Hemnauth and Rahoni drew close while on tour with the Merry Tones in neighboring Suriname.

Rahoni was from a badly broken family. She had been previously married at a very young age, religiously if not legally — a tidbit Hemnauth omits and I later learn from Hemnauth's son Kevin, who speaks of his older half-brother. Rahoni's father had long left her mother and emigrated to the United States. He was pandit of his own temple in the Parkchester section of the Bronx. Her mother, a retired high school teacher, lived in Georgetown. She had turned to rum as a substitute for a family that had scattered to the winds.

The mother lived in the house owned by Rahoni's grandmother, who was often absent. The house was large by Guyana standards and sat on a full acre of land. It was too much for an untreated alcoholic to care for, so when the Merry Tones broke up, Hemnauth and Rahoni moved in in order to tend to the house and till the acre around it. Resourceful as ever, Hemnauth fertilized it with the dung of the neighbor's cow; the neighbor had previously shoveled muck into the street to dispose of it. Within two weeks of moving in, Hemnauth planted enough beans, corn and squash to survive — all organic thanks to the proximate cow. "It was a Rasta kind of life," Hemnauth says. He could cope. "I was a vegetarian, no salt [at the time], no meat." Actually, he did more than survive. When his first crop came in, he brought part of the harvest to his mother to sell from a stall at the market. Hemnauth's produce sold briskly, to the point that his mother received offers from an exporter for two basketfuls a week.

Hemnauth's dabbling in organic farming could not really last. He did not own the plot, and his tenancy screeched to a halt when Rahoni's grandmother returned to her property. He and Rahoni left Guyana to try to find new jobs and shelter in Suriname. The venture failed and the couple returned to Georgetown. What followed was a gradual unfolding of events that led to emigration, alienation, acquittal in a felony trial, further alienation, redemption, two years of immigration detention, deportation and, finally, the long task of wiggling free of a subsistence-level existence and the sensation of living in permanent exile.

Hemnauth was staying at his own mother's house and seeing Rahoni during the day while they tried to find a place to live together. Mrs. Mohabir's home was out of the question, despite it being ample to accommodate them. She had unyielding strictures when it came to men and women in cohabitation without the benefit of a writ of marriage. To this day, Hemnauth shields his mother from the contemporary realities of out-of-wedlock relationships, or at least does his best to. Shame to her is a source of real torment. In the meantime, Rahoni coped with her mother's rum-fueled demons, until she could no longer.

There is a pause before Hemnauth continues with the story. "Rahoni had a problem." From the way he says this, I infer an accident or an illness, but he is obviously dodging. As I press for clarification, he realizes that he cannot duck the details, as much as he wishes to respect his ex-wife's privacy. They are too central to his own narrative and to subsequent events. He takes a deep breath. "Okay. Here's what happened."

What had happened was that one evening Rahoni's mother had slashed at her with a knife while in their yard. Rahoni was trying to coax her out of an alcoholic frenzy. The blade slit Rahoni's lip and opened her finger to the bone. Hemnauth apparently was in the house, unaware of the magnitude of the commotion before Rahoni was injured and bleeding.

He got her to a doctor for stitches, but it was clear that if Hemnauth was serious about keeping his girlfriend from danger, he would have to act immediately and decisively on that commitment. That meant not returning Rahoni to her mother's home under any circumstances.

His own mother had made abundantly clear that only her sons' wives were welcome. Not their girlfriends. No exceptions. Mrs. Mohabir had not even met Rahoni, so unbending she was on the matter of extramarital intimacy. Sexual prudishness is as common and uncompromising among religiously conservative Guyanese Hindus as among fundamentalist Christians, Jews or Muslims. Hemnauth quietly gathered some sheets and cushions from the house and set up a makeshift bed in the yard. They were promptly discovered, to no one's surprise, least of all their own. Rahoni was sent to sleep, alone, in the house. Hemnauth camped outdoors. His mother served breakfast and then, without opening any margin for discussion, dispatched them to the nearest priest. He married them.

Although I have never been to one, I have heard and read many accounts of Hindu weddings lasting several days and rich in ritual. There is also a short form, the Indian equivalent to the shotgun ceremony. "It is called a Jaimala wedding," Hemnauth explains. In more elaborate affairs, Jaimala is the high point in a longer process. For Hemnauth and Rahoni, it was the only point. "We exchange rings, we garland each other and we go home." The next night, they both slept indoors. "That's when I took Rahoni as a wife. I took it seriously."

Taking it seriously seemed to have suited him. For a while, they did go from pillar to post, dependent on the kindness of clan for a roof over their heads. However, Georgetown is a small town, and Hemnauth, through his music, had grown close to the country's minister of labor, a Hindu. He, in turn, negotiated with a priest for the couple to live at a temple in the city center and, in return, provide a range of services, including cooking, some grounds maintenance and teaching. It was a sweet arrangement for a young artist and his cultured wife. They kept house together in the daytime, and Hemnauth played his gigs with the Mischievous Guys, mostly nearby, at night. He also took up painting, "temple art" on Hindu themes, to add to his panoply of artistic skills. Studious meditation as well. Both he and Rahoni taught music to the children of the congregation.

Learning to draw and paint competently and channel his inspiration through the graphic medium proved more than useful later: at the jail in Passaic, he made greeting cards for other prisoners who asked him, and most likely deflected some — though not all — of the hostility swirling around him in random patterns. It also preserved him from the utter despair that threatened his soul and his sanity. The prisons did not provide him with a guitar, and had they allowed him his own, guards would likely have destroyed it during one of their punitive rampages. He made gifts of paintings on paper and fabric to the civil rights professionals who took up his cause. (Rachel Meeropol at the Center for Constitutional Rights keeps a sample in her Manhattan office, which she showed me.)

The couple stayed at the temple for two years, apparently happy ones. "It was stress free," Hemnauth tells me. He had a job he could depend on — playing with the Mischievous Guys — and, from his modest perspective, he was "making some money." He adds: "It was one of the greatest times of my life, actually. I am among good people, learned people."

Also among influential people, at least on a Guyanese scale. Hemnauth's band performed regularly in a members-only club called "The Library," frequented by the local elite. Georgetown was not exactly the Court of St. James's, and even diplomats mixed readily and casually with the citizenry. A Jamaican high-ranking official at CARICOM — the economic alliance of fifteen Caribbean nations headquartered in Georgetown — and a classical guitarist himself showed up at The Library every evening. He was a big fan of the Mischievous Boys and particularly appreciative of Hemnauth's technique and style on the guitar. He was also a self-appointed, yet effective mover and shaker. He brought Hemnauth to the attention of a trumpetist by the name of Michael Basdeo, of whom Hemnauth was in total awe.

Basdeo promptly made an offer Hemnauth could not refuse: to join a large, diverse band called "Pete's Caribbean Fusion," the expanded embodiment of an earlier reggae ensemble called the "Wailing Starliners." Pete's Caribbean Fusion was to survive many years and through many changes in personnel. The better money alone was not the main attraction, but rather the opportunity for Hemnauth to give his musicianship a boost to the next rung of its ladder. The other band members were highly trained, experienced and rigorous professionals. There were seventeen of them: multiple horns, saxophones, guitars, keyboards, percussion, four singers and a full-time sound engineer. The band's launch was well funded and the equipment a musician's dream. They played everything from calypso to big band dance music to Indian pop.

If Hemnauth had any misgivings, they were limited to a pang of guilt on leaving the Mischievous Boys and to past connections between one of the band's promoters and enlightened government policies toward the indigenous population. When Hemnauth worked at the Ministry of Mobilization and Culture, he had observed official efforts to inculcate the

Amerindians of the rainforest with western cultural values. He believed such propaganda — he called it brainwashing — damaging to the Amerindians' own cultural values and environmentalist ethos.

Pete's Caribbean Fusion could fulfill Hemnauth's wildest hopes: to play in the multiethnic company of the cream of the musical crop around him and to tour internationally. They took their show all over the Caribbean region and to Canada. Europe and the United States were in their sights. It was starting to look like Hemnauth had a career in the making. He stayed with Pete's for two years.

Hemnauth's process of immigration to the United States began before he could fully realize it. Looking through the single lens of his early adulthood, one does not imagine Hemnauth as a poster child of the immigrant's experience. His circumstances and progress through life could have kept him happily in the place where he was born, even if his outlook on the world reached beyond the borders of a small country and past the confines of adequate survival. He was a person in full: thoughtful of his surroundings, ethically sensitive, materially self-sufficient, spiritually vibrant and disciplined in the pursuit of his passion for music and composing.

A single, unexpected catalyst pulled him back into a postcolonial context that contained the seeds of the emigration imperative as it applied to Hemnauth and Rahoni.

Shortly before Hemnauth joined Pete's Caribbean Fusion, Rahoni developed a health problem, which began to fester badly. I hasten to add that since neither I nor Hemnauth are doctors, I cannot vouch for the absolute accuracy of the pathology he described, but can only relate it with some speculation as to the exact nature of her illness. That said, I am confident that the broad brush of the description is true. The consequences for Hemnauth and Rahoni most certainly were.

Rahoni had contracted an infection of the tympanic membrane — the eardrum. She lived with the irritation until she began bleeding out of her ear canal. The doctor told her that the infection had ruptured the drum and begun eating at her skull. The infected areas would have to be removed surgically. Without the surgery, the infection could spread to her brain or trigger meningitis. In short, without decisive treatment, her life was in real danger.

The hitch was the fee for the operation. It was vastly more than Hemnauth and Rahoni had, and it puts Hemnauth's assessment, that he was "making some money," into stark perspective.

It is worth examining the numbers. The cost quoted by the doctor was 60,000 Guyanese dollars. At the time, the Guyanese currency was in the midst of a protracted slide. However, a reliable approximation of the U.S. dollar equivalent is $750. Hemnauth, despite "making some money" and not spending very much of it, did not have the funds. This is unsurprising. In 1990, 40% of the Guyanese workforce was earning the minimum wage of fifty cents *per day*. Enough for six eggs.[16] Per capita annual gross domestic product was less than $554.[17]

Rahoni had set aside $250 in savings from Hemnauth's earnings, a huge feat of thrift by Guyanese standards, yet only a third of what they needed to save Rahoni's life. They appealed for the balance to Rahoni's sister and father, both American citizens living in New York, along with Rahoni's brother.

There were two consequences of note. First, the operation was successful and, indeed, saved Rahoni's life. Second, her father, who hardly knew her, since he had abandoned his family when she was a small child, awoke to her existence. The doctor was an acquaintance of her father's and, according to Hemnauth, described to him how close his daughter had come to the brink. She convalesced in the care of the mother of a man he had never met. It was time for the father to make up for the years of neglect. He filed a petition for her entry to the United States as a permanent legal resident.

Over time, they decided she should go. It was not a snap decision; the protracted U.S. resident visa application process precluded that. There seems to have been an understanding that Hemnauth would follow at some point, although a loose one, and not a topic of debate or disagreement. There was no question of their separating. They were married in the eyes of the Hindu prophets and Hemnauth's mother, as well as their own. However, Hemnauth had a job he enjoyed, and Rahoni enjoyed his having it.

---

16 "Guyana's Economic Decline During 1985–1991."
17 "Human Development Report 2000," United Nations.

Besides, he was under contract with Pete's Caribbean Fusion and the band was touring regularly, notably to Canada. For her part, Rahoni was drawn to the notion of being among family, even if that meant a father and siblings she barely knew. In Guyana, her mother — and earlier Hemnauth's father — had fallen prey to alcoholism and dysfunction. Furthermore, her life had been threatened not just by the violence of her disturbed mother and the medical fact of her infection. The couple had been unable to pay for treatment but for the money from overseas. Such was the human condition in countries like Guyana where poverty is the norm. Survival hung by a thread, whether one was fully conscious of it or not. Under such conditions, when America beckons, one answers the call.

3

SCHOOL AND HARD KNOCKS

HEMNAUTH AND RAHONI SUSTAINED A LONG-DISTANCE relationship for about a year, but clearly the moment would come for him to follow her to New York. She applied for his green card soon after she arrived in the United States and established residency at her father's home. The time went by quickly for Hemnauth, for the most part, because he was often busy. His band was on tour in Canada for much of the year, playing before sellout crowds of up to a thousand people in Toronto, Montreal, Winnipeg and elsewhere, usually cities and towns hosting sizeable ethnic communities with whom resonated the black and Indian constituents of Caribbean reggae, calypso, chutney and pop. The band declined invitations to the United States out of solidarity with Hemnauth, who could not set foot in the country as long as his application for residency was pending. There was talk of touring Europe and even Japan. It was quite exhilarating. "I realized the band was going places."

Still, his days in Guyana when he was not on tour were lonely ones. He sorely missed Rahoni. He moved out of their home at the temple and back in with his mother, a return to a nest he had outgrown, and that could only have felt like a hiatus along the path of life even if, as Hemnauth declared to me, "I could not have found a better substitute for Rahoni than my mom. My mom helped pull me through Rahoni's departure." Nevertheless, he was flirting with depression, and he probably knew it. I did not press the point, but I got the impression that Rahoni's leaving at times left Hemnauth with the sensation of a permanent breakup.

It wasn't one. After a year, Rahoni returned to Georgetown and they were promptly married in a civil ceremony. Unlike the earlier, hurried exchange of vows and garlands, it produced a wedding certificate apt to be recognized as genuine and binding by government agencies both domestic to Guyana and foreign, including the U.S. Immigration and Naturalization Service. They still had to wait another full year for Hemnauth's petition to be processed and for a residency permit to finally be issued by the INS. Under the rules, Hemnauth could not visit his wife, no matter how lawful their marital status or Rahoni's immigration status — and by then she was a permanent legal resident awaiting naturalization living with her American citizen father, sister and brother. Rahoni managed to visit Hemnauth in Canada, when his band was there on tour, two or three times during the INS prohibition on his entering the United States. Rahoni had found steady work as a nanny for a New York State Civil Court judge later to be named state Supreme Court justice in Manhattan. Her Honor was apparently a very good employer and Rahoni has continued working for her, shifting through the years from child caregiver to overall household trustee after the judge's child had outgrown the need for a nanny.

Hemnauth's immigration was deliberate and methodical, not only in its dealings with officialdom, but in the way he and Rahoni prepared it. Their legal marriage in Georgetown was certainly part of the necessary bureaucratic routine for qualifying Hemnauth to enter the United States as a permanent legal resident like his wife. In addition, it served as a renewal of the vows made earlier before a Hindu priest with no legal standing. Rahoni apparently became satisfied that her traveling musician of a husband was true to his word and to her, and that he was not about to run off with a wide-eyed fan or roadie that might fall at his feet during a Canadian tour. I can well imagine — as Rahoni apparently did — the attraction of young women to Hemnauth and his easygoing charm. He is not a large man, but would definitely have qualified in the eyes of most as a very fit and handsome one: slim, yet muscular, with rich brown skin, a gleaming smile and eyes both playful and expressive.

Rahoni's pregnancy in the month following the second wedding was neither accident nor one-sided initiative. Kevin was a child desired by both his parents. They were of one mind about what kind of son they would raise. He would take from them a spiritual disposition sprung from the challenge of an uncharitable world, and from his American birth the opportunities offered by a modern democratic society. To what extent Kevin has complied with any preconceived notions of what kind of person he would be is hardly relevant. What he has become is a young man any parents would be proud to call their son.

Kevin — his certificate name is Ravindra, of the same root as the name proposed for Hemnauth by his mother's family — was born on February 17, 1992, in New York. His father, still barred from the United States owing to the pending residency petition, was not present. Hemnauth never expressed or implied to me that being absent from his son's birth was at all traumatic to him or Rahoni. Evidently, they were resigned to following the INS's bureaucratic processes to the letter, however Byzantine and studiously insensitive they might be. In any event, Rahoni traveled to Guyana soon after the birth so Hemnauth could hold his baby son. The family reunited again in Canada before Kevin's first birthday. Then, Hemnauth's green card finally materialized. He quit Pete's Caribbean Fusion and joined his wife and child in New York. As foretold as the trajectory might have been, it was still a leap into the unknown. How much of a leap, Hemnauth could not have fully appreciated.

The threesome moved in with Rahoni's father in the Parkchester section of the south Bronx, wedged between the Robert Moses Cross Bronx Expressway and the Amtrak and Metro North railroad tracks linking New York to southern New England. A cluster of a hundred or so ten-story red brick apartment buildings, arranged in a residential park formation in the northwest quadrant of the district, dominates the local cityscape. While the neighborhood attracts people of modest means, it is adequately served with shops, services and transportation. In Hemnauth's time, the area was generally peaceful, with crime pushed to its fringes by a security apparatus in the residential complex. Rahoni's father had a two-bedroom condominium near a subway line and the expressway. I can easily picture brokers, bankers and their attorneys with homes in the southern Westchester and Connecticut suburbs zipping past places like Parkchester on their way by the commuter rail to and from Larchmont, Greenwich and Darien, faces tucked inside the *Times* or the *Wall Street Journal* and scarcely aware of the communities they traversed twice a day. I should know: I was once one of them. If I had lived in one of the same suburbs, I might have done as they did.

The living arrangement could not have been ideal, and the couple most likely miscalculated the disruption such a radical displacement — from a sparsely populated former British colony in South America to a hulking metropolis, and from free-wheeling independence to the implicit oversight of Rahoni's father — would have on their relationship. The new environment also triggered compromises in some of their personal habits, which Hemnauth believes were equally significant and harmful.

"Rahoni and I, we were vegetarians, and so on. We begin to eat a little meat when we got there, and drink a little bit, both of us. Her dad used to drink a couple of Guinness when he came home from temple. Our relationship changed, our life style changed a lot. We started getting into arguments and stuff like that. It wasn't like back in Guyana where we had our own thing. Now most of her family was around her."

Hemnauth had also abandoned a musical career, which he had every reason to believe successful, and felt very much adrift. This chapter of his story seems so emblematic of the immigrant experience as to verge on the stereotypical: the promise of a fulfillment foretold but deferred, with the hope that the bumps on the road will not be so jarring as to throw him off its course. He played an occasional gig for one or the other Indian band, using a Squier Stratocaster guitar Rahoni bought for him. Still, it was a far cry from fully booked seasons with Pete's Caribbean Fusion.

She also bought him a bicycle, the tool of a transient trade. Rahoni's father was prodding him to earn a technical degree in air conditioning maintenance and repair. He had done some research. The profession was not overcrowded with aspirants, immigrants were welcome and the skill would retain its value in a market that was unlikely ever to erode. New York summers would forever be hot and humid. It made perfect sense to Hemnauth, and he was quite willing to follow his father-in-law's counsel. There was a school in Manhattan, a short walk from the Lexington Avenue subway line that also ran through Parkchester.

The hitch was that he needed to wait a year before he could qualify for a federal loan to fund his studies. In the interim, to help with the bills, he took a job as a bicycle courier for a messenger service based on 36th Street in Manhattan and owned by a fellow Guyanese. He was paid between two and five dollars per delivery, depending on the size of the package he carried, mostly documents for publishers, attorneys and the fashion industry.

He cycled all over Manhattan. The work yielded a small income in the aggregate, and Hemnauth professes to having enjoyed riding a bike, even in the dead of winter amid the peril of New York traffic. I can hardly imagine.

There was enough of a routine taking shape for Hemnauth and Rahoni to ponder getting out from under her father, or at least not living under the same roof. His was a domineering presence. Also, they still felt committed to the vegetarian diet of devout Hindus, whereas Rahoni's father played fast and loose with his devotion, despite being a Hindu priest. Alcohol also unnerved Hemnauth — it still does — and he did not want it in the house, where the temptation to imbibe would overwhelm him. Even without beer in the fridge, the temptation did not simply evaporate.

The family moved to Ozone Park, an ethnically diverse section of Queens near the Aqueduct Racetrack and JFK Airport, and a popular destination for new immigrants, particularly Indo-Caribbeans. They shared a plain, but comfortable house and the attendant rent with Rahoni's sister, along with her husband and child, a boy Kevin's age. (Oddly, Hemnauth never mentioned to me that Rahoni had another son, from a prior Jaimala wedding in Guyana when she was only fifteen. I learned this tidbit from Kevin after he made several references to his half-brother, to whom he is close.) The move was by and large successful. They liked the neighborhood. The tension of living in close quarters with Rahoni's father was gone. So was the meat that had rocked Hemnauth's religious vegetarianism. Hemnauth and Rahoni were both working. Hemnauth did not seem to mind the menial nature of a job delivering packages on a bicycle, and that he was a faceless entity to most people he encountered over the course of a day — except at the World Trade Center in the days after the 1993 attack, where his physical appearance set off suspicions that he was the next bomber. Banter at work was mainly confined to other bike messengers, including Guyanese who hired on to the same courier service as Hemnauth.

There was another benefit to living in Queens. It allowed Hemnauth to reconnect with some semblance of a life in music. A fellow Guyanese messenger introduced him to the owners of a rehearsal space and recording studio in the nearby Jamaica section. The rehearsal space was in a garage adjacent to a warehouse on 107th Avenue at Sutphin Boulevard. It would play a fateful role in later events.

When I later located the area on a map, I felt another guilty pang at realizing the indifference with which I had bisected this neighborhood so many times in a JFK-bound car coasting — or crawling — down the Van Wyck Expressway, oblivious to the humanity who called it home. Like many in the taxis and limos around me, I was more concerned with getting to my departure gate on time than in the sociology of the urban landscape. Although, to be fair to myself, I occasionally chose to use Atlantic Avenue as my route to the airport, partly as a hedge against highway traffic, partly out of interest in the other-world-out-there that was Queens.

The rehearsal space — or band room as Hemnauth calls it — served as a gathering site for a diverse cadre of musicians, mostly Indo-Caribbean and not necessarily connected to one another. They could just show up to practice, jam or check in to see if one or the other band needed personnel for a performance or a recording session at the owners' studio. Both the studio and the band room were well equipped with amplifiers, mixers, microphones, sound processors and recording consoles. There was a lot of coming and going to the band room, which, from the street, looked like any other unmarked garage in an area whose zoning permitted residences, retail commerce, warehousing and light industry.[18] The police eyed it suspiciously. The owners have since moved from New York.

Hemnauth also befriended a neighbor, yet another Guyanese of Indian extraction by the name of Vinod and a bandleader. They had been introduced through a mutual connection at Pete's Caribbean Fusion, and Vinod appears to have had an artistic association with Hemnauth's former colleagues. He had recently founded "Angels Caribbean Band," still active today with a full calendar of performances. As I continue to discover, there is a large and durable live audience for Indo-Caribbean music within the ethnic communities with which it resonates. With the recorded music industry in the midst of decline, live acts with frequent bookings at dance parties, festivals and concerts have a chance of survival enviable to most, even as they forego a standing on the charts.

---

18 "New York City Department of City Planning Jamaica Presentation."

After a year of relative tranquility in Queens, problems between Hemnauth and Rahoni bubbled to the surface of their relationship. As is often the case, there was no single given cause, although the inevitably slow adjustment to an alien environment and the attendant anxieties could only have been an eager host to the strains between them.

The sister-in-law with whom they shared lodgings moved further out on Long Island. Hemnauth and Rahoni could not afford the rent on the house in Queens alone and had to move not just to smaller quarters, but clear back to a less expensive apartment in the Bronx and closer to Rahoni's assertive father. The move put Hemnauth at a distance from his musician buddies, the rehearsal space and the recording studio, all of which served him as an existential crutch. He did not complain, yet it was one more step in a sequence of transformations, and not the last. The next step was to go to school and take up a new career, a project he could not complete overnight and that he would not have thought to undertake unprompted.

The suggestion that Rahoni's father had made, that Hemnauth acquire a degree in refrigeration and air conditioning, was not a bad one, far from it. He could hold out for music gigs instead, but he was a smaller fish in a New York pond much bigger than Guyana's and it could take years to build up prominence sufficient for him to escape low-paying daytime labor. Pete's Caribbean Fusion toured and performed for large audiences. In Hemnauth's day, the Angels Caribbean Band hired him sporadically for shows at schools and Indian weddings. School alone could justify his quitting the messenger job.

Now that he met eligibility requirements for financial aid, he moved to enroll at Apex Technical School near Union Square.

Apex is a commercial career-training institute housed in its own eight-story building outfitted with classrooms, workshops and a large street-level space for the automotive program. Hemnauth and presumably his father-in-law learned about Apex from television commercials. The school caters especially to black, Hispanic and immigrant male students aiming for a certificate in a technical specialty.

It is easy to dismiss a for-profit training business for non-college-bound men, whose recruitment methods include placards on subway cars and TV spots, certainly inspiration for skepticism. Easy and a little unfair. The evidence — including Hemnauth's own experience and outcome — suggests that Apex's product is pretty much as advertised. I visited the school myself in April 2009, admittedly long after Hemnauth had graduated, but the place seemed true to his description. There is an earnest concern for students and pride in the sentiment that the school is doing something useful for people whose alternative might be minimum wage and uncertain employment. The recruitment tools are what they are — media advertising and direct mail (which even the most prestigious colleges use in abundance) — because they are what is available to Apex's admissions officer; he has little access to high school guidance counselors, whose agenda is often college placement exclusively and does not extend to vocational training. At least that has been the officer's experience in the New York City school system.

The certificate Apex awards in refrigeration maintenance is a genuine credential that recognizes a student's completion of rigorous requirements, plus five years of cumulative internship after graduation, before being allowed by the rules of the trade to work for his own account or to go out to the field unsupervised. Hemnauth explains to me that the institutional refrigeration and climate systems he worked on were quite intricate. To work on them safely and effectively implied a high level of understanding of interlocking components, mechanical, electrical, electronic and chemical as well as of the measurement protocols embedded in the overall systems. Further, each individual system in a large installation in a city like New York tends to be distinctive, and the technician must be able to apply a systems approach to determining the schematics of each one and break it down into each of its components before proceeding with a diagnosis or a repair.

The requirements while enrolled at the school included 900 hours of class attendance and workshop, plus a considerable amount of homework, and even research projects and papers. The gentleman who ran Apex at the time Hemnauth attended was a retired military engineer who also insisted that his students learn the fundamental science underpinning the cooling, heating, automotive and electrical systems they were training to maintain. "When I began to apply [the science], I saw that it really did help," Hemnauth told me.

School also meant that Hemnauth's contribution to the family's finances dropped to zero and Rahoni had to shoulder the burden. She, of course, knew this would happen and far preferred having Hemnauth in a full-time program than at night school. However, it was one thing to anticipate the stress, another to live it. There were arguments about household chores, which Hemnauth skirted because of his homework. "I didn't cook, I didn't pick up my son from the babysitter. She expected me to do all these things. I was unable to do them because of the seriousness of the course." Even though Apex was a hands-on technical school, the book-bound academic load was more than Hemnauth was accustomed to, and probably more than Rahoni thought he had signed up for. They found themselves unprepared, in the proverbial it-sounded-like-a-good-idea-at-the-time situation. A good idea, but no silver bullet. They had neglected to translate 900 classroom hours into the tangible commitment they represented, namely a full academic year's course load with all the homework trimmings.

Compounding the general tension between them was the hit to Hemnauth's pride of needing to ask his breadwinner wife for carfare and lunch money. The new apartment was a half-basement on Havemeyer Avenue in the Bronx near the huge freeway interchange where the Bruckner and Cross Bronx Expressways converge to meet traffic coming off the Whitestone Bridge. I asked Hemnauth whether there were adequate windows. He describes small ones, at eye level, that let in light, not the kind you look through to observe life beyond your walls. The neighborhood of Hispanic, black and West Indian families was "peaceful enough." It was what they could afford on Rahoni's slim earnings.

The arguments became part of the daily routine, and Hemnauth's grades began to slide from As to Cs. Hemnauth had acquired a reputation for being an applied student, and a caring teacher confronted him. He appointed himself as Hemnauth's mentor and offered him extensions on assignments and other relief so that he might resolve his homebound issues and not put graduation in jeopardy. The school also gave Hemnauth a job mopping classroom floors before the night students arrived. It provided enough pocket money for Hemnauth to sidestep asking his wife for carfare every morning and duck the daily reminder of his dependency on her. The monetary breathing space and some flowers lessened the tension between Hemnauth and Rahoni momentarily, but there was still a lasting dent in the marriage.

It only took one more blow to deepen the dent beyond their repair. The blow was fueled by two six-packs of Guinness stout.

"As I drink, I have a tendency to always want to drink more. This is why I never liked the idea of drinking." The couple had spent an evening with Rahoni's sister and her husband, had bought beer on the way home and proceeded to consume their entire purchase. Neither of them drank regularly, and the effect might not have been all that calamitous if they were the kind of habitual drinkers who recognize the sensation of a bit too much beer for what it is. In this instance, the alcohol was so much salt for the open wounds in their marriage. An argument over some petty item turned loud. "We both were under the influence of the Guinness."

Rahoni ran outside and started a ruckus, with the neighbors looking on. Hemnauth followed, wanting to subdue her and dampen the embarrassment of dirty laundry airing in public. Fueled by the beer, he went about the task poorly. "I raised my hand and I slapped her. She got real mad, and left and went to her dad's house. And that was the end."

Hemnauth recounts the incident quickly and in the manner of a confession. There is no real way to convey the sincerity of his regret in words that do not sound like a cliché. However, the regret is real, that he did not control a gesture of violence so contrary to his ideals and peaceable self-image. The theme returned repeatedly in his discourse over the time I spent interviewing him in Trinidad. His abhorrence of violence and vigilant distrust of his own anger when it surfaces are not rooted in fear. If they were, he might not have survived his imprisonment at Passaic. (I use the word *imprisonment* advisedly, despite the transgression to the ICE lexicon that confines itself to "detention.") Rather, the full moral and spiritual dimensions of nonviolence are ingrained within him. Certainly, his later brushes with brutality deepened his conviction. However, it is inconceivable to me that his conscious being was ever anything but at odds with the notion of striking his wife.

The fact remains, however, that he *did* strike his wife. His amplified feelings of guilt compounded the consequences beyond what was helpful for anyone.

Rahoni's father, more than Rahoni herself, insisted on a divorce. It impressed me as odd that a father who had abandoned his daughter in her adolescence would assert such control over her now that she was an adult, although in fairness I know very few fathers who would be pleased that a son-in-law had struck their daughter. In any event, Rahoni's father hired

an attorney to draw up a divorce petition claiming Hemnauth as solely responsible for the rift and culpable of domestic violence. Hemnauth, driven
by his guilt, disputed absolutely nothing, although he knew he was being
portrayed in the filing as a recidivist domestic monster. He accepted the
implied punishment as just retribution for having lost his wits, and relinquished any and all prerogatives, including custody and visitation rights.

"I signed it . . . I didn't even read the thing. [Rahoni's father] came back
to the house on a Sunday morning, in his pandit's clothes, with the papers.
I asked Rahoni if this is what she wanted. She answered: 'Yes. Daddy says
so.' Those were her words: 'Daddy says so.' So I took the paper and I signed
it. I was so upset with everything."

It is difficult to escape the suspicion that the father's ascendancy over
his daughter was a piece of the couple's cultural baggage, along with Hemnauth's masculine pride as he struggled with his material dependency on
his wife. Add to that his guilt over allowing a household dispute to turn
physical, and the potion turns lethal. Who is to say in hindsight that their
marriage was salvageable absent the extraneous ingredients? What does
seem clear — and is amply demonstrated in the eventual recovery of their
friendship — is that a less acrimonious estrangement than the one Rahoni's
father imposed was within reach, and might have saved them all from a
world of hurt.

4

POSSESSION IN THE SEVENTH DEGREE

HEMNAUTH WAS STARING HOMELESSNESS IN THE FACE as the winter of 1995–1996 blew into town. "I had two months when I still stayed in [Rahoni's] apartment." There was a security deposit he could deplete before he would have to vacate the place. "Then I went to Queens. I survived by the grace of God."

He graduated from Apex with his certificate in air conditioning repair and maintenance. However, since he had deferred completion of his degree while he was going through his marital trauma, he missed the hiring season for his specialty. Winter demand for air conditioning repair tends to be soft. He was out in the cold, with no chance of the employment he had trained for until the middle of the following spring at the earliest. His only chance for survival was to go back to his courier job, plowing through the New York snow on a bicycle. (His fellow Guyanese bicycle courier, by the name of Pots, had upgraded to his own delivery truck.) I try to imagine the suffering of a man uprooted from the hot tropics of equatorial South America, in cheap clothing and rudimentary footwear, pedaling through the northern winter.

"I found that tough. I wasn't equipped for such a task," he tells me understatedly, "in terms of clothing. I was feeling a lot of pain. I was really upset by what was going on in my life."

He slept in a friend's car.

He did speak to Rahoni occasionally, preferably when her father was not around to eavesdrop and object to her cordiality toward her *persona non grata* of an ex-husband. After a few weeks of homelessness, Hemnauth told her he wanted to go back to Guyana. Given how hard he had fallen, from the heights of immigrant hopefulness to the depths of despair, one could hardly accuse him of entertaining fickle temptations. Further, knowing what cruelty awaited him, he might indeed have been well advised to return to Georgetown and perhaps take up again with Pete's Caribbean Fusion.

Yet Rahoni persuaded him not to leave New York and surrender his residency status. It would later surface that she did not want her child so far removed from his father, but early into her divorce such a motive was effectively unmentionable. She encouraged Hemnauth to appeal to American relatives for shelter. He managed to track down an immigrant aunt with whom he had lost contact. She and her husband were observant Hindus like Hemnauth, he from a long lineage of priests. The husband's family rented Hemnauth a room in the unheated basement of their house in Queens for seventy-five dollars a week, both the least and the most they could do for a fellow certifiably devout Hindu. It was never more than fifty degrees Fahrenheit in the cellar at night, and often less, but coming in from a full ten-hour workday in the freezing elements, Hemnauth found the room positively balmy. His landlady also allowed him some access to her kitchen.

Hemnauth recollects making up to $200 a week delivering documents and small packages, and he managed to get through the winter without starving. Once the spring arrived, he was able to expand his outlook toward higher aspirations. His Apex diploma would normally open the doors to employment in his acquired field, and he had reconnected with his Guyanese buddies from the band room off Sutphin Boulevard in Jamaica.

Among them was a young man, Phillip, whom we shall designate by his first name alone. Phillip was Guyanese-born, but had grown up on the streets of Queens. He was married with two small children and drove a limo, freelance, for a living, or rather to supplement his wife's earnings from a regular salaried job. From the way Hemnauth speaks of him, Phillip was generous and fun loving to the point of mischief. One befriended Phillip at some peril, which peril Hemnauth later learned could include the attentions of the New York Police Department.

As spring neared, Hemnauth and a cadre of four friends piled into Phillip's vintage white Cadillac and prepared to set off for Florida. Hemnauth sold his guitar and four-track studio recorder to fund his share of the expenses. He had the notion that once in Florida he might find maintenance work earlier than he would staying in New York and waiting for seasonal heat to start pulling the city's air conditioning apparatus into action.

They ran into trouble on their way out of New York. They had driven to pick up one of their party, a man named Sammy, in a section of Queens popular with drug pushers. The police were watching a house on Sammy's block. As they turned a corner to leave Sammy's street, they were stopped by a patrol car out on surveillance. The police ordered the men out of their car and then searched the vehicle and the occupants' person. I am not aware that they had a warrant and, given Hemnauth's description of the incident, it is hard to banish thoughts of racial profiling. But I do not bring this up while speaking with Hemnauth, preferring that he recount the event without editorial interruption or suggestion.

One of the two cops, "a young rookie guy," was very aggressive, rifling roughly through luggage and shoving the men around. The other officer, the patrol car driver, became uncomfortable with his partner's belligerent hassling. He called Hemnauth over, intimated that they were looking for narcotics and, perhaps, guns and asked if the search would turn up any items of interest. Hemnauth explained that no, they were just a group of musicians picking up one of theirs before hitting the road to Florida. The cop asked his question over and over, until Hemnauth simply recommended that they "do their job," complete the search and get it over with.

Reinforcements showed up. Another officer, a female, joined the search. She discovered a marijuana roach in the driver's ashtray, the remnant of some past indulgence of Phillip's that his companions had nothing to do with. The officer radioed the local precinct with news of her find. Another police car showed up, this one unmarked. A detective emerged and told the assembled gaggle of cops and Guyanese that he could not care less about old roaches. His department was focusing their efforts on the stuff of violence, guns and hard drugs. The butt of a spent joint was at most evidence of a petty misdemeanor. The detective called off the cavalry.

The thought of simply surrendering was too frustrating for the tough-guy cop who had first initiated the frisking. He was not about to leave the scene with nothing to show for it. He decided to write a ticket, citing the presence of the roach. The problem was whom exactly he should cite.

Hemnauth was the only one of the men to spontaneously produce his alien registration card and it was on the top of the pile of IDs the men had handed the police, so the rookie officer wrote up the ticket in his name, despite his being the least likely source of the roach and demonstrably not the owner of the Cadillac. "He just put the ticket in my hand and said, 'I'll see you in court.'" Hemnauth had had his fill of the NYPD for one morning, so he did not fuss. He was the low-hanging fruit of the cops' labors. The five-some chalked the incident up as an early snag in the travel plans and went on their way.

They reached Florida in three days with the intention of remaining two months, except for Phillip, who would return home to his wife after a fortnight's leave with his buddies. They rented a furnished apartment near the beach and resolved to look for work. Toward the end of two weeks, Hemnauth remembered that he had the ticket in his pocket and actually looked at the content of the wrinkled document. There was a court date one month hence. His law-abiding instincts kicked in, the ones that suggested he should not dig himself into a deeper hole. He figured he had better appear and fight the ticket. He regretted needing to leave Florida where he was confident he would find work in the field he had trained for, but the last thing he needed was an interstate warrant for failure to comply with a court summons. Besides, it would be getting warmer up north and employment prospects would have improved as buildings began to prime their air conditioners for the approaching summer. Florida would have been nice, but Hemnauth did not want to risk trouble with the law.

He and Phillip made their way back to New York, driving as constantly as they could and as fast as they dared. At five in the morning of the day after they left south Florida, they pulled into an empty Kmart parking lot somewhere in South Carolina to park away from the traffic, set back the seats and sleep for a while in the car.

Hemnauth had a bad dream. As mentioned previously, Hemnauth takes the symbolism he draws from his dreams seriously. He is quick to want to interpret them and extract either premonitions or explanatory hindsight. More than mere superstition, dreams are very much part of his spiritual persona, perhaps even its bedrock. In the wake of his later ordeals, the thread of his recollected dreams has allowed him to stitch some sense into the most ill-fated period of his life.

Dozing in the white Cadillac in the shadow of a Kmart, Hemnauth dreamt that he and Phillip were arrested and taken away in shackles to prison. All the other prisoners were subject to hard labor, while Hemnauth was somehow exempted from it:

> *I was rescued by a woman with some children, and she opened the Book of Life for me. It was a large book and she told me to look inside it. I saw myself with my wife — my next wife — and a child. I had appeared as an angel and the child was sitting on my head with clasped hands, praying. The woman who was going to be my next wife, she was kneeling down at the side by my ears, praying [as well]. The [first] woman told me "keep turning the pages, you will see your entire life." I said, "I think this is enough. I don't want to see any more of this thing. I'm no angel." And I woke up.*

The "thing" he wished to avoid the sight of was, of course, a series of hapless events his premonition told him would sour his life and come close to destroying it. He thought of the dream at every bad turn to come. In speaking with me, he referred to it often and asked that I relate it here. His heed of the messages of his dreams are of a piece with his deep-seated conviction that, in his earthly life, everything happens for a reason. He returned to this theme several times as I heard his testimony, and often thereafter. This belief may also help explain his utter freedom from vindictiveness in the face of the injustices he has braved.

Back in New York, Hemnauth resolved the uncomplicated issue with the police citation and moved into an abandoned mobile home parked in the yard of an African American man he had become acquainted with, a mechanic in Phillip's neighborhood. Nothing worked, in particular not the heat, for the simple reason that the rig was hooked up to neither power nor water. He is not certain the trailer even belonged to the man who gave him the keys. Still, it had a bed and, more importantly, a roof. He occupied it for more than a year. He was also a frequent overnight guest of Phillip and his wife. He went back and forth between the two quasi-residences, the mobile home and Phillip's house, although over time he tried to impose as little as possible. The sense of intruding bothered him, although it helped that he could count on Phillip in a jam.

Soon after Hemnauth's retreat from Florida, the Apex school placement office got him a tough job that someone had to do. The vacancy was unsurprising. His new employer was a repair service for commercial hydraulic trash compactors, with most work done on site at high-rise apartment buildings — more specifically, at the termination point of their garbage chutes. The machines have a straightforward design. When the weight of recent trash sent down the chutes passes a threshold, it triggers a shot of pressure, thus compacting the volume. The work was properly disgusting. "When the [compactor] stops working, the worms and rats start taking over." You can almost hear his stomach twisting as he tells me this. Mine twists with it. A couple of months of working knee-deep in ordure were about all he could take, less out of mere squeamishness than genuine fear for his health. He was given a uniform for the job, but no mask, and he started to develop a rash. Also, summer had arrived, and its heat would not make compactor repair any more pleasant a task.

He found his own way out of the garbage predicament and edged closer to the trade he had trained for at the cost of his marriage. He was recruited by a small commercial refrigeration and air conditioning maintenance outfit with a number of accounts among Greenwich Village nightclubs, certainly a step up from being showered, quite literally, with refuse dropped from great heights. He settled into as close to a routine as he had not known since leaving Guyana: a low-paying, but steady job in safe circumstances, a set of regular destinations at the end of the workday, music practice every evening and a group of friends congregated at the band room in Jamaica. He also returned to organized worship, in spades.

Hemnauth's spirituality is dominant and deeply ingrained. He prefers to distill scripture and sip its essence rather than swallow it whole. To the untrained religious eye, such as is mine, he comes off as profoundly religious, but far from dogmatic or sectarian. He is at his most serene in the embrace of a temple and its sages, as I witnessed myself when I accompanied him to Hindu services in Trinidad. He also admits freely that he sought solace at temple from his separation from Rahoni and Kevin, all the more so that his telephone calls to her were unwelcome whilst she was living with her father, who appears to have required that Hemnauth be vigorously snubbed. Rahoni was colder on the phone toward Hemnauth than she truly desired to be, as she later demonstrated, and amply so. "She was living with her dad, so she had to talk rough to me."

Hemnauth chose as his primary place of worship the Queens affiliate of Bharat Sevrashram Sangha, a chiefly philanthropic Hindu movement based in India and founded in 1917 by its "patron saint," Acharya Srimat Swami Pranavanandaji Maharaj.[19] Another family member — the husband of a second cousin, or something like that — materialized and introduced Hemnauth to the Queens congregation. The Sangha network has forty-six ashrams in Hindu communities around the world. Its mission is heavy on community service, lighter on doctrinal pursuits. Indeed, it bills itself as ecumenical in its outlook. So ecumenical, in fact, that neither Hemnauth nor the Indian monks of the ashram saw any conflict in his simultaneous allegiance, solicited by yet another childhood acquaintance from Guyana, to the Liberty Bible Fellowship Church, whose Christian evangelistic leanings are best summarized as textbook and short on doctrinal compromise.[20]

"Krishna and Jesus were preaching the same thing," Hemnauth tells me matter-of-factly. "Why should I differentiate?" Further, Jesus and Krishna are both referred to by their followers as Lord and Supreme Being, or deity. And according to the respective scriptures, each was the issue of an immaculate conception. Hemnauth's adherence to more than one creed appears to channel Hinduism's doctrinal conviction that "the various major religions are alternate paths to the same goal."[21] It is unclear whether the Bible Fellowship Church was equally warm to multiple ritual allegiances.

Hemnauth contributed his musical ability to his ashram and his church. (Both would later intercede on his behalf during his imprisonment at Passaic.) He sprung for a new Epiphone hollow-body electric guitar to replace the one he had sold to fund his aborted excursion to Florida. He taught western music at the ashram, pro bono, and played at benefit events for the ashram and the church. Both were raising money for charitable commitments and to purchase space. He was busy enough between work, temple and church to keep his mind off Rahoni and lurking demons at bay. Or so he believed.

19 "Bharat Sevashram Sangha."
20 "International Fellowship of Bible Churches."
21 Smith, *The World's Religions*.

The day of his arrest, a Saturday according to Hemnauth's recollection, was the sweet sixteenth birthday of a girl at the ashram. Her parents had decided to hold a charity concert around the occasion rather than throw a private party. Hemnauth, by now the leading musical fixture of the temple, was naturally asked to perform, and just as naturally he accepted. He needed only procure a guitar amp for his gig. His friend Phillip was sure that Robbi, the owner of the rehearsal space in Jamaica that was chock-a-block with band equipment, would happily lend him one for the evening. They would just need to go and ask him.

Hemnauth and Phillip headed down 117th Street in Queens on bicycles, turning northeast on Liberty Avenue, riding one behind the other toward Sutphin Boulevard, Hemnauth in front. They both knew the way. Just before the overpass spanning the Van Wyck Expressway, Hemnauth stopped before crossing over the highway. He looked back to verify that he had not lost Phillip, who he expected would be close behind him. He wasn't. When Hemnauth turned around, he saw Phillip about two blocks down Liberty Avenue talking to "a big white guy." When Hemnauth later saw the man in court, he seemed a bit more on the short side with a big gut.

Hemnauth waited where he was for Phillip to catch up. He had not a clue who the man talking to Phillip was or why Phillip was listening to what he had to say. They reached Hemnauth and the "big white guy" repeated what he had already told Phillip. He introduced himself as a construction worker. He was dressed in cut-off blue jeans and was carrying a backpack. He explained that he was feeling poorly and needed a medicinal hit to restore his ability to get back to the building site where he was expected to report for work. Crack cocaine would do the trick. Hemnauth laughs at the inanity of having fallen for such a cockamamie story as he recounts this to me in hindsight taking him back a decade.

The episode, Hemnauth tells me, would have ended there were it not for Phillip's dual propensity to reflexively ingratiate himself with others and try to impress them, in this instance with his street smarts. According to Hemnauth, Phillip had stopped using hard drugs by the time they met. He had two small children to look after. Perhaps he had eschewed addiction, but Phillip's street smarts were genuine, if nothing else the product of a time in his life when his intimacy with drugs had acquainted him with the inner workings of the trade and the mechanics of dealing.

The man was asking Phillip to intercede on his behalf with the local crack merchants, that is, effect the purchase of a rock for him. Phillip boasts to his new friend of his familiarity with the neighborhood sellers and goes to some lengths to make himself seem cool and knowledgeable to the man who had accosted him. In fact, it did not require a long acquaintance — or much acquaintance at all — with sellers for motivated buyers to track them down, regardless of their purchasing history or lack thereof. The comings and goings from the band room off Sutphin Boulevard attracted petty drug retailers to the streets around it in hope, usually vain, of landing customers from among the visitors. Police stakeouts were not far behind them. Here, too, Hemnauth may have misinterpreted the full extent of his friend's motivations and been blind to the notion that Phillip's sociability toward the stranger may also have been inspired by a commercial reflex: with drug deals easy to engineer, a customer could easily migrate elsewhere. It is quite possible that Phillip had not left his home that morning in search of a drug deal, but when opportunity knocked, he answered.

Hemnauth started to ride very slowly as the two others walked a few yards behind, Phillip pushing his bike along, ostentatiously empathetic to the third man's pleading for a medicinal dose of crack cocaine. By now he is literally begging Phillip to help him acquire it. He claims that as a white guy, he cannot approach the black street sellers who are dominant in this section of Queens for fear of them beating him up and robbing him. The man was pressing Phillip with such an air of affinity with him that for a fleeting moment Hemnauth thought Phillip actually knew him from earlier circumstances. In any event, Phillip's boastfulness committed him to not simply walk away.

He caught up with Hemnauth, now on the far side of the overpass across the Van Wyck, leaving the man just beyond earshot. He had decided to enlist Hemnauth to the cause of "helping this guy out." The thought — if one could call it that — was that Phillip would stay with the man as reassurance that whoever went off to make the purchase would come back with the goods and not abscond with the funds, a twenty-dollar bill. If Hemnauth did not return, the man could take it out on Phillip. "A really stupid thing," Hemnauth tells me, this idea that Phillip would feel compelled to provide convoluted demonstrations of probity to a drug user requesting that they do his dirty work.

I believe him. It was a really stupid thing, and not only because the man's story was so improbable. So was Phillip's show of simply coming to the aid of a man in pain. Phillip's conduct had all the markings of the actions of a "steerer," the front man in charge of sizing up a buyer in a street drug transaction before activating a chain of acquisition designed to establish a set of buffers between the buyer and the location of the merchandise. The steerer's evaluation would normally determine whether the buyer was legitimate, in other words not an undercover cop setting a trap. It was also important for the steerer not to keep drugs on him, as this would facilitate a straightforward, one-two bust, often before a seller could indeed size up a customer. The street trade had become wise to the dangers of solo deals. It changed the nature of its sparring with the police into a game of cat-and-mouse, fielding teams of players rather than individual actors.

The steerer would typically relay the purchase order, and the money, to a second player, called a "hand-to-hand" or "pitcher,"[22] a role into which Phillip pressed Hemnauth. He shuttled back to the white man, got the twenty dollars and explained to Hemnauth, inexperienced in the matter of hard drugs, the misery of an addict in need of a fix to stay alive, and said it would be cruel to turn him down. Hemnauth felt indebted toward Phillip, who had kept him from homelessness and starvation in the dead of a New York winter. His unflagging loyalty toward friends and family is one of Hemnauth's salient traits of character. It was misguided in this instance. Phillip may have once showered Hemnauth with friendship and charity, earning his unbridled loyalty. But on the witness stand Phillip failed the test of reciprocal allegiance rather miserably.

"To please Phillip who had rescued me at his home . . . Remember Phillip looked after me, took me into his house, reached out a helping hand. He was the only friend who did that, and he was pretty much a stranger. If taking a little chance, if it will help him, okay, fine." Hemnauth was taking not a little chance, but a big one, gambling not only on Phillip's street savvy, but on the boundaries of his return loyalty. For openers, Phillip was exposing him to risks he may have understood at an intellectual level, but whose scope he did not fully grasp.

Hemnauth took off on his bike, the twenty dollars in his pocket, toward

22 The functioning of the street drug trade is outlined in a case heard by the New State Supreme Court, *People v. Colon* (1997).

Sutphin Boulevard. He went only a block or two and turned into a cross street. "I just came around the block, and returned." He gave the money back to Phillip, claiming that he had not come across any crack suppliers. Phillip was not satisfied with the effort and told Hemnauth to try a different block. What Phillip did not do was suggest specific locations where he knew dealers to hang out. As a steerer, he would not have divulged this information to the buyer who was standing within earshot, bolstering a reasonable suspicion that Phillip may have been more than a hapless Samaritan.

The white man was starting to worry that his new friends might be lacking in zeal. He now spoke for the first time in Hemnauth's direct presence, pressing the issue of his predicament. He pleaded with Hemnauth to "help me out."

"I was beginning to feel upset, not wanting to do this thing, but again feeling this obligation toward Phillip, because Phillip had helped me. I said, okay, I'm going to make a longer [trip] this time." He rode closer to the band room off Sutphin Boulevard, then turned back once again toward the Van Wyck overpass. On the return trip he saw a character he recognized, nicknamed "Fat Man" in appreciation of his girth. Fat Man was a fan of the musicians who rehearsed in the band room and often came by to listen. He was also known by the denizens of the band room, including Hemnauth, for being involved with narcotics on some level, and it was made clear to him that he was welcome only if he kept his drugs outside. The musicians used the premises as a rehearsal and recording space, not as a social hall of any stripe. Several were Jamaican Rastafarians who partook in the occasional puff of marijuana, including in the band room, but would not tolerate crack in their midst, lest it lead to trouble. Traditional Rastafarianism does celebrate the use of marijuana, but actually condemns hard drugs as impure substances at odds with their religious convictions.[23] Repression of marijuana possession by law enforcement was fairly mild in New York before 1996, although it stepped up thereafter.[24] Crack, on the other hand, while beginning to tail off, particularly among youth,[25] was still

23 M. Levine, "Holy Smoke."
24 H. Levine, "Legislation to Collect DNA from All People Convicted of a Misdemeanor in New York State."
25 Golub and Johnson, "Crack's Decline: Some Surprises Across U.S. Cities." The

considered an epidemic menace, destructive of neighborhoods and civil society. It was a priority for law enforcement, and police action against it had gained the approval of the public.

Fat Man called after Hemnauth, who stopped to chat. Hemnauth told Fat Man of the errand Phillip had sent him on against his will. He referred to the deprived addict as Phillip's friend, as to emphasize that he was not his. Fat Man had a ready solution. He had twenty dollars' worth of crack on him, possibly more. His inventory was no coincidence, Hemnauth knew, no more than was his loitering on the street near Sutphin Boulevard, where he was something of a fixture. He was what is known in the retail narcotics world as a "stash man," the third cog in the three-tier process of procurement, designed to obscure the drugs' point of origin. Tradesmen also reasoned that it would be easier to cover tracks in an aborted transaction if the stash was insulated from the point of sale by at least one degree of separation.

Hemnauth "got [the rock] in my hand [and] jumped on my bike." He considered just discarding the drugs. "Something was telling me, get rid of this thing, this is an illegal thing I have in my possession . . . I got scared. If someone finds me with this thing, this is jail." The choice before him does not seem complicated. Yet he was torn between the obvious illegality of holding a controlled substance in his possession, on the one hand, and, on the other, his ambivalence toward lying about what had become of the twenty dollars if he jettisoned the rock, equivalent in his mind to stealing — a conflict between the law and his personal code of honesty, even though he had been thrust into a dilemma not of his making.

When he got back to the two other guys near the overpass, he instinctively gave the rock — "this thing"— to Phillip, not to the addict directly. He was standing at a gas station across Liberty Avenue. Phillip crossed over to deliver the crack. The man told Phillip to wait; he wanted to give him something more to thank him, some kind of completion bonus. He went into the gas station office for a moment, came out and handed Phillip a single dollar, folded up. Phillip did not need the money in such a petty amount, although he commonly helped people out — jump-starting their

---

data collected in this cross section of the American urban drug landscape focused on Manhattan. We have nonetheless taken it as sufficiently indicative of the city as a whole to reference it.

cars, carrying loads or performing some other odd job of fortune — and might accept a few dollars. He did piecework as a limo driver and took care of the kids so his wife could hold her steady job. They were neither rich nor destitute. Phillip welcomed a little easy cash here and there, which might well explain his willingness to join a seemingly effortless twenty-dollar crack deal in the same vein as he might change someone's tire for the tip. He was experienced in both ventures.

Experienced or not, Phillip was surprised that the grateful man to whom he had delivered drugs had made such a show of making change in the gas station so he could offer the piddling reward of one dollar. He gave the folded bill to Hemnauth with a casual "you take it." Hemnauth smelled a rat. "I took the dollar, then I really got suspicious that something was wrong here. I said, 'Phillip, you know this man? What did he give me this dollar for?'" Hearing Hemnauth question the scenario that was playing out, the man declared, "Hey, I don't want to get locked up," and abruptly strode away toward the expressway service road.

It was now obvious to Hemnauth that something was amiss and that the man was not who or what he said he was. He threw the dollar bill on the ground, by the street corner near the sidewalk, as he left the gas station on his bike. He rode a few yards up on the sidewalk — a wide one at that point — before the patrol cars rushed up. The cops piled out, drew their service revolvers and backed Hemnauth and Phillip against the wall, guns to their heads. After subduing their captives, the police retrieved the dollar bill from the gas station grounds.

Hemnauth does not recall the police reciting their Miranda rights, but it was clear, after being handcuffed with guns still at their temples, that they were very much under arrest. (Contrary to popular perception drawn from movies and television cop dramas, police are required to read captives their rights only when they are about to question them.) Hemnauth and Phillip were placed into a van that the police had on the ready.

They made some attempt to protest their arrest as a mistake, but rapidly acknowledged the futility of appealing to arresting officers on a round-up detail. Indeed, the prisoners remained in the van for several hours, driving around Queens as the patrol car prospected for more lawbreakers. This was standard. The officers were members of a Street Narcotics Enforcement Unit. Their daily work plan would have typically called for them to conduct something in the order of a half a dozen drug arrests, deploying the same operational tactics they had just used against Hemnauth and Phillip. When the van was filled to capacity with arrestees, they would drive it in to the Ozone Park precinct house. Phillip did persuade the cop assigned to the van to loosen the cuff rings a little. The police arrested two other men found to have drugs in their possession and also picked up a troublesome trash-talking female addict who urinated in the seat.

At the station, Hemnauth was relieved of his belt, wallet and the contents of his pockets, and placed in the precinct holding cell. The arresting officer — we'll call him John F. — wrote his report, which Hemnauth did not sign, and began an interrogation in the presence of two other officers. At this point, they would have read Hemnauth his Miranda rights. They threatened him with a twenty-year prison term, but said they would help get him off the worst hook if he turned informant. It comes out that they have the band room — a large detached garage — and the adjacent yard under surveillance, convinced that they are trading floors for drugs. They want Hemnauth to tell them "everything that goes on there." What went on there, Hemnauth told them, was "jazz, rock, blues, anything you would expect a guitar player to be playing."

Officer John F. handed him a piece of paper, with a hand obstructing the text, and told Hemnauth to sign it. He tried to read it, but could not. He felt coerced into signing. Hemnauth thought the document to be his acquiescence to serving as an informant, a cooperation agreement. It wasn't. Cooperation agreements are delicate pacts, carefully worked out and drafted by the district attorney and beyond the presumed abilities of a police officer. More likely, the document was the transcript of Hemnauth's remarks while being interviewed. Some came in response to John F.'s questions and some were unsolicited, as Hemnauth was anxious to frame the incident as a dumb mistake, not an act of turpitude. It was repeated to him that to withhold his signature would land him a twenty-year sentence. He kept trying to see exactly what was on the page they were making him sign. "I was so helpless that I ended up signing it." John F.'s threats were very intimidating, interlaced with promises to "help him out," a seemingly classic good-cop, bad-cop routine played by a single actor. He intimated that Hemnauth's cooperation would get him a lesser sentence, although he had still not been informed of what charge would be lodged against him. There was no suggestion that any charges against him would be dropped, nor could there have been. The police are parties to plea bargains only to the extent that they can recommend leniency to a prosecutor for a cooperative suspect, typically one who has agreed to testify against other defendants. Plea deals themselves are the exclusive prerogative of the district attorney and the judge.

One overarching problem for Hemnauth was that the police wanted him to denounce people for drug dealing he had never observed and which to the best of his knowledge had never occurred. Another was that he would have to confirm Phillip's leading role in the incident, explicitly incriminating a man to whom he felt immensely indebted.

To Hemnauth's astonishment, the police told him that they had been watching the band room for years. They knew "something big" was going on there. They had seen limousines pulling into the yard in front of the rehearsal space, an indication to them of regular visits by a cadre of Mr. Bigs from the drug world. Their suspicions did not allow that musicians by night might be limo drivers by day. (Indeed, Phillip and several of his friends, including Hemnauth's band's drummer, worked for a limo service, based at a Trump hotel at Columbus Circle, that regularly drove name artists around Manhattan, often in stretch Lincolns and Cadillacs.) In addition, the vicinity was largely deserted during the week, whereas on Friday nights and through the weekends the street was full of cars as the regulars showed up to jam, rehearse or listen. The police also saw large bags and cases — musical instruments — that they took, speculatively, for drug luggage. Many of the musicians who frequented the band room were Rastafarians; the cops would also associate them with a drug culture.

Hemnauth tried to set them straight. The visitors to the band room were musicians, period. He expressed surprise that the police had not simply showed up and checked the place out. The band room was often open, he told them, and no one would have stopped them from walking in, although the U.S. Constitution's prohibition of warrantless searches on private property would have. (The police did later raid the place. They found nothing more suspicious than cigars in an ashtray.) Hemnauth repeated his own story consistently, including his depiction of the band room. What he failed to grasp at the time was that the police were not about to declare their long stakeout an utter futility, least of all to themselves.

By the evening of his arrest, the police gave up trying to convert Hemnauth into an informant, notwithstanding the piece of paper he had signed under duress. He and Phillip were held in the courthouse lockup overnight and taken to the Queens County courthouse for arraignment the following day. The police also managed to confuse the respective identities of the two men they had arrested, assigning Phillip's personal belongings and items found on him to be placed in evidence to Hemnauth, and vice versa. (Phillip had a small amount of marijuana in his pocket, for which he was charged with a separate misdemeanor.)

The holding cell filled up as the evening wore on. It contained a single bench that could seat maybe five people. Twenty-odd people were held in the space overnight. There were four or five other cells like Hemnauth's, also crowded beyond capacity with suspects. During the night, Hemnauth, along with the other detainees in the holding cells, was queried on his family background, living situation and means of support. Hemnauth describes his interviewer as a social worker, because of the theme of her questions. More likely she was an agent of the Criminal Justice Agency, a private, nonprofit corporation in New York that advises arraignment judges on decisions of release and bail. It also became clear during the interview that Hemnauth could not afford a lawyer and that he would accept that the court appointed one for him.

Hemnauth was arraigned the following morning, as was Phillip, after being introduced to his attorney, Marvin Landou, drawn from a pool of court-hired private criminal defense attorneys assigned to indigent clients, apparently at random. Each lawyer took several. Hemnauth tried to explain his perspective to Landou, but the lawyer focused for the moment on the written charges. They were his primer on the case, not Hemnauth's protestations. He cut off Hemnauth's attempts to speak. "You don't say anything," he ordered Hemnauth. "This is a serious thing, buddy. I'm going to take care of it for you." Hemnauth thought Landou's shutting him up imperious and a little rude. He did not appreciate something his lawyer knew from long professional experience: that anything said in court was recorded and could be placed in evidence against him.

This was neither the time nor the place for a substantive conference with Landou. They had two or three minutes at most, whose purpose was for the attorneys to learn the names of their clients before they were led up to the bench. Everything happened very quickly once Hemnauth was brought before the judge. The clerk read the charges. "I was shocked when I heard the charges," Hemnauth says, dwelling on the word *shocked*. "Sale of a controlled substance, possession with the intent to sell, possession of a controlled substance in the seventh degree."

Hemnauth recites the bailiff's words fluidly. In the state of New York, the last charge, possession in the seventh degree (Penal Law 220.03), is a misdemeanor, and among the least-grave drug offenses on the books. Hemnauth — and later the district attorney's office, as well as Mr. Landou — was fixated more on the accusation of dealing than on a misdemeanor too trivial to spend legal and court fees to contest. However, unbeknownst to him at the time, the misdemeanor charge was to change his life and come close to destroying it.

The police statement affirmed that Hemnauth and Phillip, acting in concert, had sold drugs to a police officer. Hemnauth was described as the lookout. "The story was made up. I was surprised because [the incident] had not happened at all [like the police told it]." The police did not produce for the judge the paper Hemnauth had signed and that he thought, most likely incorrectly, committed him to act as an informant. Hemnauth speculates — and this must be tagged as speculation — that showing the agreement in court could only embarrass the police, since Hemnauth had not provided any damaging leads on the band room after signing it, quite the contrary.

The judge asked Hemnauth to enter a plea and Hemnauth asserts that he is not guilty of the charges. "I had to make a decision . . . I said, 'No, no, this thing didn't happen like that. I'm not guilty of this thing.'" Presumably Landou prevented him from saying much more. He has no clear recollection of whether he discussed his plea with Mr. Landou before entering it, but that would not have made any difference; he was thoroughly flabbergasted by the accusation of drug dealing and pleading guilty would never have crossed his mind, certainly not at a hasty arraignment. The judge, noting that Hemnauth had no prior arrests or charges, released him on his own recognizance with the admonishment that he appear on the specified court date a month hence. Or else. (Phillip had to post $7,500 bail; it was not his first offense.)

Hemnauth describes Marvin Landou as an older bear of a man. He was indeed toward the end of his career — he was admitted to the New York bar in 1951 — and has since passed away. Hemnauth later learned that he had already undergone several coronary bypass surgeries. A news search using Google yields only two mentions of him as defense counsel, one in the case of a road-rage homicide,[26] the other for "one of the most destructive graffiti vandals in the city."[27]

Landou had a very peppery way of speaking to his client, which despite his irreverent demeanor and the credence he seemed to lend to the police report, gave Hemnauth some confidence that the attorney was genuinely on his side. He looked like he knew the ropes. He moved around the court like he owned the place. Henceforth, Hemnauth was not to say a word to anyone but his lawyer, unless he "wanted to end up in a fucking tin can," Landou's metaphor for the average New York State correctional institution.

They returned to court a month later for a preliminary hearing, and somewhere along the way the DA's office obtained a grand jury indictment. Landou continued to warn Hemnauth to keep his mouth shut, battling his client's urge to blurt out his side of the story, and continued referring to the prison system as the expletive-deleted receptacle where Hemnauth would spend his remaining years if he did not let his lawyer handle things.

Nevertheless, when the judge asked Landou how he wished to proceed, to a trial or to an accommodation with the district attorney, in which event his client would have to change his plea from "not guilty" to "guilty," Hemnauth did not skip a beat.

"I told Mr. Landou, 'Hey, we're going to trial.'" Landou had no choice but to confirm to the judge Hemnauth's decision to stand firm by his original plea, although he clearly had not yet reconciled himself to it and would continue to try to sway Hemnauth. The judge adjourned the case for another month after consulting his calendar.

Bryan Lonegan, the attorney from the Legal Aid Society of New York who later represented Hemnauth in immigration court, told me that Landou's initial advice to his client — to accept a plea bargain — was perfectly sound, and that he would have given him the identical guidance had he been in Mr. Landou's shoes, notwithstanding Landou's outward flippancy in the way he treated Hemnauth. The likelihood of a jury acquitting someone accused of a drug-related felony in a New York court was slim, at

26 Donohue, "Road-Rage Slay Suspect: Mom 'Deserved' to Die."
27 Onishi, "Neighborhood Report: Glendale."

best. The penalty upon conviction would be aggravated to the maximum sentence by the remorselessness implicit in the defendant's turning down a plea bargain. Trafficking in narcotics is a class B felony in the state of New York, the same level of gravity as is ascribed to rape and arson.[28] Hemnauth, Landou knew, could be put away for a very long time, his life in utter ruination. A plea bargain could reduce the most damaging charges to class C felonies carrying a sentence of five or six years' probation, with the district attorney's consent. Most lawyers would consider fighting the original charge insane.

But fight Hemnauth would.

Since he had had a difficult time getting Landou to lend an ear, he tried for his eyes. He wrote him a lengthy letter spelling out, in detail that did not spare himself frank descriptions of his own foolishness, the entire story of the incident, including ample background on who he was and where he came from. He handed Landou the letter at a third court hearing, whose purpose was apparently confined to convening the next one. Landou had the letter with him at every subsequent court audience.

On the morning of the fourth hearing, Hemnauth put on a coat and tie and headed for the courthouse. Phillip was having breakfast with his family at a diner across the street. Hemnauth did not want to join them — he was too upset and worried over being branded a criminal, and, unlike Phillip he had no family to fall back on — so he went to sit under a tree on the small lawn at one side of the court building. "I was sitting alone on the grass under a tree. I [had] bought a coffee and a donut or a bagel. Landou saw me, and he came up to me." Landou had read Hemnauth's letter, probably many times over, and taken it to heart. He also seemed to identify with Hemnauth or at least with his loneliness. He confided that he was alone in the world. His wife had died. His son — a musician! — and his daughter had moved away to Florida.

The chat on the courthouse lawn, prompted by the letter, was a turning point in Hemnauth's relationship with Landou. Hemnauth had convinced Landou of his fundamental decency, and if he, a world-weary cynic of a lawyer, could be swayed so thoroughly, so could a jury. I do not mean to suggest that Mr. Landou had ever been unsympathetic toward his client,

---

28 Lippman, *Contemporary Criminal Law.*

but that with the odds normally stacked against acquittal in situations like Hemnauth's, up to this point he had felt that his best advice was for Hemnauth to accept a plea bargain and that he should continue to press him to do so. Now, with Hemnauth's letter having convinced him of his client's essential probity, Landou began to think in terms of winning an acquittal.

One additional and critical feature of Hemnauth's determination to risk a jury returning a guilty verdict may have figured in Landou's wholehearted embrace of the notion of going to trial: his motives. Hemnauth insists, to this day, that he stood on the principle that he would never confess to the false accusation that he was a drug dealer. If the state dropped him in a dungeon, so be it. He had committed an act of foolishness, he readily admitted, not one of abomination as that with which he was charged.

However, there is no escaping that another principle was also at stake, equally in keeping with Hemnauth's ethical code: the language of any cooperative plea agreement would necessarily have incriminated Phillip, unequivocally and irrevocably. His gratitude toward the man who had scraped him off the frozen streets forbade any breach of loyalty, even if Phillip had been so heedless and irresponsible as to embroil Hemnauth in his own recklessness. There is no conflict between these two motives, as both lead to the same decision to snub a plea bargain. However, they are of differing nature, even purity, and I have confronted Hemnauth with the tension between them. While admitting that the prospect of ratting out a friend and benefactor — even one who deserved it — clearly repulsed him, he maintains that the principle that "the truth be known" far outweighed any other consideration. I believe him, as, evidently, did Landou. It is not merely a matter of blind faith. In Hemnauth's culture and upbringing, shame and humiliation are the worst of scourges. The tag of depravity the DA proposed to pin on him was more than he could bear.

Hemnauth remembers Landou mulling over a line of defense that implied entrapment, to the layman a logical path, as the facts seemed to lean that way as well: a police decoy had initiated a trade that otherwise would not have occurred.

The reality has a denser context. Many parts of greater New York in the mid-1990s still felt the grip of the crack epidemic that had emerged a decade earlier, even if, in hindsight, the data show it waning by the time of Hemnauth's arrest. Further, the mayor, Rudy Giuliani, was a lawman with a crime-fighter's agenda, responsive to the complaints of citizens from neighborhoods blighted by crack. Police "buy and bust" operations were in keeping with an accepted program of enforcement. Still, Hemnauth had a clean record tarred only by this sting designed and staged by the police.

On the other hand, Phillip, his codefendant, had a darkened rap sheet and was more vulnerable to suggestions of predisposition. So if Mr. Landou's musings drifted toward entrapment, they did not remain there. In fact, he had only three possible lines of defense for his client. One was to argue that the police were mistaken and had fingered the wrong culprit in a crime that had undeniably occurred. A second was to deny that there had ever been a crime. These two avenues were closed. There was, however a third way, which would be to demonstrate that the nature of the accused's involvement in the crime was not as alleged and not a felony. The stars must align for this device to be used successfully. They seldom do.

Landou suggested that Hemnauth, rather than sit under a tree and mope, go upstairs with him to the court library and help him research cases. "I didn't have a clue about these things or . . . where to search." Of course he didn't. He later realized that Landou wished to strengthen his paternalistic bond with this particular client, something in the manner of a father bringing his son to work. The lawyer also felt he could help Hemnauth withstand the tensions of trial if he felt party to the preparation of his defense.

Client and counsel had some time ahead of them, as the judge ordered continuances for several months running. Hemnauth contends that a police helicopter was following him around, although it seems more than a little improbable. The police knew full well that Hemnauth was no drug lord, and the prohibitive cost of helicopter surveillance confines its use to only the most high-profile and dangerous cases, for example to close the ring around a serial murderer or a notorious crime boss. Nevertheless, Hemnauth did tell me that he ran an experiment with Phillip. Seeing a low-flying chopper hovering above Phillip's house, they went from the outside front to the back yard and watched it shift positions with them. Then they got in Phillip's car and drove to Sutphin Boulevard; sure enough, the helicopter was right there with them.

Chopper or no chopper, Hemnauth was under the accurate impression that the district attorney's office took the case very seriously and was hell bent on obtaining a conviction. Landou had told him as much. Hemnauth's paranoia over the helicopter had a real menace at its roots. Mine would have been equal to it in a like situation.

Because of his unexplained absences while preparing his defense, and attending the cascade of pretrial hearings that took place over the course of a full year, Hemnauth lost his job. He was not about to disclose to his boss that he was under a grand jury indictment for a felony, so he simply forfeited steady employment in favor of freelance jobs in climate control and income from music gigs. He played "clubs and restaurants and things." He also moved in with a woman in Brooklyn, on Avenue J, who had an apartment she was willing to share on favorable terms. He had known her in Guyana. A mutual friend who attended the Bible Fellowship Church in Queens reacquainted them, another manifestation of the "it's-a-small-world" maxim.

The trial opened about a year after the arrest. The jury selection proceeded smoothly. Phillip and Hemnauth were tried jointly. While each had his own attorney, Phillip's was, according to Hemnauth, underwhelming, and Landou took the lead in questioning prospective jurors and, later, the state's witnesses.

It is tempting to credit Hemnauth's determination to risk grueling punishment by going all the way to trial for the police's sustained interest in enticing him to cooperate. In any event, during *voir dire* Officer John F., the man who had booked Hemnauth, repeatedly spoke to him in the building lobby just past the security metal detector with reminders of the benefits. These encounters were likely informal and noncommittal, again because only the DA can legally put forth any offers. For a cop to do so could expose him to sanctions. He would be risking a mistrial. Still, Hemnauth, an inexperienced criminal defendant, interpreted John F.'s casual overtures as hawking a plea deal and not taking "no" for an answer. Hemnauth also sensed jitteriness in John F.'s solicitude, that maybe the police were losing confidence in the case even before the prosecution had presented its side. Looking at the circumstances in hindsight, this was wishful thinking. Hemnauth may have overlooked the possibility, if not the probability, that Phillip's conviction was a higher prosecution priority because of his recidivism. Prison would be mandatory for Phillip if found guilty, several years if he pleaded so, plenty more if he did not. In the scope of things, he was the bigger fish. John F.'s eagerness to cement the case against him may well have driven his urge to elicit Hemnauth's cooperation.

In any event, Hemnauth was having none of it. He does not even specif-ically recall reporting Officer John F.'s overtures to his lawyer, underscoring how fleeting they probably were. Landou, meanwhile, had become a true believer in Hemnauth's honesty. He wanted an acquittal almost as much as Hemnauth did, and he thought he could get one, despite most juries' instinctive deference to law enforcement and his usual stance of advis-ing clients in similar situations to cop a plea. Hemnauth was not about to dampen his enthusiasm on the eve of the trial, especially as he was dead set on going the full distance to dismissal of the felony charge. "Mr. Landou and I had a kind of little friendship going on." Hemnauth also sensed that it was inappropriate for the police to be talking to him *ex parte* and that John F. might be trying to snare an admission of guilt. This might have been one more far-fetched suspicion, but Hemnauth's frame of mind was understandably cautious.

At the onset of the trial, the lawyer from the Queens DA's office was equally confident, if not cocky, letting loose a "Let's rock and roll!" as the various protagonists, including the men she was prosecuting, rode up in the courthouse elevator together. She apparently thought conviction a cer-tainty, what with a damning police report and no obvious holes in her case against the respondents.

The prosecuting attorney was a bright and brash young lady, but no rookie. She had to have earned her stripes to land the assignment. Although the particulars of the case seem so pathetic as to hardly register a blip in the annals of crime, the office of the district attorney was mightily attentive to it. The stakes were high. A verdict of not guilty in any drug prosecution, in the eyes of the DA and the entire law enforcement apparatus, set a dan-gerous precedent and signaled to the street that bad actors had a chance at acquittal. The pressure to obtain guilty pleas through bargaining was intense, so much so that few cases went all the way to trial. And when they did, failure to win a conviction was unacceptable.

The trial lasted one week. Landou indulged in some corny theatrics in an attempt to unnerve his counterpart at the prosecution table. His favor-ite was conspicuously leaning over and whispering into Hemnauth's ear, lending the impression that he was constantly detecting weaknesses in the prosecution's case when in fact he was commenting on mere trivia, such as what he had had for breakfast.

The asides were not all theatrics, and theatrics are not what won the case. Landou was picking up discrepancies between the transcript of the grand jury testimony given by the police and their statements on the stand, beginning with the down-and-out "construction worker," revealed to be, unsurprisingly, an undercover policeman. Little differences undermined the prosecution's narrative. For instance, one of the cops gave varying accounts of where they had recovered the dollar bill used as a wrapper for the damning sliver of crack, first from the ground, then from Hemnauth's pocket, then from his hand. The discrepancies emboldened Landou as the cops took the stand. The first witness, the "construction worker" desperate for a fix, had to confirm that he had given the twenty-dollar bill to Phillip and received the rock of crack from Phillip as well, contrary to the testimony of another squad member that Hemnauth had handed the drugs directly to an undercover agent, thus tagging him as a dealer. The written deposition of the police appears to underscore that the arresting officer confused Hemnauth's and Phillip's respective identities. In itself, the confusion did not land a fatal blow to the prosecution's argument as the police could, and did, still contend that the two men were working in concert, as is habitually true in trade deals such as the one they had disrupted.

A second witness, a cop — the "ghost" in drug bust jargon, standing by to protect the undercover and confirm the identity of the suspects upon arrest — had observed the scene at a distance from an unmarked car. In court, he situated his position in the gentle s-curve on Liberty Avenue, where the bend in the road would have buckled his line of sight. Further, Phillip and Hemnauth were similar in appearance: stature, goatee beard, long hair, plaid shirt. From the distance, it would have been difficult to definitively tell the two apart. During the questioning, it emerged that the cop at the remote observation point had seen Hemnauth's comings and goings on his bike, and had deduced he was the primary dealer who had taken money from the "construction worker" and delivered him the drugs a few minutes later. In this telling, Phillip was a lookout who had not handled money, at odds with his partner's account. The prosecuting attorney produced small pictures taken on a rainy day that were at best inconclusive, as well as a photocopy of a street map. Landou kindly and cleverly supplied — to the court and for the prosecutor's use — large, clear pictures taken on a sunny day, plus a poster-size map of the section of Liberty Avenue under examination. These exhibits showed the overall topography of the vicinity of the alleged crimes, including the curve in the road.

The jury asked to visit the scene, not a particularly good omen for a prosecution anticipating a slam-dunk conviction, although Hemnauth does not remember hearing the unusual request at the time the jury made it, unusual because there was no violence or destruction involved in the charges. Normally, the defendants and their attorneys are part of any visit to the scene of a crime, whereas Hemnauth affirmed to me with confidence that it indeed took place without him. The only way this is legally possible is if Landou gave his consent. Such visits are part of the trial proceedings from which defendants cannot be excluded.

John F. took the stand the day after the jury's field trip. He opened by contradicting his own grand jury testimony regarding the seemingly minor point of where the infamous dollar bill had been found. Absent any more glaring discrepancies, this too, on its own, would have knocked another little chink from the prosecution's armor, but nothing of a magnitude to disprove its thesis, even when combined with the police's other misrecollections. However, when Landou asked John F. to produce the dollar bill, the officer conceded that it had been misplaced at the precinct and disappeared. Landou also asked him to produce the marked twenty-dollar bill. That, of course, was gone, by way of Fat Man's pocket, because of the way the police had designed the sting operation in the first place, as well they had to. Under further questioning from the increasingly scrappy Landou, it was revealed that the cops had been given $360 in "buy money" for the day's "buy and bust" activities, but could account for only $21 of it, and even then, could not produce as much as the compulsory photocopies of either of the marked bills they had fielded in order to nail Hemnauth and Phillip. (They did produce the rock of crack from which a piece had been broken off.) John F. and his posse were starting to look just a tad sloppy. Again, the one missing piece of evidence, on its own, was probably not a game changer, but may well have provided an added boost to Landou's main theme, which he would develop in his summation.

Phillip was the last witness to take the stand. Landou did not want him to, but Phillip did have his own attorney who apparently thought that Phillip should look after his own welfare. Phillip had a police record, including car theft, drug possession and a number of petty charges, whereas Hemnauth's history was clean as a whistle.

"He told the truth up to a point," Hemnauth tells me, haltingly, still reluctant to recognize that Phillip's truth up to a point was no truth at all. While admitting that he personally received the twenty-dollar payment, Phillip denied handing the drugs directly to the undercover office, pinning that act on Hemnauth — and revealing a willingness, if not an urge, to throw him under the bus. Again, Phillip's past would aggravate his penalty if he were to be found guilty.

The prosecutor attempted to intimate that Phillip's priors were markers of the untrustworthy nature of both defendants, tacking away from the jumbled police testimony in her cross-examination. It occurred to Hemnauth in recalling the trial that she had lost faith in it. The judge sustained Landou's objections to her line of questioning, as well he would have. It is illegal to use one defendant's record as evidence against another defendant, and even without the defense's objection, the judge would have shut down any attempt to do so before it got off the ground. The inadmissible inference from the prosecutor was that Hemnauth would be guilty by an association to Phillip's past offenses that did not exist and was not alleged.

There is disappointment in Hemnauth's voice when he speaks of Phillip's demeanor during trial. The fact that he took the stand and inculpated Hemnauth — less than truthfully — whereas Landou had been representing him for all intents and purposes. That he routinely showed up late for court, a signal mark of disrespect for the judge that put Hemnauth, his codefendant, in peril. Disappointment, sadness perhaps, but not condemnation. Hemnauth is loyal to a fault to the friend who had helped him when he could have died of exposure on the mean streets. "Phillip had done some crazy stuff," he sighs, resignedly, such as, years earlier, driving stolen cars into walls while stoned, just for kicks. Not a man of constant malice, more a stunningly infantile one. Still, Phillip was out to save his own skin and was not above double-crossing Hemnauth, the man his own folly had endangered. Hemnauth who had jeopardized his own freedom — forfeited it in the end — while shielding Phillip from a mandatory prison term, if not for that sole purpose. Through his mind's eyes, Hemnauth knows Phillip had flirted with betrayal. In his heart he remained beholden to one who, in other circumstances, had come to his rescue.

When Phillip left the stand, the defense rested its case and the court moved on to closing statements. Landou knew that he had a credible argument against conviction on the felony charge of possession with intent to sell. It was fortunate that the prosecution could not produce the physical evidence they claimed they had gathered, or even the complete formal record of having gathered it. The lapse may very well have irked a juror or two and awakened reasonable doubt about the defendants' guilt. The central argument, however, lay elsewhere.

Landou told Hemnauth he was going to "play it safe," aware as he certainly was of jurors' typical hesitancy to impugn the police. Further, crack trafficking had scarred many neighborhoods around the city. Although the U.S. Supreme Court since as early as the 1920s has expressed discomfort with drug stings performed without evidence of predisposition,[29] they were popular with the New York public and, by extension, with juries. The police's handling of evidence and exhibits was shoddy; still, the chunk of crack they had shown the jury must have come from somewhere. Hemnauth's hands could not have been completely clean. It also seems likely that Landou was wary of the jury's possible antipathy toward Phillip, a man impudent enough to show up late on his own trial dates.

Playing it safe, as Hemnauth recalls Landou explaining it to him, entailed demanding acquittal on the felony charges, yet confessing to the possession misdemeanor. His legal device would allow the jury to express some opprobrium toward anyone who had gotten mixed up in drugs at whatever level of offense and sidestep a blanket repudiation of a band of New York's Finest, while at the same time avoiding delivery of a felony conviction against a simpatico first offender. Landou's strategy was entirely rational, and achievable within the confines of his most crucial task: Hemnauth's acquittal on a very serious, lock-him-up-and-throw-away-the-key felony charge. The strategy was also fateful in ways neither the lawyer nor his client would ever have imagined.

Landou indeed conceded the misdemeanor in his closing argument. The jury quickly returned its verdicts of guilty on the piddling seventh degree misdemeanor and not guilty of the felonies. In effect, Hemnauth had won his case, a statistical rarity by most accounts I have gathered of like

---

29 Urofsky, *Louis D. Brandeis: A Life*.

situations. Landou himself had expressed disbelief in Hemnauth's early refusal to plea-bargain.

After the verdict was read, the judge, as is customary, announced that jurors, attorneys and defendants were free to mingle, and mingle they did outside the courtroom. The prosecutor came out with the jury. In fact, it appeared that she had warmed up to Hemnauth, and perhaps even to Phillip. She had gone so far as to commend them *ex parte* on how courteous and gentlemanly they were, in contrast to the ruffians she had expected to be trying. According to Hemnauth, the jurors crowded around him. They wanted him to promise never again to be so foolish as to offer assistance under suspicious circumstances. In other words, don't take candy from strangers. The jury had, in fact, bought into the general idea that Hemnauth was not predisposed toward drugs or their traffic, whether or not his guilelessness was the legal basis of the decision to acquit. (It was not.) Some also voiced worry that their own children could fall into a similar ambush.

It is tempting to paint Hemnauth's acquittal on the felony charges as glorious vindication in a struggle against police entrapment worthy of a television prime-time court drama, with guilt shifting from the accused to the accusers in a rushing moment of truth, and to the jaw-dropping horror of the judge and jury. There were moments of drama, and the police's mishandling of the evidence and confused accounts of the circumstances of Hemnauth's arrest most probably helped the defense convince the jury that Hemnauth was no felon, not in deed and certainly not in spirit. However, to use entrapment as the fundamental argument for acquittal would have entailed demonstrating deliberate malfeasance on the part of the police intent on convicting an innocent man. It was easier to show that the police had barked up the wrong tree when they targeted Hemnauth, and dug in their heels at trial, not a pretty sight, but a lesser act of artfulness than blatant entrapment.

Bryan Lonegan, Hemnauth's Legal Aid Society attorney during the later deportation hearings, quickly disabused me of the notion of entrapment as the proximate grounds for Hemnauth's acquittal. It was, at most, an instructive element of the defense, not its basis. Rather, Landou adopted a rarely successful — and rarely used — strategy called the "agency defense," deemed available in Hemnauth's case under New York criminal law. The argument is technical and legalistic, which explains why Hemnauth would not have described it to me as he recounted the narrative highlights of the trial.

For all his hammy antics, Marvin Landou was not just a courtroom thespian. He was, as evidenced by his conduct of Hemnauth's defense, an astute practitioner of criminal law, particularly in view of the documented inadequacy of many state public defender programs.[30] He did his research and carefully planned his case.

To be sure, he overlooked or downplayed the tragic ramifications of the misdemeanor concession, which, in the end, overshadowed the abilities he demonstrated in getting Hemnauth acquitted. However, these ramifications are the product of the immigration code rather than criminal law. Landou was versed in the latter, not the former. In our popular imagination, warped by books, film and even some genuine courtroom history, Clarence Darrow types win cases with appeals to the emotions of juries richer in dramatic thrill than in legal argument. Our contemporary court system does not work that way. Landou may have had a touch of the Darrow in him and used it to some effect, just as a fiddler's trills embellish the melody without changing the score. But in the end Landou had to choose from a menu of legal strategies finite in number. By process of exclusion, Landou selected the agency defense and conceded the misdemeanor, as well he must.

The agency defense postulates that one cannot be a buyer and seller of the same drugs at the same time:

> The agency defense is a claim by a defendant, charged with selling drugs or possessing drugs with intent to sell, that he acted "solely on behalf of the buyer," and thus was a mere extension of the buyer in the drug sale. The rationale behind the agency defense is that an agent of the buyer cannot be convicted for the crime of selling drugs. After all, the buyer's agent is "merely transferring to the recipient that which the recipient already owns."[31]

---

30 Glaberson, "Are Lawyers for the Poor Inadequate?"
31 Simchi-Levi, "The Agency Defense: Can the Legislature Help?"

To the extent that a person purchases drugs on behalf of another party
— in this case the undercover cop posing as a construction worker — and
does not have an interest in the transaction, he is deemed, in effect, to be
running an errand for the buyer. "The agency defense recognizes that if a
person is acting only in the interest of the buyer in obtaining drugs, [under
New York State law] he cannot at the same time be acting as or in the interest of the seller. In such case, he may be guilty of the crime of possessing
but not of selling the drugs."[32]

"The agency defense can be invoked only by defendants charged with
the crimes of criminal sale of a controlled substance and criminal possession of a controlled substance with intent to sell. The defense cannot
be invoked by those charged with drug possession."[33] By pursuing a felony conviction for intent to sell in what in all appearances was a textbook
"buy and bust" operation, the prosecutor, perhaps unwittingly, dropped
the agency defense right into Landou's toolkit. That the police had been
less than adroit in both targeting as unlikely a drug dealer as Hemnauth in
the first place and in their manner of handling the items they presented in
evidence boosted its effectiveness.

The agency defense is used rather sparingly and is not available when
police stings are conducted in such a way as to establish direct contact
with the seller in immediate possession of the drugs. Such was definitely
the tack of the police in California working to infiltrate the drug ring presented to a grand jury on which I served as foreman a few years ago. In
that instance, the undercover agents directly approached drug pushers with
a stash on their person and whose activities had been observed prior to the
operation. They completed a trade using marked currency that was later
recovered. Hemnauth, in contrast, was a go-between, a "hand-to-hand"
recruited on the spot by officers of the NYPD who tailored their "buy and
bust" stings to combating dealers shrewd enough to separate the execution
of a trade into multiple segments. Since there was no evidence whatsoever
of any prior intent on Hemnauth's part to engage in drug sales or consume
cocaine himself, the agency defense applied in both fact and law.

The strategy was certainly less speculative — and foolhardy — than
to accuse the police of entrapment, and Landou was perfectly correct to

---

32 Hancock, "The People &C., Respondent, v. Carlos Andujas, Appellant" (1992).
33 Simchi-Levi, "The Agency Defense."

deploy it. He would have had a much more difficult argument if the primary seller of the source, the "stash man," had been arrested concurrently with Hemnauth and Phillip. In that event, the prosecutor would have emphasized that Hemnauth and Fat Man had been "acting in concert," joining them at the hip as mutually complicit in the sale, along with Phillip. In fact, the arresting police officer's statement at deposition specifically affirms that Hemnauth and Phillip were indeed "acting in concert" with "another." Since Fat Man — the unnamed other — was not arrested in the incident, if ever, nor even identified in the police deposition, the "acting in concert" prosecution was hobbled, leaving the DA's case vulnerable to the agency defense in the hands of a lawyer skillful enough to argue it.

There was one hitch to the strategy. The agency defense implies, per force, that the respondent invoking it was indeed, at one point or another, in possession of a controlled substance, even for a brief instant and for a small amount. Hemnauth never denied this, either to Landou or to the court or to me. Still, the risk of a felony conviction carrying a very long prison term was too great for a conscientious attorney to pursue anything less than the surest means to an acquittal on the felony charges. Further, the prosecution had misplaced the physical evidence, and the misdemeanor possession implicit in Hemnauth's agency defense concerned a tiny amount of drugs — three dollars' worth. (The police deposition gives a weight of one grain, or 65 milligrams.) The three most recent U.S. presidents have admitted to involvement with drugs of equal or greater severity in the eyes of the law. Landou could reliably calculate that the penalty imposed by the court would be trivial.

On that score he was right.

Hemnauth returned to court the next day for sentencing on the misdemeanor. The judge sentenced Hemnauth to a $250 fine and suspended his driver's license for six months. That was it.

While they were waiting for Hemnauth to be called up to the clerk's desk after the sentencing, Landou showed Hemnauth the $2,000 check he had received for his services as a court-appointed attorney, and joked with Hemnauth about how he was getting a monetary reward for the outcome of the trial, whereas Hemnauth would have to pony up $250. Landou stayed behind when Hemnauth was called to the court's clerk to make a deposit against the fine and have the suspension of his license registered. He told Hemnauth that he wanted to be sure that his immigration status would not be affected. Landou was aware of the new immigration statutes pursuant to the 1996 Illegal Immigration Reform and Immigrant Responsibility Act (IIRIRA), but his knowledge of the implications were at that point more cursory than expert, and there were few, if any, precedents of someone in Hemnauth's shoes being threatened with deportation. Attorneys in the 1990s routinely dismissed the possibility that defendants in a minor criminal case might face deportation, because in practice it did not happen.

Later events demonstrated that the comfort Landou took in the lack of any mention by the court officials of immigration consequences was illusory. He assumed that it was the court's responsibility to alert Hemnauth to any changes in his residency permit. The assumption, again, was as reasonable as it was hazardous. Reasonable in that formal notification of a sanction is customarily required. Hazardous in that, particularly after IIRIRA's passage by Congress, immigration courts did not systematically enforce notification provisions, nor did they place a burden of proof on the government in deportation proceedings to demonstrate that proper notification had been conveyed to immigrants whose status may have changed. It certainly had not been in Hemnauth's case, and the requirement that courts alert immigrants of the repercussions of a criminal conviction was not decreed until the Supreme Court's ruling in *Padilla v. Kentucky*, which we will revisit later.

Again, Marvin Landou was not an immigration lawyer, and he did, in fact, consider the possibility of ulterior consequences, albeit blithely. No official — state or federal — at the time of Hemnauth's trial ever indicated a threat to his residency permit. And no attorney or defendant would have foreseen the harshness with which the Bush administration, in concert with local politicians, would wield the new IIRIRA statutes after September 11, 2001, in an effort to persuade a timorous public that it was keeping the country safe from swarthy terrorists or to stroke the xenophobia that fear can engender. Nor could one have predicted the emergence of a web of private and local prisons, under contract with Homeland Security, with a vested interest — financial and political — in maintaining a large population of detainees awaiting deportation. Landou's concern for Hemnauth was real and deep. I would even postulate that his affection for Hemnauth fueled his grit as an attorney. He had followed the best, and arguably the only, path to exoneration, and it was a steep one at that. Sadly, his spirited and audacious defense held the seed to Hemnauth's removal and opened the gate to institutional cruelty.

It is a fact that Hemnauth is the primary source of the narrative aspect of my account of the felony trial. However, he submitted openly to questioning that consumed a sizeable part of the five days I spent with him in tight quarters in Trinidad. Answers to questions repeated and rephrased were consistent. If I harped on a detail he could not elucidate, he told me candidly; he was not about to make things up, at least not factual things. It took persistence on my part, that continued well beyond his first telling of the drug trial, for him to overcome his reluctance to volunteer the full extent of Phillip's deceit for fear of being disloyal, but neither did he duck the issue when I probed. His reading of the procedural nuts and bolts was certainly off the mark, but that was a matter of interpretation, outside the narrative thread, and he knew I would investigate the legal aspects on my own, as I did with crucial help from Bryan Lonegan and the court files. I was also able to verify parts of the story independently, in particular the topography of the Queens neighborhood where the sting operation took place. For obvious reasons, I could not interview Marvin Landou. After much sleuthing, I did manage to locate the Queens assistant district attorney assigned to argue the prosecution's case in open court, who has long since left the DA's employ. Unfortunately, as she has no recollection of the case, she declined to speak with me. (I must disclose that Hemnauth was under the impression that the prosecutor had left her job with the Queens DA partially because of her misgivings about the charges levied against Hemnauth. While he never suggested that the prosecutor had not pursued him vigorously in court, he also recalled her empathetic attitude toward him outside the courtroom. However, since I cannot verify Hemnauth's belief that she left her job in protest, I must dismiss this detail of his account as hearsay.)

Above all, Hemnauth's sincerity is as palpable as the prosecution's portrait of him as an impenitent drug merchant is implausible, let alone inaccurate. Nothing in his past, in his relationships in Guyana or with Rahoni, in his allocation of time to church, temple and art, predisposed him to enter the urban drug trade. Nothing in his story or his personal habits either before his arrest or since points to any addiction, either. I can attest to this personally. It is also noteworthy that Rahoni's divorce petition contained no allegation of drug abuse, whereas her father, who had insisted on ending their marriage, was prepared, in his anger, to demonize his son-in-law mercilessly. Even his friendship with Phillip commenced after Phillip had curtailed his cocaine use. That of course did not stop Phillip from behaving stupidly and without regard to the peril he thrust upon Hemnauth by wading into a crack sale. But nor does it indicate a drug connection as the genesis or foundation of Hemnauth's ties to him.

Admittedly, I take it to some degree on faith that Hemnauth has been scrupulously honest when speaking of the circumstances of his arrest and trial, even when his amplified code of loyalty required that I pull a few teeth to gather the full picture of Phillip's unpretty role in the episode. Nevertheless, I have that faith and could not be writing this account without it.

Then again, I must ask myself whether my personal sentiments, or anyone else's, should matter at all. A properly constituted jury in a court of law, in a setting often if not always highly deferential to law enforcement, found Hemnauth innocent of the felony charges levied against him. Years later, the Queens district attorney's office found itself in a position to impede leniency while Hemnauth was fighting his deportation in immigration court and leapt at the opportunity. (That the prosecutors were still smarting over their defeat seven years later is another indication of how rare are acquittals in cases like Hemnauth's.) When I expressed surprise at the vindictiveness, Bryan Lonegan told me that in the eyes of the prosecutor the jury had been wrong in acquitting Hemnauth. By refusing to join a procedure that would have spared Hemnauth from removal, the DA's office believed it was doing its job of protecting the public from the depredations of a drug dealer. When I reacted by telling Bryan that I was under the citizen's impression that the duties of law enforcement extended to upholding the ruling of a court, he conceded the point. I will come back to it.

5

A Father, Once and Future

THE VERY MOMENT HEMNAUTH COMPLETES HIS TELLING of the trial, the skies open and release a heavy rainfall that clatters on the corrugated roof of his apartment like hail. The rain literally drowns out the narrative for several minutes: although we are talking, it is the only thing audible on my recorder. The day has turned so suddenly dark that I cannot see to write. Hemnauth offers to switch on a lamp, but I ask him not to. The air temperature is over a hundred degrees and I have no desire to augment it.

The downpour ends as brusquely as it started, the sun reappears, drainage water rushes down the open gutters in the street to wherever it is headed and we pick up from the end of the trial.

Hemnauth emerged from his long nightmare — poverty, demeaning labor interrupted by bouts of joblessness, estrangement from wife and child, arrest and a felony trial — a chastened man. He would not permit the sanctioned knowledge that he was innocent of terrible accusations made by people sanctimoniously intent on his destruction lead to a rebirth of complacency. His heels had taken him to the edge of the abyss, his toes over it as he tilted forward. He was not free of danger, and it would take a few iterations before he would find a steady job. Still, he was determined to stay out of trouble now that he had seen it bare its sharpest fangs — or so he thought.

After his acquittal, he returned to the Apex school's career office in search of employment leads. He was quickly referred to a "top refrigeration company," JDP Air Conditioning and Refrigeration. Their lead repair mechanic needed a sidekick with at least three years' experience, which Hemnauth did not quite have. Still, he filed an application and was hired after a single interview. He was paid twelve dollars an hour and worked a standard forty-hour week. "I was still a rookie." JDP was the big time as climate maintenance goes. The company had a contract with one of the Manhattan's larger property owners and management firms. The occupants of its midtown buildings were of the sort so fully accustomed to reliable services that it would not even have occurred to them that they would ever be compromised. Accordingly, the building management company installed the largest and most sophisticated rooftop and control equipment and did not skimp on maintenance. Finally, Hemnauth had a job he had been pushed to train for — by his ex-wife's father, who had also pushed him out the door. He was assigned to the computer and security room at Madison Square Garden at Penn Plaza, rather than to the cooling tower of the Garden itself. He would return later with a different employer.

He got on well with his boss, but his boss could not protect his job from the objections of the Sheet Metal Workers union, which would not abide a colleague who had not earned a membership card. He was laid off after a year. He also broke up with his girlfriend when a friend of hers became attracted to him. "The thing started to get a bit corrupted and I decided to pull out." Hemnauth was clearly intent on deflecting trouble of any variety, to the best of his ability.

At the same time, the network of templegoers tracked him down. He had been missed, particularly at temple weddings of which there were many. With his musicianship, Hemnauth had been central to ceremony. His absence in the months of and after the trial had left a void. He confessed to the pandit who first approached him — he had known Hemnauth as a child in Guyana — that his uncommitted romances with more than one girlfriend had left him feeling guilty, "a little adulterous" and adrift. As usual, Hemnauth does not dwell on the particulars of his dating life and, as usual, I do not press the point. In any event, the pandit assured him the temple community — his ashram — would welcome him back into the fold with open arms. It did.

It also found him a place to stay, a room in a condominium apartment on Parsons Boulevard in Queens, sublet from a fellow Hindu musician and a collector of musical instruments. The rental arrangement was casual, especially with Hemnauth out of a job, and conducive to Hemnauth returning to service at and for the ashram. "We did charitable work to raise funds to build a temple in the Bronx." Despite being unemployed, Hemnauth was on the trajectory of getting his life back together. The missing piece was his son. Rahoni still gave him a very cold shoulder whenever he called her at home in the evening, and there was no discussion of her yielding visitation rights. "We were still separated." Intriguingly, her hostility vanished when he visited her at her job, away from her father's monitoring of her phone conversations. There was hope, even on that front.

It was not long before Hemnauth secured another job, and his year at JDP counted as valuable experience. His boss, Jimmy, whom Hemnauth describes as a "cool guy," owned an institutional maintenance business. His main account was Montefiore Medical Center at the Albert Einstein College of Medicine in the Bronx. Teaching hospitals tend to be valuable, but demanding clients for infrastructure maintenance services for reasons that seem intuitive. Jimmy gave Hemnauth a truck, a radio, a helper and fifteen dollars an hour.

It could have worked out, but it did not. I have mentioned that Hemnauth told me several times that he must control bouts of anger, particularly those that grew from the injustice of his deportation proceedings. At times they can overwhelm the gentleness that he nurtures by nature and spiritual conviction. The ingredients of his anger must have already been growing in the wake of his divorce and the demeaning felony accusation. It flared when Jimmy, annoyed when Hemnauth did not immediately answer a dispatch — he had left his radio on a battery charger in the company office — unleashed a barrage of curses "early in the morning." They enraged Hemnauth, who dislikes the stronger entries in the four-letter lexicon as contrary to the ethos of serenity he has retained from the teachings of the sages of his ashram. Still, he cursed back at his boss and became all the angrier for having succumbed. He did not report for work the next day. While his boss contended that he had walked off the job, Hemnauth must have received dismissal papers, because he qualified for a small amount of unemployment insurance.

The employment setbacks do not seem to have derailed him from his course of personal recovery. Between his unemployment insurance, and musical gigs at clubs and restaurants in Queens, he had enough money to live on, frugally, and welcomed the chance at a relaxed interlude from refrigeration maintenance. He also got hired for occasional reggae performances at upmarket venues in Manhattan, including SOB's and The Triad. He was decidedly no amateur; these places are picky.

Hemnauth put much of his time into the temple and two churches, attending services and doing charity work, usually with his guitar. The temple seems to have held the most sway because, as he explains to me, the learnedness of the monks appealed to him greatly, spoke directly to the here and now, relied less on revelation than western religion and gave him something he did not have. He stayed with the Liberty Bible Fellowship Church as well, out of enjoyment of the Gospel readings. He further associated with yet another place of worship, a Pentecostal church, but more as a "business relationship," as he puts it. The pastor liked his music and hired him for Sunday ritual. He even called for Hemnauth in his car and drove him home after services.

Despite Phillip's questionable loyalty at the trial, Hemnauth bore no grudge and still saw him regularly at the band room in Jamaica, where they both would rehearse and linger during the weekday. The band room was a good place for him to hang out between gigs, temple and church: groups knew where to find him if they needed another member for an ad hoc engagement or a recording project, of which there were several.

If the space had been the drug den the police suspected it was, it seems unlikely that a chastened Hemnauth would have set foot there in the aftermath of his brush with a district attorney very displeased with Hemnauth's acquittal. As it was, the police did visit looking in vain for drugs. If any of the denizens partook of a joint, they were not stupid enough to do so at a place the cops had in their tenacious sights. On one occasion, the police did take Hemnauth into custody after uncovering a bag of loose tobacco. He was released without charge. Possession of tobacco, even unrolled, is not illegal.

Hemnauth was edging closer to personal fulfillment than he had come since leaving Guyana. He had built a community around worship, neighbors and the band room. He was filling a regular calendar of music performances. He was materially self-sufficient despite setbacks and challenges.

Reunion with his son took him across the finish line.

"I saw Lo-Temp in the yellow pages. They were walking distance from Parsons Boulevard, so I decided to apply." With three years of air conditioning experience under his belt, Hemnauth easily found employment without even leaving the neighborhood. In Queens alone, there are well over a hundred cooling installation and maintenance businesses like Lo-Temp leavening the demand for skilled labor. With his seniority, Hemnauth could also be dispatched to job sites without supervision. He asked for twenty dollars an hour. They gave him nineteen along with a promise for the last dollar once he had proven his mettle. He got the extra dollar (more for overtime), and by the time of his detention by the INS, Lo-Temp had put him in charge of climate maintenance in the control room of Madison Square Garden, the arena's nerve center.

"Around that time, Rahoni moved [away] from her dad in the Bronx . . . And she came to live in Jamaica, Queens." Walking distance from Hemnauth's condo and his job. "We were living in the same neighborhood now." In any event, Hemnauth always kept in touch with her "whether she talked rough or smooth." I ask if Rahoni had had a falling out with her father, since there were many signs that he was a domineering presence in her life. Hemnauth does not know if father and daughter had a falling out, and he never asked despite the sense of vindication that Rahoni's distancing herself from her father might have brought him. He is distinctly uninterested in keeping score and scrupulously mindful of Rahoni's privacy.

Soon after she came to live in Queens, she called Hemnauth and asked, to his surprise and delight, "What kind of father am I? That I don't come and take care of the child. That he is asking for his dad." The kind of father Hemnauth was, of course, was one who had been declared *persona non grata* and unequivocally denied custody and visiting rights. True, he was not blameless in the divorce and had done little to resist or protest its explicitly harsh terms. Still, the father he had been up to that point was not the one he wanted to be. If proof were needed, he stood ready to supply it.

For all intents and purposes, Rahoni was repealing, unsolicited, the

terms of the divorce that related to Kevin, and granting Hemnauth unconditional and unlimited visitation rights to his son. Hemnauth reciprocated
with child support, without being asked to. "Not much, but something to
buy stuff for Kevin," he says, modestly. From that standpoint, the timing for a rapprochement was perfect, as Hemnauth was feeling increasingly confident in his material prospects, between his maintenance jobs
and those of his gigs that were not charities. There were no papers, court
or lawyers involved. It just happened, and to this day, Hemnauth has never
given Rahoni cause to regret it. I go a little bit out on a limb in affirming
this, but I do have the preponderance of the evidence in support, not the
least of which is the lasting bond between father and son that has remained
as tight as any to this day and lasted into Kevin's adulthood. The two years
of Hemnauth's imprisonment were an undeniable and horrible strain, but
they did not once prompt Rahoni to question Hemnauth's ability and dedication as a father. In any event, the very second Rahoni reinstated him, as
it were, Hemnauth jumped in with both feet.

"I remember it as if it were yesterday," Kevin tells me when I ask if he can
recall the moment when his father reentered his life. He is twenty-two now,
and it has been sixteen years since Hemnauth crossed his threshold for
the first time since Rahoni, under orders from her father, had made him
leave. By his own account, his vision of that first sentient encounter with
his dad is "blurred." Yet Kevin gives the distinct impression that he relives
the reunion with his father every single day with unbridled joy. "It was
Father's Day. I remember that I ran to him and hugged him." The pair immediately went off to Playland, an amusement park in Westchester County,
northeast of the city on Long Island Sound. From that day on, Hemnauth
was a reliable fixture in his son's life. They were together every weekend,
almost without exception, to the point that Hemnauth, Kevin and Rahoni
closely resembled the nuclear family the parents had once dreamt of being.
They sat often at the same dinner table. Rahoni was happy to have her ex-
husband around the house every weekend, and their relationship extended
considerably beyond the cordiality and practicality minimally needed for
shared custody of their child to function smoothly. "Kevin was happy to

see that." Hemnauth helped Kevin with his schoolwork and taught him music (although not quite as much as he would have liked) and sound engineering. He took his son fishing, and to the movies at the multiplex near Co-op City in the north Bronx. He liked comedies, like many preteen boys, as I know from experience.

Rahoni drew the line only at Hemnauth sleeping over in her home, and Hemnauth deflects my question as to whether there had ever been a likelihood of the two parents reinstituting if not their marriage, some proxy for it. In sum, once they had established a routine and built a stable rapport beneficial to Kevin, they were not about to risk upending it.

I also asked Kevin if his mother ever expressed regret or bitterness over her decision to bring Hemnauth back into her son's orbit after Hemnauth had been arrested and jailed for what would turn out to be effectively a two-year sentence, notwithstanding the official line that immigrant detention is not imprisonment. No, he says. "She was very upset. She knew I needed a father figure in my life. All that was being taken from me. She wanted to get it over with."

Rahoni may have blamed Hemnauth for making a mistake, a foolish one even, for having kept carefree company with a few people the police did not like. She never held him responsible for the injustices others dealt him. She made that explicitly clear to me when I asked her.

The routine Hemnauth had established with Kevin and Rahoni must have lasted some time, as much as three years in my estimation, before Hemnauth left on his fateful two-week journey back to see his mother in Guyana. (Hemnauth often has trouble pinpointing dates, and I have relied on Kevin's clear recollection of his reunion with his father at age six, and the known date of the trip back to Georgetown around the time of Kevin's tenth birthday.) Hemnauth's involvement in Kevin's life had an additional subtext. Kevin attended public school in Jamaica, Queens in a reasonably tranquil setting, yet but a stone's throw from Jamaica's meaner streets infested with drugs. The school itself was "so-so," but Kevin was a conscientious kid, and Rahoni wanted to keep him on that tack, away from the lure of the drugs being dealt to preteens in and around the school. Rahoni's anxiety was more than rational and consistent with the sentiments of many others in her neighborhood. At one point, shortly after Hemnauth's immigration detention, the prevalence of drugs and weapons on the junior high school property became such that police were obtaining search warrants on the students' parents' homes. Rahoni promptly removed Kevin from the school and sent him to stay with a relative in Boston until he could safely return to school in Queens. Kevin's education was a recurring theme and worry throughout his teen years, and the threats to his security and to his ability to stay his course only grew worse in high school. Thanks to our immigration laws, Hemnauth had to fret from afar, whereas he had proven in spades that he was capable of contributing decisively to his son's learning habits and value system. Against the odds, Kevin has come through admirably.

Little did Hemnauth know, at the beginning of 2002, that his life was about to crumble. The mass murder of September 11, 2001 had cast a pall over Hemnauth just as it had over the entire country and much of the world. People started to look at him with suspicion because of his skin tone — there is no other explanation — and on more than one occasion, someone in the same building as one of his maintenance sites — the Brazilian-themed music and dinner club S.O.B.'s — called security on him. He was heckled with the catcall "Bin Laden!" in the streets of Jamaica, also more than once. "That was a bit disgusting," he understates. Still, after a decade in New York, he considered himself a New Yorker and made a point of visiting Ground Zero regularly.

It had also been close to a decade since Hemnauth had seen his mother, Rawti. She was developing health problems stemming from chronic high blood pressure. With Rahoni's blessing, Hemnauth decided to go on a short leave to Georgetown to visit the mother he calls Dharti Mata, or Mother Earth, after a Hindu goddess. Ten years is a long time, and despite the reversals in his fortunes, his intention was to travel to his place of birth and youth without any notion, even a remote one, of a permanent return. By now he was materially and emotionally established in an American city where, to his mind, he was now making his mark and raising his son. Penury and the prohibitive terms of his divorce were of the past. So were his legal predicaments, or so he thought. Squirreled away in a computer file were the documents ordering his ruin and separation from his American child.

It is worth pausing if but for a moment to consider who exactly this man was, whose character our immigration statutes blithely assassinated. In 2002, Hemnauth Mohabir was a green-card-carrying legal permanent resident. He had held jobs for which America routinely imports labor for lack of citizens wanting to do them, including one fighting rodents under a shower of garbage. He gradually worked his way up in a craft he had trained for assiduously and at great sacrifice, earning a living wage from stable employment. He paid his taxes and used public services as parsimoniously as any civic-minded American, arguably more so. He had known setbacks that landed him in abject poverty and homelessness from which he clawed his way out on his own power without ever asking for a handout, a welfare check or a single food stamp. He had been acquitted of a felony charge in a court system so diffident to the police who arrested him that his refusing a plea bargain was considered lunacy. The only stain on his record on the day he left for Georgetown was a five-year-old misdemeanor conviction, trivial as measured by the penalty, and for an act no more sordid than similar ones committed by many of the people who govern us and we elect to do so. He was a devoted father to his American-born son and, once invited, a loyal helpmate to his son's mother. He enlivened the culture of the city with his skills as an artist. He was peacefully devout. He had a long record of community service.

This was the man from whose "criminal" proclivities our immigration law set out to protect us with all its xenophobia-fired and retributive fury. It would take immigration enforcement five years of dormancy to collar Hemnauth, but the trap was now cocked and patiently awaited its prey.

6

SHACKLES AND JUMPSUITS

APRIL 2002, AGAIN. THE VAN CARRYING THE SHACKLED Hemnauth Mohabir from Kennedy Airport drove up to a hard metal garage door that opened automatically and pulled past the barriers of Middlesex County Jail (officially, Middlesex County Adult Correction Center) in central New Jersey. Once inside and the door lowered, the INS transit officer stepped out, helped Hemnauth from the vehicle and brought him into a room directly inside the prison gate.

The officer removed his own equipment — the standards call for a bulletproof vest and a sidearm — and surrendered his gun to a prison official for safekeeping whilst inside the facility. He freed Hemnauth from his shackles, which he placed in a box reserved for INS gear, the same procedure Hemnauth had observed at Kennedy Airport, in reverse. Apparently, each agency in the chain of handling a detainee owns the restraints it uses, and property is not to be comingled.

Middlesex, Hemnauth's gateway to almost two years of extrajudicial imprisonment, fits into a nationwide network of detention venues comprised predominantly of state prisons and local jails. There are about 350 of them — of which Hemnauth experienced three — although the number is in constant flux as individual facilities enter and leave the system, among them

Middlesex itself, which severed its contract with ICE in 2009.[34] Also, of the total number of jails under contract, some 20% of them might go empty of immigrant detainees on any given night. The state and local facilities house 68% of immigration detainees, most under individual Intergovernmental Service Agreements (IGSAs). Another 17% reside in privately owned detention centers operated by corporate jailers such as the Corrections Corporation of America. While IGSAs are the standard pacts between the federal government on one hand, state and local on the other, they do not commit the state or local corrections institution to actually run the detention facility under its command. Operation of a state- or county-owned jail may well be outsourced to a for-profit entity and often is. Nine of the ten largest complexes under ICE contract are run by for-profit corporations; all but two are under IGSAs. Immigration detention has become an industry; its revenue stream is now safeguarded by a mandated minimum nightly occupancy of 34,000 detainees under a provision appended to the Department of Homeland Security's appropriation legislation in 2009.

The immigrant inmate population is not evenly distributed. The larger facilities — or at least the most populated ones — are concentrated along the country's southern rim, a situation partially (but only partially) explained by the high Mexican and Central American representation in the immigrant detainee population, some 65% of it. Most of the 350 state and local jails under IGSAs hold fewer than 100 immigrant inmates. However, of the five largest detention centers in the nation, housing over 20% of immigrant detainees, three have opened since 2005; the concentration in the South may have been less remarkable during Hemnauth's period of imprisonment in New Jersey.[35]

---

34 In an odd twist, the freeholders of Middlesex County cited Section 287(g) of the IIRIRA immigration code as the reason for severance. This section provides that the federal government can effectively deputize state and local law enforcement by mutual agreement, provided that agents co-opted by ICE undergo training under federal auspices. The Middlesex freeholders claimed that the costs of such arrangements were prohibitive. The irony lies in that advocates of autonomous enforcement of immigration by the states, such as the contested SB 1070 crackdowns in Arizona supplanting federal authority, often invoke an aggressive interpretation of 287(g). Another lies in the Middlesex conclusion that the immigrant detention contract was too onerous, whereas the more common assessment is that such contracts present a financial benefit as a magnet for federal funds.

35 Kerwin and Lin, "Immigration Detention: Can ICE Meet Its Legal Imperatives and

On any given night, about ten of every hundred detainees are held in federal Service Processing Centers prior to being sent on to other facilities for longer incarcerations or proceeding to a resolution of their cases. It happens that when Hemnauth was arrested at JFK, the Varrick Street Detention Center in Manhattan, a common springboard to other detention centers, had been closed after the September 11 assault. (It reopened in 2008.)

Some detainees — untallied but significant in number — are held outside the network of jails that are under explicit contract with ICE. Maricopa County, Arizona boasts, literally and proudly, one of the most fearsome detention sites: Sheriff Joe Arpaio's "internationally famous" Tent City,[36] run to a program of deliberate humiliation, intimidation, desert heat exhaustion and deprivation of inmates who, under federal statutes, are not prisoners, but administrative detainees. The sheriff has been filmed referring with endearment to his Tent City as a concentration camp.[37] (Another detention center in Willacy County, Texas is also referred to as a 'tent city' owing to the windowless Kevlar domes that serve as blocks.)

A determined and creative sheriff serially elected on an immigrant-baiting platform, as Arpaio most recently was in November 2012, will always find loopholes that permit arrest on a criminal charge by, for example, naming a smuggled immigrant his smuggler's coconspirator in a RICO (Racketeer Influenced and Corrupt Organizations Act) predicate offense. (This is the same sheriff who once arrested a citizen for clapping at the conclusion of a statement the sheriff did not like, on a charge of disturbing the peace at a public meeting.) It also helps if the sheriff has within his posse a number of officers who have received federal training under Section 287(g) of the Immigration and Nationality Act, added by IIRIRA, as cover for his vigilantism directed against immigrants.[38]

Under the 287(g) provision, the Department of Homeland Security "is authorized to enter into agreements with state and local law enforcement agencies for the purpose of delegating immigration enforcement functions

Case Management Responsibilities?"
36 "Tent City Jail," Maricopa County Sheriff's Office.
37 DeVivo and Fernandez, *Two Americans*.
38 Finnegan, "Sheriff Joe." IIRIRA added smuggling to the list of RICO predicate offenses. See: Virtue (former INS General Counsel), testimony in "Shortfalls of the 1996 Immigration Reform Legislation."

to select officers . . . The agreements permit LEAs [local law enforcement agencies] to perform immigration enforcement activities *only under ICE supervision, and allow ICE to suspend or revoke participating officers' authority at any time*" (emphasis added).[39] This language is consistent with the well-established precedent of restricting unsupervised state and local enforcement of immigration statutes to criminal matters, not civil ones. "Historically, the authority for state and local law enforcement officials to enforce immigration law has been construed to be limited to certain *criminal* provisions of the INA [Immigration and Naturalization Act] that also fall under state and local jurisdictions; *by contrast, the enforcement of the* civil *provisions, which includes apprehension and removal of deportable aliens, has strictly been viewed as a federal responsibility, with states playing an incidental supporting role*" (emphasis added).[40]

That said, Sheriff Arpaio has not been not alone in misinterpreting provision 287(g) as a federal mandate, granted to local authorities, to self-deputize at will. And he is not alone in having blurred the line between detention pursuant to a civil action by the federal government and punitive incarceration. The provision itself has been used only since 2002, and Homeland Security's inspector general has sharply criticized its application as flawed: "ICE cannot be assured that the 287(g) program is meeting its intended purpose, or that resources are being appropriately targeted toward aliens who pose the greatest risk to public safety and the community."[41]

The federal government is partly complicit in the jurisdictional trespassing by state and local law enforcement, even if it never predicted or advocated such a repercussion from programs like 287(g). State and local police have long been authorized to arrest persons suspected of having committed a federal crime. That much is uncontested. Offenses codified as crimes by the Immigration and Nationalization Act — for example, ducking an inspection at a border crossing — can legally lead to arrests by state and local jurisdictions.[42] In those cases, the respondent can invoke his constitutional protections under the Sixth Amendment, notably the right to an attorney. The law does not authorize such arrests or detention pursuant to

39 Outten-Mills et al., "The Performance of 287(g) Agreements."
40 Seghetti, Ester, and Garcia, "Enforcing Immigration Law: The Role of State and Local Law Enforcement."
41 Seghetti et al., "Enforcing Immigration Law."
42 Legomsky, "The New Path of Immigration Law."

civil violations. In 1996, the Department of Justice specifically proscribed the practice as it related to civil immigration proceedings.[43]

However, here's the hitch. Since 1986, and certainly with the enactment of IIRIRA a decade later, the punitive ethos of immigration law and the increased mimicking of the criminal justice model by immigration enforcement— absent the constitutional protections of the criminal justice system — have overwhelmed the civil nature of most violations of the immigration code. Further, in 2002, then-Attorney General John Ashcroft essentially reversed that prohibition, although Congress did not authorize him to do so: state and local police could carry out arrests of any person it thought might be deportable. Even Ashcroft's dubious finding, implicitly abandoned by the Obama administration as it fights the attempts by some states to coopt jurisdiction over immigration, refers only to arrest, not detention. In 2005, the House of Representatives, under conservative domination, did pass draconian legislation that gave the states and local police close to full authority over immigration enforcement with no preconditions such as the officer training stipulated in IIRIRA. The new House bill failed for lack of consensus with the U.S. Senate.[44]

In practical reality, 287(g) has facilitated the commandeering of immigration policy by state and local police, even if that was never the intent. "Because 287(g) jail officials are granted the authority to interrogate people about their immigration status and prepare charging documents to initiate deportation, the entire criminal and immigration process — from initial arrest to removal — can take place completely on paper within the walls of the county jail, with little or no opportunity to assert due process rights, and with minimal involvement from the local ICE office."[45]

An unfortunate irony arises from the tension between federal dominion over immigration policy and claims of jurisdiction by state and local authorities. Measures such as 287(g) acknowledge the reality that states, counties and cities enjoy more intimate familiarity with the immigrant communities residing within them than might federal regulators. The profile

---

43 Miller, "Citizenship and Severity: Recent Immigration Reforms and the New Penology."

44 Legomsky, "The New Path of Immigration Law."

45 American Civil Liberties Association of Arizona, "In Their Own Words: Enduring Abuse in Arizona Immigration Detention Centers."

of these communities can vary widely from one state or city to another. It follows that the conduct of sound immigration practices, extending to integration as well as enforcement, can benefit from the insights of state and local authorities. Additionally, "not every subfederal regulation that touches on the subject of immigration creates the sort of conflict that runs afoul of the Constitution's Supremacy Clause."[46] Unilateral power grabs, however, do. They also undermine constructive participation of state and local leadership in the formulation of immigration policy in order to advantage the politics of vilification and retribution, dear to some elected officials.

In December 2012, ICE quietly announced that it had "decided not to renew any of its agreements with state and local law enforcement agencies that operate task forces under the 287(g) program."[47] The official reasoning, which may well be truthful, is that other methodologies, such as matching arrests against a computerized immigration database, would yield "more efficient use of resources for focusing on priority cases."[48] The tone of the same year-end press release intimated that the agency would train its sights more selectively on detention and deportation candidates whose criminal profile pose a genuine threat to public safety, as opposed to an imagined or remote one.

Given machinations at the federal level during the Bush era, it is small wonder that many state and local officials, elected to office on a law-and-order and anti-immigrant ideological platform, have been drawn to immigration enforcement like bees to honey. It has given them the best of both worlds: they get to jail unpopular people *and* deny them the rights afforded to individuals arrested for criminal activity. Why? Because the government's complaint against them is technically civil, not criminal, whereas the tone of IIRIRA's approach to civil immigration infractions is pugnacious and punitive. This catch-22 trapped Hemnauth, as it has many others, in a penal netherworld. The Obama administration may wish to soften its approach to detention and deportation of immigrants with a thin record of petty offenses in the course of tuning ICE's enforcement priorities. It signaled this on several occasions in 2012, not only in ICE's year-end report. However, deportations have continued apace, and bending the IIRIRA strictures in

46 Rodriguez, "The Integrated Regime of Immigration Regulation."
47 "FY 2012: ICE Announces Year-End Removal Numbers."
48 "FY 2012: ICE Announces Year-End Removal Numbers."

the name of fitting them to the policy priorities of the moment does not rid us of them. That requires action by all three branches of government, Congress first among them.

The line between civil detention and imprisonment was first traced by the Supreme Court in 1896, in a case considered landmark among immigration law scholars, *Wong Wing v. United States*. The case tested a provision of the Geary Act of 1892, the very act that established the government's right to expel foreigners on the same grounds that determine its power to prevent the entry of those it does not deem it desirable to admit. The Geary Act extended the 1882 Chinese Exclusion Act's ban on Chinese immigration to permitting deportation. This central thrust of the Geary Act legislation was upheld by the Supreme Court almost immediately in *Fong Yue Ting v. United States* (1893), which also held that deportation is not punishment, a finding still in application today:

> The order of deportation is not a punishment for crime. It is not a banishment, in the sense in which that word is often applied to the expulsion of a citizen from his country by way of punishment. It is but a method of enforcing the return to his own country of an alien who has not complied with the conditions upon the performance of which the Government of the nation . . . has determined that his continuing to reside here shall depend.[49]

The Geary Act, named for its sponsoring congressman, prescribed a specific sentence of a year of hard labor for a Chinese citizen, without as much as a trial, if found to be in the country illegally, even in the absence of any other conviction. (The Geary Act, like the Chinese Exclusion Act, targeted Chinese in an era of strident anti-Chinese attitudes in the United States.) The hard labor penalty without trial was too rich by one degree for the justices' blood, since it

> inflicts an infamous punishment, and hence conflicts with the fifth and sixth amendments of the constitution, which declare that no person

---

49 Gray, "Fong Yue Ting v. United States" (1893).

shall be held to answer for a capital or otherwise infamous crime, unless on a presentment of indictment of a grand jury, and that in all criminal prosecutions the accused shall enjoy the right to a speedy and public trial, by an impartial jury of the state and district wherein the crime shall have been committed.[50]

However, detaining a candidate for deportation per se did not trouble the Court that decided *Wong Wing*, no more than did the overtly racist underpinnings of the Chinese Exclusion and Geary Acts. This perspective on preremoval detention has endured to this day:

> We think it clear that detention or temporary confinement, as part of the means necessary to give effect to the provisions for the exclusion or expulsion of aliens, would be valid. Proceedings to exclude or expel would be vain if those accused could not be held in custody pending the inquiry into their true character, and while arrangements were being made for their deportation. Detention is a usual feature in every case of arrest on a criminal charge, even when an innocent person is wrongfully accused; but it is not imprisonment in a legal sense.[51]

As one might imagine, the *Wong Wing* decision raises many issues, not the least of which is that it appears to open the door to imprisonment that is not recognized as such; in other words it places the threshold of what constitutes punishment beyond simple incarceration. If jailing came pursuant to a civil proceeding against a potential deportee, it was permissible. That official view persists in current law. The immigration statutes are careful to maintain the distinction between civil and criminal infraction, perhaps because *Wong Wing* also states that Congress can pass laws criminalizing illegal residency, provided that any ensuing penalty is imposed as the result of a trial:

> We think it would be plainly competent for congress to declare the act of an alien in remaining unlawfully within the United States to be an offense punishable by fine or imprisonment, if such offense were to be established by a judicial trial.[52]

---

50 "Wong Wing v. United States" (1896).
51 "Wong Wing v. United States."
52 "Wong Wing v. United States."

With these strictures on the books, it is understandable that immigration enforcement has taken the civil law route, in the process distinguishing detention from imprisonment in order to avoid the definitional tangle any confusion would put it in.

The entire thrust of the reforms advocated — but only timidly enacted — by the Obama administration to the immigrant detention regimen is to reverse its close resemblance to a penal system within the strictures of IIRIRA. The idea is essentially that the legal distinction between detention and imprisonment should transfer to a practical one, rather than rely on the fantasy of detention not being punitive simply because the government decrees it is not. Since the IIRIRA statutes are careful to avoid equating detention to imprisonment in their formulation in order to impede detainees' access to the courts of the federal judiciary system, the door is theoretically open to the kinds of reforms the Obama administration wishes to implement. A first detention center designed and built to noncorrectional standards of custody was completed in March 2012, in Texas, with the capacity to house 608 male inmates deemed to be low safety risk[53], although who makes that determination, and how, is unclear. Since Hemnauth had a criminal record from his misdemeanor, duly inflated by the formulas embedded in IIRIRA, it seems doubtful he would have benefitted. A few more similarly designed facilities are in the works, and ICE has hired additional on-site monitors for the largest existing detention locations.[54]

This is a step in the right direction, perhaps, yet a drop in the bucket, considering the expansive network of jails with immigrants under lock and key. The difficulty in generalizing the Obama reforms to immigrant detention lies in the punitive thread thickly woven through the immigration and deportation system. A further impediment is their reliance on both a high ranking among policy priorities of whoever is president at any point in time, and Congressional budget appropriations that mandate a minimum detention target of 34,000 detainees per night, but little in the way of detention standards. Not to mention the hardening of anti-immigrant hearts, the irresistible opportunity it offers for electoral gain and the cash incentives for private jailers, counties and their sheriffs to keep things just the way they are. Hispanic American and Asian American voters repudiated

---

53 Semple and Eaton, "Detention for Immigrants That Looks Less Like Prison."
54 Semple and Eaton, "Detention for Immigrants."

immigrant bashing by conservatives in November 2012 and contributed mightily to the defeat of Governor Mitt Romney's presidential bid and his vision of "self-deportation" as a basis for immigration policy. As a result, many in conservative circles have discovered a new appreciation and burning affection for constituents of recent foreign heritage.

On the other hand, Sheriff Arpaio was reelected.

The guards at the prisons serving as federal immigration detention wards do not carry guns, at least not for the routine work of a normal day. For raids, they are more amply equipped, as Hemnauth would later experience. They do always wear a thin layer of body armor under their shirts that to Hemnauth's eyes, in hindsight, is not designed to stop bullets, but rather to deflect blows or stabs. "And maybe some pepper spray," Hemnauth adds. Hemnauth would not have known this, but it is now common protocol for prison guards to carry pepper spray rather than guns, even in high-security prisons like the notorious San Quentin in Northern California. Like many newer or renovated prisons, Middlesex has alarms always within easy reach and an armed brigade on standby, but out of sight of the prisoners unless summoned to intervene. In which case "they'll rush in and kick the shit out of everybody," to use Hemnauth's recollection of protocol at Middlesex. Hemnauth was being shown no special deference as an administrative detainee of the immigration service — his first exposure to the blurred line between civil custody and correctional incarceration.

Two prison officials, one man and one woman, then went through the motions of booking Hemnauth into Middlesex County Jail. They began by signing a document the transit officer handed them on a clipboard confirming that the INS "had delivered his body." When I heard the phrase from Hemnauth's mouth, I immediately asked if he was editorializing. But no. "He said that. That is the term they use, actually."

Since I had just begun questioning Hemnauth about prison life as an INS detainee, I was eager to drill down on the idioms used by those with authority over him, as a measure of the ethos of the system, beyond Hemnauth's own interpretations. I did not need to. Hemnauth dwelled on the terminology without any cue from me.

"Yes, that is the term they use," he repeats. "When they are taking a group to the courts and stuff, they'll say, okay we have twenty bodies." On the day he arrived at Middlesex, they "had one body. My body . . . That's a common theme, the body theme. They don't address you as a person." He pauses a moment. "It's a kind of way that they make you feel like an animal," he says, in a way that suggests I should not be surprised.

"Or not even that?" I ask.

Hemnauth's mood darkens for a fleeting moment. "A dead person. A carcass." The distinction was deliberate. A dead person is still a person; a carcass, not necessarily.

I was not surprised, or if I was, should not have been. After all, I had heard Daniel Zwerdling's reporting and talked to him about it. Still, to face the man who can describe, firsthand, how he had experienced a deliberate campaign of dehumanization — or animalization, to be more specific and true to a sentiment he will evoke many times as we sit in his cold-water flat in Trinidad — gives a poignancy to his account that no prior knowledge could have prepared me for.

The male officer booking him was a young white man. "He started really harassing me," while the lady officer, also white, was filling out forms. She asked him "the normal things": health history, dietary restrictions, allergies, next of kin. She also asks for his name, which presumably she had in front of her, and his address, which the INS is heartily intent on rendering irrelevant. Also ironic are inquiries about his family status; IIRIRA does not consider Article 16 of the Universal Declaration's proscription of the forced dislocation of families to be a concern in deportation cases. "She's just doing her job." She did not inquire about the old misdemeanor charge or the circumstances around it.

The male officer, on the other hand, "started treating me like the Taliban, yelling and cursing at me." He barked commands such as "Answer the woman!" each time the woman read a question from her checklist, although Hemnauth was responding politely and without embellishment. The man berated Hemnauth abusively for his posture as not as appropriately akin as it should have been to an enlistee facing a drill sergeant at boot camp. He addressed Hemnauth sneeringly as "you people," which in the context Hemnauth heard as a racial slur. "It was disgusting."

The officer did not strike Hemnauth, yet, but when it came time to move even a few steps he manhandled him and "tossed me around." Lest we forget, Hemnauth had been picked up for a civil violation of the immigration code, which he was unfamiliar with, pursuant to a six-year-old misdemeanor. The INS bureaucracy had taken some twenty-four hours to process him, during which he had not been given a meal he could eat, let alone a bed. His INS handlers had insisted to an almost comical degree on labeling him a "detainee," not to be confused with a prisoner. Yet, at the gateway into his administrative custody, he was treated as someone just arrested for some grievous criminal misconduct.

It would appear that conflating detainees with criminals was a prescribed psychological tactic intended to deflate the detainees and erode any will and ability to resist their treatment by convincing them that they are, indeed, criminals.[55] In keeping with this logic, Hemnauth was to be presumed a terrorist inherently belligerent toward his captors or an equally hostile common criminal.

He was, of course, neither.

I record this first encounter with an irascible prison official not solely for its narrative value. There is a larger significance to the male officer's demeanor that I find particularly striking as I recount it here in writing. One might be tempted to chalk up the officer's verbal abusiveness to a lack of training or slim pickings among the candidates for his job. However, it appears to me that there are inescapable ramifications to deputizing jailers, be they state, county or corporate, as custodians for administrative detainees. Not to put too fine a point on it, once a jailer, always a jailer. Sure, there are regulations applicable specifically to detainees, but they do not protect people like Hemnauth from the jailer's mindset that considers anyone in his keeping a danger to be subdued, whether he is one or not. I shall leave aside, for now, the question of whether the distinctive rules drafted by the INS and later ICE are anything more than mere fig leaves, so many boxes to be checked in those seemingly rare instances when the INS and ICE have tried to highlight their deference to the supposedly nonpunitive nature of

---

55 Dow, *American Gulag: Inside U.S. Immigration Prisons.*

immigration detention. In fact, ICE also has explicit rules that allowed Hemnauth's custodians to treat him preemptively as hostile because of the nature of his prior misdemeanor conviction, let alone that it involved no violence, no resistance to arrest, no suggestion of jail time and no attempt at evasion of either his fine or the suspension of his driver's license that went with it.

Beyond weighing the effectiveness of any safeguards ICE may offer specific to detainees as distinct from prisoners, lies the ethos of the jail-house. A jail is a place in which the state incarcerates persons it deems too dangerous or ill deserving to be released into society. To hold people in that same bad guys' place for a reason other than public safety or retribution equates to requiring of their jailers that they split their manner if not their personalities. On top of that, there is little evidence that ICE, and before it the INS, ever did require that jails observe the distinction between immi-grant detainees and prisoners otherwise than to maintain separate quarters under the same roof and, perhaps, a separate squadron of guards. Even these requisites have been loosely heeded.

By contracting state, county and private jails as custodians for its immi-gration detainees, the federal government has let more than one genie out of its bottle. It has, by extension, hired sheriffs answerable to an elector-ate easily seduced by tough law-and-order rhetoric, attitude and actions. Selective toughness is not on the ballot, nor, often, are the finer points of ultimate federal authority over the detained immigrant population. Just ask Sheriff Joe Arpaio of Maricopa County if he draws a distinction between immigrant detainees and the general prison population in how he should treat them. Or better yet, ask the people who have voted for him, up to this day, or the legislators who approved the self-designation of the state of Ar-izona as ICE's posse whether the federal government requested it or not.

To be sure, the federal government has teased local authorities with mea-sures drawing them closer to participation in immigration enforcement. The USA Patriot Act enlists the vigilance of local governments in spotting and detaining suspected terrorists, leaving the door open for local law en-forcement to "suspect" immigrants on grounds other than actual evidence of terrorist activity or even sympathy. Let your imagination wander.

More recently, the Secure Communities initiative implemented by ICE checks data on persons "arrested for a crime and booked into local law enforcement custody" against ICE's immigration records.[56] To the surprise, and dismay, of many of his supporters anxious for the immigration reform he has championed, President Obama has stepped up the use of Secure Communities to identify candidates for deportation and remove them from the country. In fact, the administration has characterized Secure Communities as compulsory, leading to a surge of immigrant detentions. The administration has gone so far as to attempt to prohibit states from opting out of the program, amidst a rising chorus of law enforcement experts worried over the negative repercussions of Secure Communities on the willingness of immigrants, both documented and not, to report crimes against themselves and others, for fear of entrapment by ICE. Says one Illinois sheriff, who identifies himself as a Republican critical of Secure Communities: "Law enforcement works best when it's engaged with the community . . . To have the community not working with you, that's a frightening proposition."[57]

The Obama administration's tough stance on enforcement, reflected in the record number of deportations it has set, is, according to the president, necessary to establish credibility as he attempts to land a bigger fish: comprehensive immigration reform more attuned to human rights concerns and American ideals. We have no grounds for doubting his intentions, since Secure Communities has risked driving away as much or more Latino support than it could possibly have won him among other constituencies, notwithstanding his success with Hispanic voters in November 2012. Nevertheless, Secure Communities' stated emphasis on dangerous criminals has been lost among the reports of people stopped for broken taillights, and subsequently detained, deported and separated from immediate families, American-citizen children and spouses among them. The Obama administration has taken the corrective measure of instituting "prosecutorial discretion," and ICE in December 2012 published a list of focus areas for enforcement as means of distinguishing high-priority candidates for deportation, for example violent and recidivist criminals, from more benign offenders of immigration law, such as students immigrated as minors with no criminal record. Still, Secure Communities is in operation, the sweeping list of criminal offenses deportable under IIRIRA has been left unamended

56 "Secure Communities," U.S. Immigration and Customs Enforcement.
57 Sheriff Mark Curran (Lake County, IL) in Young, "Lost in Detention."

by Congress — who alone can alter it — and prosecutorial discretion has thus far benefitted only a relative handful of removal cases.

The data assembled by ICE show that only 14% of the immigrants apprehended and removed by ICE in the 2013 fiscal year were serious offenders convicted of either a single count of an aggravated felony — as expansively defined by IIRIRA — or multiple crimes carrying a sentence of more than one year.[58] Also in fiscal year 2013, assault, sexual assault, weapons offenses, homicide and kidnapping accounted for 10% of those deportees with a criminal record and 6% of the total.[59] According to analysis by the Chief Justice Earl Warren Institute on Law and Social Policy at the University of California, Berkeley, the share of "aggravated felons" among arrests under Secure Communities is only 8%.[60] Secure Communities begins to resemble fishing for salmon in a river teeming with trout. Still, ICE has highlighted the policy as a cost-effective alternative to 287(g) compacts that are both costly to the federal government and have led to public displays of cruelty.

The various measures engaging state and local law enforcement are not the wholesale abdication of federal authority over immigration policy and its implementation the authors of legislation in Arizona, Alabama and other states construe them to be. However, in the twisted reading of a sheriff or politician feeding at the trough of anti-immigrant fervor, they can read mightily like an invitation to usurp that authority or unilaterally appoint himself an effective agent of the Department of Homeland Security. Federal law clearly states that it does not work that way, although teaser initiatives, like Secure Communities, IIRIRA's general affection for collaborative enforcement or tendentious readings of the IIRIRA statutes dating to the Bush era have been convenient tools to local officials goosing their own authority.

Then there is the financial genie floating off, hand in hand with its ideological twin to local enforcement nirvana. The contracts with the states and counties have created a source of money to which many have become addicted if not entirely beholden, particularly in communities with low tax

---

58 "FY 2013: ICE Immigration Removals."

59 "Secure Communities and ICE Deportation: A Failed System?"

60 Kohli, Markowitz, and Chavez, "Research Report—Secure Communities by the Numbers."

bases further hurt by recession, strapped for cash and eager to attract jobs provided by the growth industry immigration detention has become. Save for a few exceptions, state and local jurisdictions are not about to surrender federal funds, as long as they can escape, deflect or, in the exemplary cases of Arizona and Alabama, defy scrutiny. Jurisdictions who have taken on debt in order to build or expand detention centers are even less likely to welcome reforms that might undermine their ability to service them.

The federal government pays a fixed per diem per detainee and leaves it to the jailers to manage their own costs while imposing few standards specific to immigrant detention, certainly none more onerous than those applicable to the general prison populations. Arguably less so, since the policing of those standards by a distant ICE has been demonstrably lax in the past, as I shall illustrate. After all, it took a National Public Radio report to alert ICE that one of the facilities under contract with it was loosing attack dogs on detainees. (Canine use was subsequently addressed in published ICE detention standards.) The bottom line is just that: the bottom line. Revenues are fixed and costs are variable. The lower the costs, the better the net profit. So why serve three meals if you can get away with two? Why pay for genuinely qualified personnel when you can hire a brute for less?

Add it all up. Sheriffs elected for their law-and-order credentials. Politicians from local to state to federal officeholders and candidates preaching uncompromising treatment of immigrants, particularly those with brown skin. Financial rewards for filling jails and skimping on the care of detainees in custody. What we get, in more cases than not, is too good a deal for county sheriffs and other beneficiaries of the system to turn down. Or to give up.

After taking the officers' abuse for a while, Hemnauth tried a different tack in an attempt to deflect some of the prejudice the male officer was exhibiting. At this point he has no idea what awaits him, in what company he is to be kept. He had seen enough thus far to conclude that gracious hospitality was not a salient feature of the internment being arranged for him. So he felt it was a matter of survival to provide some definition of who he was, rather than to be summarily tagged a terrorist or predator, which was now emerging as the default hypothesis of his bookers at the jail. And if there were terrorists and predators in this place, he certainly did not want to be lumped together with them.

With this in mind, he tried to explain as best he could, given his state of exhaustion and confusion. "Listen, man," he said, "I'm a musician."

The few words he spoke awakened some curiosity in the male officer. He could not place Hemnauth's accent. This signaled to him that, perhaps, there was something different about this new inmate that might set him apart from others. He asked Hemnauth where he was from, a tidbit he might have picked up had he been listening to Hemnauth's answers to his colleague rather than obsessing over whether his toes were turned straight or outward. Hemnauth told the man he was from Guyana and, combined with his status as an artist, that "calmed him down." (Why it befell to the prisoner to calm down a guard is a question almost funny to ponder.) The officer had racially profiled him as an Arab; the deviation from the profile just as racially relieved him. It also made him curious about Hemnauth, for instance about his music, and even the music scene in Guyana, and he let some humanity poke through his enforcer's carapace. The coarse reception with which the officer had greeted Hemnauth yielded to "a friendly conversation." I conjure up the comforting image of prison officials predisposed to amicable discourse given half a chance, but it credits the immigration detention system with too much and Hemnauth with too little. The truth is that he possesses a disarming and gentle charisma that worked in this case. It did not always, and as time went by, even his natural charisma would recede, like a turtle into its shell, under the constant assault of hopelessness.

That the officer had relented and decided to treat Hemnauth with a modicum of respect emboldened Hemnauth to ask to use the phone. The man acquiesced to a collect outbound call, the only kind permitted, warning Hemnauth that it would be expensive. At that point, Hemnauth did not really care, and he was not envisioning two years of dependency on a parasitical phone company out to bleed inmates.

He had no idea of the extent of the telephone racket prevalent in INS/ICE detention centers, designed to serve the twin goals of denying inmates access to their lawyers and families and of enriching a monopoly carrier charging usury rates. Hemnauth may have had no idea, but the prestigious law firm Latham & Watkins certainly did. In a 2003 memorandum assessing conditions at Middlesex, the firm euphemistically reports that "telephone access at the Middlesex facility is a serious problem," and, more to the point, that "use [of telephones] is extremely cost-prohibitive." (The memo notes charges of seventy cents per minute for collect calls, a possibly illegal two-dollar connection fee for local calls and a five-dollar charge for dialing out of state, which, of course applied to Hemnauth with Rahoni and Kevin living across the state line in nearby Queens.) Published federal detention standards prescribing free calls to consulates, legal aid services and the immigration courts went unheeded or were logistically impeded. The memorandum also suggests that phones at Middlesex were tapped.[61]

The communication problem turned out to be widespread throughout the detention system, causing considerable hardship to people *not* being detained on a criminal charge, including, of course, to Hemnauth: after he was moved to Passaic, Rahoni refused the collect calls to her and Kevin, not from spite, but because of the crippling financial drain they triggered.

The outlandish telephone practices by the jails and whoever benefited from the communications contracts they awarded were not fully investigated by the ICE inspector general until 2008. Right then and there, Hemnauth needed to contact Rahoni, and cost was not the object. He steeled himself to remain strong and serene and not give way to the despair that now bared its teeth. He wanted to save his inner peace from the practical and physical hardships of his impending ordeal the better to confront them. This was more easily resolved than accomplished.

Hemnauth reached Rahoni from the booking room. "Hey, girl, I'm in jail," he announced. "They've got me in a big jail down in New Jersey." Rahoni and her older sister had been driving — wandering, really — around northern New Jersey looking for Hemnauth. He does not know exactly where they went, only that someone at immigration at Kennedy Airport had told them that he would likely be taken to New Jersey, as the detention facility on Varick Street in Manhattan had been evacuated after 9/11 because of the attack and the building's location in lower Manhattan. Whomever they talked to declined to provide any more substantial information than that or help them to determine how they might go about getting it.

---

61 Latham & Watkins LLP, "Review of ICE Detention Standards at Middlesex County Jail." The names of the attorneys who drafted the memorandum are redacted, although one is identified as a litigation partner.

Again, inhibiting contact with families has been one of the arrows in the immigration service's intimidation quiver. Withholding information is another of the preferred tactics, right up there with pricing telephone calls beyond the reach of most inmates' means. Hemnauth suspects that the two women went to the immigration court in Newark, to no avail. The court would not have been aware of Hemnauth's case so early in the process. That would occur only upon the case's assignment to a judge.

Hemnauth's vow of serenity shattered. "Rahoni's voice began to sound like she was crying. I started to cry . . . I knew then I would never see this girl and my son again." The way the words come out of his mouth confirm to me that their divorce was the mirror image of a sham marriage, that there was more to hold Hemnauth and Rahoni together than there ever was to drive them apart. "The thing I was trying to suppress just came out of me. That made it *real* difficult" to face his conundrum as he had silently resolved to do. If he were alone in the world, his jailers could "beat me up, chop off my hand" without damaging his determination to "fix this thing." He had figured that this was the first time he was in jail and he would not be there long. (Even after his felony arrest, he had been released without bail pending the trial that acquitted him.) He had never tested the brick wall that is IIRIRA, and his detention seemed so inane that he easily convinced himself it would ultimately be judged in error.

Now, hearing Rahoni's despair awakened his own. A prison officer stood by to observe while it blanketed him.

The receiving officer walked Hemnauth to the jail's infirmary for his medical examination. A nurse took blood samples and a urine sample and asked questions about his medical history. He was taken into another side room by two other male officers and ordered to strip naked, to "bend over and shake my dick and open my butt in front of them." I wonder about the medical rationale for requiring that detainees perform such maneuvers with the intimate zones of their bodies. However, this is a topic Hemnauth is not inclined to dwell on. "It was a strip search," the first of several. "That should tell you everything." It is embarrassing to him to talk about the searches, and he prefers to imply that the scope of the humiliation is self-evident and in no need of further elaboration, even if he acknowledges that in this first instance humiliation may not have been the intent. "Actually, it was a procedure. A normal thing in jail."

On later occasions the strip searches did not strike him as so normal, and I would postulate with some confidence that the one conducted as part of a medical probe upon his induction at Middlesex was neither normal nor medically indicated. Rather, it was an early mark of a deliberate assault on his dignity and a preemptive rebuff of any claim to it he might stake. In any event the "procedure" was, as Hemnauth correctly observed, similar if not identical to that imposed on criminal inductees to the general prison population, certainly at Passaic where he was later interned. The federal courts have increasingly tended to view arbitrary prison strip searches as violations of the Fourth Amendment to the Constitution. The courts view them as intentionally designed to humiliate, degrade or frighten people into submission — or any combination of the above. When they are carried out immediately upon arrival at a detention facility, they must be seen in the light of a deliberate policy of intimidation, codified in ICE standards, beyond even what is specifically spelled out in IIRIRA. In ICE's defense, the statutes the agency acts under have invited the punitive disposition of detention policies and practices.

We should also consider the possibility that Hemnauth's inaugural strip search at Middlesex was not, in fact, part of a medical examination protocol but simply concurrent with it. In other words, that strip search was just that. The detention standards for strip searches published in December 2008 state: "Staff shall not routinely require a detainee to remove clothing or require a detainee to expose private parts of his or her body to search for contraband. To the extent reasonably possible, the inspector refrains from touching the skin surface of the detainee; however, the inspector may request that the detainee move parts of the body to permit visual inspection."[62] Hence the moving and shaking that Hemnauth reported to me. Since Hemnauth showed no provocative behavior during his induction to Middlesex, one might assume the search was, in fact, routine and therefore forbidden by ICE's own formal rules. It wasn't. There was a catch. According to these standards, Hemnauth falls into a predefined, cookie-

62 U.S. Immigration and Customs Enforcement, "2008 ICE Operations Manual: Performance-Based National Detention Standards."

cutter category of persons automatically subject to reasonable suspicion of hiding contraband by virtue of a drug-related misdemeanor. Reasonable suspicion triggers a conditional license to strip-search, more permissive than probable cause. Personnel at Middlesex appear to have dispensed with the prescribed alternatives they are directed to attempt, such as pat-down and interview, and moved straight to nudity.[63]

Hemnauth would not wear his own clothes for two years. The officers took them and placed them in a plastic bag, which they handed back to Hemnauth, making it clear that was where they would remain for the duration. The moment was a threshold for Hemnauth, past which any rights he may have been so delusional as to think he still possessed vanished over the horizon. Any hope he may still have harbored evaporated, that his captors would concede that the whole episode was grounded in abject silliness, and send him on his way to job and kin. He had been tossed into rapids so strong there was no chance of swimming upstream no matter how powerful his stroke. "Basically they were telling me I had no rights. [From that moment] whatever they said, you do." They gave him an orange jumpsuit and instructed him to put it on. After he dressed, the officers took him to a storage room. They took the bag with his clothes and made him a prison photo ID card right then and there. He was admonished to wear it at all times. They handed him his immigration paperwork and told him he would have the cash they found in his wallet placed into a jail account to buy whatever sundries might be made available for purchase at the jail commissary during his detention. His driver's license, green card and social security card were confiscated by the INS. That was the last time he would ever see them up close.

When Hemnauth characterized the features of his welcome to Middlesex as normal for jail, he probably did not realize how poignantly accurate he was being. Years after Hemnauth's deportation, the Obama administration declared its intention to reform the conditions of immigration detention. Many, myself included, cheered when Dr. Dora Schriro, ICE's Director

---

63 U.S. Immigration and Customs Enforcement, "2008 ICE Operations Manual."

of the Office of Detention Policy and Planning in 2009, unequivocally described the immigrant detention system Obama inherited as the imprisonment it was not supposed to be according to the law: "With only a few exceptions, the facilities that ICE uses to detain aliens were built, and operate, as jails and prisons to confine pre-trial and sentenced felons. ICE relies primarily on correctional incarceration standards designed for pre-trial felons and on correctional principles of care, custody, and control."[64]

The casual reader of the statement or the reporting around it might arrive at the reasonable conclusion that the resemblance of detention conditions to criminal incarceration was the evolutionary result of the haste with which the system was devised, in response to September 11, and the urgency imposed by immigration politics. In other words, the government, primarily concerned with cost and expediency, hired local and corporate jailers ill versed in detention standards specific to immigration law — a logical underpinning for Dr. Schriro's rather obvious, albeit important, declaration.

However, a closer look reveals that the conditions Hemnauth encountered, first at Middlesex, then at Passaic and Hudson County Jails, were no accident of history. They were federal policy. As the deputy secretary of Homeland Security has noted, the body of national immigration detention standards that took effect in January 2001 was "based on the then-current INS detention policies, Federal Bureau of Prisons ('BOP') program standards, and the widely accepted American Correction Association's ('ACA') Standards for Adult Local Detention Facilities."[65] If immigration detention standards looked like criminal incarceration standards, it is because they were in large part copied from them. Let alone that what looks, paddles and quacks like a duck might reasonably be taken for one.

With his induction completed, Hemnauth was moved to a residential hall, of sorts, that occupied a floor behind a main door, with twenty to thirty individual cells arrayed around its perimeter. They were locked. They each had their own metal door, not bars, and a tray slot, about ten inches wide

---

64 Schriro, "Immigration Detention Overview and Recommendations."
65 Lute, Deputy Secretary of Homeland Security, in a letter to Wishnie and Shah.

to Hemnauth's recollection. Modern correctional facilities have swapped out bars for solid metal doors in order to offer more safety to guards from assault by inmates. There was no window to the outside, he tells me emphatically. The inmate can neither see outside nor into the common area, except through the tray hole. Nor can he see into an adjoining cell. Each one was completely enclosed. Hemnauth would have preferred bars; better a cage than a box, he told me, if those were the only available options. As any viewer of cable channel MSNBC's documentary series *Lockup* will know, solid doors, not bars are the current correctional standard. Bars are a feature of antiquated prisons — of which there are many — and period movie sets.

By the time Hemnauth was taken to his cell, it was well into the evening of the second day since his arrest at Kennedy Airport, around nine or ten o'clock. A cellmate had taken the bottom of the two bunks. Hemnauth remembers him as a Hispanic man who "kind of welcomed me," although gruffly and visibly displeased that he would have to share the accommodations. The man also took a stand on who was boss in the narrow eight-by-twelve cell, using the first-comer's assumption of lordship over the space, assigning a confined area where Hemnauth could put his few belongings. These included the paperwork the immigration officers had completed, his wallet — absent his green card — and the belt he had been asked to remove. There was a table in the cell, but only one stool, a sink, and a tankless toilet kept under enormous water pressure as a means, Hemnauth speculates, of keeping it clean without regular use of a brush and detergent. There was no hygienic privacy such as a curtain around the commode, another indication of penal standards of detention, if one were needed.

Hemnauth jumped onto the upper bunk. He tried to sleep, and after a thirty-six-hour ordeal, he was certainly exhausted enough. "I'm tired, but I can't recognize that I'm tired. I'm hungry, but I can't eat." He was still far too agitated to eat — he had been given a tray with fixings for another bologna sandwich and he might have eaten the bread — or sleep, and the echoed clunk of the guard closing and bolting cell doors set him to panic. He felt the walls closing in around him every time he shut his eyes, a sensation enhanced by having the ceiling, a slab of unfinished concrete, a mere three feet from the top of his bunk. "I started to stifle." He could not breath, his heart was racing and the veins in his temples throbbed with spiking blood pressure. He slid down from his bunk and paced back and forth from the far end of the cell to the tray hole. He opened its flap and sucked at the extra air through his nose. "I kept on doing that all night," back and forth between the bunk and the tray slot. "You feel like you're dying, life coming out of your body. This is a weird, weird experience . . . like there's no oxygen there."

After several hours, while peering through the hole, he finally saw a guard making the night rounds. Hemnauth speculates that it was shortly after a shift change when the officer just coming on duty would walk the floor as part of a routine check.

"I called him over. He seemed very pleasant, neatly dressed, nice combed hair, young, moving slowly." Nobody had as yet fully explained the lay of the land, and Hemnauth thought that, perhaps, if someone described the normal protocol for him, he might feel a little better. Confinement to an eight-by-twelve cell worried him particularly. No one had ever brought up to him that he would be under such a punitive regimen, and yet he had been delivered immediately to a cell in a locked-down area worthy of a high-security penal establishment.

Hemnauth was prepared to allow appearances inform his forecast of the guard's demeanor, and his confidence was rewarded with a straight and courteous answer. "Listen, buddy," Hemnauth said, "I just came in here and I want to ask you a question, buddy. Will I be locked up all the time in this little room here? Is this the procedure?" The guard tried to be reassuring. He told Hemnauth that usually the door was open during the daytime hours, but there had been an altercation between some inmates and a social worker. It appeared that the cells were normally shut during the night, but the guard was leading Hemnauth to anticipate that the lockdown conditions would spill into the following morning, depending on what the warden would decide.

Indeed, the area remained in lockdown with detainees in their two-man cells until lunchtime the following day. The jail did not exactly call off the lockdown, but rather escorted Hemnauth and a small number of immigration prisoners to a mess hall for the general prison population. There were over a hundred inmates there. "They are not supposed to do that," Hemnauth informs me. By "that" he means comingling immigration detainees and prisoners jailed pursuant to a criminal charge. "They were a rough crowd," he adds a moment later.

Although the ICE detention standards do not explicitly proscribe overlap among immigrant detainees and correctional inmates, the general practice is to keep the two groups segregated, if for no other reason than to maintain the appearance of separate, and wholly unrelated regimens and context of detention between the penal and administrative varieties, even if in practice they are often, if not always, indistinguishable. ICE's detention standard on admission and release does state that "each newly admitted detainee will be kept separated from the general population until classified and housed accordingly."[66] The standards remain vague to silent on when the mixing of detainee and general populations should be permitted.

International standards tend to frown on the practice. The comingling of common prisoners and detainees violates United Nations guidelines drafted in consideration of asylum-seekers: "The use of prisons should be avoided. If separate detention facilities are not used, asylum-seekers should be accommodated separately from convicted criminals or prisoners on remand. There should be no co-mingling of the two groups."[67] (I should point out that the UN High Commissioner for Refugees guidelines do contain a disclaimer referring back to other conventions and national law when examining the cases of detainees other than those officially classified as asylum seekers. I shall leave it to others to argue why the guidelines should not apply to an immigrant under administrative detention like Hemnauth.)

More pointedly, the UN's Universal Periodic Review of the human rights records of all member states observes, disapprovingly and among other objections, that "noncitizens detained in prisons and county jails that contract with DHS [Department of Homeland Security] frequently are mixed with the general population of criminal inmates."[68] The Obama

---

66 U.S. Immigration and Customs Enforcement, "2008 ICE Operations Manual."
67 Office of the UN High Commissioner for Refugees, "Standards Relating to the Detention of Asylum-Seekers."
68 "Human Rights Violations in the Immigrant Detention System," Ninth Session of the Working Group on the UPR Human Rights Council.

administration has voiced its specific intention to terminate the assimilation of immigration detention and criminal incarceration,[69] but the immigration service was considerably less scrupulous in disassociating criminals
and immigrants during Hemnauth's period of detention. And given the
thick web of contracts between ICE on the one hand, and local and private
jailers on the other, extricating those caught in it will be a long, complicated
and politically vulnerable process in times of harsh anti-immigrant partisan
rhetoric. As Sheriff Joe Arpaio boisterously refuses to comply with federal
subpoenas, arguing in effect that public documents pertaining to federal
statutes can be withheld as privileged at his discretion, his constituents
cheer him on. The Obama administration's implementation of new detention standards proceeds at a snail's pace.

There were just a few empty seats in the mess. Hemnauth picked one at
random at one of the long tables similar to those that figure in prison movies like *The Shawshank Redemption.* "I went up to a guy, and sat down on a
chair [next to him] to eat."

The crowd, Hemnauth repeats, is a rough one.

"Yeah, the real deal. Big strong guys." There were a few white prisoners
mixed into a general population black and Hispanic in its majority, none in
immigrant detention. "A guy came and yelled at me and ordered me to get
up." The guards were not about to enforce rules of civility in the mess hall,
let alone promote socialization among their charges. "A big strong guy," he
repeats. The inmate who confronted Hemnauth told him, in no uncertain
terms, that he never wanted to "see [Hemnauth] sitting at this table again."
Hemnauth got up as ordered by the tough and went to sit with his tray — a
bona fide vegetarian one in this instance — on a stairwell step.

As he had spoken a few words during the seating altercation, another
detainee heard him and picked up on his accent. He came up to Hemnauth
when he had finished eating. "Hey, you from where, man?" He was a black
West Indian, from Jamaica or Trinidad, Hemnauth recalls, although with a
little uncertainty, so he may also have hailed from one of the other English-

69 Schriro, "Immigration Detention Overview."

speaking Caribbean islands. This was the very first person Hemnauth could relate to on an equal human plane since his arrest at Kennedy Airport, and the man, in turn was very happy to talk to Hemnauth, with whom he felt some cultural kinship. Like Hemnauth, he was an INS detainee.

The man took it upon himself to instruct Hemnauth on the survival skills he would need when he found himself amid the general prison population. The environment was self-segregating between INS detainees and the general jail population, in addition to territorial cliques, and with an ethnic component thickening the line between the groups, not to mention the overall atmosphere of suspicion in the mess hall.

Hemnauth's assorted handlers over the prior two days had meticulously adhered to the drumbeat reference to him as a detainee, not a suspect under arrest. That the distinction was so often repeated was understandable since it was not obvious from the treatment the various INS agents had visited upon him thus far, and might otherwise have been lost on him. Hemnauth was still new enough to the detention universe to be surprised at finding himself and a few other detainees interspersed with jailed convicts and suspects under criminal prosecution. Notwithstanding the shackles, strip search, indifference and shouted orders, the semantics of his capture never strayed from INS code. He tried to get this friendly new acquaintance to explain why, apart from his perfunctory introduction to his bunkmate, his first encounter with his fellow detainees was occurring among prisoners of the criminal justice system. (To which, by the way, he had no recourse, as was made abundantly clear to him. There had been no mention of Miranda rights; they did not apply to the civil case brought against him by the INS.)

All the other man could do was agree that it was not supposed to happen, in fact did not occur very often, but sometimes it simply did. He could offer no further explanation than that. For Hemnauth, the comingling with sentenced and arraigned prisoners had been arguably a less damaging episode than the cuffs and shackles, the endless night of waiting tethered to a hard bench, the swings from sheer indifference to the presumption of turpitude on the part of the officers who inducted him, his swift and deliberate dehumanization, or the panic of not knowing what was to become of him. Still, the grievance stood apart because, however degrading the other bits of the process, this flippant deviation from what he thought were the INS's own rules meant that other deviations were likely and that he would be subjected to arbitrary treatment and decisions he would be powerless to contest.

Late that afternoon, a guard returned to Hemnauth's cell and cuffed him for the walk back to the medical ward. Nurses administered a few more elements of a standard medical examination, drawing blood for a lab test and measuring his blood pressure. There was little discussion of what was being done, why, whether the results would be disclosed to him and what the range of outcomes might be for his detention.

When Hemnauth was returned to his block, the individual cell doors had been opened, indicating the end of the latest lockdown. He was grateful for this. He could walk around the floor's central common area rather than being confined to a small cell with a mate he had not befriended and who had been a shade less than comradely. This open arrangement was infinitely more conducive to socializing, one of Hemnauth's singular skills, to which he owes his survival through the months and years of his incarceration.

As it was, he did not remain long in the cellblock. Rather quickly he was taken to an area more resembling a dorm. On the surface, conditions complied slightly more to the notion of detention rather than criminal imprisonment. The relief would be far from permanent, and further yet from unconditional. The new block contained three floors of what the prison called cubicles, sleeping pods accommodating four detainees in each, in two stacked bunks, and separated from each other by partitions without doors. Each cubicle had a table protruding from the concrete wall and a single fixed stool. Each had a window. Hemnauth guesses that the block housed about a 150 men per floor. Bathrooms were more plentiful than in the cellblock. There was a weights room on the floor and a small indoor handball court. Hemnauth describes the residency amenities as "comfortable," certainly compared to where he had been held the two previous nights.

The architecture of these ostensibly kinder and gentler detention floors was no more an accident than the choice of metal doors over bars in the conventional cellblocks. It complied with a deliberately implemented program. Middlesex County Jail is one of a select few (about a hundred in the country) to deploy a relatively modern concept of incarceration known in the prison métier as "direct supervision" or "direct inmate supervision," promoted by the National Institute of Corrections, an agency of the

Department of Justice. As the name suggests, the direct-supervision model prescribes the presence of a corrections officer among the inmates at all times as a better recipe for behavior control and peaceful cohabitation, at least among prisoners not addicted to violence. In return, the inmates are relieved of the stress induced by tighter confinement overseen by more distant guards. They can also spend more time in a common day room and sleep in open cubicles.[70] Middlesex County's government website proudly states: "Since opening in 1984, the Adult Correction Center has been recognized as a leader in Direct Supervision Jail Management. Through the years, jail leaders from all around the country (and even overseas) have visited Middlesex County."[71]

So, if there was a coincidental ingredient in this picture, it was not in the existence of the seemingly more lenient setting, but rather in its having been available for federal immigration detention despite its relative rarity. The regimen remained correctional in its essence. Furthermore, from Hemnauth's perspective at the time, the change in living conditions would make his detention tolerable, but only because he did not imagine remaining imprisoned for long. He was thinking days, not weeks, or months . . . or years.

Hemnauth's pod mates were others of Caribbean origin, a Guyanese man and two Jamaicans. "All three Rastas," he specifies for the sake of completeness of his description, not as a value judgment. The officers had performed a certain amount of triage among their charges, postulating in the process that cube mates of similar origin and language would make for fewer disputes and less trouble on the floor. They also grouped Asians and Middle Easterners. In hindsight the pairing decisions seem consistent with the general principles of direct-supervision jailing.

During the first two weeks of the now-settled regimen at Middlesex, Hemnauth was summonsed to several departments for visits. He was taken back to medical, but also to sessions of questioning with a social worker and INS officials. Each time he was cuffed for the trip away from the dormitory block and down the corridors of the jail to either the medical department or an interview room, the cuffs a clear reminder, if indeed one were needed, that his detention should not be mistaken for a stay at the Ritz, notwithstanding the improvements over the dungeonesque

70 Zupan, *Encyclopedia of Crime and Punishment* Vol. 4.
71 "Adults Corrections," Ed. Middlesex County, NJ.

beginnings. Furthermore, he could still see the double row of high fences from the dorm, not a standard feature at finer hotels and resorts. Word among the detainees was that the fences were electrified, although I could not verify this and rather doubt it.

Hemnauth had every reason to feel humiliated, as he did, by the hand-cuffs. For reasons that were to remain a mystery to him — but very much in keeping with the prescribed handbook assumption that he was by defi-nition hostile because of the ancient drug misdemeanor — he was being singled out. There was a constant to and fro of untethered inmates in the hallways. For all he knew, those inmates could well have included members of the general prison population, and he was being treated as more crimi-nal than the criminals. He also felt that the showy precaution of walking him in cuffs would set him up for later ostracism, although when I probe, Hemnauth tells me that this did not happen at Middlesex, and such intent would have run counter to the direct-supervision model. Certainly none of the guards or corrections officers ever explained the logic of the protocol. In fairness, no INS handbook ever stated that the jailers ever had to explain much of anything to do with the mode of detention of INS inmates. In ad-dition, the guards did not know the details of the charges, past or present, against Hemnauth, nor how trivial they were. "They were not concerned with that. All they know is that the INS is bringing in a whole lot of Middle Eastern people. They view it like that."

"I realized [the use of handcuffs] is unusual . . . [Everyone] was staring at me . . . I felt like a terrorist." When he says this, it is hardly the first time that he registers his particular distress at being tagged a terrorist real or potential, even tacitly, by the way others might look at him. There is more to Hemnauth's vexation than his matter-of-fact observation that his skin tone colored the attitude of his escorts who, in Hemnauth's Middlesex experience, associated men of real or imagined Middle Eastern appear-ance with imminent danger. No, there was more to it than his suspicions of racial prejudice. Hemnauth harbors a strong ethos of nonviolence, all the stronger that he senses in himself a hidden silo of anger that he very consciously bundles away like an evil genie he must keep sealed in its bottle. That ethos is both religious and deeply personal. He is studiously gentle and naturally affable. His flashes of anger are rare, many of then a legacy of his confrontations while in detention.

"At this point, I don't want to make any kind of an argument with the officers, because I am new to this thing. So I was just observing, and moving along and wondering what was happening." Other inmates informed him that Middlesex was a maximum-security facility, although that does not appear to be the case. (I found no records that designate Middlesex as a maximum-security facility or one specifically tuned to maximum-security programs, and the audit cited above by the Latham and Watkins law firm[72] describes the jail as minimum to medium security.) From an objective perspective, the classification of the jail is really neither here nor there. Middlesex covers 132,000 square feet of prison space and was built to contemporary standards for a corrections facility, which implies a security apparatus that leaves little doubt as to its function. These standards include, as Hemnauth experienced, blocks of barless jail cells secured by solid metal doors, as well as invasive searches and lockdowns that kick in whenever ordered by prison officials. The more dorm-style "direct supervision" floors where Hemnauth resided during most of his stay at Middlesex exist to comply with an alternate doctrine of criminal incarceration.

"My Guyanese friends and Jamaican friends were pretty strong people." The floor guards appointed them as de facto prison block trustees to deter and, on occasion, stop fights. The other inmates were careful not to cross them. "They were respected, there, you know. They were respected." The incentive of Hemnauth's friends was not to curry favor with the guards, but rather avoid lockdowns on the floor. No one on the floor enjoyed lockdowns, as the tightened confinement would typically be accompanied by searches, disregard for the inmates' belongings and the brutal reminder of the stark delineation between rights, of which they had few, and privileges, whose distinctive feature was that they could be lifted at the will and whim of prison officials.

At this point, Hemnauth reached out to the other inmates and tried to make friends among them, in addition to his cubicle-mates, the Jamaican and Guyanese trustees, who had taken him under their wing. It was his way of battling the depression that, Hemnauth tells me, was settling in

---

72 Latham & Watkins LLP, "Review of ICE Detention Standards."

more and more. There were a few musicians on the floor, game for *a cappella* singing and drumming concerts that Hemnauth instigated. One of the Jamaican trustees, nicknamed John Crow for his facial features and who was in charge of serving food on the floor, would collect whatever surplus might accumulate over the course over a day or so and concoct a shared late-night meal for his fellow inmates. For Hemnauth and several other inmates, creative socialization became a means of survival. "We'd stay up late," Hemnauth told me. Late is a relative notion, since Hemnauth did allude moments later to a ten o'clock curfew.

The cordiality between Hemnauth the newcomer and the other detainees progressed rapidly, and talk moved naturally to discussion of their individual plights, although they tended not to share — at least not immediately — documents they may have received from the INS, immigration court or, if they had one, their lawyers. "From the time you get in there, they are going to ask."

Each inmate had a purpose in mind: to weigh the magnitude of his charge against those of the men around him as a way to gauge the likely outcome once they were in front of the immigration judge. It was a rather futile exercise in that they all shared a common charge in the view of the INS, that is, being in civil violation of the immigration code. They were ostensibly not being held for past offenses, for to do so would expose the immigration detention system to formal scrutiny for the double jeopardy that, as a practical matter, indeed was being imposed. The underlying circumstances of the immigration violation, including past criminal convictions, served the purpose of providing background to a detention or deportation order. The relative gravity of the circumstances bringing them to immigration court correlated only partially with the deportation outcome. Having said that, as we shall see, the immigration statutes took care to conflate trivial and graver crimes as felonies in their eyes in order to tilt the playing field toward easier deportation. It is simpler to deport someone labeled a felon than someone whose conviction compares in gravity to jaywalking.

Among his fellow inmates at Middlesex, Hemnauth was the jaywalker. He does not recall any of the inmates as having a record of violent crime, but many of them had committed offenses for which they had served jail time under sentence. One had jumped a one-million-dollar bail. Hemnauth being in detention as a result of the pettiest of misdemeanors strained the credulity of those around him. That he appeared to be an outlier among detainees with more serious criminal records might tempt us to view his case as the exception to the rule, and consequently to absolve the system as one that works equitably in all but extreme and extraordinary instances that the Congress could not possibly have foreseen when drafting the current immigration statutes. Certainly the kindly immigration judge — to whom we shall return — viewed Hemnauth's case as an isolated hiccup rather than a systemic shortcoming of the law. He told me as much. Even Bryan Lonegan, no fan of IIRIRA, referred to Hemnauth's circumstances as a "perfect storm." However, Hemnauth's story dispels any such temptation. All of the immigration detainees were treated as the prisoners they were not supposed to be according to the law's own verbiage. And compared to other jails, conditions at Middlesex were benign.

Still, it was Middlesex: a jail, not freedom. And, as he was informed by a social worker at the jail, Hemnauth would wait a month, if not longer, before being granted a hearing in immigration court. A month was the average delay, and it has since lengthened. The social worker had called a meeting so a group of freshly minted detainees could be read their rights and told how privileged they were to be housed and fed at the government's expense. There was an INS officer present, identifiable by his uniform, not by his subdued participation in the meeting. The list of rights was short, and boiled down to the "right" to counsel that detainees had to pay for themselves, as well as minimum standards of detention strikingly similar to common imprisonment standards, and bare-bones ability to communicate with the outside world, also on the detainees' nickel and at great expense. It sounded to Hemnauth more like a recitation of rights they did *not* have, in particular the one to contest detention prior to a hearing that would occur only after a month had passed, if not longer.

At the gathering, Hemnauth would make the acquaintance of a detainee from another floor of the block, a man of some past and future notoriety and something of a cause célèbre for immigrants' rights advocates: Farouk Abdel-Muhti. Farouk was a stateless, undocumented Palestinian who, to the government's annoyance, had evaded immigration sanctions for many

years. After the September 11 attacks, as Islamophobia and Arabophobia
were on the rise, Farouk was given his own morning talk show on Pacifica
Radio's WBAI-FM station in New York. He advocated for the rights of
Palestinians, and in so doing attracted the escalated attention of the INS.
Farouk's personal history contained a few episodes of questionable behavior. He had been arrested on several occasions for disorderly conduct during public protests and had pled guilty in 1993 to an assault charge arising
from a domestic dispute, instances that licensed an assistant U.S. attorney
to brand him, with more than a trace of hyperbole, "a convicted criminal
several times over."[73] Farouk's detention by the INS was later ruled unlaw-
ful. Hemnauth witnessed himself the undertreatment of Farouk's serious
health condition while in detention.

Farouk was outspoken by nature, and during the meeting with the INS
officer and the social worker aired his feelings unequivocally. According to
Hemnauth's account, Farouk yelled at the presenters that their referral to
detainees' rights was a sham and that the conditions of their incarceration
amounted to those of a "concentration camp."

"I wondered: who is this man?" Hemnauth says. The social worker and
the INS man were, in fact, somewhat apologetic as they tried to assuage
Farouk, impressing upon him that they "were just doing [their] job." A
logical response since, as Hemnauth notes, "They had no answers to give."

"Later on we became friends because I admired his courage," Hemnauth
says of Farouk. Like Hemnauth, Farouk would also be later jailed at Passaic
and Hudson County Jails.

After the group session, Hemnauth finally got to talk to the INS field
officer privately, who confirmed the one-month estimate of how long it
would take to get a hearing before an immigration judge.

What strikes me with some vehemence when Hemnauth recounts how he
learns of the month-long delay for as little as a first hearing is the double-
jeopardy implicit in the imposition of jail time as a result of a prior conviction for which he has already paid the full penalty, not to mention that

73 Fisher, "Stateless, Man Avoids Deportation from U.S."

said conviction did not carry jail time in the first place. In hindsight, the one-month of detention at Middlesex prior to his court hearing was but the opening episode in his imprisonment, and Hemnauth does not dwell on the double-jeopardy aspect as I do. Rather, what has stayed with him is the INS agent's view of detention as subsidized housing. Where Hemnauth saw a high-security jail, complete with handcuffs and jumpsuits, the INS man saw a resort hotel and three free meals a day. The other ramifications were lost on him as he wandered his alternate reality.

7

A Very Tight Box

With his first hearing a month away, Hemnauth resigned himself to settling in for a longer haul than he had ever imagined, while still imagining far less than he would ultimately endure. He was learning "how to cope, how to survive." He laughs as he tells me that one of the first rules of coping was hiding food under his mattress, since the jailers prohibited inmates from holding back items from their food trays like fruit and individual milk cartons. The evening meal would be brought in — I hesitate to apply the word "served" in this setting — anywhere between five and seven p.m., and the men valued a snack just before curfew. So they stashed food. If they were caught, the bounty was confiscated. Why the detainees had to squirrel away food from their own trays in the first place and forfeit it if they did not consume it immediately should raise some questions, particularly once considered that food service in jails is often outsourced to private firms with an eye on the profitability of their contracts. Hemnauth recalls the boyish mischief surrounding the detainees' theft of their own apples and half-pints of milk with some amusement. The inadequate diet at Passaic was less of a laughing matter.

Nothing major happened in the month before his hearing. No violent incidents, and no lockdowns or strip searches that he could recall. He had not yet struck up his friendship with Farouk Abdel-Muhti, who resided on a different floor. That would come later. He socialized mainly with the other West Indians.

Hemnauth did not have an attorney, nor did he foresee that he would get one. It had already been made abundantly clear that his right to counsel extended only to permission to hire his own lawyer, at his own expense and with no help in finding one other than the provision of a list of seemingly random names. Neither the immigration court nor the INS-screened lawyers presenting their credentials for minimum competency or ethical standards. Detainees are not directed to pro bono services, and pro bono lawyers do not line up inside the detainment centers to take on indigent clients. Some, like Bryan Lonegan, held periodic group meetings with inmates in detention centers in northern New Jersey to explain the adjudication process and give general legal advice. Bryan would later acquire Hemnauth as a pro bono client of the Legal Aid Society. Others, like Rachel Meeropol of the Center for Constitutional Rights, took an interest in the treatment of immigrant detainees and advocated for them beyond the immigration court proceedings. (At the time of this writing, she still does.) There are simply not enough pro bono resources to provide individual legal representation for more than a small minority of detained immigrants. As far as Hemnauth knew, he was on his own.

Hemnauth had one short leg up in the legal defense department over other inmates, given his past travails at the Queens County Court. He knew his way cursorily around law books, and the jail, as prescribed by ICE standards, had to provide access to a rudimentary law library. Hemnauth went twice a week.

Given the intricacies and rigidity of the immigration statutes, particularly since the adoption of IIRIRA in 1996, he could not have gotten far on his own devices. During his felony trial, his tenacious hours in the courthouse library, rather than giving him the tools to conduct his own defense, inspired his attorney to look beyond the usual plea bargain outcome and work on winning an acquittal. Still, the time he spent at Middlesex reviewing past cases and reading statutes, to whatever level of fluency he could possibly have attained, did help him focus his mind on fighting his detention and deportation, even if he could not get far without expert counsel. "It was kind of difficult to navigate the law books," he confesses to me. He did receive advice from some "long term" inmates who had been back and forth to immigration court many times, but it was unclear how much help he could get from men whose cases had not progressed in their favor.

Perhaps it served his emotional balance better that he did not realize what he was up against. The forces arrayed against him were powered by the twin engines of disenfranchisement and dehumanization. Disenfranchisement from his right to counsel, from his job, from the material means to mount an adequate defense, from his freedom, from any presumption of innocence. (Even payments he made to his Social Security account have been confiscated, as he will receive none of the benefits he paid and qualified for under the system; it may seem like a petty detail, but it illustrates the all-encompassing scope of his disenfranchisement and the absence of any effort at mitigation.) Dehumanization embodied in a drumbeat of humiliations, from the cuffs and prison garb to the stingy access to information provided by the INS and inhibited communication to the outside world — a way of telling Hemnauth and others that no one needed to hear from them any more than they needed to hear from a cinder block. It seems the only barrier to the complete stripping of his humanity was the usefulness of his "criminal alien" identity as a target for the enmity of others, driven by fear, xenophobia and the zeal with which politicians mined prejudice for votes and federal contracts.

True to the estimated schedule the INS handlers had given him, Hemnauth saw a judge approximately one month into his captivity. He was driven to Newark by special transport, fully shackled, chained around the neck and waist, cuffed and in his jumpsuit stenciled with the name of the jail in large letters. "That part was a little extra humiliation," he tells me, speaking specifically of the chains (a word he spits out in disgust), "as if the handcuffs weren't enough." When I ask if the guards were at all sheepish about enforcing the surfeit of shackles, Hemnauth answers emphatically: "No, man! They enjoyed it!" Once outside the jail in transit to the hearings, the guards "could be nice," playing the excursion a bit like a grade-school field trip, but could turn "on the slightest little mistake and start beating the shit out of everyone." He starts to recount a later incident, but decides to save it for its chronological place in the narrative.

I need not picture the scene at the immigration court building, nor the humiliation Hemnauth described to me. In April 2009, I went to the Federal Building in Newark, New Jersey, on the corner of Broad and Court Streets, which houses the immigration courts, to see them myself. A week before, I called the court to state that I wished to observe hearings as documentation for this book and that, as I was coming from afar, needed to check when the courts would be in session and the protocol for attendance. The court clerk told me I had to get permission from the Department of Homeland Security, and he took my mobile phone number. I received a prompt and rather breathless call from an official at the Department of Justice's Executive Office for Immigration Review (EOIR) in Falls Church, Virginia, who went to painful lengths to emphasize that hearings were public, that I was very welcome, and that I need not provide a justification. I took this as an indication that the department is careful to present the trappings of a real court of law even as it operates largely outside the reach of the judicial branch. The EOIR is a branch of the Department of Justice, which separates it in theory from Homeland Security, the cabinet-level department housing the INS and now ICE. Both, however, are part of the executive branch of government, not the judiciary.

There is a subtext to the EOIR's sensitivity to fears that an observer might be denied access. While the rules clearly specify open hearings, some immigration courts are located inside detention facilities, including some run by corporate jailers. Some hearings are conducted by videoconference. The same rules caution that "When planning to observe an open hearing held within a detention facility, however, you should contact the detention facility in advance to learn of any security clearance requirements for entry to the building."[74] This loophole in the open hearings policy has been used to inhibit access.[75] Luckily for me, the Newark immigration court is located within a federal building housing several government departments with which any person may have business.

Immigration judges are administered by a section of the Department of Justice, the aforementioned Executive Office for Immigration Review (EOIR). There are two categories of court hearings each business day, one for detained, the other for nondetained immigrants under the threat of

74 U.S. Department of Justice, "Observing Immigration Court Hearings (Fact Sheet)."
75 Stevens, "Lawless Courts."

a deportation order. The "nondetained" hearing I attended first was the more intimate and conversational between the judge and the respondent, who spoke through a court interpreter. What I heard there was clearly emblematic of the latter-day immigrant experience — a young woman from Peru brought to the U.S. by an abusive older man who made promises he knew he could not keep — but outside the scope of my research. I proceeded to the "detained" hearing.

As prepared as I was for the spectacle I was to witness, it hit me like a thousand sorrows. It was quite as Hemnauth had described to me. About thirty men stood in shackles outside the courtroom. They looked like a chain gang. They wore jumpsuits, mostly orange, some either green or blue, stamped "Hudson County Jail." A cadre of armed officers watched over them and made sure they were lined up in orderly fashion, as if set to march. The officers also ensured that no one came near them, and kept shouting that there would be no talking to persons in the hallway — that order intended for both the inmates on the one hand and family, friends and advocates on the other. While orders were barked, particularly the admonition that there should be no contact between detainees and anyone other than the officers, the guards did conduct some friendly banter with a few of their charges. The men shuffled into the courtroom and took seats assigned to them individually as they entered. There was one detained woman in the group from Haiti, but I saw her only once inside the courtroom.

I took a seat on a bench a couple of rows behind the lawyers. The family of a Middle Eastern detainee, including two children, sat in the row in front of me, but heeded the no-talking rule.

The judge, a lady, walked in, dressed in a judicial robe. She had been in the judge's job for only a year, and I later learned that she remained for less than two. She looked quickly around the room, saw me in a middle row, and asked if I was representing any of the detainees as counsel, although without a coat and tie I would have stood out as quite casually attired for an attorney trying to win favor for a client with low odds of prevailing. She reiterated that hearings were open without condition by law, but still was curious as to my interest in them. I stood and stated I was there to observe the proceedings to document the narrative of a past case, now closed and unrelated to any of the detainees present. She welcomed me with some bemusement.

The hearings I witnessed in her court that particular day did not, by and large, delve into the substance of the detainees' cases. Most appeared to address the issue of their release bond — none were granted at the hearing — and to set a date for a future hearing pursuant to a continuance. The judge was perfunctory in her rulings, and for good reason. She had two hours to dispose of over thirty cases that morning, a normal half-day's docket. She was not the only judge to be working under the pressure of a crushing caseload. In 2009, for example, 390,000 deportation cases were initiated before 238 immigration judges presiding over fifty-nine courts around the country.[76] (As of March 2014, the total number of immigration judges had risen to 248 including 15 in management roles.)

Only one case gave this judge pause and led to a sharp exchange with the lawyer for the only woman among the detainees. For consideration of her bond, the court required certain documents that could only be obtained from Haiti, not a jurisdiction particularly noted for expeditious bureaucratic responsiveness. The attorney stated that it would take thirty days to obtain them. This upset, even angered the judge because she saw the detention of a woman as a particular hardship and wanted the tools by which she might be able to order her release. No one, certainly not I, would dispute the premise that the woman whose case the judge was examining faced dire hardship as a female detainee. What I found puzzling as I digested the scene was that the cruelty of the entire detention system was not a matter of similar consternation, even dampened.

The Haitian lady's case provided the only moment of debate in the courtroom, but not the only drama, at least not to my eyes.

As each detainee was called, a guard escorted him to the front of the court. The guard unlocked one hand from the cuffs, attaching the now loose end to the chain wrapped around the prisoner's back. This was performed in order to allow him to raise his right hand as he took the oath swearing to tell the truth. He was then recuffed and allowed to sit by his attorney and interpreter, if one was needed, at the table placed directly below the judge's bench. The uncuffing and recuffing may not strike anyone as particularly dramatic when described on paper, but the sequence of clicks of those cuffs drives home the grimness of the loss of liberty of people

76 Stevens, "Lawless Courts."

imprisoned for reasons other than a crime.

Upon concluding the business of each detainee, a perfunctory affair in most instances, the judge looked him straight in the eye and said, "Have a great day, sir, and good luck to you." She even emphasized "great." This flourish of cordiality startled me, more than I can adequately describe in words. As my jaw dropped, I wondered if the judge was a cruel cynic, but she clearly was not. She meant what she was saying in utter sincerity, all the while peering down at a man in handcuffs, chains and an orange jumpsuit. How does a man in shackles have a great day? How is the liberty or exile of a person under the control of a government engaging in extrajudicial detention a matter of luck?

Hemnauth was assigned to Judge Alberto J. Riefkohl immediately upon having his case introduced in immigration court. This is the same affable judge who handled the case of the Peruvian lady in the undetained hearing I observed in 2009.

When I walked into his courtroom, he was alone, sorting through papers on his desk in advance of the court session that was yet to commence. He wore a cardigan over a shirt and tie, not the judicial roles favored by some of his colleagues, including the justice presiding over the detained hearing I attended later that same morning. I asked if I was in the right place, that is, Judge Riefkohl's courtroom. This of course invited the question as to who wanted to know and why. I asked if he recalled Hemnauth's case and in fact told him that Hemnauth had asked me to send his greetings, despite the poor outcome over which Judge Riefkohl had presided. The judge indeed remembered Hemnauth, rather clearly. Immigration judges are under strict orders not to talk about their cases. Nonetheless, Mr. Riefkohl was willing to comment on Hemnauth's, partly because, as he told me, he had already talked off microphone to NPR, gotten into some mild trouble for having done so, and besides Hemnauth's case was closed *sine die*. He also remembered Kevin, Hemnauth's son.

"This is the one case I've had where the system didn't work," Riefkohl said in explaining his regret over Hemnauth's exile. I do wish I could have debated whether the outcome was a matter of an anomaly in an otherwise sound system or a system that was fundamentally deficient. The judge had been quite forthcoming, and I thought it wiser not to press my luck on that point, especially since engaging him on the wider issue of the fairness of the deportation statutes would likely have been inconclusive, given his position and the strictures against immigration judges speaking to anyone about virtually anything to do with their jobs.

Had I felt able to pursue the discussion, I might have asked the judge whether a salient feature of established immigration law is that it deprives judges like him of any latitude to apply context to the cases before him. Context, in Hemnauth's situation, could include the simple fact that deportation would annihilate his union with his American son, both a right according to Article 16 of the Universal Declaration of Human Rights and an oft-proclaimed principle of government policy in the United States if not, as I later came to realize, a fundamental right under the U.S. Constitution. It might also include the observation that Hemnauth was neither a threat nor a cost to a society to which he contributed productively, once considered the pettiness of an old misdemeanor plea and absolutely no suggestion of recidivism. I might also have asked Judge Riefkohl whether the enormity of the penalty — and double jeopardy — the system wished to impose on an originally legal immigrant, namely exile, was collateral damage or a deliberate cruelty of IIRIRA that he was powerless, as a judge, to weigh. In short, whether the constraints placed upon the immigration judge's discretion are of a piece with "the most ferocious assault on judicial review of immigration decisions," renowned immigration law professor Stephen Logomsky's assessment of IIRIRA's court-stripping provisions.[77]

Judge Riefkohl has a reputation for evenhandedness, which, from the information I have gathered, is not undeserved. Data compiled by the Transactional Records Access Clearinghouse (TRAC) at Syracuse University seem to bear this out. For the period 2000–2005, which coincides with Hemnauth's detention, of the 208 immigration judges working for the Executive Office for Immigration Review with a total caseload of greater than 100 candidates each for deportation, Judge Riefkohl was ranked 183rd in frequency of asylum denials as a percent of cases heard. The sternest of

---

77 Legomsky, "Fear and Loathing in Congress and the Courts: Immigration and Judicial Review."

the judges refused to grant asylum in 97% of the petitions that came before him. The median was 65%, about double Judge Riefkohl's 38% rate of denial.[78] The judge's denial rate did increase in the 2002–2007 period to 42% under the impact of cases arriving before him subsequent to Hemnauth's deportation. The mix of nationalities represented in a given judge's caseload can affect outcomes, as can the percentage of respondents represented by counsel. Nevertheless, "decisions also appear to reflect in part the personal perspective that the judge brings to the bench."[79]

Appointments to the immigration bench are covered by federal civil-service laws and are supposed to be politically neutral. However, from 2004 to 2007, when the practice was uncovered, appointments became a reward of patronage that disqualified liberals and Democrats in favor of loyalists deemed reliable by White House political operatives. It seems likely that the denial rates in the Syracuse University data mirror a resulting bias.[80] Judge Riefkohl's appointment preceded the politicization of the immigration courts and may explain why his record stands out as lenient relative to others. Importantly, this perceived leniency in the data is comparative to a moving target drifting toward sterner outcomes, rather than absolute. Judge Riefkohl, as demonstrated in his interpretation of Hemnauth's removal as an exceptional perfect storm, does not dispute the principle of an immigration code with deportation provisions.

More anecdotally, Judge Riefkohl, by merely fostering a climate of respect and empathy in his courtroom even toward respondents he rules against, appears to have earned the affection of local immigration advocates. He has also attracted, on at least one occasion, the ire of the more punitive-minded. In that instance, Riefkohl ordered the release of a Muslim cleric accused, unconvincingly in the judge's view, of having withheld disclosure of past membership of Hamas.[81] The outcome of this case did demonstrate Judge Riefkohl's willingness to challenge ICE's presentation of evidence. He did not seek to circumvent the requirements of immigration law.

On the whole, Hemnauth does remember Judge Riefkohl fondly, and

---

78 "Asylum Denial Rates by Immigration Judge: FY 2000–FY 2005."
79 "Judge Alberto J. Riefkohl." Eds. Long and Burnham.
80 Savage, "Vetted Judges More Likely to Reject Asylum Bids."
81 Henry, "Terror Claims Against NJ Muslim Leader Rejected."

recounted to me the many occasions when, in court, Riefkohl appeared
if not to overtly advocate for Hemnauth, to at least express a favorable
personal opinion of him and try to guide his first attorney in his approach
to the case. Still, in a rare moment of rancor — and very mild rancor at
that — Hemnauth compared Judge Riefkohl to those among the guards
who could be very friendly in the right setting, but ultimately carried out
the commands of a callous system.

Even more tellingly, Hemnauth recognized as early as his first hearing
that the judge, as an employee of the executive branch, did not have the
judicial prerogatives one normally associates with judges. He could adjudicate within strict factual boundaries, but could not weigh the merits of a
respondent's case against any standard of fairness other than what IIRIRA
defined as such. "Judge Riefkohl was helpless . . . The "district attorney . . .
was calling the shots." The lawyer representing the INS was, of course,
not a district attorney but rather a legal advisor or counsel for the government in a civil proceeding. That Hemnauth conflated the INS lawyer
with a district attorney is somewhat understandable given the prosecutorial
setting of the hearings as well as other small details such as the respondent's confinement to a jailhouse and appearances in court in shackles and
a prison jumpsuit. ICE, the successor agency to the INS formed on March
1, 2003, retained the title of counsel to designate its attorneys. Immigration prosecutors are under the authority of the Department of Homeland
Security's Office of the Principal Legal Advisor and are the department's
exclusive legal representatives before the immigration courts. There was
no single district attorney or prosecutor or INS counsel assigned to Hemnauth's case, but several — to the point that they seemed interchangeable
to Hemnauth, unlike his experience in Queens County Court where he
faced a single prosecutor throughout an argumentative trial.

Adding to the impression that he was confronting a stacked legal deck
was the apparent overlap of the role of judge and attorney seeking a deportation order, notwithstanding the indisputable empathy of this particular
judge, Mr. Riefkohl, and his record of turning down a greater-than-average
percentage of requests for removal. It is telling that, to this day, a large number of immigration judges are former INS or ICE prosecutors. While three
of twenty-three judges appointed in 2010 had previously been immigrant
advocates, thirteen have been ICE attorneys arguing for removal, prolonging

a trend.[82] The law, upheld by federal courts, even allows the immigration judge to serve as both judge and prosecutor at the immigration hearing.[83]

Hemnauth's initial hearing was brief, amounting to the reading of the government's motion for removal, and Judge Riefkohl inquiring of Hemnauth whether he had an attorney, which he obviously did not since none was present in the courtroom. The judge gave him a list of attorneys who might take his case, but, in keeping with the INS's prohibition on providing legal assistance to those it wants to deport, there was no guidance on securing free or even low-cost representation beyond providing the list of providers, let alone an assessment of the competency of the lawyers available as defense counsel. None of the lawyers on the provided list accepted pro bono work. This is not to say that there are no pro bono attorneys working on behalf of immigrant detainees. When I visited the courts myself, I was under the clear impression that some of the men had secured free legal representation, as, ultimately, Hemnauth did himself when Bryan Lonegan took his case under the auspices of the Legal Aid Society of New York. However, finding pro bono immigration counsel requires overcoming the hurdles imposed by immigration jailers such as obstructed communications with the outside world, building a broad web of advocacy and convincing a pro bono lawyer or a nonprofit law center of the merits of one's case.

This is easier said than done. The obvious fact, of which I should have been more aware than I was when researching this story, is that attorneys take cases they believe have merit and turn down obvious losers. If I had any doubts, Bryan Lonegan disabused me of them most explicitly. Organizations like the Legal Aid Society do what all good law firms do: they choose their clients and their cases with care. They cannot afford to do otherwise, and would do a great disservice to the fundamental justice they are trying to attain for creditable cases if they tried. Bryan was one of the only free attorneys available to immigrant detainees in New Jersey. He would accept as many clients as he humanly could, provided there was some basis for relief. Most of the organizations offering free legal aid dispensed by attorneys tend to restrict individual representation to persons in

82 U.S. Department of Justice, "Executive Office for Immigration Review Swears in 23 New Immigration Judges."

83 McWhirter, *The Criminal Lawyer's Guide to Immigration Law.*

special circumstances, such as children or survivors of torture. The Executive Office for Immigration Review, the governing body of the immigration courts, has also constructed a hierarchy of non-attorneys it allows to represent immigrants who are contesting their removal and maintains a list of organizations and representatives so empowered. The loosest designation is "qualified representative," a category that includes, among others, "reputable individuals of good moral character who have a personal or professional relationship with the represented alien (e.g., relative, neighbor, clergy, co-worker, or friend)."[84] On the surface, the liberalization of immigrant representation seems a good thing, what with the penury of free or affordable immigration defense attorneys, and the EOIR, at least on paper, requires either a basic level of fluency in immigration law or supervision by an attorney who presumably does. In practice, the cryptic complexity of immigration law creates an insurmountable barrier to the effectiveness in immigration proceedings of persons armed chiefly with zealousness and who, unwittingly, pave the road to immigrants' hell with their good intentions. Bryan observed such "disasters" as he did his rounds in immigrant detention facilities.[85]

Hemnauth's first hearing lasted a matter of minutes. The judge then issued a continuance that sent Hemnauth back to jail to serve another month, neither indicted nor convicted, at Middlesex, nor even with the option of immediate deportation rather than being thrown back in jail. There was no question of being freed on bond. This was not exceptional punishment leveled at one man; it was, and is, the system.

The scenario repeated itself for five months, each month producing a hearing with no substantive decision, a deferral for another month and remand back to detention. Hemnauth asked Rahoni to "scrape some money together to get a lawyer." By this time Rahoni had started to visit him regularly.

---

84 U.S. Department of Justice, "Representation of Aliens in Immigration Proceedings: Attorneys, Recognized Organizations, and Accredited Representatives; Qualified Representatives; Free Legal Service Providers."
85 See: Lee, *Legal Ethics in Immigration Matters: Legal Representation and Unauthorized Practice of Law*, and Dolnick, "Removal of Priest's Cases Exposes Deep Hole in Immigration Courts."

It was during one of the repeat visits to the immigration court in Newark that the incident with the guards Hemnauth had started to tell me about earlier occurred.

"[The guards] were pushing a guy. I think he was African." The detainees were downstairs in the underground parking lot, "all chained up," although individually, not to each other. The guards had lined them up to take the elevator in formation. The African detainee, an older man, in his sixties according to Hemnauth's recollection, made some kind of request to the officers, one a man, the other a woman. Hemnauth does not recall exactly what the detainee was requesting other than it was something within the ordinary, like to visit the bathroom.

Whatever he was asking was met with a curt denial, which the detainee protested, invoking his rights. He may have raised his voice to be heard by the officers, who were guarding a fairly long line of their charges and may have been at the outer edge of earshot. The officer came back over to the detainee he now regarded as insubordinate and told him: "I'm going to show you that you have no rights." (Hemnauth is confident those were the exact words: when I read back what he has just told me in paraphrase, he corrects me.) The officer grabbed the detainee and pushed him onto the hood of a parked car. The man fell backwards. Since he was in a full set of restraints, with his hands pinned to his chest in the position of someone praying, he could not cushion his fall, let alone prevent it. The guard began punching and slapping him in the face without quarter, certainly hard enough to bruise, in effect beating him up. The officer had clearly crashed through his self-control, and there was no one to stop him. He kept up the assault. Both men began to slide off the car hood under the weight of the officer, and the detainee landed on the ground, awkwardly because the chains and cuffs constrained his movements and balance. The blows kept coming. The guard straddled the detainee and "continued to beat the shit out of him," while the female officer did nothing but block the elevator door, hold it open and stare at her feet as if expecting the incident to play itself out and everyone to proceed quietly upstairs to the court.

Some onlookers, people who had just parked their cars, gathered. "They were just regular people. They don't normally see something like that." Hemnauth could no longer contain himself. "At that point I got real emotional. I began to yell at the officer," calling on him to stop. The other detainees on the line kept still, out of fear of jeopardy to themselves, either in their court appearances or once back at Middlesex. Hemnauth was bolder, and though far from a natural-born troublemaker, he is prone to react when pushed beyond a threshold. "'Hey! It's about time you stopped now. You know, you have no right to be beating this man like this.' The man looked like he wanted to kill me, too." The guard was otherwise occupied, and Hemnauth was probably fortunate that he did not have an accomplice. When he did not cease mauling the African detainee, Hemnauth insisted the female cop intervene. She was close enough that he did not have to shout to her. She must have realized that the situation had gotten far out of hand. She let the elevator door go, walked toward her partner, who finally relented, and lifted the man up off the ground before she said anything. The detainee was taken to a holding cell in the building, whose existence I have verified.

Hemnauth later learned from Farouk Abdel-Muhti, whom by then he had befriended beyond casual acquaintance, that the victim of the beating had been placed in solitary confinement as punishment once back at the detention center he was assigned to. (It was not Middlesex.) After hearing of the incident from Hemnauth, Farouk — who was moved several times by the INS and ICE during his confinement — was somehow able to follow up on the story and meet the victim. He appeared before his warden and a sergeant to answer to a charge of assault on the guard. "Jails have their own little court thing going on." The guard claimed that the detainee had attacked him and that he had retaliated to defend himself. That an unarmed man in tightly fitted and heavy restraints could have endangered a guard so as to attract such savage repressive force strains credulity. However, in the parallel universe that is immigration detention, what people who inhabit ours are willing or not to believe is well beside the point.

Hemnauth speculates that the man, constrained by limited English, may have had difficulty answering the accusations leveled against him back at the jail. Still, to Hemnauth, grounded in the reality of shackles and handcuffs, the whole episode "was an unbelievable thing." The more such instances of abuse he witnessed, the more believable they became.

Rahoni discovered John Charles Allen, esquire, in the New Jersey yellow pages, she somewhat sheepishly told me when I met her in New York. Hemnauth did not remember "how the hell she found him." The immigration court had provided no guidance to detainees for selecting effective counsel, and it is difficult to shake the sensation that the IIRIRA statutes were deliberately intended as hostile toward the notion of legal defense for those whom the INS and later ICE had tagged for removal. Lawyers representing respondents seem to be tolerated chiefly as a carapace against suggestions of violation of due process.

Neither Rahoni, let alone Hemnauth as he sat in the Middlesex County Jail, possessed the resources to make a fully informed selection of an attorney and, if the list provided by the court did not turn up someone they could use, had to rely for their choice on the luck of the draw from sources like the phone book. The one prerequisite they could screen for was acceptance of a credit card in payment. Mr. Allen is the apparent sole practitioner of the law firm he runs, since no other attorneys are listed as partners or associates. He lists thirty-eight practice areas on his rudimentary website, in an alphabetical scroll, from adoption and elder law to sports law and wrongful termination. Immigration is a little further than halfway down the list, between fraud and intellectual property. In flashing capital letters, he announces a commitment to return his clients' phones calls as a distinctive qualification.

And yes, he does take credit cards. The home page features the logos of those he accepts, right next to the animated waving American flag. The whole site is atmospherically akin to a late-night TV infomercial produced on a tight budget.

There is a modicum of prominence given to immigration law on the site: one of four large buttons links to a page with further claims of expertise. Mr. Allen is a member of the American Immigration Lawyers Association; however, its eligibility requirements do not include an actual record or evidence of specialization in immigration law.[86]

In any event, Rahoni retained Mr. Allen on Hemnauth's behalf, and the attorney traveled to nearby Middlesex County Jail to introduce himself and offer some lawyerly words of reassurance. He looked the part of the slick,

---

86 American Immigration Lawyers Association, "Application Process, Eligibility."

confident lawyer in a nice suit, and sported a briefcase and "fancy toys," like a personal digital assistant. He told Hemnauth that his opening initiative would be to get him out of detention on bond, and did not go any further in outlining a strategy for fighting removal. Hindsight is, of course, twenty-twenty, and Hemnauth now claims that he read Mr. Allen as a jack-of-all-trades, prone, in Hemnauth's words, to "playing people for fools." Hemnauth's displeasure with Mr. Allen may have swollen over the years; however, he did express misgivings to Rachel Meeropol of the Center for Constitutional Rights in June 2003, while he was still in detention.[87] The business card Mr. Allen handed to Hemnauth, like the website, highlighted the disparate nature of his practice. He actually gave Hemnauth several cards and asked him to share them with his detention mates. Nothing works for business like referrals.

Nonetheless, at the moment, the lawyer had a comforting effect, and Hemnauth wanted to believe that he would be released quickly, if only on bond: "He kind of gave me that impression." Mr. Allen did not at the time comment on an actual strategy for enabling Hemnauth to post a bond and meet its cost — the minimum is $1,500 — or for obtaining definitive relief from deportation. He would have needed a damn good one, since the IIRIRA statutes place very rigid strictures on bonding, to the point that mandatory detention cases like Hemnauth's are very specifically disqualified.[88] Mr. Allen would need to plumb the statutes with the finest of legal combs to uncover a device for getting Hemnauth free.

Any generalist can be forgiven for being confused by the web of statutes governing deportation. Immigration law is often compared to the tax code for its complexity. Provisions adopted in each new set of immigration laws refer to prior immigration code, particularly the Immigration and Nationality Act of 1965, itself a modification, albeit a very substantial one, of the 1952 legislation of the same name. Provisions of current law also invoke diverse legislation in other areas such as that criminalizing behavior related to controlled substances, including the Controlled Substances Act of 1970, in turn subject to various legal definitions included in Title 21 of the United States Code. IIRIRA itself was adopted by Congress in tandem with the Antiterrorism and Effective Death Penalty Act (AEDPA), and the

87 Hemnauth Mohabir, in a letter to Rachel Meeropol, 2003.
88 Siskin, *Immigration-Related Detention: Current Legislative Issues.*

two acts are intimately associated with each other. Finally, IIRIRA so drastically expanded the grounds for, and enforcement of, immigrant detention and deportation as to take the contrast of immigration law with the judicial canon of the rest of the legal system to unprecedented extremes.

So it may not surprise everyone that Hemnauth's generalist attorney might adopt the logic that a release on bond would be available. What is more puzzling is why any attorney, given the level of complexity of immigration law, would want to hop among, say, closing real estate transactions, arguing personal injury cases and defending Hemnauth against exile in the face of extraordinarily intricate and rigid federal statutes. Against government counsel steeped in immigration law, a nonspecialist would be severely handicapped, particularly before the extrajudicial, discretion-deprived body that is the immigration court.

Hemnauth did not share his misgivings with Rahoni. She seemed to have confidence in Mr. Allen. Hemnauth did not want to rattle her or show her disrespect by second-guessing, especially as Rahoni had already paid Mr. Allen a retainer, and buyer's remorse on top of the substantial financial sacrifice she was making might have caused her useless anguish. Later, after Mr. Allen began charging for every filing and "every piece of paper he wrote on," Rahoni did indeed question her selection. He called repeatedly demanding more fees, typically in chunks of around $200, and before making any court appearances. Later still, in 2009, when Hemnauth wrote Mr. Allen to authorize him to release his files on the case to me, he responded with a supplemental invoice for $16,478.59 — including interest compounded at 18% annually — and claimed a lien on Hemnauth's file. For all practical purposes, Mr. Allen had curtailed his representation of Hemnauth long before any final outcome and prior to the Legal Aid Society taking the case. Rahoni ended up spending about $6,000 on Mr. Allen's fees and putting herself into substantial debt.

Hemnauth remembers only two court appearances with Mr. Allen at his side. At the first one, "he didn't know where to start." He asked for a bond. It was quickly denied by Judge Riefkohl after the INS attorney (the "D.A." in Hemnauth's perception) opposed it on grounds of ineligibility according to the immigration code. Hemnauth's interpretation, which is generally accurate, is that bond was denied out of hand because he was apprehended as an inadmissible arriving alien. Under these circumstances, the immigration judge simply lacked the authority to grant bond.[89] Had the attorney known this, he presumably would not have made the request. Parole, on the other hand, was theoretically available. Parole applications must be made to the Department of Homeland Security, specifically to a ranked official with the discretion to grant or deny parole as stipulated in the Code of Federal Regulations.[90] The guidelines for parole are deliberately restrictive. "Most arriving aliens are not eligible for parole . . . In general, parole is available on a 'case-by-case basis for urgent humanitarian reasons or significant public benefit.'"[91]

Judge Riefkohl, as an immigration judge, had no authority under the code to grant parole, and urged Allen to submit a petition to someone who did. We have no record of his ever having followed this guidance or indicating to Hemnauth that he would.

Without further argument as to why certain provisions within the statutes might allow for bond in Hemnauth's case, denial was bound to be swift. Mr. Allen did not attempt to present justification for Hemnauth's release beyond the request. In fairness, he would have been hard-pressed to find any within the law's uncompromising, one-size-fits-all strictures binding the immigration courts. However, this does beg the question as to why the attorney did not move immediately to seeking avenues for definitive resolution in his client's favor rather than petition for an elusive release on bond. Petitions for which he was charging his client. They amounted to spinning wheels. And if he did not know of any avenues to deflect ultimate removal, why was he taking the client's money? No lawyer can guarantee an outcome, but he might owe it to a client to know and convey fairly which actions are futile and which might have even a slim chance of succeeding.

While the immigration code is of Byzantine complexity, proceedings in immigration court follow a fairly clear three-step pattern to which an attorney would normally refer when developing the grounds for relief.

In step one, the government, through the INS (now ICE), must show that the respondent is inadmissible, removable, or both. The evidentiary burden is fairly light. The candidate for deportation must be indisputably

---

89 "In Re Jesus Collado-Munoz, Respondent" (1998).

90 "Parole of Aliens into the United States," National Archives and Records Administration.

91 Siskin, *Immigration-Related Detention,* citing 8 Code of Federal Regulations §212.5(b).

an alien, not a citizen, a fact easily demonstrated in Hemnauth's case by his green card, a document that is issued only to foreigners. The government must also show a criminal conviction, for Hemnauth the misdemeanor conviction from the Queens criminal court, again easily documented. Once the immigration judge confirms these two observations, the respondent is deemed to be removable.

In step two, the burden shifts to the alien, who must satisfy the court that he is eligible to apply for one of the limited forms of relief that can lead to a cancellation of his removal. In order to pass this hurdle, the alien must meet the specific statutory requirements for relief.

Only in step three of the standard roadmap does the judge exercise any discretion, by deciding whether, once an alien has fulfilled the statutory conditions, he is deserving of relief from deportation, or not.

Hemnauth, as we know, never got this far. He remained stuck at step two, and his lawyer had no idea what device he might use to try to help his client past it and into the tightly constrained realm of judicial discretion afforded the immigration judge.

At the second hearing, in August 2002, Judge Riefkohl decided to intervene more pointedly on Hemnauth's behalf. He began to question Hemnauth himself, leading the witness in order to plant in Mr. Allen's mind some ideas he might pursue in advocating for his client. "The judge became my attorney . . . He was trying to help me, but he couldn't really call the shots. The D.A. [sic] called the shots. [Riefkohl] was in the judge's seat; he could help by advising us, so he was doing that.

"He asked me where I was from. I answered from Guyana. He asked me what kind of political situation they had there." Political asylum was, in the judge's mind, something worth exploring, as well as other possible forms of relief from removal in response to a tangible fear of abuse. Unlike many other human rights treaties, including the articles of the 1947 Universal Declaration, the main stipulation of the Convention Against Torture is self-executing,[92] meaning that it has force of law in American courts by virtue of an enabling act of Congress, including in immigration court. Hemnauth

---

92 Kurzban, *Kurzban's Immigration Law Sourcebook*. Some courts have found that the treaty as a whole is not self-executing, although the Foreign Affairs Reform and Restructuring Act of 1998 requires enforcement of its Article 3(1) banning extradition and deportation to countries where a respondent might be tortured.

outlined to the best of his ability the polarization in Guyanese politics between the two political parties, the People's National Congress and the People's Progressive Party associated, respectively, with each of the ethnic communities, black and Indian. At the time of Guyana's independence, the reins of power evolved to Forbes Burnham's PNC and stayed there until 1992. However, since then, the presidency has been held by the PPP with the backing of voters of Indian extraction. (Bharrat Jagdeo was Guyana's president at the time of Hemnauth's removal hearings and remains in office today.) "'Then it's your government now. Your people are ruling now,'" Hemnauth remembers Judge Riefkohl saying, or something clearly to that effect.

Under these circumstances, Judge Riefkohl discounted fear of persecution as a lever for obtaining relief, although Hemnauth's treatment immediately upon returning to Guyana indicates that this assessment was only partially informed. It posited that political or ethnic affiliation was the only basis for gross, and perhaps even predictable, human rights violations that Hemnauth was likely to invoke.

There are three permutations of grants of relief from removal on human rights grounds. The gold standard, and one that is unique to the United States, is what the law terms outright asylum. It provides a path to permanent residency and eventual citizenship to its beneficiaries, who must document a well-founded, individualized fear of stiff victimization (such as torture or imprisonment) for reasons of race, religion, political opinion, nationality or membership in a social group. Civil war or generalized violence may also bolster a petition for asylum.[93] In any event, the burden of demonstrating a significant likelihood of persecution falls to the petitioner, and the application requirements are daunting. Hemnauth had no obvious claim of eligibility for asylum, since he could not demonstrate a likelihood of individual persecution based on his experience in Guyana prior to his emigration. A step down from asylum is "withholding of removal," which imposes the same conditions as asylum, but in cases where it cannot be granted, either because the petitioner had delayed filing beyond a year or had been convicted of a particularly serious crime as defined by law. In this case, deportation is deferred until conditions in the country in question improve. The third avenue is the Convention Against Torture. It simply

---

93 "Asylum Law, Asylum Seekers and Refugees: A Primer."

restricts the U.S. government from sending people to countries where a government or its agents engage in torture. There are no explicit ramifications for a petitioner's residency status. Even in CAT petitions, the government places restrictive boundaries on the definition of torture that were upheld by the federal appeal court, in the case of a Haitian deportee fearful of the general brutal prison conditions in his homeland: "We hold that in order to constitute torture, an act must be inflicted with the *specific intent* to cause severe physical or mental pain and suffering"[94] (emphasis added).

At the time, Hemnauth himself may have been unaware of the brutality that could greet deportees returning to Guyana and would have been unable to document it on the fly. He would personally confront the brutality a year and a half later, and discover that his membership in what can be construed, in all honesty, as a social group — returning deportees — placed him in danger of persecution. Also, the judge's first written ruling against Hemnauth later suggests that he researched the situation in Guyana himself:

> The respondent is correct in asserting that the control of police power is concentrated and controlled by the Afro-Guyanese population even though the PPP (Indo-Guyanese party) has won the last three elections . . . The differences in both parties or groups have brought about violence and deaths.

Mr. Allen's brief in support of his motion to have Hemnauth's removal from the country cancelled was, well, brief, although he did reference materials he had consulted in drafting it. These included a memorandum from the U.S. attorney general that, Allen claimed to the court, identified mitigating criteria in drug-related convictions applicable to Hemnauth's case. The striking feature of this argument is that it attempts to exempt Hemnauth from deportation by advancing the notion that his misdemeanor was not a "particularly serious crime." While the phrase reads like a personal assessment, it is also a term of art. It appears in the text of the Immigration and Nationality Act, referring to discretionary asylum that may be granted by the attorney general, but this discretion is subject to severe preconditions that Mr. Allen did not address. In short, the motion appears to confront

---

94 Fuentes, "Auguste v. Ridge No. 04-1739" (2005).

the immigration statutes head on, without a finding of fact other than the ones the INS had already considered, thrusting Hemnauth's case under the sharp blade of the law's cookie cutter.

Indeed, Mr. Allen's motion to cancel the proceedings against Hemnauth missed the central point. The INS knew full well the nature of Hemnauth's misdemeanor and its piddling magnitude. The judge himself acknowledged that the "criminal infraction" Hemnauth had committed was "minute." However, IIRIRA was specifically designed to be inflexible and to deflect exceptions. Further, the framers of the law went to great lengths to redefine the relative gravity of past offenses for the purposes of deportation, and indeed to dilate them with the inflammatory designations of "aggravated felony" and "crime of moral turpitude," even in cases when the underlying offense is not a felony at all, let alone an aggravated one, and when the term "moral turpitude" was totally absent the verbiage of any prior indictment. The law even states that the gravity of an offense triggering deportation may be irrelevant. It also seems unlikely that an attorney general who regarded his department as instrumental in building the Bush administration's credentials in the still-young war on terror would have been prone to promoting leniency in removal proceedings. A set of stern deportation rules fit the objective of demonstrating to the public that the government was on a "war footing," a phrase favored by Vice President Dick Cheney.

In Hemnauth's case, his misdemeanor involved a controlled substance other than marijuana in an amount of less than thirty grams, and he had been in the country for a period of less than five years when he pled guilty to the offense. As far as IIRIRA was concerned, in letter and in (mean) spirit, Hemnauth was deportable, period, full stop, end of story. To debate whether relief was available under the same provisions of the statutes that declared otherwise was an exercise in futility that most fully informed immigration advocates would not have performed.

"Judge Riefkohl tried another thing then. Rahoni had given me a letter written by my son. I handed it over to the judge." Kevin was ten years old at the time. The letter was addressed to Hemnauth. Riefkohl read the letter, then handed it to the bailiff or guard and asked that photocopies be made.

He then gave a copy to the government's attorney, and another to Mr. Allen. He kept a copy for himself and returned the original to Hemnauth.

"He kept on questioning me on all sorts of things, about my career as a musician and as a technician." The judge had clearly taken an informed and rather thorough interest in the individual appearing before him, as he did years later when I observed him receiving the testimony of the lady from Peru in nondetained removal proceedings. He turned to John Charles Allen, who had been silent for some time, and said, in Hemnauth's recollection of the words, some of them purposefully flippant in order to get the point across to the lawyer: "The place is getting warm, and we need air conditioning people. Why don't you get this man out of jail? Get him out of jail. We need this man." Whether he knew it or not, the judge was only half joking about the need for immigrant air conditioning technicians; if attendance at the Apex school is any indication, immigrants make up a large share of its graduates in refrigeration maintenance. Hemnauth told Rachel Meeropol that the judge stopped the tape recording of the hearing as he made his most candid remarks and appeared to rebuke Mr. Allen. Since the government denies that detainees are imprisoned, it would be noteworthy if the judge actually referred to Hemnauth's incarceration as "jail," regardless of the practical reality that he was, indeed, in jail. He may well have used the J word: in his written decision, Riefkohl stated that Hemnauth had been "held in prison" by the INS.

Mr. Allen reacted by once again bringing up a request for release on bond. The government attorney reminded the court that the question of the bond had already been settled. Since the issue fell beyond the immigration court's jurisdiction, the judge did not even need to formally deny it and may not even have had the authority to do so.

"Mr. Mohabir," the judge continued, "I find you to be an extremely honest man." Hemnauth then remembers him stating the obvious: "Your attorney does not seem to be helping you too much." Hemnauth does not stand by those exact words, but certainly by the fact that the judge expressed his disappointment in Mr. Allen. "He embarrassed Mr. Allen, but in a diplomatic way." He could not do much more. Courts do not question the basic competency of a lawyer who has been admitted to the bar and cannot disapprove of the presence of such a lawyer in court, including immigration court. This rule and consequent practice are anchored in the

Sixth Amendment to the Constitution.

Judge Riefkohl also addressed Rahoni, who was present in court and had written a letter as well pleading for Hemnauth's release. He recognized the sacrifices she had made hiring an attorney and taking leave from her jobs to come to court and offer support with her presence. The letter from Kevin had obviously affected him, and he said as much to Hemnauth and Rahoni.

Hemnauth also told me that the judge invoked the fact that the couple had divorced and that this would have to count against Hemnauth's petition for relief. This is slightly odd, and Hemnauth's recollection of how the judge addressed the topic of marital status may have clouded with time. Indeed, as Bryan Lonegan, the Legal Aid Society attorney who later represented Hemnauth, told me, the case never got so far as to examine Hemnauth's family situation. It would have been a nonissue, since the statutes commanding deportation in Hemnauth's case bar mitigation owing to family hardship or human rights conventions protecting family integrity. One would also expect that if family matters had warranted consideration, Hemnauth's "emotional and monitary [sic] support"[95] for his American-born son would have more than offset the ultimately amicable separation of his mother and father that Riefkohl purportedly raised as a strike against relief. In fact, divorce or no divorce, Kevin qualified as Hemnauth's child: not only was he born to Hemnauth in wedlock, the Immigration and Naturalization Act as well honors as valid the parent-child bond when "in the case of the father, a bona fide parent-child relationship exists."[96] And, as the judge explicitly acknowledged, there was no faking the letter from Kevin to his dad.

The hearing concluded with Judge Riefkohl announcing to those before him that, to his regret, he would allow Hemnauth's deportation to proceed. He was apologetic, and there is no reason to doubt his sincerity; quite the opposite. He did not wish to do what he was doing, but the statutes left him no choice. He told Hemnauth that he expected the deportation order to be carried out within three months, presumably counting from issuance of the written ruling. "That was the end of the hearing. I lost the case then."

There is one significant detail Hemnauth omitted when I interviewed him, but that he related to Rachel Meeropol in the narrative of the case

---

95 Rahoni Sharma, in a letter to Judge Alberto Riefkohl, 2002.

96 Kurzban, *Kurzban's Immigration Law Sourcebook,* referring to INA Section 101(1)(b).

that he wrote for her about nine months after the August 2002 hearing. In it, he quotes the agitated judge telling Mr. Allen: "This is a stupid charge, a stupid case, and I have to make a stupid decision on this man, get him out of detention, go vacate the [misdemeanor] charge or file [for] parole." He gave Mr. Allen two months to follow his advice and suggested an appeal following the formal publication of the deportation ruling. The advice is meaningful for a couple of reasons. First, getting the Queens district attorney to vacate the misdemeanor drug charge was indeed one of the avenues Bryan Lonegan later pursued, with some creative twists. Second, Mr. Allen did not pursue it, despite the clear suggestion from the judge that he do so. Nor is there evidence that he ever submitted a petition for Hemnauth's parole to ICE, as the judge had urged him to do.

Hemnauth saw his attorney one more time. "Mr. John Charles Allen showed up at Middlesex correctional center and said that he works for $200 dollars an hour, and that the money has finished, but he'll see me through this. I was ordered removed from the U.S.A. on the 25th of September. I learned this from an INS officer. Mr. Allen then filed a notice of appeal to the BIA [Bureau of Immigration Appeals] and sent the bill to Rahoni. We never heard from him again."[97] The appeal was later dropped. The lawyer did not tell Hemnauth that he had filed the appeal, also an important detail. The appeal triggered a suspension in the deportation process, leaving Hemnauth to languish in jail with no information forthcoming on the disposition of his case while his lawyer took a powder.

At the risk of damning with faint praise, I should point out that Mr. Allen's derisory effectiveness was hardly exceptional, and more a paragon of the quality of representation detained immigrants often receive when they resort to a private attorney. Immigrants fare better in immigration proceedings when legal aid foundations or pro bono lawyers take their cases.

Until recently, such an assertion would have been hazardous and founded upon anecdotal evidence. However, in late 2011, the Benjamin N. Cardozo School of Law of Yeshiva University published an extensive study[98] of the

97 Mohabir, in a letter to Meeropol, 2003.
98 Markowitz et al., "Accessing Justice: The Availability and Adequacy of Counsel

adequacy of representation in immigration court, in both quantitative and qualitative terms. The quality survey underpinning the report was conducted in July 2011, well after Hemnauth's case had been closed; however, the study was undertaken to test suspicions of poor representation the authors had harbored for years based on isolated observations, and there is no reason to believe that the quality of the legal defense of immigrants by private counsel has varied materially over the past decade. The study focused on respondents residing in New York at the time of their alleged immigration violations, as Hemnauth did. The detained among them were often held in jails outside New York.

The findings of the quality survey are devastating, with a full 47% of the responses from New York immigration judges rating the overall quality of representation of the defendants appearing before them as either "inadequate" (33%) or "grossly inadequate" (14%).[99] Further, these assessments cover all attorneys, including those working pro bono or in nonprofit legal aid practices, which have a different stake in the outcome than monetary compensation. When asked to grade attorneys by category, pro bono counsel scored much higher than fee-earning attorneys and firms, 8.41 versus 5.22 on a ten-point scale,[100] implying greater incidence of inadequate or grossly inadequate performance of the private bar, "the epicenter of the quality problem."[101] The wording of the study's conclusion is worth quoting at length as we attempt to understand the ramifications of the quality of service detained immigrants might receive when, in desperate straits they fall into the hands of a private lawyer they do not know:

> These findings — most critically that nearly half of removal-case representation is inadequate — are of serious concern . . . These findings are particularly alarming because minimally adequate representation is essential to the fundamental fairness of removal proceedings, particularly since it affects a class of people that is likely to be unfamiliar with the law, the procedures, and the evidentiary rules. When

---

in Immigration Proceedings." The New York Immigrant Representation Study underpinning the report is an initiative of Judge Robert A. Katzmann of the U.S. Court of Appeals for the Second Circuit.

99 Markowitz et al., "Accessing Justice."
100 Markowitz et al., "Accessing Justice."
101 Markowitz et al., "Accessing Justice."

representatives fall short of basic standards of representational adequacy, as the survey findings indicate is too often the case, the consequences to a person's case can be devastating and, as a practical
matter, often irreversible.[102]

Judge Alberto Riefkohl issued his written decision on September 25, 2002.
The document is both unsurprising in the context of the IIRIRA provisions and astonishing in its willingness to assert that the application of the
law in the case before him was frankly unfair. The judge had also looked
into the human rights profile of Guyana on his own initiative in search of a
lever under the Convention Against Torture. Hemnauth was in a very tight
box. The post-IIRIRA Immigration and Nationality Act's section 212(a)
(A)(i)(II) governing controlled substances other than small amounts of
marijuana mandates deportation, and the conditions for cancellation of removal are narrow, in particular the stipulation that an immigrant convicted
of any drug-related crime within seven years of his or her arrival in the
United States does not qualify. The choice of the seven-year threshold is
entirely arbitrary. Regardless, Hemnauth had been in the country for fewer
than four.

The best Judge Riefkohl could do in his legal ruling was to confirm, as
he went through his procedural checklist, that Hemnauth was not an aggravated felon, sparing him the label's insult and its kiss of death for any
appeal. Also, under the law Hemnauth's simple possession of a controlled
substance was officially not a "crime involving moral turpitude." Not that
escaping either of these distinctions was of any practical consequence,
since the section prescribing Hemnauth's removal treats him the same or
worse than someone guilty of utter depravity. (A later ruling by the Supreme Court in 2006 specifically barred the government from designating
simple possession of a controlled substance as an aggravated felony, contrary to ICE's wishes.[103])

---

102 Markowitz et al., "Accessing Justice."
103 Justice David Souter, "Jose Antonio Lopez, Petitioner v. Alberto R. Gonzales,
Attorney General No. 05-547" (2006).

I do not know how unusual it is for an immigration judge to express, in official rulings, empathy toward a deportee as Judge Riefkohl demonstrably did. "The respondent is an honest individual who did not embellish his facts," he writes. Language such as this might be common. To raise an objection to the law itself in a written decision must be rarer, but that is what Judge Riefkohl did: "I honestly believe that the respondent's criminal infraction is minute and should have no bearing in the respondent's right to remain in the United States."[104]

The judge also recognized that he was powerless to show any leniency in his ruling. A judge in a genuine judicial setting, that is in an actual court of law, has a number of levers at his or her disposal to ensure that punishment is proportional to the crime, to make an individual judgment as to what form and magnitude of penalty is most appropriate, to take into account both aggravating and attenuating circumstances.

Bryan Lonegan was not impressed when I offhandedly commented to him that immigration judges were not real judges. "They're not Article III judges," he corrected me, invoking the section of the U.S. Constitution that establishes an independent judiciary. I ceded the point. After all, Bryan is an eminent legal scholar and I am not. Also, the task of adjudicating between exile and relief is nothing if not real, for many judges painfully so. But in retrospect, after reading Judge Riefkohl's poignant admission to being forced to do something he felt was wrong because he was specifically stripped of discretion, I would maintain that immigration judges, indeed, are not independent judges as most of us would understand the title to mean. They are part of the executive branch of the federal government, not the judiciary, and report to a boss who can fire them.

The remaining salient feature of Judge Riefkohl's decision is its apparent admonishment of Hemnauth's lawyer for not attempting to have the misdemeanor charge vacated. Without the misdemeanor charge, the INS would have no grounds for detaining Hemnauth, and Riefkohl could order him released. "At the end of the testimony, I indicated [that the misdemeanor should have no bearing on Hemnauth's right to remain in the country] and allow[ed] a period to the respondent's attorney to find out whether he could find a way to vacate the respondent's conviction . . . The

---

104 Alberto H. Riefkohl, "In Removal Proceedings of: Mohabir, Hennauth [sic], Decision of the Immigration Judge" (2002).

court has not received any communication from either side."[105] The district counsel representing the government and intent on Hemnauth's removal would, of course, have had no interest in seeing the old misdemeanor charge erased, so the rebuke must have been aimed at Mr. Allen. There is, indeed, no indication that Allen ever approached the Queens district attorney's office.

Although the judge downplayed the possibility of relief from deportation by virtue of the Convention Against Torture, Mr. Allen did take the hint, if that is what it was, and made Article 3 of CAT the motive of the appeal:

> Appellant respectfully submits that the Immigration Court erred in determining that Appellant's fear of suffering from persecution and torture, as well as danger to his safety and life if he is required to return to Guyana does not satisfy the requirement for relief under Article Three of the Convention Against Torture. Appellant prays that circumstances in Guyana are such that his stated fear of prosecution, torture and for his safety are well founded fears.

This was a fair statement as later events demonstrated, although very general. Upon returning to Guyana, Hemnauth discovered that it was common practice for pictures of returning detainees to be published in the government-controlled newspaper as a green light to whoever might harm them. However, with little meat on the bones of Mr. Allen's appeal, it was a dead letter. The filing measured a total of five typed lines and included no documentation, substantiation or reasoning, nor has any evidence of a subsequent brief from Mr. Allen surfaced that might have enumerated dangers specific to Hemnauth. There was no other communication to the immigration court or the Board of Immigration Appeals. Relief under CAT was almost certainly a long shot. Still, there was discoverable evidence of abuse of deportees returning to Guyana, and Mr. Allen's appeal could not have taken more than a few minutes to draft.

The rules of professional conduct for lawyers in the state of New Jersey imply that the courts will frown upon abandonment of a client by an attorney. However, the specific regulations regarding termination by an

---

105 Riefkohl, "In Removal Proceedings."

attorney seem remarkably open to interpretation and therefore equivocal. For instance, an attorney must take steps "to the extent reasonably practicable" to ensure his client is not harmed in the transition to succeeding counsel.[106] What is "reasonably practicable"? We can also speculate that Mr. Allen's repeated phone calls to Rahoni demanding additional payments constituted in his mind the fair warning mandated by the rules that he would stop representing Hemnauth unless she came up with the money first. What is unequivocal is Hemnauth's perception that the attorney had abused his trust and abandoned him when he ran out of money. He said as much in a sworn statement to the ICE district director in New Jersey when he finally applied for parole in May 2003 under the aegis of a community advocate alerted to the case well into Hemnauth's hellish residency at Passaic County Jail. He told me in Trinidad, without my asking as much, that he would sign written testimony confirming what he had said about Allen if I asked him to.

Mr. Allen's representation of his client may seem puzzling or inadequate, in light of its outcome and the judge's impatience with the uninspired defense Mr. Allen offered. As much of a problem as the lawyer may have been, the bigger problem was the IIRIRA statutes he confronted. In fact, his largest failure was in not recognizing how effectively IIRIRA couples intransigence with downright cruelty. While these pages are intended as narrative, not treatise, the narrative would be incomplete without a brief detour through the "gotcha" ethos of our current immigration law, particularly its sections commanding deportation. The most peculiar, even spectacular feature of the law is the set of barriers it erects against any and all appeals to basic fairness. IIRIRA is so thoroughly cleansed of any concern for justice or empathy that one gets the sense that its framers looked upon these fundamental American values as so many stains to be scrubbed. For all his undeniable, even quantifiable compassion, I still find it astonishing that Judge Riefkohl could characterize Hemnauth's deportation as "one instance when the system did not work." Upon examination, it appears that

---

106 "Rules of Professional Conduct," New Jersey Courts.

the system worked exactly as was intended, as a deportation machine that spews out binary, take-no-prisoners removal decisions. Mitigation would just gum up the works.

Barriers to mitigation are the very spirit of the law. Before IIRIRA, the process for ordering deportation was analogous, if certainly not identical to the practices of the criminal justice system for all individuals charged with an infraction. The process contained two determinations: first, whether an alien was a candidate for removal, and second, whether the totality of circumstances warranted such removal. Observation of an event that could spell removal, followed by a reasoned judgment as to whether it should.

IIRIRA summarily eradicates the latter. Under the immigration code superseded by IIRIRA, "When the balance of equities counseled against deportation, a permanent resident could be granted relief from deportation."[107] Evidence of remorse or rehabilitation, family ties in America, the person's honesty in the proceedings, if the crime triggering deportation hearings was not "a particularly serious one" threatening the nation's security, a favorable employment history: these are all factors that could and did routinely weigh in that balance. They all, not coincidentally, apply to Hemnauth's case. In a 1978 ruling, *In re Marin,* the Board of Immigration Appeals actually set forth a laundry list of mitigating factors — alongside obvious aggravating circumstances — that the INS could use in its decisions, everything from service in the military to community service.[108] Again, Hemnauth would have satisfied most of them if he had gotten that far. Pre-IIRIRA, Hemnauth would in all likelihood have been allowed to stay in the United States and care for his son.

No more. Discretion still exists in theory, but it has been kicked upstairs and can be invoked only if all the preconditions embedded in IIRIRA have been met, such as the minimum of seven years residency including five as a permanent resident. Catch-22. Even if the preconditions have been met, an immigration judge can order removal if there are grounds for it. In that

107 Morawetz, "Understanding the Impact of the 1996 Deportation Laws and the Limited Scope of Proposed Reforms."
108 Hing, *Deporting Our Souls: Values, Morality and Immigration Policy.*

case, the immigrant must take his case to the Board of Immigration Appeals and assume the burden of proof of his good character, rehabilitation, and the like.[109] IIRIRA blocked Hemnauth from ever getting to that point.

Hemnauth's case stumbled on two blocks aligned with each other. The first mandates deportation for crimes of any severity involving controlled substances other than small amounts of marijuana. Immigration law categorizes such offenses of simple possession as equally if not more worthy of retribution as aggravated felonies and crimes involving moral turpitude, tarring the character of someone like Hemnauth in the same strokes as it would a pimp or a thief.

The second imposes a seven-year blemish-free record of residency regardless of status and five years of legal permanent residency before consideration of relief, let alone granting of it since it can still be denied. These thresholds appear plucked from thin air and do not make reference to any documented correlation between an alien's length of residency and public safety. The seven-year yardstick is also subject to a stop-time rule: even though Hemnauth did not receive a Notice to Appear from an immigration court prior to his detention at Kennedy Airport in 2002, the law says that the accrual of a record of residency halts on the date of the crime triggering removal. In Hemnauth's case, that was six years before he was threatened with deportation.

The one-size-fits-all approach thoroughly permeates the law. It prescribes mandatory deportation in myriad circumstances that, while differing from Hemnauth's, nonetheless subject an immigrant with a minor offense on his or her record to an unforgiving sentence of exile from home, spouse, children, friends, job, future and, often, political and personal security. The law favors labels such as "criminal alien," "aggravated felon" and "moral turpitude" so broadly that one can only suspect that the language of the statutes was deliberately designed for rhetorical effect.

Like Hemnauth's drug misdemeanor, an "aggravated felony" as defined unilaterally by IIRIRA triggers mandatory detention, deportation and sky-high barriers to effective appeal. In his testimony before Congress in 2007, the former general counsel of the INS cited real-life examples of infractions reclassified as aggravating felonies, such as the theft of a ten-dollar

---

109 "In Re C-V-T, Respondent" (1998).

video game and hair-pulling during a fight over a boyfriend.[110] He was not making this stuff up.

It gets worse. IIRIRA has a long arm, and its provisions apply retroactively. If the INS and now ICE were to discover an ancient criminal record, even one for a petty crime committed years or decades earlier when the immigrant was a juvenile, he or she can be placed into deportation proceedings without recourse to a statute of limitation for the simple reason that there isn't one. The Supreme Court, in one of its decisions at the edges of IIRIRA, *INS v. St. Cyr*,[111] did rule that a removal candidate was eligible for a waiver if his deportation order was pursuant to a crime committed when the old immigration code was in force and permitted such a waiver. This was a typically narrow ruling, with little practical bearing on the forward thrust of current immigration law.

There are also provisions that use length of sentencing, as little as one year, as a trigger for deportation even in cases when charges have been expunged. Others allow the government to use the *potential* of a prison term under sentencing guidelines as indicative of an aggravated felony even when no jail term was imposed. Under IIRIRA, ICE can count a suspended sentence as equivalent to a served one. The potential for abuse is wide enough to drive a truck through, and political attitudes in, say, Arizona, demonstrate eagerness in some local quarters to get into the deportation-enforcement business. It is easy to imagine, particularly in an atmosphere where ever-stiffer sentences play well to the electorate, that the threat of a harsh punishment for a relatively minor crime increases the appeal of a plea-bargained suspended sentence. Under IIRIRA, a prosecutor can obtain an iron-fisted sentence of exile — after a period of incarceration by ICE that can easily run longer than the term of the suspended sentence, especially if the immigrant has the audacity to contest his or her removal — whereas otherwise he might exact only a fine or short jail term, let alone an acquittal. This is a variant of what happened to Hemnauth.

Like its partner label, "crime involving moral turpitude," the "aggravated felony" designation indiscriminately trawls for deportation candidates whose offenses are vastly different in nature, intensity and threat to society.

---

110 Paul W. Virtue, testimony in "Shortfalls of the 1996 Immigration Reform Legislation."

111 Supreme Court, "Immigration and Naturalization Service v. St. Cyr" (2001).

An eighteen-year-old noncitizen who has consensual sex with a sixteen-year-old girlfriend falls into the same sexual abuse rubric as a statutory rapist under IIRIRA and is automatically deportable as an aggravated felon. Forget that a majority of girls in the United States are sexually active before their eighteenth birthdays. Bryan Lonegan related to me the case of a man who faced deportation for having neglected to reregister as a sex offender when he moved across the street. His sex crime? Many years earlier he had slept with his underage girlfriend — who later became his wife and mother of his two American children.

One might easily be tempted to view such cases as exceptional, as aberrations, as the small price we (or rather someone else) must pay in collateral damage in order for our immigration laws to operate correctly. Such is the position Judge Riefkohl took when he characterized Hemnauth's case to me as a rare instance when the system misfired. However, the whole point of IIRIRA, its operating principle, is that there are to be no exceptions, no room for interpretation or special cases or challenge other than, narrowly, on findings of fact. If the drafters of the law had wanted it to provide for exceptions, its provisions would have included some method to measure the actual circumstances and severity of an immigrant's offense or to review cases for mistakes outside an onerous appeal. Instead, current immigration law specifically abjures such measurement, which was permitted in the Immigration Act prior to IIRIRA, in favor of all-encompassing tags. Or are we to believe that the members of Congress and their staffers who drafted IIRIRA in 1996 were in such utter denial of the possibility that exceptional situations such as Hemnauth's might arise? In fact, in addressing "crimes involving moral turpitude," — an expansive and very consequential category comprising "conduct which is inherently base, vile, or depraved, contrary to the accepted rules of morality" — the law explicitly states it does not give a damn how trivial an offense might be: *"The seriousness of a criminal offense, the severity of the sentence imposed, or the particular circumstances of the crime's commission do not determine whether the crime involves moral turpitude."*[112] Until the Supreme Court intervened — thank Heaven for small mercies — ICE equated simple controlled-substance possessions to drug trafficking, and driving under the influence as a crime of violence,

---

112 "212 Crimes Involving Moral Turpitude," U.S. Department of Justice.

in order to name removal candidates aggravated felons.

It is difficult to pronounce which provision of IIRIRA is the most draconian. There are so many choices: deportation, demeaning labels, double
jeopardy, denial of the right to counsel — by classifying deportation proceedings as civil rather than criminal — tight-jacketed judicial discretion,
cordoned avenues of appeal, systematic overreach, the seemingly deliberate feeding of political hostility toward immigrants implicit in the vocabu-
lary of the legislation. Take your pick.

Still, mandatory detention occupies an elemental spot in the lineup, even
setting aside the conditions of incarceration in ICE detention facilities,
which Hemnauth's story illuminates and to which we will return. The ramifications are devastating. A person who has never done time, whose crime,
like Hemnauth's, was not punishable by jail time, can wind up serving what
amounts to lengthy prison terms alongside violent criminals, in the same
exact conditions of incarceration and restraint. The period between apprehension and a first hearing before an immigration judge can be months,
as it was for Hemnauth, so even an immigrant who chooses not to contest
his or her removal in the wake of a very first appearance may have served
significant prison time without ever having been sentenced to jail.

The system hides behind the terminology disqualifying administrative detention as imprisonment, but this should fool no one. ICE, under
President Obama, has described detention standards as correctional rather
than administrative, and even the immigration judge in Hemnauth's case
referred to his confinement as jail and prison, orally in open court and in
writing. Mandatory detention like that imposed on Hemnauth is proscribed
by ratified international treaty, in particular the International Covenant on
Civil and Political Rights. When the question of immigrant detention was
put to the Human Rights Committee of the United Nations — whose
readings of international covenants are specifically recognized as valid by
the United States, even if we claim the right not to abide by them — it
declared that prolonged *"remand in custody [of persons in deportation proceedings]
could be considered arbitrary if it is not necessary in all the circumstances of the case,
for example to prevent flight or interference with evidence: the element of proportionality
becomes relevant in this context."*[113] What is arbitrary is, of course, contrary to

---

113 Bhagwati, "A (Name Deleted) v. Australia, Communication No. 560/1993."

the relevant provision of the covenant, in this case its Article 9, which addresses arrest and detention.

So, for openers, we have a clear portrait of sanctioned double jeopardy, even if the federal courts have yet to fully counter immigrant detention practices in light of the Fifth Amendment's prohibition of double jeopardy, and have given little to no indication that they are inclined ever to do so. The issue of constitutional limits on preremoval detention has been addressed in part and narrowly. Under Supreme Court rulings, ICE cannot detain an individual under a deportation order indefinitely if he does not contest his removal and ICE cannot find a country to deport him to within six months. More recently, in 2009, the Court in *Padilla v. Kentucky* affirmed an alien's right to know the consequences for his residency status of a criminal conviction. This is particularly important for people tempted to plea bargain or drop challenges to a conviction, as Hemnauth did in 1997 vis-à-vis his misdemeanor.

But consider this: mandatory detention, paired with severe restrictions on the granting of release on bond, amounts to a system of coercion tantamount to official blackmail. Fighting words, perhaps, but can they really be disputed? On the one hand, an immigrant facing deportation has no right to court-appointed counsel and is remanded to jail as he seeks a fee-for-service attorney he hopes might be effective, figures out how to pay for him and prepares his legal defense, all the while facing the barriers and often prohibitive cost of communicating with the outside world. If there were a right to counsel as there is in criminal proceedings, the individual could see a lawyer as often as necessary for the adequate conduct of his defense without bumping against financial constraints after a few hours with one. This situation improves when the immigrant detainee secures pro bono representation, but such a benefit is far from guaranteed.

And even when a detainee has a pro bono attorney, time is on the side of the government: the longer the detainee languishes in jail, the more desperate he becomes to be released, even if this condemns him to exile. In addition, if an immigrant has a constitutional claim or wishes to appeal the reading of a statute by the immigration court, he or she will have to clear a long sequence of administrative hurdles and jurisdictional boundaries. As long as a person is contesting a removal or pleading for its cancellation, he can remain in jail, without bond, indefinitely until final resolution of his case. The detainee "must in effect agree to incarceration, for an indefinite period of time, while he or she pursues claims of non-deportability or eligibility for relief."[114] That is where the blackmail comes in. In practice, the government often can, and often does, keep a deportable alien in detention until he or she breaks and accepts removal. This is precisely what happened to Hemnauth, as we shall see. A person convicted of a minor misdemeanor in a prior life who finds himself incarcerated for months or years, under the same correctional standards of confinement as the general prison population, alongside jailmates not of his choosing, vulnerable to brutality, isolation, depression and inadequate health care, on a lousy prison diet, under the thumb of prison guards untrained to distinguish between detainees and persons held for criminal behavior, administered by sheriffs who benefit politically from cracking down on immigrants and under jurisdictions that benefit financially from it, what person in these circumstances will not, sooner or later, cry uncle, give up his or her rights and accept deportation? When a successful outcome under our intransigent immigration code is so uncertain? Add to this menu that a detainable alien can be sent to a facility thousands of miles and hundreds of dollars removed from family elsewhere in the United States. None of this is an exaggeration or a rarity. Mandatory detention is at the root of immigration enforcement. With so many political and money interests contingent on perpetuating it, it is likely to remain so.

To my nonjurist's mind, the constitutional issues Hemnauth's case and that of so many others raises are the proverbial elephant in the room. The ideological and partisan conduct of the conservative majority of the Supreme Court has convinced me that while you or I may be ill-equipped to assess the strictly legal reasoning of decisions based on theory or precedent, when it comes to gauging the fundamental fairness or ethics of legislation and court rulings defending it, many of us are as competent readers of the Constitution as several of the black robes I could name. In that vein, although the federal courts, be it by omission or head on, have not declared

---

114 Morawetz, "1996 Deportation Laws."

mandatory detention as contrary to the Fifth Amendment's proscription of double jeopardy, or Joe Arpaio's Tent City "concentration camp" under a 135-degree sun cruel and unusual punishment in violation of the Eighth, I, for one, feel entirely secure doing both. The Court has left me or you with little reason to feel bashful. I also do not mind calling the denial of the right to counsel a sham from the perspective of basic fairness, notwithstanding the legalistic pretext that immigration transgressions fall under the civil rather than the criminal code, as implicitly commanded by the Supreme Court in 1896 (in *Wong Wing v. United States*) if the government is to avoid judicial trials for establishing guilt.

Thankfully, and before I get carried away, recognized legal scholars and practitioners have questioned the constitutionality of IIRIRA, or at least its compliance to the rule of law we have relied on, as Americans, as the bedrock of a peacefully functional society. For instance, Professor Hiroshi Motomura, then of the University of North Carolina School of Law at Chapel Hill and currently at UCLA, told Congress in 2007 that "[IIRIRA's] enforcement-*only* approach creates some real problems that actually undermine the rule of law"[115] (emphasis is Motomura's). Several tangible failings in the law trouble him as contrary and damaging to the rule of law. From there, it is but a short leap to wonder about the law's constitutionality. The whittling of judicial discretion has automated deportation decisions, exposed us to uncorrected mistakes and upset the balance one might expect in an American system of adjudication. The law goes beyond omitting the right to counsel in a civil procedure by instituting a mandatory detention regimen that severely impedes the very access to counsel by detainees, paid or unpaid. The barriers to judicial review compounds the bias against the immigrant threatened with deportation. It also means that decisions made by ICE personnel without extensive legal expertise, for example agents at ports of entry, are less likely to be challenged in a discretionary review of their actions. Not to mention potential jeopardy to those apprehended within the "Constitution-free zone" of 100 miles of a land border and deported under the rules of expedited removal. The "overall effect" of the erosion of due process "has been a pervasive reduction in the quality of justice."[116] If that is not a constitutional alarm bell, what is?

---

115 Motomura, testimony in "Shortfalls of the 1996 Immigration Reform Legislation."
116 Motomura, in "1996 Immigration Reform Legislation."

There were many elements in Daniel Zwerdling's NPR reporting of Hemnauth's ordeal back in 2004 that startled me, as they should have startled anyone listening. I did, however, fixate on one aspect I feel others have overlooked. I am certainly not the first or only one to deplore the separation of a father from his child imposed by a government as an insufferable cruelty. My personal perspective on it, however, may have been more singular than others, and relates to the question of constitutionality, even if I do not like the answer I have gotten from legal scholars and literature.

After I heard the Zwerdling report's two installments, I consulted the full text of the Universal Declaration of Human Rights, adopted by the United Nations General Assembly on December 10, 1948. The United States was, of course, a leading proponent and anchor signatory. Its Article 16, paragraph (3) states: "The family is the natural and fundamental group unit of society and is entitled to protection by society and the State." The Universal Declaration engendered a multilateral treaty, brought into effect in 1976, called the International Covenant on Civil and Political Rights, ratified by the United States in 1992. Better late than never. The wording of its Article 23, paragraph (1) is identical to that of Article 16 in the Universal Declaration.

I have never thought we needed to draw a picture. For the State to remove a parent from a child is contrary to a charter of human rights that the United States helped draft and signed. Better yet, Article 16 invokes protection of family integrity by society as a right. It is hardly a leap to infer that resistance to political or societal pressure to abrogate this right is an obligation of the State.

My recollection from the time I lived in Europe was that immigration of family members was accommodated with little to no debate or fanfare because it was a commonly recognized human right, as codified in the Universal Declaration. Attitudes have changed, as we know, in Europe, not always for the better, with more anger gathering against certain immigrant and minority groups such as the Roma and Muslim communities. Politicians hostile to immigrants in France and the Netherlands, to take two examples, have gathered a significant and durable following. And notwithstanding the relevant international conventions and treaties, international bodies have been reluctant to challenge national immigration policies, particularly in response to claims by individuals, and not just those of the

United States despite the unusual magnitude of our deportation apparatus. A foreign government suing for relief in the case of one of its citizens on the basis of international treaties theoretically might stand a better chance of having its standing recognized to file a legal motion, since treaties are agreements between nation states, not between individuals and any governing body. The operative word here is "theoretically."

All this does not change the perception I had, while living in Europe, of immigration practices aligned with Article 16. It would have been inconceivable to me that an immigrant would be forcibly separated from a member of his immediate family, let alone an underage child, under a deportation order, except, perhaps, in the event of a documented security threat. That was my frame of mind, informed by unrelated personal experience, when I first heard of Hemnauth Mohabir years later and his Gordian entanglement with American immigration and deportation policies. In short, I imagined that Article 16 had the force of law in all countries that had signed the treaty, and would be generally respected by all signatories representing modern democracies.

Silly me.

The first question I asked Bryan Lonegan, who handled Hemnauth's case with the full benefit of his expertise, was why no one had ever argued that his deportation was not a violation of the Universal Declaration of 1948, whose language transferred to a treaty the United States had signed with other nations. Surely the intent of Article 16 was not a matter of equivocation. I realized then as I realize now that U.S. law trumps international law when the two collide. Under Article VI of the U.S. Constitution, "all treaties made . . . under the Authority of the United States shall be the supreme Law of the Land."[117] The wording of the article does not mean that treaties and conventions outweigh federal laws passed subsequent to the adoption of a treaty, but rather the contrary. As part of the supreme law, a ratified treaty enjoys the *same* standing as any other statute, not a higher one. "For that reason, just as one statute would supercede a prior statute, a statute will clearly supercede a prior treaty."[118]

But was a covenant adopted by the United States — as opposed to the more generalized canon of international law — not enforceable, or at least

117 U.S. Constitution, Article VI.
118 Legomsky, *Immigration and the Judiciary: Law and Politics in Britain and America.*

worthy of consideration in an American tribunal?

I am grateful to Bryan for not having laughed at my idealistic credulity. He patiently explained to me the distinction between self-executing covenants and those that are not. A self-executing treaty or article of a treaty is indeed the law in the United States, because Congress has specifically consecrated it as such. The prime example of a self-executing treaty is the Convention Against Torture, which Hemnauth did ask Judge Riefkohl to consider as grounds for relief, and which Riefkohl addressed in his decision to deny it. However, for a provision of a treaty, convention or covenant to be admitted as lawful or relevant in an American court — including immigration court — it must be affirmed by specific subsequent "implementing legislation." The Convention Against Torture complies. Article 16 of the Universal Declaration and Article 23 of the International Covenant on Civil and Political Rights (ICCPR) do not, placing us in the stunningly hypocritical position of signing treaties we have no foregone intention of enforcing inside our own borders and feel free to overrule without batting an eyelid. Further, when it finally ratified the ICCPR, the United States registered a record number of "reservations, understandings and declarations," some of which undermined the U.S. commitment to the covenant and affirmed its non-self-executing status for purposes of enforcement.[119] An attorney who pleads on the basis of provisions contained in treaties such as the ICCPR will be barking up a tall and slippery tree.

Few bother. The most headway a plea based on sanctioned human rights has made was in *Beharry v. Reno* (later *Beharry v. Ashcroft*).[120] A federal judge in New York ruled that the INS must conduct a relief hearing for an individual, Donald Beharry, whom the immigration court ordered removed from the country for having committed an "aggravated felony." Although the IIRIRA provisions barred all avenues of relief, the judge invoked international law, notably the ICCPR, to order that the government nonetheless consider the human rights implications of forcibly separating Mr. Beharry from his American child and legal resident spouse.[121] Again, a situation very analogous to Hemnauth's, although Hemnauth was not labeled an

---

119 Ash, "U.S. Reservations to the International Covenant on Civil and Political Rights."
120 "Beharry v. Ashcroft" (2003).
121 Parker, "Forced Apart: Families Separated and Immigrants Harmed by United States Deportation Policy."

"aggravated felon" even in IIRIRA's Alice-in-Wonderland glossary. It was a quixotic effort on the part of the district judge, and it failed when the government successfully appealed. He might as well have fallen on his sword. To be complete, the appeals court neither endorsed nor rejected the substance of the lower court's references to international law. Rather, it sanctioned the government's right, under IIRIRA, to require that all administrative appeals be exhausted by a candidate for deportation — as arcane as they might be — before he or she is permitted access to a court of law.[122] *Beharry* is the most progress international law has ever made resisting the fangs of the immigration statutes, and meager progress it was. In a telling testament to the federal courts' deference to enforcement over the rights of those who might be harmed by a deportation order pursuant to a civil, not criminal, complaint, the *Beharry* decision was ultimately rejected by none other than Sonia Sotomayor when it arrived before the U.S. Court of Appeals for the Second Circuit.

In any event, the issue of what standing an individual like Hemnauth Mohabir might have in American court to contest the government's neglect of international treaties and laws is, at best, unclear. Unless Congress has passed a law providing for the enforcement in the United States of treaty provisions, the customary practice has been to bar private parties from suing on the basis of international law. Rather, violations of international treaties are generally considered state-to-state matters, to be resolved as such: "International law lacks a coherent set of principles that define when a private person is entitled to rely on an international obligation against a state."[123]

For all this, the substantive issue does not necessarily evaporate. There is, at the very least, a tradition in American law, society and policy favorable to the protection of families and to the preferential prerogatives of family over the State. The phrase "family values" comes up in every election cycle. Immigration law itself has embedded family reunification in its selection of admissible immigrants. "After the 1965 reforms," writes Bill Ong Hing of the University of California at Davis and the University of San Francisco, "family reunification was the major cornerstone of the immigration

---

122 Sonia Sotomayor, "Don Beharry, Petitioner-Appellee, v. John Ashcroft, Attorney General" (2003).
123 Nollkaemper, *Domestic Courts and the Rule of International Law.*

admission system."[124] The disconnect occurs when the same family integrity factors guiding admission under the immigration code are disregarded, wholesale, in removal proceedings, as they are under IIRIRA. It is also troubling that kinship-based immigration practices have come under more attack as more Asian and Hispanic immigrants enter the country legally as kin to legal residents.[125]

To paraphrase the admonition in Article 16 of the Universal Declaration, that the State is obligated to protect family integrity, no government should separate spouses from each other or parents from their children if it can avoid doing so. There is no exception for whomever a government might tag as "illegal" or "undocumented." Nevertheless, when it comes to immigrants, current U.S. federal law sanctions insensitivity to Article 16, and judges routinely order our marshals to carry out deportations that fragment families. Under our immigration law, the special-purpose judges who adjudicate immigration cases often have no choice, and no recourse to any declaration of human rights — including the one we promoted and ratified, with great fanfare, in San Francisco in 1948, in the wake of the greatest human rights violation of all time. In short, an established, universally recognized and very basic tenet of human rights commands that a government shall not split up families.

Ours does it anyway. To the tune of 108,000 deported parents lost to their American children in the ten years between 1998 and 2007[126] — the period covering Hemnauth's struggle — with no indication that the practice has halted. Indeed, quite the opposite: in the six-month period from January to June 2011, ICE deported 46,486 parents of American children.[127]

---

124 Hing, *Deporting Our Souls.*
125 Hing, *Deporting Our Souls.*
126 Bernstein, "The Making of an Outlaw Generation."
127 Yoshikawa and Suárez-Orozco, "Deporting Parents Hurts Kids." At the time of this writing, the U.S. Senate was to receive a draft proposal outlining the elements of a new immigration law. The proposal includes a provision allowing some deportees with no criminal convictions and with immediate family members resident in the United States to apply for readmission. See: Preston, "Beside a Path to Citizenship, a New Course for Immigration."

The constitutional question is a vexing one. If "our immigration law, like our family law, endeavors to keep families together"[128] and is particularly reluctant to split children from parents, is there a constitutional underpinning to this well-established notion? If there is, why have Hemnauth Mohabir and so many others been deported without their sons and daughters, many of them U.S. citizens? Why have our removal guidelines been so militantly insensitive to the bonds between parents and children? Hemnauth's with Kevin was a demonstrably strong one, eagerly cultivated by both father and mother to the point of their burying for its sake any residual vindictiveness from what had been an angry divorce. The judge saw the strength of the filial affection so clearly as to pronounce it exemplary in his court.

Despite a historical inclination of society and, to some extent, the law to uphold the integrity of the nuclear family, and of candidates for elective office to declare unwavering fealty to family values, there is no section of the Constitution or specific legislative text that reflects, unequivocally, the substance of Article 16 of the Universal Declaration. The U.S. Constitution does not even contain the word *family* let alone formally pronounce it indivisible. In fact, the practice of subordinating parent-to-child bonds to other law traces some of its roots to pre-emancipation legal custom. As the story of Sojourner Truth illustrates, a freed slave living in New York in 1827, could not exercise her claim to parental custody if it conflicted with the property rights of a master who still owned the child, even if that child was entitled to freedom upon reaching age twenty-one under New York law.[129] The sanctity of family ties was an essential principle of the abolition movement.

Over the years, there have been teaser judgments by the Supreme Court upholding family rights that flirt with family integrity as an aspiration deserving of constitutional protection. Flirt and no more. The specific rulings and the majority opinions that accompany them have been frustratingly narrow. For instance, reversing infringement by the State on the educational prerogatives of parents on the principle that parents' bond with their child took precedence over state policy. In *Santosky v. Kramer*, the Supreme Court's majority went a little further, declaring: "The fundamental

128   Morawetz, "1996 Deportation Laws."
129   Davis, *Neglected Stories: The Constitution and Family Values*.

liberty interest of natural parents in the care custody, and management of their child is protected by the Fourteenth Amendment." There, as well, the context was narrow, nothing like the exile of a parent far from his child, but a situation where the State had claimed custody of children from their parents for reasons of insufficiently demonstrated neglect.[130] In an earlier custody case brought by an unwed father in 1971, the Supreme Court held (in *Stanley v. Illinois*) that the "Constitution prohibits removal of children from parental custody without first addressing the parents' fitness."[131] In a 1977 Court decision discussing the definition of the family for purposes of access to housing, the majority spoke, comfortingly, of "the strong constitutional protection of the sanctity of the family established in numerous decisions of this Court."[132] So, the Supreme Court has tilted toward interpreting the Constitution as protective of family integrity against interference from the State, or so it would seem.

Close, but no cigar. That protection is not absolute. The Supreme Court has pointedly declined to characterize the State's interest in family unity, legitimate as it might be, as an overarching, fundamental right.[133] Typical of a posture hedging the judicial commitment to family integrity is a 1975 Supreme Court pronouncement that a parent "has a constitutionally protected right to the 'companionship, care, custody, and management' of 'the children he has sired and raised, [which] undeniably warrants deference and, *absent a powerful countervailing interest, protection*"[134] (emphasis added).

If that were not enough, championship of family integrity comes to a screeching halt at the gates of immigration law. In fact, even prior to IIRIRA the INS and the immigration courts realized that many deportable parents would claim relief on the basis of the harm family separation would inevitably trigger, and have moved vigorously, and successfully, in the federal courts to deflect the argument. Should they ever lose it, the floodgates of derivative asylum — cancellation of removal for the conflicting purpose of protecting family integrity — could open.[135]

---

130 Supreme Court, "Santosky v. Kramer (Syllabus)" (1982).
131 Thronson, "Choiceless Choices: Deportation and the Parent-Child Relationship."
132 Supreme Court, "Moore v. City of East Cleveland" (1977).
133 Legomsky, "Immigration Law and the Principle of Plenary Congressional Power."
134 Brennan, "Weinberger v. Wiesenfed" (1975), quoting "Stanley v. Illinois, 405 U.S. 645."
135 Thronson, "Choiceless Choices."

The official reasoning against derivative asylum borders on cynicism. The rulings in favor of the INS (and by extension to the present ICE) acknowledge the potential for harm to children and then address it by setting an insurmountably high standard of "exceptional and extremely unusual hardship." In addition, the courts, when faced with the question of families fractured by the deportation of a parent, have ascribed responsibility for the decision to leave a child behind in the United States to the parent, not to the government, since the law does not prevent a child or spouse from accompanying a deported parent into exile. So the State is deemed not to be interfering with family unity as forbidden by the Constitution, or so goes the theory that, thus far, has translated seamlessly into practice. Nor does any law prevent a child who is an American citizen from later returning to the United States. In this manner, the immigration system inoculates itself against charges of insensitivity to family integrity while shielding the deportation machine from disruption. Relying on federal court decisions that treat family integrity as a matter of custody, not immigration, it reaffirms the sanctity of the child-parent relationship in theory, while in many cases, like Hemnauth's, shattering it in reality. It has its cake and eats it, too.

There is a yet bigger elephant in the room. It dwarfs the issues of the narrowness of federal court decisions sanctioning family reunification, of the agility of immigration law in circumventing them and of the pegging of the family bond as, at best, a State interest among others rather than an individual right. This elephant is named the doctrine of plenary power. The doctrine proclaims almost total deference of the judiciary to congressional will in matters of immigration, and, by extension, to the agencies that enforce it. One might argue that deference is owed Congress in the normal course of the nation's business, subject to checks and balances that the judiciary provides as a coequal branch of government. The principle of plenary power goes far beyond normalized fealty of the courts to acts of Congress. It stipulates that "immigration is an area in which the normal rules of constitutional law simply do not apply."[136] In adopting the doctrine, the courts have forfeited their role in policing compliance of immigration law with constitutional provisions, even when fundamental rights are at stake. "When regulating immigration, Congress may discriminate on

---

136 Legomsky, "Immigration Law."

the basis of race. It may discriminate on the bases of gender and legitimacy. It may restrict aliens' political speech without having to establish a clear and present danger. With some qualifications, Congress may disregard procedural due process when excluding aliens."[137]

The language the Supreme Court has used, in many cases, in sustaining the principle of plenary power has been stark and, in some cases, almost shockingly vehement. One would expect as much from the decisions in the Chinese Exclusion Case of 1889, reiterated in *Fong Yue Ting*, sanctioning racial discrimination and, in so doing, permitting the government by act of Congress to bar or deport aliens as it saw fit. There, the power of Congress over immigration and removal was deemed "conclusive upon the Judiciary,"[138] that is, irreversible by the federal courts.

What is a bit more surprising to the layperson is the consistency with which the Supreme Court has affirmed, time and time again, its allegiance to the principle of plenary power, becoming, if anything, even more explicit over time. In 1953, the Supreme Court held that the "courts have long recognized the power to expel or exclude aliens as a fundamental sovereign attribute exercised by the Government's political departments largely immune from judicial control."[139] In 1953, the National Origins Act had not yet been repealed, and the clouds of distrust of immigrants were still near their darkest, so perhaps these words were unremarkable at the time they were written. However, in light of Hemnauth Mohabir's case and the prejudice he suffered, I shall admit that it is disconcerting to read the following from the pen of Justice John Paul Stevens, in a 1976 ruling:

> In the exercise of its broad power over naturalization and immigration, Congress regularly makes rules that would be unacceptable if applied to citizens . . . The reasons that preclude judicial review of political questions also dictate a narrow standard of review of decisions made by the Congress or the President in the area of immigration and naturalization.[140]

---

137 Legomsky, *Immigration and the Judiciary*.

138 "The Chinese Exclusion Case, 130 U.S. 581" (1889); Gray, "Fong Yue Ting v. United States" (1893).

139 Clark, "Shaughnessy v. Mezei" (1953).

140 Stevens, "Mathews, Secretary of Health, Education and Welfare v. Diaz et al." (1976).

In other words, federal courts, hands off immigration even if substantive rights have been denied. And even if the Constitution does not distinguish between persons and citizens in granting them.

In 1977, the Supreme Court again reiterated its reluctance to scrutinize congressional immigration statutes in a case, *Fiallo v. Bell*, which is often considered the established modern endorsement of the plenary power doctrine by the Supreme Court. It is not seminal in its affirmation of the doctrine, but its approving references to a long string of precedent lend it a veneer of finality:

> It is important to underscore the limited scope of judicial inquiry into immigration legislation. This Court has repeatedly emphasized that "over no conceivable subject is the legislative power of Congress more complete than it is over" the admission of aliens . . . Our recent decisions have not departed from this long-established rule.[141]

The irony of such unequivocal phrasing from the Supreme Court resides in the faith it expresses for a principle of plenary power over immigration and deportation that is not firmly grounded in any constitutional commandment. Arguments claiming constitutional vindication of plenary power fetch their substance from afar, in particular from the clauses of Article 1, Section 8 establishing congressional authority over naturalization and commerce with foreign nations, although it takes daring semantic contortions to conflate naturalization, external trade and immigration.

Rather, plenary power derives its potency through force of repetition and from a set of extra-constitutional theories, many of which also present remarkable leaps of logic.[142] For example, a common theory surfaces in several of the decisions supporting the doctrine's assimilation of immigration policy with foreign affairs,[143] pushing it into the realm of political issues beyond the reach of judicial review or second-guessing. "The plenary power doctrine . . . assumes that immigration matters necessarily generate

---

141 Powell, "Fiallo v. Bell" (1977).
142 For an extensive exposé on, and critique of, the theories and externalities underpinning the plenary power doctrine, see: Legomsky, "Immigration Law and the Principle of Plenary Congressional Power."
143 Legomsky, "Immigration Law."

the kind of foreign policy problems that defy judicial resolution."[144]

Leaving aside the issue that the courts *have* intervened in foreign policy on many occasions, it defies realism to posit that the pursuit of a just outcome for Hemnauth Mohabir through judicial review of the circumstances of his detention and of the order to exile him from his American child would have had any effect whatsoever on relations between the United States and Guyana, such as they were.

Other theories include the notion that immigrants are guests from whom harbor, protection and hospitality can be withdrawn at will and without recourse.[145] Another assumes that the loyalty of immigrants is necessarily suspect, obviating their access to constitutional safeguards[146] — despite the fact that the naturalization many seek (as Hemnauth intended to do) is a process requiring lengthy residency on American soil as an immigrant, and that other ties, such as Hemnauth's parental bond with his American child, inspire robust allegiance to the country. Even more uncomfortable, yet very pertinent to Hemnauth's ordeal, is the empirical evidence that the courts, knowingly or not, are influenced by public attitudes and social trends, inspiring all the more deference to the political branches: "Unhappily for immigrants, the periods in which their large numbers make their presence all the more unpopular tend to be the very periods in which they are the most frequently before the courts."[147]

Somewhat more happily, there is one boundary over which the Supreme Court has been slightly more reluctant to allow Congress and the Executive to venture: due process. Such misgivings led to the decision — *INS v. St. Cyr*[148] — to allow a waiver from deportation for an immigrant who had been convicted of a crime before IIRIRA decreed it a deportable one. More recently, the Court recognized that the failure of a defense attorney in a criminal case to warn his client of possible deportation should he be found guilty amounted to a lapse of due process.[149]

The doctrine of plenary power, combined with a climate vacillating

---

144 Legomsky, "Immigration Law."
145 Legomsky, "Immigration Law."
146 Legomsky, "Immigration Law."
147 Legomsky, "Immigration Law."
148 Stevens, "INS v. St. Cyr" (2001).
149 Stevens, "Jose Padilla, Petitioner v. Kentucky" (2010).

between ambivalence and hostility toward immigrants, set the ideal stage for IIRIRA. Its proponents jumped upon it with both feet. Since its enactment, restrictionist politicians — and corrections industry lobbyists — have bolstered its defenses against reformists. In some ways, it was the perfect arrangement. Congress was able under the guise of law and order to cast a very broad trigger for deportation with the assurance that the federal courts would hide behind an opaque wall of deference and peek out only rarely.

In attempting to trace a constitutional trail that might have led to relief from deportation for Hemnauth and others like him, we simply run into a brick wall. The wall may have some cracks, for instance in wobbly assertions by the courts that harm to small children of deportee parents can be avoided and that the State does not force them into their parents' exile.[150] However, the immigration system has been remarkably adept at filling those cracks, spawning a lengthy repertoire of court decisions favorable to it in the process. Also, while the Supreme Court has not eternally repudiated the role of judicial review, it has, in practice, restricted its scrutiny to matters of due process rather than substance, at the same time granting broad latitude to Congress, in IIRIRA, to define due process pretty much as it pleased. The attitude of the federal courts has been that Congress can do whatever it wants in immigration legislation, without consideration of the substantive rights of aliens threatened with deportation, as long as the rules it wishes to enforce are explicit. IIRIRA is nothing if not explicit.

In sum, we are back to where we started. Kevin Mohabir was ten years old when his father was jailed, fundamentally because of a long-past petty misdemeanor for which he had already paid the prescribed penalty. The INS and ICE severely restricted contact between father and son by detaining him hours from home — on this front, ICE has abundantly demonstrated that they could have made things far worse by sending Hemnauth to, say, Louisiana — and outsourcing phone service to an intermediary that gouged detainees. Kevin had just turned twelve when Hemnauth was removed permanently, confiscating his opportunity — the Universal

---

150 Thronson, "Choiceless Choices."

Declaration says his right — to grow up in the company of his father.

That the courts have found no constitutional remedy to this sort of situation does not alter its inherent injustice. I, for one, do not believe they have looked that hard for one. If anything, they have bent over backwards in promoting as reality the immigration system's fictional respect for family integrity, sacrificing kids like Kevin and fathers like Hemnauth on the alter of an ill-conceived, punitive lust for deportation.

There is a further irony, if one were needed. In his *Padilla* opinion, Justice John Paul Stevens wrote, "Our law has enmeshed criminal convictions and the penalty of deportation for nearly a century . . . And, importantly, recent changes in our immigration law have made removal nearly an automatic result for a broad class of noncitizen offenders. Thus, we find it 'most difficult' to divorce the penalty from the conviction in the deportation context."[151] To my reading, this comes tantalizingly close to the admission, in a Supreme Court decision, of double jeopardy and to rejecting the notion of deportation as a mere collateral consequence analogous to, say, the repeal of voting rights of convicted felons. An immigrant convicted of a crime can have added to the sentence proclaimed by the presiding judge an additional sentence imposed by another party when this was not the intent of the verdict, certainly not in Hemnauth's case. And since, according to *Padilla,* removal is both a penalty and "an automatic result for a broad class of noncitizen offenders," how can one not conclude that Hemnauth's right to the Fourteenth Amendment's guarantee of equal protection was not violated, since a citizen offender similarly convicted would not have been banished? The equal protection language in the amendment applies to "any person" within the jurisdiction of any state.[152] True, public order and protection of national sovereignty are legitimate interests of the State that may, at times, conflict with the guarantee of substantive rights for all persons present on U.S. soil. But is that always the case? And when these other prerogatives are not in jeopardy by any objective tally, is it not in the national interest to affirm an individual's substantive rights in order to reinforce the constitutional principles that engendered them?

---

151 Stevens, "Jose Padilla, Petitioner v. Kentucky" (2010).
152 U.S. Constitution, Amendment XIV, Section 1.

With little help from the keepers of the Constitution, we must look else-where for genuine defense of families from human rights violations pro-hibited by treaties we have signed, let alone our conscience. The Constitu-tion as currently interpreted may not recognize as a consecrated right the extension of family integrity protection to the likes of Kevin and Hem-nauth. More to the point, the current majority of justices in the higher courts is more inclined to defer to restrictions of rights formulated by leg-islators and federal agencies than to plumb the Due Process Clause or the Fourteenth Amendment for the means to parry political overreach. To the point of postulating that severing the bond between a parent and a young child does not lead to hardship.

But nor does the Constitution prohibit enactment of legislation and pol-icy in closer alignment with basic fairness. For openers, legislation or policy that would have allowed Judge Riefkohl the judicial discretion he needed to avoid issuing a ruling he himself called "stupid." Of course, many mem-bers of Congress, trolling the electorate's myriad frustrations for votes, are more than happy to leverage the ensuing proclivity to focus its displeasure on society's most vulnerable. Ostracism toward immigrants is, after all, the gift that keeps on giving. Or will be until the growing segment of voters that identifies with the immigrant experience begins to overwhelm the re-strictionists. The results of the 2012 presidential and Senate races suggest that a wave of resistance to the anti-immigrant temperament of conserva-tive politics has begun to swell.

Letters like Kevin's to his imprisoned father, the one that affected Judge Riefkohl so profoundly, may yet illuminate a path to a little more enlighten-ment, a little more justice, a little more humanity, a little more adhesion to ideals we call our own.

It would not take a lot. Just a little.

June 25th, 2002

Dear Dad,

I miss you and I hope to see you soon. Today Tuesday was my award ceremony and I wish you could have been there, I recived 5 awards and a special prize of $35.00 on a gift certificate for a perfect score on my science test which you helped me with. I am also letting mom take the awards with her for you to see them. I was very happy that mom was at the ceremony but upset you couldn't come.

Anyway I miss you very much and hope too see you soon becouse I have alot planned for the summer and something special for your birthday. I miss our walks and little talks that we used to have and I am looking foward to doing more of that.

Love,
your son Rajendra K. Mohabir

A letter from Kevin Mohabir to his imprisoned father, dated June 25, 2002

Hemnauth (center) with Pete's Caribbean Fusion, a musically
sophisticated touring band

A versatile musican, here on traverse flute

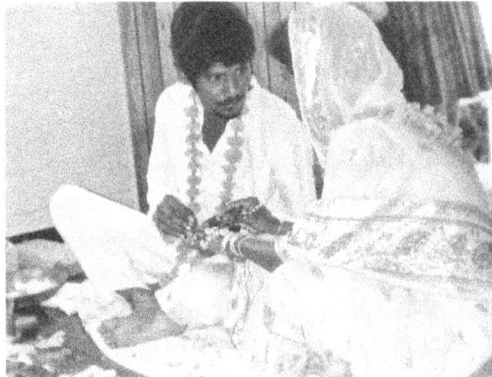

With Rahoni on their wedding day

Hemnauth at temple. Spiritual vitality sustained him during his detention.

With son Kevin as toddler

Rawti, Hemnauth's mother, with Kevin in New York at the time of Hemnauth's detention at Passaic

8

OFF WITH THE GLOVES

AND THEN, SILENCE.

The last information Hemnauth possessed as he was remanded back to Middlesex County Jail was that his case was closed and that he was under a deportation order that would be executed within about three months. "After January, I should have been removed, but I was not. A year and a half followed after that. That's a long time." Indeed. When Daniel Zwerdling surveyed a larger group of immigrant detainees around the country, he discovered that one of the largest causes of anguish among them was simply not knowing how long they would be confined: days, weeks, months or years.[153]

Hemnauth began to suspect that perhaps Judge Riefkohl's order was not the very last word in the case, although he knew of no specific action being pursued on his behalf. John Charles Allen promised that he would "see me through this" without really saying how, other than to remind Hemnauth and Rahoni that the payments had run out. Allen did file an appeal, without Hemnauth's knowledge, for relief, quixotically based on the Convention Against Torture. The appeal went dormant, as did Mr. Allen's representation. "He disappeared." For a short period after the September 25, 2002 ruling the lawyer maintained some contact with Rahoni, primarily if not exclusively regarding his billing and tactics he might try if she paid him more money, which she no longer had after paying him several thousands. "She had already exceeded six grand" in payments to Mr. Allen.

---

153 Zwerdling and Casciato, "Investigating Abuse."

Back at the jail, Hemnauth tried to carve out a life for himself. Jail is jail — or, rather, in this case, "detention" is jail — with all the restrictions and languishing that incarceration minimally implies, not the least of it confinement to a building ringed by barbed wire. The detainees received visits from INS agents assigned to social work who would inquire, without apparent irony, if he was "happy," if his needs were being met. The script of each of these visits included a disclaimer asserting, again without face-tiousness, that he was a detainee as distinct from a prisoner. These meetings happened, Hemnauth snickers, in full view of "an electric fence."

Still, Middlesex lacked the Shawshank ambiance of other detention facilities, including the one Hemnauth would transfer to shortly. Hemnauth set out to preserve his sanity by occupying his time as productively as he could. The day room was spacious, and there were few, if any, compulsory activities or restrictions on whatever recreational assets were available outside of curfew hours. He started lifting weights, the stereotypical prison pastime, facilitated by a "couple of strong Jamaican guys" who offered themselves as trainers. He also began helping the other inmates prepare for their court hearings. Having been through a series of procedural steps himself, he had become familiar with the most standard forms as well as the jargon of immigration rules if not the gamut of gotcha properties of the law. His language skills were superior to those of many around him, so he helped draft letters and decipher incoming correspondence for inmates who had trouble with the English of officialdom. His bunk area became the place for others to "hang out," a kind of social magnet I can easily imagine Hemnauth creating. "It was better than sitting around playing cards all day. Most of the people played dominoes and cards [to pass the time]. Or watched TV."

He also read. He had a favorite book, the gift of a fellow Guyanese inmate nicknamed "Fish," who was released on a bond posted by his father after a few weeks at Middlesex. Hemnauth recalls that Fish's bond was predicated on some form of probation and regular reporting to the immigration court; Hemnauth later saw him at the court in Newark after Bryan Lonegan obtained new hearings.

The book was *Autobiography of a Yogi* by Paramahansa Yogananda, a renowned swami, or religious teacher. Indian-born Yogananda was the founder of a self-realization movement in 1920, the year he migrated to the United States, where he spent the bulk of his working life. He later founded the Self-Realization Fellowship in Hollywood in 1942. He was very influential as a motivational speaker, appealing to audiences with a nonsectarian message, including luminaries like botanist Luther Burbank, the inventor Jagadish Chandra Bose and Gandhi. *Autobiography of a Yogi,* Yogananda's magnum opus, seems tailor-made to Hemnauth's mindset at the time he read it. Here he was, cut from the outside world, with no tangible indication of his ultimate fate other than Riefkohl's dormant court order expelling him from the country. Nobody had given him a formal date when the order would be carried out. He did know that his file had been transferred to a deportation officer at the INS tasked with organizing his removal, but he has no recollection of ever having met him at the jail. Hemnauth wrote letters of inquiry to the INS that went without answer. Rahoni tried repeatedly to call a number that was indeed that of the deportation officer, but never got past his voice mailbox. "He seems to be an extremely busy man. You can't find him."

The statutory three months between judgment and removal would pass without a peep from the INS. So, as far Hemnauth knew, he could be confined to Middlesex forever, or be moved and never heard from again. This was not the home he chose, not by any extent of the imagination, but it was the only one his captors permitted him. Since it would be at least several months before he got out, he had to make a life for himself in the crucible of a jailhouse, so those months might count for something when he looked back on them.

Autobiography's chapters do not preach self-realization in verses or commands, but weave its spiritual lessons into stories of the pilgrimages and voyages the author made and the people he met along the way, including Rabindranath Tagore, the poet and sage who inspired Hemnauth's parents to give him the name they did. Imprisonment has never been a prerequisite for Hemnauth's attraction to spiritual discourse. He has always had fertile and active spiritual faculties. Still, I can easily picture him reading as personally relevant and revelatory passages like this one:

> The starry inscription at one's birth, I came to understand, is not that man is a puppet of his past. Its message is rather a prod to pride; the very heavens seek to arouse man's determination to be free from

every limitation. God created each man as a soul, dowered with in-
dividuality, hence essential to the universal structure, whether in the
temporary role of pillar or parasite. His freedom is final and immediate, if he so wills; it depends not on outer but inner victories.[154]

"That book gave me the strength to face everything."

Fish was not the only detainee held at Middlesex for shorter periods than
the more permanent residents like Hemnauth. Hemnauth distinctly recalls
an influx of Middle Eastern men around the time of his expulsion order
from the court in Newark. One night, late, "when everyone was asleep," an
INS transit crew came in, very quietly, and removed several dozen of these
men. "That was, like, almost fifty people. They did it secretly. We were all
there, but no one knew this had happened. When we woke up for breakfast,
we found that the place was kind of empty . . . Like half of the population
had gone." The bunkmates of the men removed were the unavoidable witnesses. The INS men told them "to shoo, don't make a sound."

Hemnauth later learned from human rights groups in New Jersey in contact or correspondence with Middlesex inmates that the men removed that
night were put aboard a chartered plane and flown to Egypt. Hemnauth and
others were able to confirm that a large group of people had been taken en
masse from Middlesex under cover of night. After their arrival in Egypt,
they were apparently driven to the border with Gaza and commanded to
walk across it. "Four of [the deportees] were from India [or Pakistan] and
for some reason their photographs showed up in the news media, that they
were terrorists living in the United States." The men and their families re-
settled in South Asia. "We knew them. They ended up on the television one
night when we were looking at the BBC." On the news clip, the men claimed
that they had learned, to their surprise, that they were terror suspects wanted
in the United States. They countered the story with the obvious retort that
they had been deported from the United States and that it made no sense
that the INS would have removed them from federal custody if they were
under investigation as a national security threat. The point of the BBC story
was specifically that their reporters had found people fingered as dangerous
that the American government had had ample opportunity to scrutinize
and prosecute. Instead they had been released and placed in deportation

---

154 Yogananda, *Autobiography of a Yogi*.

proceedings. The BBC saw a newsworthy irony in the occurrence.

I have been unable to verify the pieces of this incident that Hemnauth learned secondhand, in particular the detail of the removal to Gaza by way of Egypt of men detained at Middlesex County Jail. What is clear, however, is that an operation conducted by the INS in the middle of night involving a large contingent of inmates was not a release. It could have only been a transfer to another prison or, more likely, the simultaneous deportation of several people to the same overseas destination, and one that could not be easily accommodated by a commercial airline.

Significantly for our story, it was Hemnauth's first exposure to the physical logistics of deportation, at least the opening steps.

By all appearances, including those that impressed the judge who ultimately ordered him released, the INS had also tagged Farouk Abdel-Muhti as dangerous, but more in a political than in a security vein. The official justification for his arrest and placement in deportation proceedings was based on factual findings of immigration violations. These were irrefutable. Farouk had been living for many years, undocumented, in Queens, New York since the 1970s. He also had a police record, which included a 1993 charge of attempted assault against his former wife. There had been several instances of illegal entry into the United States, and one prior deportation to Honduras, which had issued him a travel document that was probably not a passport as he was not a Honduran citizen. The INS had abandoned his trail in 1982, and Farouk continued to live in Queens in plain sight — so much so that in 2002 he was given his own morning radio talk show on the liberal WBAI-FM, despite his halting English. His appeal to WBAI was his ability to feature interviews of people under Israeli occupation in the West Bank. Once the INS refocused on his case, he was promptly detained and sent to Middlesex, the first of several jails he would inhabit until he was freed under the stipulations of a landmark Supreme Court decision, *Zadvydas v. Davis.*

Under the ruling — lamented by Antonin Scalia in his dissent — the INS (and now ICE) has six months to find a destination country willing to accept a deportee from the United States. If none has been found, the detainee must be released. It does not relieve him from the deportation order, but the fact that the government cannot find a place to send him is deemed, theoretically, to be its problem, not the detainee's under the ruling. Implicit in Stephen Breyer's opinion for the majority, as I read it, is the equating of immigration detention to punishment, at least once detention is imposed for more than a reasonable amount of time. In Scalia's dissent, also as I read it, he views detention not as punishment but as simply a denial of asylum in keeping with national desires expressed in legislation to keep certain people out of the country. Once again, the Kafkaesque notion dating from the *Wong Wing* decision resurfaces: detention is not prison simply because the government decrees it is not. Kafkaesque is also the term the immigration judge assigned to the case used to describe the INS attorneys' tactics in the agency's efforts to keep Farouk in detention.

In practical reality, *Zadvydas* contains loopholes big enough to drive a fleet of trucks through, arrayed side by side. There is no absolute prohibition on indefinite detention, but rather discomfort in the terms in which the statutes imposing it are formulated. Even though *Zadvydas* was decided before September 11, 2001, the ruling provided an exception for terrorism cases and other special circumstances. After 9/11, and the hasty passage of the USA PATRIOT Act, the Bush justice department sped through the loophole without so much as blinking. Under the act, terrorist activity as defined by Congress extends to the use of any weapon or dangerous device "with the intent to endanger, directly or indirectly, the safety of one or more individuals or to cause substantial damage to property" other than for "mere personal monetary gain."[155] The new terrorist designation is "narrow enough to exclude a bank robber who seeks monetary gain," but broad enough to include just about anyone else the government wishes to detain for as long as it sees fit.[156]

Farouk Abdel-Muhti was a poster child for *Zadvydas*, at least until one reads between the lines of the prevailing opinion. Indeed, his case turned on the simple fact that he had nowhere to go, no place that would take him. He was born before the creation of the State of Israel, in the Palestine of 1947, and before the annexation by Jordan of the West Bank. He left some time before the Six-Day War, subsequent Israeli occupation and the end of Jordan's claim to the West Bank as part of its territory in 1988. He

---

155 Richsbourg, "Liberty and Security: The Yin and Yang of Immigration Law," quoting U.S. Code Title 8, Chapter 12, Subchapter II, Part II, Section 1182: Inadmissible aliens.
156 Richsbourg, "Liberty and Security."

was left stateless[157] and, according to Hemnauth, confused about where he belonged. The only country that could issue him an inbound travel document in 2002 was Israel, which displayed no interest in doing so. Farouk, although he did not call for violence against Israel, was a vocal proponent of Palestinian rights, including on WBAI.

Hemnauth befriended Farouk at Middlesex. Both were still far from the day their detention would end. Hemnauth had just begun to await the outcome of his case in the wake of Judge Riefkohl's ruling, and the INS did not feel bound by *Zadvydas* in Farouk's. Although their minds lived on different planes, Hemnauth's a spiritual one, Farouk's more political and analytical, they were kindred characters.

In addition, the other inmates were wary of Farouk, with his dissident's history and outlook, of which he made no secret. Many of the other inmates sought admission to the good graces of the guards and officials, although to little avail, with expressions of flattering bonhomie. "A regular jail thing. Good behavior." Part of the charm offensive consisted of treating Farouk as a marked man, speculating that his past was viewed as particularly reprehensible by the INS and, by extension, his jailers. "He had friends, but [many] people would try to stay away from such a man." They were afraid "of getting beaten up or deported faster." Farouk was not hostile, but certainly outspoken, the latter attitude easily mistaken for the former by those among the officials who had no interest in distinctions. He would hector officials about the violation of his rights, falling on deaf ears, but never giving up. It was evident to all that Farouk would never seek a way to the guards' hearts. Given his suspect background, it would have been a futile quest had he attempted any rapprochement, and an unlikely one since "he did not like the guards. Neither did I."

What Hemnauth had caught on to, even without Farouk's help, was the role of various agents in softening up detainees like sheep bound for slaughter. "Even Riefkohl who was trying to help me? He was helpless." And by extension a cog in a machine beyond his control or influence. "I realized this was all a stupid joke . . . The whole thing about these INS guys and social workers coming to talk to us, telling us 'Hey. Man, you're not [really] in jail. You happy? You okay? You're not in jail.' [Meanwhile] there's a

---

157 Fisher, "Stateless, Man Avoids Deportation from U.S."

big electric fence outside, there's handcuffs going on, guards beating people up. They're trying to instill in our minds that we are happy here, everything is good. So they can make a report" about inmates lying on comfortable beds and lifting weights and singing. Inside the facility, the immigration inmates wore civilian clothes, a superficial concession that padded the message that immigration inmates were not treated as prisoners. "But nobody was coming and giving us our rights. We had no rights over nothing." Even the purportedly liberal dress code was controlled: only plain T-shirts were permitted, no decorated or inscribed ones.

Hemnauth was not one to condone the ostracism of some inmates toward others, let alone join it, even had he and Farouk never associated in a mission to both understand and protest their detention and pending removal in human rights terms. For Hemnauth it was an entire education. Had one asked him at any point in his sentient life if he was a human rights advocate, he would have certainly affirmed he was. In racially polarized Guyana, he had seen himself as a bridge between the country's two dominant communities, Indo- and Afro-Caribbean. However, he had never really engaged in political discourse or argument, preferring, instinctively, spiritual explanations of what was and what ought to be. Farouk, on the other hand, was versed in political interpretations of the world at large and the events of the day, drawing explanations from history and theories. They included Marxian analysis, although when I asked Hemnauth if Farouk was a Marxist, he told me, in all sincerity, that he did not know. From where he stood, encircled by guards and fences, it simply did not matter.

What did matter was getting the word out and regular people sensitized to the injustice of standing immigration law and the policies it engendered: incarceration that did not speak its own name and deportation pursuant to adjudication scrubbed of judicial discretion.

"Farouk and I, we kind of spoke the same language in terms of our curiosity about our situation. We really got along well. His conversations were about history and politics and human rights and stuff . . . We talked about so many things that I don't even remember. He had known so much . . . He actually traveled the world. The whole night we would talk."

They also wrote, mainly letters and newsletters for the various human rights organizations interested in the plight of immigration detainees and the conditions inside the jails where they were held. Farouk got "bags of mail" every day, acknowledgement that he was communicating effectively with advocates on the outside, who were sending him correspondence, but also tracts and newspapers. Sometimes the bags were so heavy he could not lift them. He kept it all.

"I would sit with him and he would talk. He spoke broken English." This is odd for someone with a radio talk show, but true, as is apparent from interviews with Farouk recorded after his release. His imperfect fluency would have kept him from keeping up the outbound correspondence without help from Hemnauth. Hemnauth would compose it for him based on their discussions of the content, and Farouk would copy it back in his hand. "We would speak and I would write" often late into the night, including personal letters to Farouk's son and temperate love letters to a "Jewish lady named Emma" with whom he had a romance Hemnauth suspected was platonic. "He would write these loving kinds of things." Any bitterness, Farouk reserved for the INS. "I did, too. We shared this bitterness, but we had this love for everyone else." Hemnauth even transposed some of what Farouk wanted to say into poetry for Emma and others. He had, after all, written a song or two himself.

"In January, I was removed from Middlesex County." The January date is unlikely, since it diverges from other indications, including correspondence between Hemnauth and civil rights advocates. While Hemnauth's memory for detail is remarkable, his chronology is sometimes off. It appears that he was actually transferred to Passaic County Jail in Paterson, New Jersey in October 2003, about a month after Judge Riefkohl's written decision. One morning the guards came into his dorm at Middlesex and called out names of men who were ordered to "pack up your shit." One of the detainees stood up to ask, in what Hemnauth remembers as a confrontational tone of voice, what was going on. The tone aside, it seems like a reasonable query that someone who is not a prisoner of the criminal justice system would make to know where he is being taken by an agent of the state. After "slapping him around a bit," the guards took the man outside for what Hemnauth describes as a beating. Perhaps less severe a corporal punishment than others Hemnauth would witness, but still a chilling concept that a guard would lay hands on someone for asking a directly pertinent question. The guards may have been on edge precisely because they were as much in the dark as the prisoners they were handling.

The first thought to run through Hemnauth's mind when he was commanded to pack was that his deportation had come through and he was on his way to exile. However, the INS was moving a fairly large number of men of different nationalities at the same time, so he deduced that he was going not to Guyana, but somewhere else. The guards returned the belongings the jail had confiscated and held in storage (minus, of course, his green card and Social Security card, which had been destroyed) in exchange for his regulation Middlesex-marked jumpsuit. The more likely explanation, Hemnauth now surmised, with logic on his side, was that the INS had singled out detainees whose deportation had been stayed by the INS because their cases were on appeal, as was Hemnauth's, unbeknownst to him. Residency at Middlesex tended to be brief: days or weeks, maybe a few months. A different detention center would be assigned, if not specifically equipped, to house longer-term detainees. "A whole bunch of people at Middlesex were fighting their case[s]." He also speculates, with logic and subsequent events to bolster his thesis, that the INS had a strategy of "breaking" whoever contested their deportation by tightening the screws on the conditions of detention. The place where he was going had the tightening-of-the-screws routine down cold.

Along with the other detainees in transit, Hemnauth was handcuffed, shackled and put on a bus. No one said anything, preferring to take in the scenery — even if it was merely the drab landscape along the New Jersey Turnpike — and maybe catch a glimpse of free people or spot some pretty girls. Being on a bus for ninety minutes "was like a privilege." Until they arrived at Passaic County Jail on Sheriff's Plaza in Paterson. Some of the prisoners aboard the bus were familiar with Passaic and became visibly rattled when the bus made the turn through the prison's gates. "They were disgusted," Hemnauth said. They had convinced themselves that they were bound for a clean facility in the Middlesex mold somewhere in New York State. Since no one at Middlesex had volunteered any information, they had let their optimism wander way too far.

Passaic County Jail was party to an Intergovernmental Service Agreement (IGSA) signed in 1985 with the Immigration and Naturalization Service, making the facility a contract jailer for the federal government. During the time Hemnauth was in residency, the prison operated under the authority of the county's high-profile, publicity hound of a sheriff, Jerry Speziale. Speziale ultimately left his elected Passaic office in 2010 for a senior security post at the Port Authority of New York and New Jersey. By then, he had accumulated some B-list notoriety for his indisputable moxie, not just as chief cop in a rough corner of New Jersey, but also for prior stints as a bona fide undercover agent fighting the Cali drug cartel for the U.S. Drug Enforcement Administration. He also possessed a marked talent for self-promotion, capped by a small role in a high-adrenalin action movie called *Brooklyn's Finest* with Ethan Hawke and Richard Gere. Speziale's real undercover feats of drug-busting became the central theme of the autobiographical thriller *Without a Badge*, featuring prominent appearances by former New York mayor Rudy Giuliani — still basking in the self-stoked glow of his post-9/11 glory when the book was published in 2003 — and Bernie Kerik, the hapless nominee for secretary of Homeland Security later convicted of tax fraud.

Speziale was the first Democrat to occupy the sheriff's office in Passaic when he was elected in 2002, shortly before Hemnauth arrived at the jail. The sheriff enjoyed the limelight, and his bluster bolstered his popularity in the county despite the legal and human rights complaints against him and the prison over the course of his tenure. Indeed, he used bombast as a foil to demands for improvements in conditions at the jail — for both immigrant detainees and the general population — and to accusations of abuse of his office. Instances of tempestuous behavior and patronage were legion. In one well-publicized incident, Speziale excoriated as unworthy of his badge a police officer in Virginia who had stopped two Passaic officers for speeding while returning from Hurricane Katrina relief in a patrol car. The car was traveling 95 miles per hour with its emergency lights flashing in the total absence of any emergency and a thousand miles from New Orleans. They were simply in a hurry to get home to New Jersey. Speziale's phone rant against the Virginia cop who stopped his deputies was made public. It is laced with invective, such as, "You know what? It's a disgrace and I don't know who your sheriff is, but I plan to find out who he is and speak to him. It's a disgrace. If you think that that's not a disgrace you should take the badge off your shirt and throw it in the garbage."[158] In the same call, Speziale stated that he did not normally lower himself to dealing with deputies from other police departments, only fellow chiefs.

Far from being embarrassed by such disclosures, Speziale wore his bluster as one more medal to pin on his own blue shirt. It did not hurt him with the voters, no more than did his co-bashing immigrant detainees with Lou Dobbs, cable television's erstwhile über-immigrant-basher who marketed his railing against immigration as the distinctive feature of his long-running anchor position on CNN, until other conservative talk show hosts horned in on the game and the distinction faded. He doubled down on his anti-immigrant fulminations, adding, for good measure, empathy with the discredited "birther" movement's efforts to brand President Obama a foreigner, as well as with other unsubstantiated conspiracy theories. (His indignant objections to the hiring of illegal aliens by others did not stop Mr. Dobbs from hiring some himself, to help care for his daughter's horses and to garden for him.) In 2009, his boss at CNN, queasy over his extremism, tried to rein him in. He quit instead.

When Speziale terminated Passaic's contract with ICE, in 2006, under pressure from a pending unfavorable report from ICE's inspector general, he appeared on Lou Dobbs' CNN show, blaming human rights groups for disrupting the smooth performance of his immigrant detention duties. According to the sheriff, they had made the jail's federal outsourcing contract far more trouble than it was worth, a strange assertion for a boss whose jail ended up grossing some $114 million in federal contracts[159], immigrant detention prominent among them. Tellingly, Speziale joined the chorus chanting the stereotype of immigrant detainees as uniformly dangerous criminals deserving of mistreatment and, from his language, opprobrium as human beings. It was facile to hide behind the government's own classification of virtually anyone in INS or ICE detention as a "criminal alien," conjuring up images of villains, be they genuine recidivist criminals or petty

---

158 "Reckless NJ Police Convoy Escapes VA Justice."

159 Goldberg, Mitchie, et al., "Angel Colon, et al. v. Passaic County Jail, et al." (2008). The complaint filed by the plaintiffs' attorneys uses the phrase "over a hundred million dollars." The more specific figure of $114 million was cited to me orally by Emily Goldberg.

one-time offenders. It fit the anti-immigrant narrative better if all were painted with the same righteous brush and if whoever wielded it willfully ignored the distortions it left behind. Witness this exchange:

> Speziale: *See, what happens here is the INS detainees, the perception is that most of the people are someone that crossed over a border or overstays on a visa to be here for the American dream. In reality, these are people that crossed over that border and then stole the American dream by committing a felony, by committing a murder, by committing a rape, or a sodomy, and we can't even discuss that.*

> Dobbs: *Sheriff, you're committing truth here. The fact is everybody wants to believe that illegal aliens in this country are simply coming here to do America a favor, yet the figures show that at 400,000 criminal illegal aliens, that is besides the crime of crossing our border illegally, are at large in this country?*

> Speziale: *Yes, Yes. And that is just the problem. The perception is that these people in my jail are people that just came over for the American dream. And that is . . . not the reality. The reality is the fact that these people are criminal aliens.*[160]

The discourse pursued by Dobbs and Speziale is chillingly reminiscent of the terms of the immigration debate in the late nineteenth century, when the politics of exclusion of a certain category of immigrant — ethnic Chinese — needed the ideal scapegoat to bolster the case for expedited removals. Then, as now, the irresistible urge inflicting proponents of aggressive deportation was to tar an entire group as a criminal underclass (for example, prostitutes and opium pushers then, "criminal aliens" today), better to deflect any opposition to indiscriminate removals.[161] The inflammatory phrase "criminal alien" sanctified in current immigration law is a handy device for doing much the same thing. In that perspective, Speziale was just a messenger. He did not even have to coin the phrase himself. "These people" Speziale refers to were prebracketed as a lumpen criminal group in the inflammatory glossary of federal immigration law, whether they were actual criminals or not by any objective accounting at the time of the Dobbs' interview. So the sheriff did not even have to go to the trouble

160 "Transcripts: Lou Dobbs Tonight January 3, 2006."
161 Kanstroom, *Deportation Nation: Outsiders in American History.*

of separating truth from fiction, let alone explain to Dobbs' viewers that many of those with long past offenses had paid their penalty in full before detention by the INS and had not been charged with any subsequent offense in years.

Better yet, Dobbs might have asked Speziale about the nature of his contract with the federal government, which was to house administrative detainees and to keep the public and his charges safe, including from one another. He had no correctional function beyond that. Yet, like some before him and many afterwards, he interpreted the rampant permeation of the civil justice model by the punitive themes of criminal law as license to turn a housing contract into a correctional mandate. Why wouldn't he, if it worked to his political advantage and, to top it off, Attorney General John Ashcroft, seizing on the nation's post-9/11 anxiety and confusion, said he could?[162]

Hemnauth encountered Jerry Speziale directly on only one innocuous occasion, when the sheriff made a grin-and-greet tour of the section of the jail housing ICE detainees. Speziale made other visits to the jail, but Hemnauth believes the sheriff deliberately avoided him as his protests, all of them peaceful, gained visibility both inside and outside the prison, thanks to the involvement of New Jersey–based human rights groups. In reality, the problems at Passaic ran much deeper than Jerry Speziale, even if he embodied an epitome of the detention system's studied indifference to the welfare of the nonprisoners it held prisoner, referring to his immigration detention operation as "my jail."

The problem with Passaic was not limited to its sheriff. The problem with Passaic was Passaic.

Hemnauth did a little typecasting of his own, as he described his arrival at Passaic. The guards who greeted his bus, to his eyes, were of two types. The dark-haired Italians were easier to get along with, striking him as "roots people," a phrase apparently used in his community in Guyana to denote people conscious of their families' origins and imbued with heritage.

162 Miller, "Citizenship and Severity."

(Redheads of, say, Irish descent might take issue with being excluded from that particular typecast.) They were also not as large of body as several of the others, whom he describes as "Vikings," of inhibitive dimension and physical strength, towering, as they did, over someone of as slight of build as Hemnauth. The INS transit detail left immediately after "dropping off the bodies," as Hemnauth overheard them describe their duty, entrusting the immigrants to the watch of prison guards and officers in dark blue uniforms. Their demeanor was one of ominous mockery. One of personnel chided the new arrivals with a faux-jovial "happy to have you" as he booked them and took possession of their belongings.

As at Middlesex, the inaugural ritual of arrival at Passaic was the strip search, although this time with a collective twist. The pretense of a medical examination threw off one more veil as the new inmates were prodded, and probed naked, four at a time rather than privately. The anal search appears to have been a hallmark of the booking process at Passaic. In fact, Sheriff Speziale's website — taken down when he left office and no longer available — featured a number of video clips presented as instructional. One of them follows a group of high schoolers on a field trip to the jail to be briefed, graphically, on the downside of poor behavior. A reformed recidivist offender addresses them, recounting the discomforts of his several dozen arrests, the "probe up my ass" initiations to Passaic the most memorably painful of them, so much so that he finally abandoned his life of crime to avoid them.

They were memorable to Hemnauth, as well, for the humiliation they brought that was all the more vexing that it served no other function, except if one credits the amusement of the guards as a worthwhile purpose. Certainly the opportunity for the inmates to smuggle any forbidden items in their private orifices was remote; they had boarded a secured bus, shackled, at Middlesex, been driven directly to another prison and taken off the same bus in another prison yard an hour away without crossing state lines. "They were mocking us," Hemnauth recalls. With the others, Hemnauth was ordered to "shake that dick. Let me see you shake that dick." In addition to bending over so the officers could "look up my ass." No reference was made to a medical protocol or requirement, and no doctor was present. "They were laughing over the whole thing." Once again, as happened frequently over my time listening to Hemnauth tell his story, his tone turns from the chuckles of hindsight to a darker shade of deep-seated anger, subtle, but unmistakable. The notion that he could be commanded by anyone in an official capacity to strip naked in front of other people and present his anus to a nonmedical stranger for penetration by a probe without the slightest concern for his dignity, and despite the fact he was not under arrest for a criminal offense, let alone a violent one, shook Hemnauth to the core. True, he had inherited a faint prudish streak from his mother and his culture, but prudishness had very little to do with his reaction. Rather, the idea that others could be so desensitized to the act of dehumanization they were performing boggled his comprehension and does to this day.

"That was a horrible thing. That alone told me this was going to be a disaster . . . That was a way of [the officers] entertaining themselves." There were senior prison officers present, but in the background.

Hemnauth's impression of guards entertaining themselves at the expense of detainees' dignity cannot be summarily dismissed as an emotional response to an unpleasant experience reluctantly imposed by a government agency. It is true that INS procedures in force when he arrived at Passaic prescribed a strip search for each arriving detainee, and the logic for these searches was left vague. The relevant section of the standards document does, however, focus on contraband as the overarching concern being addressed, whereas the opportunity for such contraband was so scant with the detainees arriving from Middlesex as to fail any test of reasonable suspicion.[163] That "shak[ing] that dick" would reveal any contraband fails the most basic giggle test. Even the liberal standards governing the jail's strip-searching called for privacy, a command Passaic blithely ignored. If further evidence was needed that INS-appointed jailers were abusing their strip-searching mandate, the INS provided it itself. Indeed, shortly after Hemnauth's induction to Passaic, the INS issued a directive forbidding strip searches except in instances triggering reasonable suspicion, such as a discovery during pat-down or evidence of gang affiliation.[164] In Hemnauth's case, even after enactment of the new directive, the old misdemeanor drug conviction could have been construed as a "reasonable suspicion" by a jailer eager to engage in strip-searching. However, that is not the point.

---

163 "INS Detention Standard: Admission and Release," U.S. Department of Homeland Security.

164 Tangeman, "Strip Search Guidelines."

Rather, the INS would have had no incentive to curtail strip-searching absent a record of abuse by the jails the agency hired.

The booking, the strip search and a further, perfunctory medical session consisting of a health history interview took the entire day. The inmates were given prison garb, a two-piece green canvas suit, shirt and pants. Some had plain white T-shirts from the Middlesex commissary, which they were permitted to keep but not inscribe or decorate in any way. They were also issued an inmate number.

"Then the canines showed up." He did not mean Chihuahuas.

The jail was not wasting any time bringing out the stars in its arsenal of intimidation. After the booking procedures, Hemnauth was herded with the others into a corridor or lobby. The dogs were employed by the guards to force the new prisoners into a line and keep them there. They were barking at the men. "We were all kind of tired and frustrated" and ready "to go to the dorm and relax for a minute, you know." The dogs looked like "they wanted to eat you up. Very fierce and aggressive. [They] keep jumping," lunging at the inmates until the guard holding a dog just within reach of one of them pulled the animal back by its leash, "just before he touches you. The mouth would come real close so you could see the [bared] teeth." Hemnauth positioned his hand right in front of his nose to demonstrate how close everyone felt to being bitten in the face. The dogs were very muscular and strained on their leashes, testing the guards' ability to hold them back. As the inmates advanced in a line, the dogs were positioned to the side and the back of the formation. This just made them scarier: the prisoners had gotten a clear sense of their ferocity, and not being able to anticipate a charge they felt all the more vulnerable to being attacked. "If they came from the front, you might be able to make a little move, but coming from the back they put more fear in you."

This was Hemnauth's first glimpse of the attack dogs, but not his last. They were used "day in and day out," reported another Passaic inmate,[165] who was ultimately bitten on the arm when one guard told another who

---

165 Zwerdling et al., *Exposé: An Inside Job.*

was restraining a dog to loose the animal on the detainee. Hemnauth never saw the canines being used solely for their stated purpose of sniffing contraband, like they might at an airport. The use of dogs was exposed by Daniel Zwerdling in his November 2004 NPR piece, contemporaneously with the reports and pictures of canine attacks and intimidation against prisoners at Abu Ghraib in Iraq. "The problem in the Passaic County Jail in New Jersey was much greater than the problem at Abu Ghraib," Zwerdling later told an interviewer. "The guards used their dogs on a daily basis."[166] Zwerdling's reporting would quickly lead — notwithstanding government denials of cause to effect — to a Homeland Security directive ordering that canine-based control of detainees come to a halt. However, this was not before Hemnauth witnessed and experienced many more episodes of vicious animals sicced on handcuffed detainees.

True to form, Speziale's spokesperson denied abuse and maintained that dogs were used "strictly for security and contraband detection purposes" and that their handlers "act in a professional manner when interacting with inmates."[167] "Security" is the convenient skirt behind which to hide any form of prisoner control. And what better way to justify any repressive practice than to conflate it with "contraband detection," read drugs?

The cornerstones of professional police employment of dogs are trained reaction to specific stimuli and turn-on-a-dime obedience. Each encounter Hemnauth witnessed with the dogs at Passaic suggested that the jail's canines possessed the attributes of ferocity and strength common to the breeds generally used for patrol dogs, as distinct from detection dogs. The former respond to imperilment of their master or the object of his protection from, for instance, an armed criminal on the loose. The latter pick up a scent they are trained to recognize in even minute amounts, locate it and alert their handlers without necessarily aggressing whoever might be carrying it. Luggage-sniffing beagles of the kind I have encountered at airports are a perfect example, and I have not felt threatened, nor have I had reason to. Some police dogs can possess the attributes of sniffers and patrollers, but the soldiering qualities of patrol dogs would not have been needed to detect contraband at Passaic, as Speziale affirmed was the primary purpose of his canines and the only use ever sanctioned by ICE. Even if inmate

166 Zwerdling and Casciato, "Investigating Abuse."
167 Bernstein, "9/11 Detainees in New Jersey Say They Were Abused with Dogs."

control by dogs were a legitimate aim — and it certainly was not — Passaic's canines were evidently ill trained, if trained at all, in instant obedience to verbal commands from the guards who handled them. The leashes and the guards' ability to overpower the dogs at their ends were evidently all that kept them from mauling detainees.[168]

The guards packed their new charges in a room so densely that they could not sit on the floor for lack of surface, despite having been on their feet essentially the whole time since arriving at Passaic. Every half an hour or so, the guards would come and escort five people out of the holding room and bring them to their block. After a sufficient number had left, the remaining prisoners had enough space to sit. "On the floor, we're talking."

The strain in the room ultimately triggered pushing and near-fights among them. The "aggressive inmates were able to reach the door [first]." There was no method to how inmates were called up to be taken to their detention quarters. They were not called out by name, so the pushier ones got to move on before the more orderly prisoners, leaving behind a trail of resentment as the mark of the first day at Passaic. Hemnauth ended up waiting almost three hours in an empty room with no seating. He was not about to get into a fight in order to reach the door before someone else, although one of the Jamaican inmates he had befriended at Middlesex was urging him to assert himself.

Having nowhere to sit but a hard floor — and that only once over-crowding in what amounted to a large holding pen had thinned — sounds like small beer for outrage, but only if one ignores the prior context. Here is a group of detainees — who are supposed to be distinct from criminal prisoners according to the statutes that placed them in detention and that abjure the prisoner designation — removed from one jail to another without prior warning, without the opportunity to inform either their family or advocates, subjected to a humiliating and pointless search of their naked bodies in the presence of an amused audience, exposed to the unprovoked scoffing of police officers, referred to as "meat" by INS transit officers,

---

168 Burkhard, "Beware of the Dogs: Can New York's Canine Units Keep the City Safe from Terrorism?"

robbed of their very identity as humans and threatened from within inches
by snarling dogs trained for aggression. All that and more in the span of
the first day at Passaic. A long day to be sure, but one the jailers made sure
to pack with hardship.

That Sheriff Speziale conflated Hemnauth's ancient misdemeanor with,
in his words, "murder," "rape" and "sodomy" is highly symptomatic not
only of the intellectual shortcuts of local officials the federal government
has entrusted with the care of detainees, but also of the self-delegated
license to abuse them based on a distorted portrayal of their past offenses
and outright character assassination. More than hyperbole, the assertion
that Hemnauth and his peers were all killers and rapists is also morally if
not legally libelous. According to ICE, only 51% of detainees are convicted
felons, which Hemnauth was not, and only 11% of these violent ones, according to the standards contained in the FBI's Uniform Crime Reporting
Program.[169] (In fact, Bryan Lonegan of the Legal Aid Society later told
me that according to his observations when he held guidance meetings
with the detainees, about half the detainees were awaiting deportation at
Passaic pursuant to immigration violations alone — a civil offense — and
had no police record whatsoever.) Rounding upward, that means that Speziale in the TV interview where Lou Dobbs praised him for "committing
truth here" was tarring the entire detainee population with the crimes of
roughly 6% of them, based on statistical likelihood. Also according to ICE
estimates, crimes of homicide and sexual assault — murder and rape —
were committed by 2.5% of detainees who, like Hemnauth, were parents
of a child.[170] Even allowing for the fact that the ICE data breaking down
crimes committed by aliens collected in 2009 might be different from that
collected in 2006 when Speziale was interviewed by Dobbs, or in 2003
when Hemnauth arrived at Passaic, and that further variances, even relatively large ones, might occur among different detention facilities around
the country, the characterization of the majority of immigrant detainees as
bloody-handed is a wild exaggeration past the point of mendacity. So much
so that it leads to legitimate questions about the motives of those who, like
Speziale, would spread such fantasies. After all, if they are so convinced

---

169 Schriro, "Immigration Detention Overview and Recommendations."
170 Outten-Mills, Islam, and Kelch, "Removals Involving Illegal Alien Parents of
United States Citizen Children."

of the rightness of their punitive treatment of immigrant detainees, why must they lie in order to justify it to the public? "Sodomy" on the part of detained immigrants "stole the American dream"? Really? (Sodomy, incidentally, is not listed as a tabulated offense in the Uniform Crime Reporting Program.)

This is not to say that all of the detainees in immigration custody are angels, but rather that the sheriff's framing of his duty as one of maintaining order in the face of the violent proclivities of the detainee population deliberately ducks the point. It also evades the issue of the government's failure to protect peaceful detainees from belligerent ones, some of who arrive in immigration detention directly from incarceration by the criminal justice system. Also, the inclusion of a small minority of violent inmates in Passaic's detainee population brought out survivalist instincts in those who never resorted to physical force in the normal conduct of their lives. Hemnauth witnessed this phenomenon all around him and eventually felt animal reflexes grasp hold of him as well. If the sheriff felt his charges were unanimously dangerous, he might have paused to ponder how much of the menace the Passaic penal regimen created on its own.

The threat of violence surfaced the moment Hemnauth set foot in Passaic, with some inmates willing to physically intimidate others to get what they wanted, in the first instance early assignment to their living quarters. The overhang of imminent violence among inmates, instigated by a minority, is a constant feature of immigration detention, part of the punitive flavor that, by law, it is not supposed to have. In the criminal justice system, violent criminals who pose a risk to physically vulnerable inmates are routinely segregated into facilities with beefier standards of security. The most venal white-collar criminal is not likely to serve his term within reach of Charles Manson.[171]

The official propaganda of the jailers would have us believe that the behavior of the most violent inmates is common to all detainees and that,

---

171 In 2009, Bernard L. Madoff, the most infamous of financial criminals, was sentenced to 150 years, which he is serving in an unlocked cell at a medium-security federal prison complex in North Carolina with a reputation for excellent staff and medical facilities. He was denied residency in an even lower-security prison because of the impact of the length of his sentence on the Federal Bureau of Prison's scoring model. See: Smith, "Madoff Arrives at N.C. Prison."

therefore, all must be dealt with sternly. This attitude certainly transpires from Jerry Speziale's statements to Lou Dobbs, but he is hardly the only jailer in the country to have staked out that position.

Please.

Far from a justification for the treatment of immigrants detained in ICE facilities, the threat of violence of some of them upon others is, quite to the contrary, a component of that treatment, one more brick in the edifice of abusiveness maintained by the ICE detention system and the contract jailers entrusted with operating it. A chapter of a Department of Justice Office of the Inspector General's report on Passaic clearly shows jail officials being evasive when queried about the comingling of various categories of prisoner: "The housing records we reviewed did not contain information about inmates' criminal history."[172] In short, the climate of fear was part of the punishment inflicted on the detainees simply for being there. The likelihood of violent altercation, exacerbated by the despair — and in some instances mental illness — of some of the detainees is a major theme of Hemnauth's experience at Passaic. It is one more twist in the process of dehumanization the detention system champions. At best, the life of a detainee is so unworthy of protection that the distinction between dangerous inmates and peaceful ones is simply ignored. At worst — as when Jerry Speziale shows his hand — erasing the distinction feeds the deceitful narrative of immigrants in deportation proceedings as uniformly vile. There were many ramifications of this prejudice during Hemnauth's time at Passaic. It was common that an altercation between two detainees would lead to an equal presumption of guilt for both the violent aggressor and his victim, particularly if the victim had the audacity to physically defend himself. All the more grist for the narrative's mill.

Hemnauth was finally escorted from the induction holding space to a prison supplies office, again with barking dogs standing guard, although less primed for attack by the guards than they had been in the holding area. Hemnauth was given a rolled mattress, a sheet and a pillow. He also received a "little cleaning pack" composed of a small piece of soap, a

---

172 Office of Inspector General, "Conditions of Confinement at Passaic County Jail in Paterson, New Jersey" in *A Review of the Treatment of Aliens Held on Immigration Charges in Connection with the Investigation of the September 11 Attacks.*

toothbrush and some toothpaste. So equipped, he was led up several flights of stairs, with a bag of personal items from Middlesex, including documents, letters, cards, books and a couple of T-shirts, along with the mattress roll and bedding. He may also have still had some chocolate from the Middlesex commissary. Clothing from his suitcase was not returned to him, nor was his wallet, his belt or shoes, but kept in storage as ordered by the INS. In any event, his few personal belongings were scanned and searched when he first arrived at Passaic before anything was surrendered back to him. He had also been issued shoes by the jail, soft "Kung Fu" boots. His green card and Social Security card were long gone. When Judge Riefkohl declared Hemnauth deportable at his last hearing, the government's attorney ceremoniously held each in the air as he cut it into pieces with a pair of scissors, on hand for the occasion, a kind of breaking-of-Captain-Dreyfus's-sword moment the lawyer had seemed to relish for the dishonor it served upon the pending deportee. Hemnauth felt suitably humiliated. "My driver's license was probably in the garbage a long time ago," so he was spared a third assault on his identity.

Hemnauth's residency quarters reminded him of the hold on a ship. He was taken to the top floor, of four according to his recollection. It was divided into quartiles, or pods, delineated by iron bars and gates. There was a guards' station in the middle of the floor, an office enclosed behind tinted glass. Passaic had not adopted the "direct inmate supervision" model Middlesex is so proud of, perhaps rightfully so. Hemnauth estimates that there were about 200 inmates per floor, 50 per quartile.

The jail did make sure that each inmate had a bunk, that there was never a situation whereby two inmates were sharing a bed and that no one was sleeping on the floor. I was surprised that Hemnauth even brought it up, but there was a reason. In the general population at Passaic, some inmates were indeed sleeping on the floor. Hemnauth observed this later in his stay at Passaic, when his protests became more troublesome to the management of the jail and the route to isolation blocks, medical units or meetings with officials took him through the general population sections. Evidently the sheriff and the warden did not wish to trigger scrutiny of their immigrant detention operations (although they eventually would) by so gross a violation of the service agreement with INS as a lack of beds. After all, jails are paid per night per bed, and the deals were —

and are — sweet ones. As we have seen, the threshold of violation was comfortably high. Still, admitting an inmate without a bunk would have crossed it.

Every trip to and from a detainee's residency pod was patrolled by at least one guard assisted by a dog. The dogs were never friendly, and no one among the detainees was ever tempted to pet them. The animals were conditioned as police dogs, and how aggressive they turned during a routine movement of a small number of prisoners depended on how experienced a handler the particular cop was. Their behavior on a quiet day ranged from alert passivity to ominous growling. The dogs were conditioned to see the prisoners as a constantly pending threat, and any hint of disturbance in the blocks was a stimulus to attack. "In shakedowns and things, the dogs would get real angry . . . They respond to police behavior."

One of Hemnauth's Middlesex friends had reached the pod a little earlier and saved the bottom level of a two-tier bunk for him, speculating that they would be assigned to the same floor and quartile. That was about the best arrangement that could be hoped for, the worst being the top level of a three-tier bunk stack inches from the ceiling. The lower bunk "gives you kind of a cozy feeling."

That was the only time the word "cozy" came up as descriptive of anything at the jail. "The place was kind of dirty. We tried to keep it clean," Hemnauth told me, making plain the challenge of succeeding. "But it's an old building, a very old building."

"Each dorm had a large ventilation fan. There was no real fresh air intake." Here Hemnauth speaks like the climate control expert he is. The pods were almost hermetically sealed. There were bars separating them one from the other, but between the bars and the dorm, the prison had installed an iron door. The windows were more like slits glazed with thick bulletproof panes of a polycarbonate-like material. The "windows" stood four feet off the floor and were about six feet high and only a few inches wide, four in Hemnauth's estimation. There would be one for every two bunks or so, but only at the back wall of the building.

"Could you see out?" I ask.

"No," Hemnauth says, again with that flash of anger at certain recollections. "They scratched it [up]. In a way that we won't be able to see outside." He firmly believes that scuffing the panes was a deliberate initiative of the jail, with no other purpose than to ratchet the cruelty up one more notch.

"There is a heat and ventilation system, but it doesn't work." Surprise. "No fresh air. So the place had a smell, all the time, a foul air smell." In the close environment, the dogs that accompanied the guards on all the regular patrols in the cellblocks also contributed noticeably to the rank odor. Only some of the vents' fans used to extract the spent air functioned, and overall the HVAC system was defective and neglected, as Hemnauth was professionally qualified to observe. Since they were on the top floor, just below the roof, some outside air would "seep in" through the ceiling vents, but certainly not enough to clear the foul odors. These were a composite of perspiration of a crowd of men in close quarters, the smells of rotten wood and other decay from the old prison building they were in and whatever the buildup of filth in the ducting systems gave off. "They don't clean those things for years," to the point that the induction system was so clogged as to obstruct the flow of air in the vents and soil whatever ventilation might manage to pass, if by chance the HVAC was to come on. There was just enough air "to keep you alive." Hemnauth tried to unclog the HVAC himself with a pen, unsuccessfully.

The place was completely mildewed. "The walls were all moldy. Green stuff would be growing on the wall," and the spores of mold would circulate. Periodically the prison smelled of gas.

"We were living under extreme conditions now." The air that would seep in beneficially in moderate conditions, would stifle the quarters in the extremes of summer and chill them in the winter, because the vent and exhaust dampers were either defective or worn. When the inmates complained, the jail responded not with repairs to the HVAC, but with blankets in the winter.

In the washroom, the area around the sinks and the toilets was infested with mosquitoes, the showers a little less so. "I got some infections on my head, through my hair. I began to get sores and boils on my head, on my scalp." Another inmate contracted a skin disease that spread over his body. The showers were defective as well, running either ice cold or so burning hot that Hemnauth and others would wet and clean themselves with the steam rather than be burned by the water. The men hung a sheet to trap the steam so it would at least be effective, but the guard removed it during one of their periodic raids. The inmates provided their own cleaning crews.

Hemnauth saw this as an infinitely better alternative to relying on the same jail management that was allowing the entire physical infrastructure at Passaic to crumble and rot.

"When I first saw [the quarters], I thought damn, what a filthy, stinking place! Right away, my mind started to waver. It was so old, like eighteenth century; maybe they used to keep slaves here or something, in the old days . . . You begin to feel *this* is jail. In Middlesex [by comparison] it looked like more of a housing thing." Such was the contrast, notwithstanding the same presence of guards and the same security fences encircling him. "But now you get the sense, you are in jail for real, here, now." Most of the people on his pod came from Middlesex, so the impression of the contrast was widely shared. The transferees from Middlesex occupied two dorms at Passaic, Hemnauth's and an adjoining one. Farouk Abdel-Muhti was among the transferees.

It was about two in the following morning by the time the new inmates could unpack their few belongings, spread their mattresses and bed down for the night. Two officers accompanied by two more with canines erupted through the "cage door thing they have there," immediately followed by yet two more guards armed with pellet guns and pepper spray canisters.

They "began to curse, real nasty," addressing the detainees as "motherfuckers" as was their entrenched habit. The officer ordered them to get up and stand against the bar that ran along the rows of cells separating them from the guards' control space with their hands on it, their backs to the officers. The point was to prevent the prisoners from seeing what any of the officers was doing or if any of them was approaching. "If you tried to look, they had a dog jumping at you." The protocol specified the dogs be used for control and intimidation, to be pulled back on their leashes before actually biting an inmate. In this instance protocol was followed, which did little to ease the terror the dogs inspired. "They were barking and just running wild." The sergeant, "the main officer," who was commanding the apparent raid on Hemnauth's pod, "stepped onto a steel table and began stamping his feet and cursing" as a way of introducing himself and the other guards, and proceeding to perform a shakedown. "If you don't like it, call your congressman," he declared. "This is how we do things here." The inmates would have to get used to it. He did not provide instructions for reaching the switchboard at the Capitol. Rather, the guards went on a rampage, "started going wild," pulling mattresses off bunks and searching the cells without regard to any damage they might inflict on the inmates' possessions, "throwing mattresses all over the place, and all our commissary clothes and things." The raid was entirely unprovoked, which was sort of the point. "We were newcomers" and the sergeant apparently thought he would show them who was the boss.

One of the cops pointed a pellet gun directly at Hemnauth, and others, although there was no immediate threat or likelihood of one arising from a group of exhausted and disoriented inmates. The other officers used the dogs, strung high by the fabricated commotion, to prevent any inmate from turning around and looking behind him at what the guards were doing in the sleeping pods.

"Things were happening fast." While Hemnauth observed what he did by looking at reflections in glass, one of the inmates did turn around. Hemnauth recalls that he may have been trying to tell the guards that he was feeling ill; several men were. "He was new to this kind of thing, kind of sickly, [although] I was new, too." The man was dragged away and beaten. Not a gentle slap on the wrist — not that even that would have been justified. Although Hemnauth could not watch the blows being delivered under the threat of the pellet gun to his head, he heard the screams. "They were hurting him." To top the beating, the man was sentenced to "probably ten days" in solitary confinement for disobeying a direct order from a guard. "They treat him rough to send a message to us: 'Hey, don't disobey us, because you are going to have a hard time.' . . . When the cops are in shakedown mode, they are like robots. They get real horrible and beat you up . . . [They are] like savages." Meet them on the outside, "they talk like regular people and carry on regular conversations. They can be very nice people." Or, Hemnauth corrects himself, "pretend to be very nice people." He specifically cites encounters when the inmates are escorted to the gym or the basketball court.

There was no schedule to the shakedowns. There could be as few as one or two in a month. Sometimes when things were "running smoothly" and the guards faced boredom, they would stage a shakedown to relieve it.

So went Hemnauth's introduction to Jerry Speziale's Passaic County Jail. The gloves were off. So was the mask.

Daily life at Passaic between incidents of repression by the guards was remarkably confining in light of the inmates' status as detainees, not criminal convicts, or even "364s," the colloquial designation given to incarcerated individuals either awaiting trial in a criminal court or sentenced to a prison term of less than a year. These types made up the other section of Passaic's inmate population.

The only outdoor time allotted to the immigrant detainees was a visit to the rooftop basketball court, twice per week for a total of an hour. The whole space was "caged up. You could see outside to a certain extent, but we were in a cage." Again, Hemnauth's emphasis on one word, "cage," is a measure of his lasting outrage at a particularly offensive feature of the prison regimen. He repeats the word several times.

"Sometimes in the winter, they would take you out late in the evening, when it was damp and cold. You would still want to go." Besides diminishing the detainees' enjoyment at being outside by subjecting them to the cold and dark, we are left to ponder why the jailers would choose to erode the value of the already puny ration of outdoor recreation if it were not yet one more a reminder of their unmandated punitive aims. Indeed, the detention standard for recreation in application at the time of Hemnauth's detention at Passaic provided one hour outdoors every day for each detainee "at a reasonable hour."[173] Passaic violated the standard in at least two ways: the time to be allotted and the permissible segment of the day. The only other possible explanation is hardly an excuse: overcrowding. On average, the jail would have needed to spread its entire population of immigrant detainees and members of the general population over twelve hours of daylight and two basketball cages. With a total population of some 1,700 inmates, and sometimes more, and even assuming that a sizeable portion of the people in custody chose not to benefit from an outdoor period, were ill or under

173 "INS Detention Standard: Recreation," Immigration and Naturalization Service.

disciplinary restriction on any given day, the jail would have had to cram more inmates onto the two basketball courts than they or the security protocol could accommodate, upwards of a hundred men at a time. Further, we would have to assume that it never rained, snowed, froze or baked. The jail would have been hard pressed to comply with detention standards even if it wanted to, leaving us to wonder why the INS and ICE licensed Passaic to house administrative detainees in the first place, if it lacked as much as the basic infrastructure required to come close to meeting the standards under federal law.

If anything, Hemnauth was understating Passaic's skirting of its obligation to provide opportunities for physical recreation. A review of compliance with immigrant detention rules conducted by the American Bar Association in 2004 confirmed Passaic's violation of the standard for recreation, as well as ICE's failure to admonish the jail for not meeting it. ICE awarded Passaic with a rating of "acceptable" on the recreation measure. The ABA noted that an HIV-positive detainee, for all practical purposes, had to choose between receiving his medication and his exercise: if he was absent from his cell when the nurse came by, no meds.[174] Passaic was one of forty-one detention facilities providing inadequate recreation time when the ABA and the UN High Commissioner for Refugees scrutinized them in a study, using ICE's own standards as their benchmark.[175]

The other furloughs from the dorm area included an hour in a weight room and one in the law library. Pretty quickly, Hemnauth came to see the trips to the law library as "one more little [weekly] outing," although the same recreation standard for detainees specified that law library time could not substitute for recreation.

Detainees were not provided with a dining hall. Meals were delivered to the dorm. Men lined up as individual trays — including Hemnauth's vegetarian one — were passed through a slot in the bars securing the space occupied by inmates. Yet another degree of confinement added to the others that seems to underscore the punitive regimen ICE jailers could impose, willy-nilly, on administrative detainees, without regard to any distinction among prisoners between those who may have required restrictive residency

174 Tumlin, Joaquin, and Natarajan, "A Broken System: Confidential Reports Reveal Failures in U.S. Immigrant Detention Centers."
175 Tumlin et al., "A Broken System."

and those who did not. Some indeed did, and some, under the pressures of being treated like prisoners, started acting the part over time, according to Hemnauth's own account. However, none was being held at Passaic under criminal sentence and many, Hemnauth included, were treated as inherently prone to disorderly and dangerous behavior without any police record of criminal violence — in addition to not being charged with any crime, felony or misdemeanor, violent or not, whose penalty he had not already paid.

"Some sat at the table [to eat], some sat on their bunk." There was not enough table space to accommodate everyone, nor were meal times staggered so everyone could eat at a table.

There were two television sets in the dorm. One was tuned to Spanish television. Both showed commercial television exclusively, whereas at Middlesex they had been entitled to movies on a VCR. Newscasts and sports were popular, and boxing when shown, generally late at night. "Whatever showed up." Hemnauth was not particularly interested, nor were most of the other detainees. Even those prone to throwing their weight around did not waste much willpower in imposing their channel selection, notwithstanding an occasional conflict. "Everybody was thinking about getting out of that place," he exclaims, and not about having the outside world piped in through a cable. "That place was very smelly," he said, returning to the theme emblematic of the constant vexation of life in a very bad jail. "Nothing was nice there," and the best TV programming on the planet was not going to change that. "You can't even see a tree, you know . . . They scratched up the windows in the entire building."

When I asked Hemnauth about coping with boredom, he answered that the bigger problem was stress. "It was difficult to get used to the surroundings, because at any moment you can get this shakedown thing." While over the course of his stay at Passaic there could be lulls of infrequent raids, they could come "every week, or twice a week, day or night. It was quite often." And always with the attack dogs. Guards might stage a raid on no other pretext than to reclaim the mattress or sheets of a departed detainee who left the jail for deportation, transfer or, in rare cases, release. A pod mate who remained behind might use a former inmate's mattress to double his own. Much of life at Passaic consisted of seeking small increments to one's comforts, since the jail provided the barest of minimums. This was a place where detainees ate on their bunks for lack of space at a table, not out of preference for breakfast in bed.

"We liked to save the sheets." The sheets of an inmate no longer in residence could be torn into strips to make clothing lines or, better yet, curtains for the bathroom "so we could poop in private. The bathroom had a wall in front of it with some big holes so that the man in the control room [guard], he could see in the bathroom, too." For some reason, they allowed the curtains between shakedowns, but during raids "they would rip everything apart." Hemnauth almost envied the prisoners in the general population in conventional cells. At least they could "pull in the door and take a leak or something" without someone watching. The immigrant detainees were continually subjected to exposure of their nudity and intimate bodily functions at the whim of the guards. There is little explanation for this obsession for nudity other than the deliberate abasement, the better to exert control, and keep the inmates in the constant companionship of anxiety and stress. Hemnauth's narrative tells us that the tactic succeeded.

A particularly brutal beating took place about one month into Hemnauth's imprisonment at Passaic. "It happened during the day." When the guards arrived for a shakedown, one detainee happened to be showering. The inmates were ordered to the bars. The inmate in the shower asked for a moment's reprieve so he could put some clothes on. His request was taken for a provocation. The guards seized the man. Hemnauth explained to me that as soon as a guard grabs an inmate, a beating always follows. "If they hold you, you're going to get licked." The letter of the Passaic rules, if not their spirit, as conveyed to the detainees, permitted a guard to liberally interpret as hostile virtually any physical gesture by an inmate they are touching. A prisoner who as much as tensed a muscle in reflex to being restrained was construed by the Passaic guards to be resisting. The guards could then step up their use of force. In other words, beat the detainee. This fairly describes the scene Hemnauth observed. The man was dragged, naked, out of the shower and along the floor, his hands over his genitals to protect them as the blows and kicks rained down, including on his face. "They beat him real bad. He had injuries . . . He was yelling. He was feeling pain." The guards pulled him across the block, into the cage by the entrance to the block and through the sealed door into the passageway, where the beating continued. "We heard it. [Once the victim was beyond the door to the block] we couldn't see him. But we heard him." Once the guards had taken the prisoner into the blind passageway, there would have been no more witnesses. One of the guards stepped back inside and grabbed a sheet at random from a bunk to cover the lower body of the still-naked man they had dragged away. When they opened the door to step back out, Hemnauth caught a glimpse of two guards holding up the man they had hurt badly enough for him not to be able to stand on his own.

The one perk Hemnauth availed himself of was a weekly visit to the medical facility, "to check my eyes, check my teeth. Because that was paid for by the INS." He found some mischievous pleasure in making the INS pony up the little it cost to comply with the mechanical provisions of a rules manual. Mischief was not his only purpose. "And I had these boils on my head. I wanted to check my health a little bit because the place was filthy." Rachel Meeropol of the Center for Constitutional Rights, reporting on her first visit with Hemnauth in February 2003, indeed recorded that Hemnauth had not complained about medical care up to that point. The comment refers to the surface adequacy of the nurses' interventions early in Hemnauth's experience, not the limited access to it or other evidence of startling deficiencies.

The full story reflects very poorly on INS and ICE medical practices, particularly if one extends the examination from the limited context of interaction with the nurses to the appalling sanitary conditions at Passaic. Rachel's notes to her files address them in some detail: "The air is making everyone unhealthy. For the last two or three weeks [Hemnauth] has felt this mucus in his throat that he can't swallow . . . All the detainees cough all the time, and take and exchange Vicks' all day long . . . The place is infested with roaches . . . The COs serve [Hemnauth's] cereal with their hands."[176] Also, Hemnauth had entered prison fit and in reasonably good internal health, hence a candidate for perfunctory diagnosis of any discomfort, including the rashes on his scalp from the various infestations that flourished at Passaic. Others, such as Hemnauth's friend Farouk Abdel Muhti, would suffer greatly from the limitations of the medical care offered INS detainees.

Cursory is the most charitable qualifier I can apply to the medical progress

176 Meeropol, "Visit with Passaic Detainees."

notes kept by Passaic while Hemnauth was detained there. Various pains are noted as no more than that, without attempts at formal diagnosis, although, ironically, Hemnauth was given Zantac for the heartburn triggered by the prison food. He was also given an unspecified analgesic cream for muscle pain. He was told, without a written entry to the medical record, that pain and bleeding in his throat was "normal." Much in the notes is completely illegible. Signatures are scribbled without further identification of the attending practitioner, making medical assessments impossible to trace back to whoever made them. Nothing in the medical charts suggests that improvements in sanitary conditions and diet a notch above dismal might deflect the health problems a relatively healthy man like Hemnauth would not otherwise experience, like boils, chronic heartburn and ear pain. There is no record of the blood in his throat that Hemnauth reported to the infirmary that dismissed it as "normal," nor to the damp and freezing dorm where some detainees slept in wet sheets.

Excerpt from medical records of Passaic County Jail medical department

One gets a clearer picture of the jail's — and through it the government's — apathetic approach to the health of inmates from Hemnauth's description of the space that served as makeshift antechamber to the offices where he met with doctors and nurses. Its purpose was to ensure that immigration detainees did not come in contact with the general population should any of its members be visiting the medical facility common to both groups. The jail feared, perhaps with some justification, that such contact could produce friction and physical confrontation. The antechamber in question was one long room fronted with impact-proof glass that had once been a visiting area, with prisoner and guest on either side of the glass barrier as one might see in a television series set in a prison, but abandoned and with the phones removed. The most salient feature of the room was its double duty as both medical waiting area and kennel for the prison dogs, which were simply removed during nurses' and doctors' hours. "When you went in there you found dog pee all over, and dog hair and dog smell." Dog urine stained the walls. Inmates with long waits for medical consultation or treatment sat on the soiled floor between puddles of animal waste. At first, Hemnauth believed that the jail had moved the kenneling operation elsewhere and that eventually the space would be sanitized. He was quickly disabused and curtailed his medical visits for fear of disease.

The universe of medical neglect of immigrants in detention, particularly acute in the five years after Hemnauth's arrival at Passaic, reaches far beyond indifferent treatment by doctors once sick inmates actually gain access to them. A *Washington Post* investigation in 2008 "found a hidden world of flawed medical judgments, faulty administrative practices, neglectful guards, ill-trained technicians, sloppy record-keeping, lost medical files and dangerous staff shortages." And, as if to confirm Hemnauth's apprehension at visiting Passaic's grubby medical facility, such as it was, the investigation noted "evidence that infectious diseases, including tuberculosis and chicken pox, are spreading in the [detention] centers."[177] The kitchen area

177 Priest, Goldstein, and Washington Post Staff Writers, "System of Neglect:
As Tighter Immigration Policies Strain Federal Agencies, the Detainees in Their Care

produced a constant, overpowering stench that Bryan Lonegan, despite his frequent visits to Passaic, never got used to. The harbingers of infection at Passaic — mold on the dormitory walls, air ducts spewing filth, guards dishing food with their bare hands, dog urine on the floor of the medical waiting area — were certainly emblematic of the health neglect that pervades the immigration detention system. They were also a tip of a growing iceberg.

At the latest count made public as of this writing, there have been 122 deaths of immigrants in detention.[178] With an average daily population of over 30,000 detainees, 122 deaths over eight years might seem statistically unremarkable. ICE has cited the statistic as evidence of its good stewardship of immigrant detainee health.[179] However, such an aggregate measurement does not hold up as an indicator of the quality of health stewardship by ICE and its contract jailers. The reality is much more somber than the implications drawn from a raw mortality rate. Under scrutiny, ICE's boast of healthcare prowess falls somewhere between silly and cynical.

Of the deaths in detention that have occurred since the government began tabulating them in 2003, well over half were of people under fifty years old, and a vast majority of this group was under forty. Life expectancy for men in the United States is seventy-five years, an age reached by only two of the 122 recorded deceased. The average age of the dead in immigration detention is forty-six, the median forty-seven. The cause of death for one 24-year-old detainee in California is listed as "natural."[180] The ICE list does not include people who have died prematurely subsequent to their release or deportation.

Beyond any data suggestive of how mortality in immigration custody may or may not be statistically predictable lie too many testimonies to

Often Pay a Heavy Cost."

178 "List of Deaths in ICE Custody, October 2003–July 28, 2011," ICE Health Service Corps.

179 Priest, Goldstein, and Pelley, *Detention in America*.

180 "List of Deaths in ICE Custody."

denial of care, lackadaisical response to emergencies, concern with costs over outcomes, callous accusations by prison staff of fakery on the part of sick detainees, false or vitiated medical charts, cover-up of circumstances of detainee deaths, stonewalling of media investigations and routine exoneration of ICE personnel . . . by ICE.[181] (Much of this abuse occurred before the Obama administration began examining conditions of detention with view to reforming them. The "death roster" — ICE's jargon — has been corrected for missing entries, and the pace of deaths in custody appears to have slowed. However, some ICE officials involved in deflecting media scrutiny still have their jobs, and resistance to reform within an entrenched bureaucracy is predictably stubborn.)

Some of the stories of neglect and abuse of ill detainees that have emerged since Hemnauth's time at Passaic are well documented and spectacularly gruesome.

In 2007, a green card applicant from Guinea who had attempted to re-enter the country was placed unconscious in an isolation cell at Elizabeth County Jail in New Jersey after suffering a skull fracture and brain hemorrhaging. He remained there for thirteen hours before the private prison officials called for medical help. He died in a coma four months later as ICE officials scrambled to pass off the hospital expenses to someone else, including the victim's cousin. Meanwhile, his family was denied access to his medical records and information on the circumstances of his injuries.[182]

In 2008, a detainee in Rhode Island in excruciating pain from cancer and a spinal fracture was accused of faking his discomfort by his jailers and actually taken for a jolting two-hour car ride to Hartford, Connecticut to be pressured to accept deportation. He died shortly thereafter, while still in ICE custody. Originally from Hong Kong, he had arrived as a teen with his parents, had an American wife and child and was picked up for overstaying his visa.[183]

In 2007, another man in detention in California was denied a biopsy of a lesion for ten months, even though the medical department observed a bleeding lesion two days into his detention. When a doctor finally

181 Bernstein, "Officials Hid Truth of Immigrant Deaths in Jail."

182 Bernstein, "Officials Hid Truth"; Bernstein, "Few Details on Immigrants Who Died in Custody."

183 Bernstein, "Ill and in Pain, Detainee Dies in U.S. Hands."

ordered a long overdue biopsy, ICE released him before the biopsy was performed. One can only suspect the agency realized that the detainee's treatment would be very costly for it having neglected the man's condition and its progressive horror. The man underwent penile amputation and died shortly thereafter. In 2010, a unanimous Supreme Court denied his family the right to sue the health officials responsible for his well-being, ruling that the family could sue only the federal government, not individual health personnel.[184] And since death occurred after release, it is excluded from ICE's tally.

An eighty-one-year-old Baptist pastor and *temporary* asylum applicant from Haiti fled extreme gang violence, to Miami, where he was detained by ICE, which also confiscated his medication. His church in Haiti had already been torched and gang leaders had threatened to behead him. He was repeatedly accused of fakery by an ICE medic after falling into medical distress at his asylum hearing, and waited twenty-four hours in an emergency room before being seen by a doctor. He died shackled to his hospital bed, his family denied permission by ICE to visit him in hospital, including his niece, the acclaimed writer Edwidge Danticat.[185] A government inspector general exonerated ICE of any delinquency in fulfilling its duties.[186]

There are reams of further evidence of ICE practices that severely compromised the health of detainees, particularly between the time Hemnauth entered custody and 2008. The evidence ranges from Division of Immigration Health Services (since rechristened ICE Health Services Corps) schedules of savings achieved by denying care to detainees, to a treatment request form requiring detailed answers to eight diagnostic questions in a space measuring less than an inch, to demands for medical records that are nearly impossible to obtain, such as ancient charts and mammograms from a date when a detainee was in custody.[187, 188]

Notwithstanding the oddity of a purportedly trained medic so insensitive as to insist that a frail and frightened eighty-one-year-old man was

184 Barnes, "Immigrant's Survivors Cannot Sue Federal Health Officials, Supreme Court Rules."
185 Danticat, *Brother, I'm Dying.*
186 Priest et al., *Detention in America.*
187 Thomas, "Division of Immigration Health Services (DIHS)."
188 Priest et al., *Detention in America.*

putting on an act, one need not impugn the professionalism of doctors actually administering treatment to inmates in order to question the adequacy of the medical care prescribed by ICE. The best doctors and nurses in the world cannot ensure favorable outcomes when access to them is denied and when the broader health context is one of apathy, neglect and contempt for hygiene. How else does one explain a medical waiting room doubling as a kennel, an unmaintained one at that?

There have been too many other sordid examples throughout the immigration detention network to write them off as mere aberrations. While the official standards for detainee health as revised in 2008[189] have been expanded and tightened as compared to those previously on the books,[190] the Department of Homeland Security's 2009 review of ICE detention conditions outlines in muted but unmistakable terms how woefully inadequate they remain. The report cites, among other failures, inconsistent "management of pandemic and contagious disease," an absent "medical classification system other than a limited use coding of healthy and unhealthy" and the "relaxed professional credentialing procedures" of the contract personnel who make up the predominant share of health care providers in immigrant detention centers.[191] Whatever the improvements currently on the drawing boards, ICE's default practices in terms of prevention, access, diet, hygiene and overcrowding have been so lackadaisical as to appear deliberately callous. One more extrajudicial punishment to add to a lengthy roster.

"Did they know the inmates by name?" I ask Hemnauth.

"They all knew *my* name. I was popular [with the other inmates]." More importantly, "they didn't like me and I didn't like them." What sparked the guards' distrust of Hemnauth was that he had begun to receive regular visits from human rights activists, most frequently from members of the local New Jersey Civil Rights Defense Committee who, along with Rachel Meeropol of the Center for Constitutional Rights, were documenting the

189 "ICE/DRO Detention Standard: Medical Care."
190 "INS Detention Standard: Medical Care."
191 Schriro, "Immigration Detention Overview."

conditions of immigrant detention at Passaic using information passed along by Hemnauth and a few others.

Hemnauth's tone is fairly upbeat when he begins speaking of the regular visits he received from civil rights groups and Rachel in particular. Indeed, his leap into activism and peaceful resistance against the detention regimen at Passaic came to dominate his life and give it the purpose he felt was being stolen from him.

But then, abruptly, his mood swings to one that can be described only as heartbreak as he recalls the visits he received from Rahoni and Kevin and, once, unexpectedly, from his mother. Rahoni had sent for her in Guyana. He speaks at a hushed volume, and I can barely hear him over the whir of the electric fan standing next to us. Kevin, on the few occasions he visited Passaic County Jail, looked "wide-eyed and sad," and scared. Hemnauth did not speak to him directly very much, unable to explain to a ten-year-old how his father had abandoned him for a filthy dungeon, and had to talk to his son from the other side of a partition. He was also afraid of breaking down himself and causing further damage to Kevin. "I didn't want that." Rather, he concentrated on Rahoni, remaining as jovial as he could as he deflected attention away from himself and inquired what was going on "outside." He hoped that Rahoni, later, would be able to explain to Kevin what was going on with his father and shield him from fear, grief and spite.

By all indications, she was successful. The singular victory they all won over the intransigence of the detention and deportation apparatus was that Kevin never for a single instant blamed his father for the ordeal they all went through, nor even considered that he, as his son, had been abandoned. Later, Kevin would tell me that he knew his dad had "messed up" with the drug arrest, but to his mind that neither explained nor justified the arbitrary wreckage the system had sought to inflict.

Hemnauth's mother's one visit to the jail was unbearable, and he could hardly stand to speak of it years later as I sat with him in Trinidad. "I saw my mother cry man, that was the worst . . . I didn't want her to see me like that. Talking through a glass window. I hated it. It was the worst moment in my life." The moment left him shaken. He wrote a note to Rachel Meeropol in July 2003, telling her how worried he was about the effect of his imprisonment on his mother. "I would be really glad if you can at least talk to my mom and let her know that I'm OK . . . I left her last year [in Guyana] looking good and rosey [sic] and when she came to the jail. It looks like what happened to me has really took [sic] a toll on her."

During a break in our conversation, I ask Hemnauth if he has a picture of Kevin. He shuffles through some documents and finds a snapshot of his son and mother taken at the time of her trip to see Hemnauth at Passaic. They are posing in the breeze, on a ferryboat, with Liberty Island and its iconic lady of welcome, beacon raised high, as their backdrop.

9

CODE OF CONTEMPT

HEMNAUTH BEGAN ORGANIZING HIS RESISTANCE TO the conditions at Passaic about a month after arriving. The key was getting messages to the outside world through channels that were equipped to garner media attention and legal resources. Hemnauth assumed the task of gathering and formulating those messages and assembling them into a lucid and persuasive portrayal of Passaic as a den of abuse. Early on he recognized that his experiences alone would not suffice to rally support for concerted action against the Passaic regime, and through it condemnation of the immigrant detention gulag in its entirety.

He had a full plate: fighting his despair as his own case settled into official oblivion, tending to his spiritual calling, maintaining his health and strength, remaining artistically engaged, providing the legal advice he could by drawing from his own ordeal in immigration court, cultivating a semblance of unity among like-minded detainees, taking notes, recording stories, writing letters, establishing connections to activists willing to help him and his co-inmates.

Just like at Middlesex, he teamed with Farouk Abdel-Muhti. Farouk knew whom to call as the first cog in a possible network of advocates: Dr. Flavia Alaya, a Fulbright scholar, retired college professor, social historian, preservationist and prolific author. She was also a tireless and passionate civil rights activist. She had cofounded the New Jersey Civil Rights Defense Committee (NJCRDC), a grassroots league that nonetheless proved effective in organizing for the Passaic detainees. She also sat on the board of the Bill of Rights Defense Committee, prominent in due process protection. Since she knew of Farouk, she readily accepted his collect calls.

At first, Hemnauth's system was a clandestine one. Word got around to the other blocks that he wanted to pass reports of abuse to sympathetic ears outside the jail, who would then attempt to build a civil rights case against Passaic and bring legal resources to individual detainees. Detainees, particularly those who had been subjected to beatings by the guards, passed along accounts of incidents to Hemnauth. Flavia had easily impressed upon Hemnauth the need to document as many incidents and other examples of ill treatment as possible. For her part, she enlisted several people from within the NJCRDC and elsewhere to regularly visit Hemnauth and Farouk and amass a body of evidence.

Since the immigrant inmates lived in tightly confined quarters with few excursions away from their dorm — they did not have a mess hall to go to for meals, and recreation hours away from the dorm were awarded stingily — the jail did not impose a curfew on top of it all. "There is no lockdown time, because we are permanently locked down." The inmates could stay up as late at night as they wanted, which is precisely what Hemnauth and Farouk did in order to work once the dorm fell quiet. "When everyone had gone to bed, we would go the tables, sit down and write some letters . . . while everyone was sleeping." The noise during the day could be deafening and constant and was a real impediment to accomplishing anything that demanded lengthy concentration, such as the letter writing. Farouk and Hemnauth lived in the same dorm area, although the guards "separated us a couple of times" when they became suspicious of what the pair was up to. Farouk was transferred from Passaic about five months into their stay. Hemnauth would catch up with him much later at Hudson County Jail. Once Farouk left, Hemnauth continued his resistance to jailers' behavior on his own.

The visits from representatives of civil rights groups placed Hemnauth in a category distinct from his jailmates in the eyes of the guards. Hemnauth was not seeking and never did solicit dispensation from the officers above what he was advocating for everyone. Still, since he was receiving regular visits from people intent on action on behalf of the immigrant detainees, the guards were more likely to think twice before assaulting him physically — although they were sorely tempted, as subsequent altercations document. A man with bruises and scars would add graphic evidence to the already compelling testimony Hemnauth was compiling on the conditions of detention. That was the good news.

The bad news is that visits other than those from an attorney could be monitored. Rahoni's apparently were.[192] "They don't get a contact visit, just through a very small glass window. One time [Hemnauth] was on the [visitor's] phone telling his wife about how bad conditions were at Passaic and the officers cut his line right then. It wasn't time [for Rahoni] to go, and everyone else's phone was still operating normally. Then they put him back through, but he could still hear all this clicking, and the line kept going in and out."[193]

Hemnauth gradually became the designated spokesman for his jailmates, along with Farouk until he was transferred, first to another floor of the prison apparently segregated for Muslim inmates, then to jails in York County Jail in Pennsylvania, Bergen County and ultimately Hudson County, the last two back in New Jersey. Even before Farouk's removal from Passaic, while Farouk was in partnership with him, Hemnauth assumed most of the duties for communicating with the outside world. In addition, not only was he skilled in laying out his testimony, but his honesty inspired confidence in the civil rights advocates who were envisaging a class action lawsuit against the jail and the INS. Rachel Meeropol's first impressions of Hemnauth are telling: "Hemnauth is a great guy. He was very easy to talk to, and had an amazingly laid back and sunny disposition, considering his present circumstances. He is a musician and still composes music. He has done charity work for churches his whole life. I think he would make a fabulous plaintiff." For anyone preparing to file a plea, a certain quotient of charisma in the lead plaintiff is an indisputable asset. However, Rachel, to be sure, was

---

192 In 2004, the American Bar Association noted Passaic's violation of ICE phone standards by "failing to post notification by the telephones when calls were being monitored." See Tumlin et al., "A Broken System."

193 Meeropol, "Visit with Passaic Detainees." Other quotes from and references to statements by Rachel Meeropol in this chapter are sourced from memoranda to her files at the Center for Constitutional Rights between February 6, 2003 and September 8, 2003 and from correspondence addressed to Hemnauth at Passaic. Copies were kindly provided by Ms. Meeropol with Hemnauth's permission under rules commonly governing client-attorney relations.

not relying on charm over substance — which Passaic provided in spades. Still, even the most legitimate grievances, such as those against Passaic, are most effectively voiced by plaintiffs who can best withstand extraneous attacks on their credibility. From that perspective, Hemnauth, the very picture of guilelessness, devotion and community involvement was, indeed, a fabulous plaintiff.

In the meantime, an alliance of the human rights groups honed in on the conditions at Passaic. The began a campaign of protests and appeals to various authorities, informed in large part by Hemnauth's detailed insights covering everything from the deficient ventilation to the use of dogs, "the whole works." The areas near the jail in Paterson, New Jersey include residential and commercial streets, such that there were a fair amount of passers-by in the vicinity who were bound to notice activity or commotion by the prison gate. As an irritant to the sheriff, the protests were just getting started. Hence Speziale's later appearance "to commit truth" on Lou Dobbs' CNN program through fabrication, and deflect blame for prison conditions on the overarching need to treat criminals harshly, a penal responsibility that was not his to assume. Nor did Speziale discuss how malnourishment, appalling hygiene and medical neglect complied with an effective correctional program, even if the design of such a program indeed fell under his jurisdiction, which it did not. The early demonstrations and letters from detainees, many written in Hemnauth's hand, triggered a meeting with the county freeholders, the designation given to elected county supervisors in New Jersey. The meeting was arranged by Jeannette Gabriel and Flavia Alaya.

In speaking with me, Hemnauth confused the term *freeholder* with the word *shareholder*, ironically believing the members of Passaic County's governing body to be the owners of the jail building and beneficiaries of the profits it generated. *Freeholder* has its etymological roots in the notion of property ownership. While the members of Passaic's legislature obviously do not hold title to public assets, Hemnauth was not as wide of the mark as one might think, if for no other reason than the existence of a federal contract that paid Passaic County per inmate and per day. The detainees were certainly aware of the administrative degree of separation between the INS and a county sheriff, just as they were even more keenly attuned to the stinginess in the provisioning by the jail of food, living space, safety, hygiene, phone calls, visitation, recreation and health care. A later investigation preparatory to a civil action against Passaic County Jail in 2008 confirmed that the county received substantial revenues for housing federal detainees.

"Of course, they did not allow them to speak to me," Hemnauth recalls, speaking of the visit to the jail by the freeholders. He was clearly the witness his jailers wanted to keep far from any opportunity to air grievances within earshot of county officials, not just his own, but of the consensus he represented far too effectively to the taste of the prison brass. "But they did provide a few detainees to speak" to the meeting of protesters, warden, sheriff and freeholders. Jeannette Gabriel did produce letters Hemnauth had written on behalf of the immigrant detainees and signed by many of them, and turned them over to the freeholders present. The sheriff also led a prison walk-through and allowed the freeholders to speak to an additional small number of detainees, but Hemnauth was studiously excluded from any contact with the visitors. Nevertheless, the meeting produced some effect, loosening the relative secrecy and impunity in which Passaic operated. The cat was out of the bag or, more accurately, the canines. "The dogs were the big thing," Hemnauth says. The freeholders had not imagined attack dogs as central to Passaic's control procedures.

After the meeting, Hemnauth did get some respite from the mayhem of his surroundings, although it would be short-lived. He got a "pack up your shit" order from an officer — another customary mark of disdain for anything a detainee might value — and was transferred to another floor with quarters the jail had set apart for Muslim detainees. (This may have been a temporary arrangement during Ramadan.) Farouk was there; he had not yet been relocated to Hudson County Jail. Apparently the guards were not fully aware that he and Hemnauth had been resisting conditions at Passaic in concert. The space was quieter and less exposed to shakedowns and other repressive conduct on the part of the guards. It was also Ramadan, which may have inspired the jail to allow Muslim inmates some contemplative serenity. Farouk and Hemnauth continued their advocacy, with some emphasis on assisting individual inmates with their legal filings. The beneficiaries included a detained nuclear scientist by the name of Ali whom the INS had been moving from jail to jail, reluctant to return him to Pakistan. Hemnauth carved out some time to exercise his technical knowledge of climate conditioning systems by drawing A/C wiring diagrams. He was preparing for his release to wherever that might be. He knew he would be eager for employment.

Hemnauth's immediate surroundings may have changed — temporarily — but the abysmal food did not. In fact it was made worse in the new quarters, where inmates were denied a kettle to heat water for tea or for the ramen noodles the commissary carried. The data we have on food expenditures at the prison clearly suggest that cost was the variable driving the policies and practices of Passiac's pantry and kitchens. Under those circumstances, uncooked canned corn or boiled beans as a main course were to be expected. More puzzling was the kitchen's refusal to add salt or seasoning to anything they cooked, if what they produced can qualify as cooking. The imposed blandness appears to have been deliberate, another way of wearing the inmates' spirits. What other motivation could there possibly have been? Certainly a pinch of salt would not have dented the provider's profits on the meal plan in any perceptible measure. Even spaghetti was cooked without salt and served plain. "They just boiled it in water and handed it to you." More forage than human fare. "Everything is tasteless. It was like that every day."

Hemnauth knew that the food service had been outsourced to a private company, and he readily recognized the name Aramark when I mentioned it. "I had a meeting with them" to voice his complaints. Ironically, "a big, fat guy," who was the head cook and designated "dietician," along with an INS agent. The "dietician" attempted to assuage Hemnauth and his confederates with a presentation claiming that the meals included all essential nutrients "for a balanced diet," and outlining what those nutrients were. Hemnauth simply responded that what the Passaic kitchen served was barely fit to feed animals: they also receive essential nutrients, he told them. "We hit him real hard. He said he would try to improve it, but he never did. You would get a good meal Christmas, Easter and Thanksgiving," and that was all. Actually, Hemnauth's first Christmas menu of his detention consisted of cold beans straight from the can sprinkled with vinegar, with a supper of the leftovers the following day.

The unhappiness over the food was "a big issue," and Hemnauth pinpointed the purposefully repressive nature of the stingy and cheerless diet. His years of poverty had inured him to frugality, and he neither expected nor even desired haute cuisine. After all, this was a man who had lived successively in a van and an unheated basement and worked a job knee-deep in rats. So the dissent over the jail food was serious and no whim. Not even close. Against a landscape whose features already included separation from his son and surrender of his future, the numbing indignity of the Passaic diet seemed consciously designed to further dehumanize him and erase all vestiges of hope. As stern as IIRIRA is, there is nothing in the law that ever precluded the INS, its successor agency ICE and Hemnauth's jailers from treating their charges like human beings. Rather, they chose to compound the misery of detention by debasing so much as the fundamental act that kept their prisoners alive: eating. They have never answered for it.

Simple budget analysis suggests that the food policy at Passaic blended low cost and poor nutrition. In 2002, Passaic hired Aramark Correctional Services to feed its inmates, a division of a large multinational corporation specializing in, among other things, institutional food services for everything from university campuses and company canteens to prisons and sports arenas. In 2002, reports in the food service trade press announced an annual $2.3 million contract to supply meals for 1,900 Passaic inmates, a number that would include the general population and INS/ICE detainees. The contract price covered food provisioning, meal preparation, depreciation and Aramark's operating profit expectation.[194] It does not take higher mathematics to derive the daily expenditure on calories per inmate: about three dollars for not one, but three meals. Less on days when they served a fraction of a bag of chips and an ounce of peanut butter for dinner.

I was able to question a former Aramark corporate executive whose candor and familiarity with Aramark's prison business I have every reason to trust. I recounted the reports of immigrant detainees receiving a spoonful of beans cold from a can for dinner, and asked if Aramark's business

---

194 "Aramark Corporation Form 10-K," Securities and Exchange Commission.

strategy was contingent on serving stingy rations devoid of any attempt to make them more than marginally palatable to a human being. No, I was told, and I believe truthfully: beans dished straight from a can onto a plate would not meet Aramark's corporate guidelines for the division, which included prescriptions for calories, protein, fiber and vitamins.

However, this executive did not deny the plausibility of what I reported. The reality of Aramark's correctional business reflected a reliance on literally thousands of individual contracts between the jailers and the company. The company's ethos dictated that each Aramark manager entering into a contract had to strike a balance between the prerogatives of the jail and the satisfaction of the people eating the food Aramark served. However, each contract was different, and each Aramark manager essentially acted at his or her own discretion as long as the deal was profitable. On the other side of the table from the Aramark representative sat, ultimately, a local official typically under political pressure, at least tacit, not to be seen as coddling prisoners with gourmet cuisine. Hence, it was entirely possible that in some cases — which the executive characterized as in the small minority if not entirely isolated — a manager might surrender to local politics and deliver meals far below the Aramark corporate standard in order to hit a depressed pricing target. The executive did not refute the idea that this is precisely what may have occurred at Passaic and did not appear surprised by my depiction.

The implicit abuse is stunning on several levels, most of them obvious, such as serving food to inmates much in the same manner as one might pour kibble into a dog's feeding bowl, except with less affection and concern for the subject's health. Equally remarkable, however, is the notion that the official negotiating the food service contract would even consider as pertinent the local public's reaction to how lavishly, or not, immigrant detainees were nourished. The detainees at Passaic were not in custody pursuant to any offense committed against any party in Passaic County or the state of New Jersey. They were not prisoners of Passaic County or the state of New Jersey. They were there because Passaic wanted them there as a source of federal contract revenue for the county. Full stop. Period. The citizens of the county had absolutely no standing to determine whether federal immigrant detainees were being coddled, even less to complain if they thought they were. Somewhere along the line, officials acting on behalf of the county's fiscal interests violated the boundaries of their juris-diction. Why? Because they could. Passaic would be neither the first nor the last local jurisdiction in which such trespass would occur, and diet would not be the only matter in which local authorities would exert abusive power over immigrant detainees in their care under federal contract and extract political benefits for doing so. ICE for its part failed to impose its own authority, and not only in this instance.

Reading Hemnauth's letters and testimony regarding the diet at Passaic, I had an epiphanic recollection of a medieval history course I took as a student at the University of Brussels. One lecture was on monastic life in the Middle Ages. There was, given the period, a socioeconomic element to men being attracted to abbeys as insurance against the dire ravages of penury. I also remember clearly the professor's comments about the role of sitting down to meals in the monks' daily routine. In a life of numbing mo-notony and confinement — spatial, social and aspirational — dinnertime was the one slice of the waking day that provided any diversion or measur-able gratification. It followed that the quality of the monks' food and drink was of cardinal importance to them, almost a matter of survival against despondency. (A byproduct of the paramount relevance of food and bev-erage for men in a restrictive institution is available today wherever finer brews are sold: beer from Belgian abbey breweries founded half a millen-nium ago and more.) When Passaic, acting as an agent of the federal gov-ernment, substituted pleasureless, minimalist feedings for meals — without as much as adequate space at a dining table — it was, in effect, fostering despondency and injury to the mental health of the people in its care.

Hemnauth began his first hunger strike — not his last — specifically in support of Farouk. "He was sickly," Hemnauth explains. The strike was specifically over the food. Hemnauth's later strike encompassed the other brutalities of the jail regimen. Farouk aimed to be released. Ramadan had just ended. Hemnauth had joined the Muslim inmates in fasting. It seemed natural to do so as resident in (except for him) an all-Muslim block. The month of fasting during daylight hours dampened the transition to a full-blown hunger strike. It lasted eight or nine days, but neither Hemnauth nor Farouk had said their final word.

They were once again separated. Hemnauth was sent back to the dorm he had left when he was moved to the Muslim block. As the first winter set in, so did the cold in the dorm where Hemnauth was confined, adding to the vexation of the livestock-grade diet. "It was extremely cold. There was no heat. We were living in winter without heat and [with] cold air coming in" through the broken vents. Actually blowing in from Hemnauth's description. Water, too, and with the overcrowding, some inmates would need to sleep adjacent to the dripping from the ceiling. When word of the Siberian cold got to the INS, but not before, the officers distributed blankets. Not that the INS became overly concerned. "They said they would take care of it," but rather than order the prison to repair the building and its heating system, it was they who suggested blankets as a remedy. The jail apparently had a supply in inventory. The inmates would remain wrapped in them all day. "The blankets didn't work." In one protest, the inmates in the freezing block staged a sleep strike, standing for an entire night in "shakedown position."

The warden saw where this might be going: to a prison riot or scrutiny by the INS that could put the federal contract in jeopardy. He thought it wise to heed this particular grievance. He moved the prisoners from the heatless dorm to a conventional cellblock, two bunks per cell, connected to a common room with tables and a couple of television sets. Farouk was not among them. He had begun another hunger strike to win his freedom and had been isolated from the other inmates. He was moved to Bergen County Jail shortly thereafter where, Hemnauth later learned, he continued to strike, was placed in solitary confinement and endured beatings. For two months, correspondence between Hemnauth and Farouk mysteriously disappeared. They put the pieces together when they were reunited at Hudson County Jail before Farouk's release and Hemnauth's deportation.

"The cells were the best part of the jail." Being moved there "was a good thing." The configuration differed radically different from the dorm blocks in that there was no control room in its center robbing the residents of all semblance of privacy. "Most of the time I spent by myself" writing, drawing, painting and otherwise keeping occupied. He was assigned a cell-mate by the name of Michael, a fellow Guyanese by origin, but clearly American in every other aspect, particularly his speech and upbringing. "He talked like a Yankee." Hemnauth describes him, somewhat affectionately, as a "bad boy," who tangled frequently with the guards. "He was very strong. He was the strongest man among everybody." So strong that the guards gave him a trustee job in the general population until the INS got wind of it. He was also, in Hemnauth's assessment, sharply intelligent. Hemnauth encouraged him to kick his penchant for physical altercations and fight with his brain instead. The man later sued to demand monetary damages for wrongful arrest and won, according to what Hemnauth later learned from Bryan Lonegan.

With Farouk gone, Hemnauth began to forge closer ties with the relatively large contingent of Jamaican and Dominican prisoners, who were growing increasingly anxious about gaining legal representation and fighting their removal. "They began to listen to me, then." Farouk had used a more confrontational verbal style that was not always effective in mobilizing others. Hemnauth's manner was more persuasive, even if he urged the other inmates to protest their condition as forcefully as Farouk had. Now when Hemnauth envisaged a collective hunger strike out loud, many more inmates would listen and agree with its premises even if they were reluctant to commit to joining one. It was also true that months into their detention at Passaic, virtually none of the transferees from Middlesex was making progress with his case or petition for parole. "We were stuck inside." With Farouk's removal from Passaic, the group became wary of being moved around as well. Not that they enjoyed Passaic, but rather that they saw the transfers as an ICE tactic intended to disrupt contact with the outside world, including attorneys and civil rights advocates, and blot the little shards of light any of them might have seen at the end of their tunnels.

The relative tranquility that reigned in the cellblock could not insulate it from fights when a belligerent inmate was determined to provoke one, and others were predisposed to meeting force with force. Anyone else, Hemnauth among them, would be caught in the middle with no escape path. Even if a majority studiously avoided joining any violence, it poisoned the prison atmosphere and brought collective retribution from the guards, who inferred some level of collective guilt in any disturbance.

As winter drew to an end, so did the residency in the cellblock, with its relative comfort. The removal of the group of immigrants from the cells may have been in retaliation for a fight sparked by racial taunts from one of two Russian inmates during a card game with a West Indian detainee, a friend of Hemnauth's named Marcus. Once the verbal altercation had run its course, the Russian put on his boots in a gesture called "strapping up," a signal that he wanted to brawl. The onus shifted to the other Russian — who happened to be a boxer, as Hemnauth knew from seeing him work out — to either broker a peace or take sides. He "strapped up."

The guards came quickly with their dogs "and the works." They placed Marcus in solitary confinement and moved the Russians to a different location in the jail. The fight also spelled the end to the idyll in the cellblock as the other inmates in it got assigned to a dorm with triple-bunk sleeping partitions, the high one twenty-four inches from the ceiling. It was impossible to sit up for lack of clearance. The dorm was too small for the number of residents, but the jail did not dare place them back in the heatless space that had almost provoked some real trouble. The common toilets were open along a passageway in full view of prison personnel passing through it, including women. The presumed purpose of limiting hygienic privacy was to be sure all could be accounted for during roll calls.

The guards gave no reason for moving the inmates from the cells. Hemnauth believes it was a combination of penalty for the fight and the jail reserving the area for more "celebrity" detainees, such as a suspected terrorist who was held in permanent cell lockup. He arrived shortly before Hemnauth left the cellblock. "He did not come out [of his cell]," which he occupied alone, except at night when guards would take him for a walk and to shower. When I asked him if he ever talked to the alleged terrorist, Hemnauth told me that he preferred not to. The man's cell door did not open like the others, and Hemnauth felt it was undignified to approach another person as one might an animal in a zoo cage. "You have a reflection of your own self."

As real as was Hemnauth's neighborly disposition, beneath the surface some real despair had begun to surface and simmer. His legal case lay dormant. His dread of being in lockup at Passaic forever joined a genuine fear for his person and the clear-headed apprehension that he might get dragged into fights simply in order to defend himself. While there is no reason to believe that the majority of immigrant inmates at Passaic had a record of violent offenses, mixing even a small minority of violence-prone detainees into the overall population and then imposing a prison regimen that stoked some very raw survival instincts amounted to lighting a slow-burning fuse. About four months after his transfer to Passaic, Hemnauth wrote that his block had become overcrowded — a perennial complaint against Passaic, and a major component of the later lawsuit against the prison and the county — with a predictable impact on "noise, arguing and fighting." The jail had also moved at least one physically aggressive man with very obvious mental disorders to Hemnauth's ward. "I don't think I can spend the summer here . . . I can't believe what is happening to me. It's very depressing." Ominously, he wrote to Rachel: "I'll let you know if I go on a hunger strike."

He was not kidding. However, his early inspiration for another strike was triggered not by general depression, but again by the abysmal quality of the food, so bad that it is impossible to dismiss his persistent protestations against it as the least bit trivial. "The food has gone sloppy," Hemnauth wrote the following February, and went on to describe a meal comprised of one-fifth of a small bag of potato chips and one tablespoon of peanut butter. The "diet people" refused to eat it, that is, vegetarians like Hemnauth, or inmates with other dietary limitations, such as halal strictures, that would have compelled them to turn down the standard-issue tray. Assuming, generously, that the regular meal was of acceptable quality, serving chips or cold beans as the main culinary event for those who required an alternative diet was paramount to imposing an additional punishment on inmates with religious or health requirements. One more entry to the litany of unsanctioned retribution visited upon immigrant detainees.

With evidence accumulating, Flavia and her coadvocate at the NJCRDC, Jeannette Gabriel, attracted several others to the cause of the Passaic detainees and to Hemnauth's predicament in particular. One was an organization by the name of Desis Rising Up and Moving, or DRUM, which acts on behalf of South Asian immigrants with a twin focus on immigration rights and wage abuse. Another was the Center for Constitutional Rights, represented by Rachel Meeropol. Rachel, as a CCR attorney, undertook to compile materials supportive of a civil rights class action suit. She and Jeannette Gabriel also solicited legal assistance for individual detainees from other lawyers. (Rachel, herself, did not specialize in immigration law. She is a recognized expert in the legal ramifications of prison conditions throughout the United States and at Guantánamo Bay, and in the racial profiling by law enforcement.) Rachel began to make regular visits to Passaic, encouraged to find in Hemnauth a counterpart both outspoken and capable.

Client-to-attorney rules insulated the conversations between her and Hemnauth from eavesdropping by the guards. "We ended up in a room where we could shake hands" as opposed to speak by phone on opposite sides of a glass barrier. It would take the jail the better part of a year to realize that Hemnauth was supplying evidence for a legal complaint, even as the relationship of trust and genuine friendship grew between Hemnauth and Rachel. She confided to Hemnauth that her interest in combating government-sanctioned abuse was inspired by the fate of her grandparents, Julius and Ethel Rosenberg, at the hands of the state.

"I was enjoying giving information about what goes on inside." Rachel also gave Hemnauth guidance on how to draw other inmates into collectively voicing their grievances against jail conditions and the behavior of the guards. It was not always a simple matter to overcome the inherent cautiousness of many of the other inmates fearful of the consequences of being perceived as stirring up trouble. There was also some clustering by national origin, with certain groups more intrepid than others. "I was able to convince my Jamaican friends to be partners with me in this thing." By this, he means getting others in the immigration wards to sign letters and testimonials. "They're the big bad boys, so when they sign everyone signs." Hemnauth had designed a process by which everyone would agree on a portrayal of prison conditions or the circumstances of an incident or set of incidents. "A whole lot of things." Hemnauth would then draft a letter to Rachel for use as evidence and gather signatures. One such letter attracted over a hundred signatures, a large majority of the two adjacent dorms. Hemnauth either passed them on to Rachel during a visit or mailed them using his stamp allowance.

I was a little surprised that Hemnauth would drop a letter in the jail's outgoing mailbox, lest it be inspected by the officers and leveraged against the detainees who had signed a detailed and pointed complaint against them. Apparently, the officers believed the letters addressed detainees' legal situation, not the conditions of their detention. (Hemnauth was also unaware that his letters to Farouk at Bergen had been misplaced, and vice versa.) "Remember, they don't care about our immigration problems. All they care about is that we stay quiet at their place and they make money off of us." Or, if they did care about the disposition of the inmates' cases, they were confident that most pleas for relief would not be heard. Hemnauth suspects that later on, once the jailers had caught on to the airing by Hemnauth of serious grievances against them, they began to read letters and destroy some of them. Regardless, the Passaic detainees had been allowed enough leeway to get their cat out of its bag. At one point, Hemnauth also made an appeal by phone to a free-speech radio station.

None of his activities endeared him to the guards, with the exception of one sergeant: a cousin of one of the human rights militants who frequently came to visit Hemnauth on his way to or from his work.

As averse as he was to violent confrontation, Hemnauth could not always dissuade every inmate determined to pick a fight with him. Sadly, his first physical altercation pitted him against a young inmate from Africa who was so deeply disturbed that he was later released on a mental health discharge. Naturally, the fight started over something very silly. Hemnauth had objected to the other inmate's removing Hemnauth's belongings from a vacant bunk where he had stored them. By this time, Hemnauth's bunkmate, Slate, had impressed upon him that letting matters slide in a disagreement with another detainee was a sign of weakness and detrimental to one's chances of survival in the charged and overcrowded prison environment, where territorial boundaries are sacred. Hemnauth stood by his objection, and the other inmate threw a punch. Hemnauth caught his arm, gripped it tightly and grabbed his neck with his free arm in order to hold him off. Slate egged Hemnauth on, urging him to stand his ground: "This is jail, man!" As a crowd of inmates gathered, Hemnauth yelled at Slate to help him stop the fight. Slate's jailhouse wisdom, acquired apparently through experience, was that it was better for two men to settle a score then to risk a broader melee and a particularly vigorous shakedown by guards on riot alert and armed with pepper spray. When the other inmate would not relent, Hemnauth's temper started to flare and he began to fight back more vigorously. "The madness came over me, and I hurt him then," Hemnauth confesses, although "not badly." The guards arrived with the dogs, separated the men and placed them in individual isolation cells, or "bull pens." The dorm got its shakedown, absent the pepper spray. "It was an opportunity" for the guards.

"Some of the guards treated me with respect. They knew I was having lots of visits. [Sometimes] two a day. Some of the other inmates were there for years with no visits" in unspeakably sad abandonment and complete exposure to the whims of the jailers. "They knew I had people behind me. They would avoid ill-treating me then. They would speak nicely and everything. Those visits meant a lot." (Rachel, Flavia, Jeannette and another human rights activist by the name of Tommy Silva came by routinely.) A sergeant on night shift was assigned to sentencing Hemnauth to some retribution for fighting. A typical sentence would have been five or six days in solitary confinement. Knowing Hemnauth and doubting he would have willfully provoked a rumble, the sergeant sent him back to his block.

The respect from the officers would not last, with a few exceptions. It was grudging and defensive in the first place, also with one or two exceptions. The officers quickly came to realize that Hemnauth would not reward any charm offensive with complacency in his reporting to his visitors or in his letters of prison conditions, and of the brutality and constant menace around him. Some of the guards could not or would not contain their hostility under any circumstances, regardless of the disciplinary slaps on the wrist some would occasionally receive. More rarely a guard might be laid off, and in one instance Hemnauth reported that one was fired and a sergeant demoted, temporarily. From Hemnauth's observations, there was no perceptible method to the prison taking such consequential action against a guard as dismissal or suspension. And in any event, occasional disciplining of the officers may have offered brief moments of reprieve in the oppression of the inmates. They were never sustained.

Hemnauth's clash with the troubled fellow inmate was not the gravest he would be pushed to, and it was relatively benign compared to other skirmishes he had already seen and to the beatings he had already witnessed guards mete out to their targets. The supervising officer had effectively exonerated him of guilt in the incident by waiving a penalty he could have imposed.

Nevertheless, the fight was a signal moment in his slide toward despair. He was probably headed there anywhere, because it is hard to believe that the very purpose of Passaic, evident in its contrast with the relatively benign regimen at Middlesex, was not to break him. However, the fight bespoke a tide of dehumanization. It was rising and now lapped at his feet. For all his determination to deflect and defuse any violence that arose around him, and despite his example of peaceful resistance to the Passaic order, he could not stop the wave. Slow it perhaps, but not stop it.

He was well past the six-month milestone at Passaic, and his case had fallen into a quicksand of oblivion. He was completely in the dark, unaware of any movement. For all he knew, he might be at Passaic forever.

Outwardly, he remained occupied between gathering evidence of jailer abuse for the human rights committees who now had Passaic on their radars, composing music and lyrics (albeit without the benefit of a guitar), drawing and painting on paper and bits of textile. He carved out time for prayer, something of a challenge in the noisy and reverberant jail block. Much of Hemnauth's art is inspired from Hindu scripture and tradition, but not all of it. His paintings, he says with pride, are of his own personal inspiration on contemporary themes.

He crafted greeting cards, including the poems, and other illustrations for his fellow detainees happy to have something cheerful to send to loved ones. Hemnauth remembers a Vietnamese detainee who wanted gifts to send his wife and children as evidence that he had not forgotten his head-of-household responsibilities toward them, even if he was not in a position to fulfill them. A Jamaican inmate credited a Valentine card Hemnauth made for him for salvaging his relationship with his girlfriend. Hemnauth normally donated the work solicited of him, at least until some of his friends convinced him he was being too much of a patsy and that receiving a little extra commissary money or payment in kind would not be improper. So "whatever they gave me, I accepted," including five dollars' worth of chocolate bars in appreciation for the heroic Valentine card.

The Valentine story was my cue to ask Hemnauth how inmates coped with sexual starvation, a delicate question given his own modesty and discretion on the topic. "Actually, in there, your mind has been taken up. You really forget about that," he answered. Celibacy is, of course, a consequence of any imprisonment, yet Hemnauth's reaction is revealing both of him and the atmosphere. "They [the inmates] don't try to remind themselves of [sex] . . . like that doesn't exist. You look to learn more about yourself. Lust is eliminated. You always have this tension, looking out for the police and the dogs. I took my mind away from things by writing poems and songs and painting. Others played cards, lifted weights. They never mention their sex life." Inmates who had served time prior to immigration detention talked about their prison experience "and how to survive in it," a topic that gained everyone's attention.

Hemnauth also worked an occasional prison job, folding the laundry the jail took in from a nearby hospital. The position was shared among about ten inmates who solicited a sergeant after a social worker encouraged them to do so. The jobs were mostly intended for men with "nothing else in their lives" or absolutely no source of money for the commissary or the highway-robbery phone calls, no marketable skill such as Hemnauth's for illustration and verse. He also offered to use his documented technical qualifications to repair the A/C system. The jail actually considered the idea — or claimed to have done — but rejected it on the grounds that such a job would require that he be issued tools and might expose the jail to medical expenses, which the INS would not cover should he be injured in the practice of an unsanctioned activity. Folding clothes entailed no such danger. Hemnauth appeared to accept the explanation he was given for not being allowed to fix the jail's dysfunctional heating and cooling apparatus, despite the jail's studied indifference to the misery it was causing the detainees. Perhaps he was even more inured to litigiousness in American society than he was suspicious of his jailers' motives. Similarly, inmates were not allowed to work in the kitchen, ostensibly to prevent them from cutting their fingers.

In any event, Hemnauth figured that he was more useful as a scribe and advisor to other inmates than as kitchen patrol, in addition to spearheading advocacy on behalf of Passaic's detainees. Sometimes his assistance in filing motions and other papers would extend to members of the general population who shared the law library with the immigrant detainees. Notwithstanding his eagerness to help others with their cases, his effectiveness as a paralegal was, per force, infinitesimal given the impenetrable architecture and jargon of the legal code, especially as it applied to immigration. Still, for what it was worth, he had learned to recognize similarities among various cases and what elements pertinent to a filing were transferable from one to another. His knowledge was certainly very rudimentary compared to an attorney's, but more than that of the average Passaic inmate. By regulation, contact with any non-INS inmate had to be mediated by a trustee, one of whom was Hemnauth's friend Marcus who had been drawn into the fight with the Russian inmates. Marcus habitually signed the letters of protest Hemnauth drafted.

Normally, the immigration and general populations are to be strictly separated, and there is good reason for this. General-population inmates are either serving time or awaiting trial for a crime. By legal definition, immigrant detainees are not. For their protection, they cannot be in contact with convicts. The reality is that jails that neglect this separation —

Border drawing from a handwritten letter from Hemnauth to Rachel Meeropol. "The flower and the hands in prayer is man in the flesh. The body is like a flower: it grows, it beautifies and it dies. It is in the duration of that time that we have to use it to do the right things."

and many have — place detainees in further jeopardy from the frequent hostility toward them on the part of inmates from the general population. Transgression of the rule to the detriment of the detainees did occur at Passaic, but comingling was not the worst of the jail's malfeasance. Hemnauth's contacts with the general population were specific to the men he helped with legal papers and research, and therefore benign. Fees for his services would often come on a food tray or book cart as chocolate or a bag of peanuts in the time-honored tradition of jailhouse barter.

Still, as forthcoming as was his solidarity with the plight of other detainees, Hemnauth's personal anguish grew with each passing day and as his own helplessness sank further in, for having been "lost in the system." In letters written to Rachel and a colleague of hers, beginning shortly after they began visiting as representatives of the Center for Constitutional Rights, the unmistakable signs of distress appear. "I don't mind going back to my country, but I've got a son to raise, a woman [Rahoni] to take care of." Kevin and Rahoni struggled with Hemnauth's absence and the material support he could no longer provide. This weighed on him constantly. "I am trying to fight my case because I want to be there for my son. It is my duty to take care of him. It's a hurt I'll have to live for the rest of my life that I did not do my duty as a father if I have to leave him." Thanking Rachel for a subsequent message from her, he wrote, "It feels real good getting a letter in here. My son broke his hand and his mom is finding it very hard to survive. It saddens me to know what is happening to them, and it saddens them to know what is happening to me."

Again, Hemnauth's sorrow and distress over having had his son torn from him is not unique, but symptomatic of a hardship inflicted with breathtaking indifference on a large population of detainees around the country. It hurts most when the detainee is moved to a faraway location, often without the ability to alert his or her family. The financial burden of visits an airplane flight away is most often prohibitive, between the cost of travel and absence from jobs. Kevin and Rahoni's plight were a harbinger of things to come. Today, the number of families with U.S. citizen members affected by Secure Communities alone has reached the tens of thousands, representing close to 40% of detainees under the program.[195]

---

195 Kohli et al., "Secure Communities by the Numbers."

In his letters, Hemnauth also frets over forfeiting "the music I have lived my whole life for . . . If one person enjoys listening to it or learns from it, my heart's desire would be fulfilled." When the INS arrested him, he was on the cusp of being able to make music his primary occupation, with gig offers coming in steadily from elite venues in New York. His equipment and master tapes, including one for a nearly completed album, lay stranded in his landlord's garage. "I would like to ask of you to help me get out [of jail], so I can accomplish my dreams and finish the album." And escape his accidental career as a commercial refrigeration mechanic, however skilled at it he was, and is: "Everything went downhill when I tried to be an A/C mechanic in the U.S.A."

Hemnauth's dreams were not the artistic fantasies of an idle man. He had worked jobs — one of them knee-deep in rats and refuse — few Americans know exist, let alone imagine performing themselves, in order to assume responsibility for himself and provide for his son and former wife. The forced separation from his highest aspirations was a serious hardship with lasting repercussions past his imprisonment and removal by the INS and ICE. One more instance of jeopardy in which the government placed him, heedless of the collateral damage it wreaked. Aspirations did not matter. Punishment that dwarfed by many orders of magnitude past offenses for which he had already paid and atoned did not matter.

Living under the thumb of officers and guards who would not dream of acknowledging that the men they addressed interchangeably by their name or a graphic epithet might actually have aspirations, that did not matter either. The graphic epithets may have been part of the "culture" of prison guards and officers, but there was little to justify the gratuitous scorn levied upon all of the detainees. The language was a code of contempt, a way of marking the distinction between the masters of the jail and those they held under their thumb. It was used constantly, lest the mark fade. The detainees were not people, they were "you people." They were not immigrants, they were "fucking immigrants." A man who tied his long hair back with a length of string was a "fag." Although Passaic did not perform routine strip searches after induction — only nonroutine ones — the foul language was of a piece with the guards' fixation on the detainees' intimacy, insisting, for instance, that the bathroom and toilets offer no privacy. Or that they take down towels hanging to dry from a bunk railing on the pretext that detainees might be practicing sodomy under cover. Naturally, they would need to observe it.

Hemnauth had indeed assumed a role of ringleader in protesting the conditions at the jail. He was undeniably bold by any tally. That does not mean that he was without fear. He was frightened all the time, he worried all the time, he battled dejection all the time. Part of his motivation for remaining feverishly active was to bolster his defenses against depression. That he overcame his fear and anxiety to stand up for himself and for others, far from lessening the extent of his courage, is a testament to the effort he put into it. Beatings were not restricted to a finite number of chronically unruly detainees; they could be inflicted on anyone on virtually any pretext, including lese-majesty toward the guards.

Hemnauth received his worst pummeling while confined to the "bull-pen" for having declined food in protest over a spate of particularly harsh brutality. This gesture was one of several precursors to his later sustained hunger strike. Hemnauth had responded "present" to a roll call, a perfectly normal protocol for inmates in a contained cell and in full view of whoever passed it. However, the guard expected him to mark his deference by coming to swift attention by the cell bars. "I was moving a little slow because I was feeling weak" from hunger. The lead guard was a more senior official, a "white shirt" by Hemnauth's description, with the rank of lieutenant. He began cursing loudly, first barking, "You little motherfucker! Get off the bunk, and come up and stand in front of me!" The only discrepancy in Hemnauth's two accounts of the incident is between the epithets the lieutenant may have chosen: "motherfucker" or "fucking asshole." Either way, Hemnauth pointed out to him that his language was uncalled for. He does remember that he was upset by the implied insult to his mother, for whom he has always felt an abiding reverence. Hemnauth's objection did not sit well with lieutenant. With his fellow guards, he entered the cell with two attack dogs and began hitting Hemnauth with an open fist, a technique that was less likely to leave knuckle marks — material evidence of excessive force — than punching. The lieutenant was good at it, since he easily succeeded in knock the breath out of Hemnauth. Hurting and struggling to recover his breathing, Hemnauth apologized and asked him not to hit him again. The officer feigned to acquiesce, then struck him again hard in the ribcage with a dog at his back, "jumping very close to us," fangs bared. "It's a very scary thing, it's hard to describe." The episode quickly degenerated into a full-scale police riot, now directed at all of the inmates in Hemnauth's immediate vicinity, with manic dogs adding to the terror. The guards threw T-shirts and towels in the toilet, destroyed commissary items and soiled sheets and mattresses, which they pulled off the bunks into one huge pile. The destruction or confiscation of commissary items was not only punitive; it was a sadistic infliction of hardship upon many inmates who could barely afford the toothpaste they had to purchase from the prison, which did not provide it.

After the guards left, with the cell in shambles, the detainees who had been assaulted refused to put the mattresses back on the bare bunks and sat up all night on the concrete floor in protest.

The next day, Hemnauth placed collect calls to Flavia Alaya and Rachel Meeropol to relate what had happened in the night. One irony is that physical access to the phones was easy. There were two in the normal detention blocks and even one in the "bullpen" cells. Hemnauth shrugs off my astonishment with a reminder of Passaic's signature method of monetary extortion: "The more phones there are, the more money they make."

In the meantime, the jail warden, aware that a disturbance had broken out, decided to actually ask the inmates what the ruckus was for. He listened to Hemnauth's grievances about the prison conditions, the dogs and the brutality in particular, and to his demand — one of many — that he be transferred to another detention facility more reminiscent of Middlesex. By comparison to Passaic, memories of Middlesex were like an image of Eden. The warden listened but did not hear, although even if he did, the situation at Passaic was so entrenched—everything from the mold on the walls to the barbarity of many of the guards — that there was little a warden could do. So he took the most predictable tack: he dismissed the police riot as just an isolated incident and tried to persuade Hemnauth and his cohorts that the conditions were not what they appeared to be; that, what with food and bunk, they were to be envied for the comforts Passaic provided. The disturbing part of this otherwise comical elevation of Passaic County Jail to the ranks of the Ritz is this: if the warden were trying to sell the inmates the notion that they were living a life of leisure on the taxpayers' dime, what were he and his bosses telling the taxpayers? Presumably the same thing, at the risk of inflaming the public's antagonism toward aliens with the charge that they were freeloading while in detention.

In any event, the victims of the riot were not buying it and demanded to see an INS officer. The warden acquiesced, and an INS agent came the next day. Hemnauth remembers him as Mr. Rodriguez. "We were stilling living in the mess that the police had created, so we were able to show him what they did." He was unacquainted with Hemnauth's case or his petition for parole, and his job did not require him to be. He was, as Hemnauth recalls, a staffer in charge of prison relations and transportation of detainees. One more cog in the detention machinery with little individual authority, but with a loose mandate to try to resolve conflicts that were at risk of festering. If there were any doubts about the boundaries of his authority, when he asked the jail to produce the surveillance tape from the cameras trained on the cells, the jail authorities refused, claiming they could not find it. (At Passaic, cells housing hunger strikers were video monitored.[196]) An oddly convenient excuse, given that the tape would have been little more than a day old, and the warden was keenly aware of the behavior of his guards, the kind of behavior likely to attract scrutiny. Still, there was no avenue for appeal. Hemnauth drafted an affidavit that he and his fellow victims of the assault in the cell signed. He gave it to the INS officer and demanded copies be made for himself, Rachel Meeropol and the NJCRDC, so the "INS could not throw it in the trash." He need not have bothered. The idea that a detainee's complaint over guard brutality would percolate up the ranks of the INS on its own power and shock the brass into action was a naïve one.

---

196   There was no explicit INS standard prescribing — or prohibiting — video monitoring of inmates on hunger strike; the cameras appear to have been specific to Passaic County Jail. The newer ICE standards are marginally more assertive about monitoring inmates held in isolation in the context of hunger strikes, still without mention of cameras. The placement of cameras in Passaic's Special Detention Units — the cells of Hemnauth's description — is confirmed in an inspector general's report dated June 2003; see Office of Inspector General, "Conditions of Confinement" in "A Review of the Treatment of Aliens."

Still, Hemnauth would not be deterred. "Things started to happen" as a result of the letters Hemnauth was writing over the signature of multiple detainees. "We were getting one out every week." The various civil and human rights groups alert to the gulag-worthy immigrant detention operation at Passaic County Jail mobilized around the affidavits Hemnauth was gathering and scribing along with a few of the other detainees proficient in written English. To build a court case, as was Rachel's original intention, would take a considerable amount of time to organize, as such is the nature of any civil proceeding, where the only possible arbitrator is a sitting judge. At the same time, the rights' activists could also put immediate pressure on the governing bodies of the jail if they had enough evidence to demonstrate embarrassing malfeasance that could be of interest to the media.

The evidence Hemnauth assembled[197] was plentiful and shocking beyond mere embarrassment. That the letters are handwritten and susceptible to errors of grammar and spelling makes the content all the more poignant, giving them the aura of clandestine messages from kidnap victims:

A detainee, for having the audacity to speak to the prison ombudsman on his way to the law library, is threatened with a deadly beating by a sergeant reminiscing nostalgically about former prisoners he had sent to the hospital with injuries he had inflicted. A complaint to the captain brings amplified threats in retaliation for "snitching."

A detainee, mistaken for another inmate, is randomly beaten by a guard in the nurse's office, taken to a "bullpen," punched, kicked, spat on and left in segregated confinement for two days without medical attention. His smuggled message: "I am feeling pain every night and day, and I have bruises all over my body. I was trying to get medical treatment ever since, but was denied. Please help."

Hemnauth transcribed these testimonies and seconded them with an appeal to Rachel and her colleague to "watch over the detainees, 'cause we are all scared. They can just come up and call you out and beat you up." And sic the dogs. Meanwhile, the incidents piled up:

---

197 Hemnauth submitted his handwritten affidavits in the form of letters to Rachel Meeropol, who kindly passed them onto me with Hemnauth's permission. Along with Hemnauth's oral narrative delivered directly to me, they are the basis of the present reporting of incidents he observed while in the jail.

A Muslim detainee, protesting an arbitrary change to his name by staging a hunger strike, is dragged from his dorm by the collar, beaten to swelling in the face and refused a visit from an attorney . . . under the pretext of mismatched names.

A posse of guards performs an unsupervised shakedown after one of them admonishes a detainee for wearing a sleeveless sweat top to the weight gym. The response to the detainee's offer to remove it back to his dorm was met with a "you fucking Jamaican" and confiscation of basic hygienic items like soap and toilet paper from the entire dorm.

For trying to back away from a lurching police dog, an inmate is grabbed by the neck, punched in the head, pulled down, his face pushed against the floor, handcuffed and beaten while manacled by two officers. Hemnauth tried to intervene, but was threatened by a guard for opening his mouth. "The rest of the police started running around like [they were] crazy." In this instance, a small group of inmates, including the abused man and Hemnauth, were given two minutes to pack their belongings. The guards never offered an explanation of why it was necessary to rush the move to the standard of a fire evacuation, nor why they showed up with the dogs.

A fellow Guyanese inmate is denied care for a visibly infected foot, placed in "the hole" instead and not permitted to bathe. The infection worsens. The man was on crutches when Hemnauth last saw him just prior to his deportation. (Why peaceful individuals under administrative detention, like Hemnauth, are anywhere near a facility that even possesses a "hole" as a design feature is a question ICE did not address until its leadership changed under the Obama administration.)

Funds disappear from commissary accounts as a result of fictitious charges. In an environment where food is scarce, tasteless and contaminated, this was no trivial matter.

The "jail is highly roach infested, which is very disgusting waking up with crushed roaches on your bed. No matter how much we sweep and mop up, they keep coming from all parts of the building."

The roof leaks into the dorm. It was periodically patched, but never adequately repaired, so the leaks always returned. Some inmates had to sleep in damp bedding because there was so much water penetration.

A dietician working at the jail tells Hemnauth and a group of hunger strikers protesting the dismal food that it is his job to "save money." The statement at least had the virtue of being ostensibly true.

The guards enlist pandering detainees as informants whose accusations against fellow inmates are never challenged and lead to disciplinary action against the accused. "I would like to warn you," Hemnauth wrote to Rachel, "that not all the detainees are on our side. There are some who are working with the police."

It was also common practice for the guards to heave mattresses from the bunks and trail them across the dirty floor — of course, the mattresses were filthy to start with, so the jail might argue no harm, no foul — and to scatter detainees' legal documents and other belongings knowing full well their value to men without the means to replace them. The guards were constantly inventing new modes of oppression and adding them to the repertoire, everything from emptying bottles of skin lotion onto detainees' sheets to ripping out pages of a bible and — as Hemnauth was not alone in experiencing — flushing towels and clothing purchased at the commissary down the toilet.

As gut-wrenching as are the episodes Hemnauth witnessed and experienced, violence and abuse of this nature were not exclusive to Passaic. The one distinction Passaic may have had over other detention facilities was the state of its building, likely more decrepit than the norm. Otherwise, the regimen at Passaic was depressingly unexceptional, both in time and in space. Guard-on-detainee violence was common for many years prior to Hemnauth's incarceration, even before IIRIRA created a body of immigration law emphasizing retribution against wayward immigrants as the dominant theme of immigration policy. Common not only in New Jersey, but across the country from Louisiana and Florida, to Texas and California. At a different facility in New Jersey, new detainees were subjected to a "beat and greet" upon arrival that extended to pushing inmates' heads into toilet bowls and ordering that they perform sexual acts on each other. In a corporate jail in Colorado, inmates the guards suspected might be suicidal were placed in four-point restraints.[198]

---

198 Dow, *American Gulag*.

Worse, reports of brutality have continued to flow forth well since Hemnauth was deported. In 2008, in California, a female detainee fearful of her male cellmates, for having requested protection had her arms yanked up hard behind her back by the guards after being cuffed, ripping her shoulder from its socket; she waited twelve hours in a holding pen before receiving medical attention.[199] In 2011, another female inmate, detained because of an expired visa, reports having been sexually assaulted by a male guard, who attempts to silence her with death threats. A female official at the huge Willacy Detention Center in Texas, in whom the inmate confided, confirmed to her that she was at risk of retaliation if she filed a complaint with ICE. She consented to deportation and separation from her four American-born children rather than face further assault. Others report beatings and "being chased down like animals" at Willacy.[200]

I could go on. There is a rich body of survey research into the abuses tolerated at ICE detention facilities and its contract jails around the country that I need not replicate. Rather, there are two important observations I draw from this catalogue of horrors.

First, Hemnauth's experience at Passaic County Jail, far from being exceptional, fits a pattern of mistreatment at the hands of guards molded to a mentality of enforcement prevalent in the criminal justice system. This is not to suggest that mistreatment is ever a virtuous undertaking, especially when such mistreatment approaches what we understand as torture in its systematic application, but rather to underscore the inescapable fact that ICE has not trained its guards or those of its contract jailers in the distinction between sentenced criminals and administrative detainees. It did not do so in Hemnauth's time at Passaic, and apparently has continued to fail, badly, in this regard.

Beyond the mistreatment is the ingrained indifference to it, up and down the chain of hierarchy. Perhaps not at the level of the president or cabinet secretaries, but across so many other layers that executive policy of the sort Obama has proposed seems almost powerless to reverse it. Of course, it does not help if one policy, Secure Communities, in its zeal to hit numerical deportation targets, enlists state and local law officers, ready hosts to the

199   Amnesty International, "Jailed Without Justice:."
200   Young, " Lost in Detention"; Review of *Immigrant Detainees: The New Sex Abuse Crisis.*

old mentality of harsh criminal-style enforcement.

The second is that, in parallel fashion to the slack protection by the state of family integrity, there has been no successful challenge to the detention system on constitutional grounds. The plenary powers doctrine notwithstanding, I find this puzzling.

Perhaps I should not. When I scoured references to case law for clues as to why the courts have not protected families from being ruptured by deportation, even when a member of a deportee's family is a citizen, unsurprisingly I found several pronouncements upholding family integrity as an interest of the state. However, the discovery of an unequivocal court decision, or underlying opinion, prohibiting deportation on the constitutional grounds favoring family unity proved elusive. The context of relevant cases and subsequent profamily rulings was simply too narrow to inhibit the mandate of the INS and ICE to deport whomever Congress said they could, even before taking plenary powers into consideration.

Similarly, as I poke around for Supreme Court decisions contrary to administrative detainees being held in clearly punitive conditions, such as Passaic's were, the rulings I find encouraging are also frustratingly narrow, and their context one step removed from immigration matters. Nevertheless, the wording in several of them clearly suggests that Supreme Court precedent does not condone punishment for administrative detainees as distinct from convicts,[201] certainly not at the Passaic level, and supports the limitation of administrative detention to measures necessary to ensure public safety and prevent flight. If there is a public safety objective met by beatings and other violence, verbal assault, comingling of peaceful and violent detainees, libelous ostracism (like Passaic Sheriff Speziale's on CNN), denial of medical treatment, unsound hygiene, confiscations, forced nudity, purposefully soiled bedding, freezing and dungeonesque quarters, contaminated and woefully inadequate food, gouging for telephone calls, retaliation for filing grievances, roach infestation, constant humiliation, false accusations, eavesdropping and forbidding a father from hugging his ten-year-old

---

201 Kalhan, "Rethinking Immigration Detention."

child; if there is any such justification in the name of security and flight prevention, I would sure like to know what it is, if not punishment. And that was just Passaic.

One intriguing decision offers some clues as to the delineation in the eyes of the law between justifiable conditions of confinement and proscribed punishment. *Bell v. Wolfish,* a case taken up by the Supreme Court in 1979, addresses complaints of pretrial criminal detainees over various aspects of living conditions, including double bunking, cavity searches and the receipt of packages. Pretrial detainees share in common with ICE detainees the fact that both are subject to preventive incarceration, not imprisonment as a result of a criminal conviction. The court ruled largely in favor of the jailers, noting that elements of incarceration designed to ensure safety and the detainee's presence at court hearings were permissible. It even admonished the courts against becoming "enmeshed in the minutiae of prison operations,"[202] including disciplinary matters. However, the ruling contains some notable clarifications limiting the prerogatives of detention to nonpunitive objectives, a tighter leash than the Eighth Amendment's ban on the cruel and unusual punishment of convicted prisoners. The Court begins by noting that the detention facility defending its practices in the case before it "differs markedly from the familiar image of a jail,"[203] a claim Passaic and other ICE or ICE-contracted facilities would have been hard-pressed to make, unless, like Sheriff Arpaio in Arizona, they wished to underscore how much worse they were. Referring to the Due Process Clause of the Constitution, the Supreme Court affirmed that the government may subject a nonconvicted detainee "to the restrictions and conditions of the detention facility *so long as those conditions and restriction do not amount to punishment*"[204] (emphasis added). Further, "if a restriction or condition is not reasonably related to a legitimate goal—if it is arbitrary or purposeless—a court permissibly may infer that the purpose of the governmental action is punishment that may not constitutionally be inflicted upon detainees."[205]

---

202 Rehnquist, "Bell v. Wolfish" (1979).
203 Rehnquist, "Bell v. Wolfish."
204 Rehnquist, "Bell v. Wolfish."
205 Rehnquist, "Bell v. Wolfish."

In the decision, even cavity searches are legal to the extent that they are implemented as a safeguard against contraband. When Hemnauth was strip-searched upon induction to Passaic, the likelihood of contraband was remote, since the detainees had been transported under guard from one jail to another, and therefore should have been disallowed. And, not to nit-pick, the opinion also rejects saving money as a permissible objective if it leads to abusive conditions, casting as a smoking gun the Passaic dietician's admission to Hemnauth that the jail was doing just that with its meal plan.

Protesting the conditions in the immigrant detention system on constitutional grounds presents a real conundrum. First, a jailer caught, say, beating a detainee or staging a superfluous strip search need not dispute the Supreme Court's disapproval of punishment threaded through decisions like *Bell v. Wolfish,* but simply defend an occurrence as disciplinary action necessary to ensure security and therefore deny it is punishment by invoking the Court's reluctance to intervene in the management of detainee custody or in immigration matters. Or testify to the nutritional integrity of meals, using calorie and vitamin allowances as evidence, again dodging scrutiny by a judiciary that has explicitly voiced its reluctance to interfere, at the Supreme Court level no less. In a system generally deferential to law enforcement, the burden of proof shifts inexorably to the detainee, with a very high hurdle. Indeed, the prevailing benchmark in determining abuse of noncriminal detainees remains the Eighth Amendment's prohibition of cruel and unusual punishment, not of punishment as an impermissible component of a detention regimen.[206] We should also harden ourselves to jailers arguing, narrowly, that no Supreme Court ruling has conferred any rights specifically upon immigrant detainees and that decisions benefiting comparable classes, such as pretrial detainees, do not apply.

Second, demonstrating that the immigration detention system in its entirety is in violation of constitutional strictures might entail separate actions against more than 200 detention centers and jails. It is unclear what court might order the entire system shut down or radically reformed, as opposed to imposing piecemeal modifications on a case-by-case basis, provided the courts agreed to intervene at all. Rather than contest the principle

---

206   Gorlin, "Evaluating Punishment in Purgatory: The Need to Separate Pretrial Detainees' Conditions-of-Confinement Claims from Inadequate Eighth Amendment Analysis."

that detainees cannot be punished, the system is set up to circumvent it. In fact, the Obama administration has agreed, quite explicitly, that the current custody arrangements for immigrant detainees are punitive, but without strong congressional support in term of budget appropriations and policy endorsement, achieving the overhaul Obama seeks will be an uphill struggle fraught with political risks. Still, while *Bell v. Wolfish* does not assimilate pretrial inmates with immigrant detainees in so many words, and I can easily imagine anti-immigrant militants speciously contesting its applicability to ICE and its contractors, it is tepidly gratifying to see policy objectives that purports to abide by the decision's unabridged implications.

It is important to remember that Hemnauth's detention was longer than most, so he would see several rotations during his time at Passaic. With each new batch of arriving inmates at Passaic came a new set of mutual adjustments, particularly since the jail did little to segregate those in the habit of provoking others or turning to confrontation men who would normally avoid it in the conduct of their daily lives. It was a question of time before a wave of violence among inmates would engulf Hemnauth, despite his vigilance against it.

As is often true, the latest fight arose over something trivial. One of Hemnauth's older bunkmates, a Mr. White, suggested to an incoming detainee that he join a pod of other Cubans. From Hemnauth's description, many if not all the Cuban detainees at Passaic had arrived in the United States as young men with the 1980 Mariel boatlift, which Fidel Castro had bloated with common criminals from Cuban jails. Mr. White's suggestion may have come off as more imperious than deferential. The newcomer took offense, and others from the Cuban contingent came to witness a brawl in the making. Hemnauth saw a weapon, some kind of pointed object, perhaps as simple as a pen or pencil, get passed forward. Seeing Mr. White defenseless against a possible stabbing, he threw him a bunch of pencils, the only armament readily available. One of the longer-term Cubans, a big strong man with a long experience of jailhouses, turned to Hemnauth with glee: "Oh, yes! I have been looking to fight you for a long time."

Animosity had been brewing. The Cubans, on the whole, declined to sign Hemnauth's petitions and letters, and looked askance at his resistance to the Passaic regime. Hemnauth's impression of the Cubans, by contrast, was that "they sucked up to the police. They knew they could not be deported" and would eventually be freed. It was in their interest to play for early release. The *Zadvydas v. Davis* decision proscribing indefinite detention applies eminently to Cuban detainees whose homeland or another host country will not receive them, often for lack of diplomatic relations with the United States. Ironically, many of the Cubans came to Hemnauth for assistance with their petitions for leniency, although Hemnauth did insist that any assertions he made on their behalf were truthful and could be documented, for example allegations of assault as justifying fear of future injury and claims of crime-free living prior to being detained. Hemnauth found himself working around a plethora of rap sheets rich in firearms and burglary convictions.

Appreciation for his legal assistance was not on this day's agenda. The provocateur had his *casus belli* . . . and was armed with a hand-fashioned blade, quite serviceable as a knife, likely the same one intended for use against Mr. White. Hemnauth walked up to his declared adversary. To try to duck the situation would have been either impossible in the close quarters or a lethal sign of weakness, like blood on the water. The man flashed the makeshift knife at Hemnauth to let him know what he was up against. Hemnauth, now realizing that he could bring nothing more than a pencil to a knife fight, acted nonchalant and unintimidated: "Oh! You have a knife!" He walked over to the bars by the passageway to wait for an officer. When one appeared, he called him over, told him there was a knife on the loose and requested to be transferred out of the dorm. The man who had threatened him also walked up, presumably after having entrusted the knife to a confederate, and spoke to the guard in Spanish. The guard heard him out and simply walked away.

Hemnauth had taken up the habit of napping by day and staying awake at night, drawing and writing under the cover of calm. The routine now came in handy, since he had to mount a vigil lest he be stabbed in his sleep. "That night, I sat up all night on my bed." His bunkmate did the same, to the dual effect of deflecting a surprise and possibly deadly assault, and intimidating the man determined to launch it, by having him suspect that

Hemnauth's lookout was a prelude to a preemptive strike on him should he nod off. "That was a jail kind of technique . . . He freaked out."

This was no game. Hemnauth had committed to defending himself if need be, even, he thought, if that meant throwing the first punch in a fight, although he never did. But the resolve brought him no joy, no pride in himself, no sense of empowerment, no macho conceit, nothing of the sort. Quite the contrary. He felt like a gladiator thrown into combat to please his masters. It sickened him. "From a humble, peaceful, quiet musician I have gotten this angry, aggressive attitude like everybody else . . . This jail changed me, it made me into a different kind of human being."

Not one he liked.

10

THE MOST WICKED OF THE CAST

THE NEXT DAY PASSED AND NOTHING HAPPENED. Then another day. The guards ignored his appeal to be transferred away from danger. Rachel Meeropol came to visit and, in Hemnauth's recollection, relayed the request to the prison authorities. If anything, Hemnauth understated to me the effort he put into negotiating a transfer. Rachel's memoranda to her files indicate that Hemnauth made his appeals both verbally to at least two sergeants and in writing to one officer and to the Passaic warden. All remained unanswered. One sergeant he approached for acknowledgement of his requests just laughed at him. Meanwhile, Rachel noted, "Hemnauth is very depressed, and feels like his life is in danger." With a shank in the hands of someone who wished him harm and guards indifferent to the fact, it was.

Around this time, early June 2003, ICE denied his parole application. Desis Rising Up and Moving, the rights organization assisting South Asian immigrants and detainees, had filed for parole on Hemnauth's behalf. Apparently the ICE opinion, which was not subject to judicial oversight, was sent to Hemnauth's old lawyer, John Charles Allen. If he received it, he never forwarded it to his former client or Rahoni. Although Hemnauth submitted a written release to him, Allen demanded payment of bloated arrears before he would release any documents in his files to me.

"So the next day I started a hunger strike." At first, Hemnauth simply declined meals without fanfare, beginning with breakfast the night after he made the decision to starve himself. Without a declaration, the guards finally came by and asked him if he was on strike. There was an official protocol for handling inmates who refuse food. He answered that he was. The on-duty sergeant informed him that he was to be isolated from the rest of the inmate population, to which Hemnauth responded, "Fine, I don't care. You put me wherever you want." Hemnauth remembers the exchange with the sergeant as very matter-of-fact and dispassionate: "It's a procedure." They were, by Hemnauth's account, going by the book, an assessment that appears to be generally accurate.[207]

Tensions would rise as Hemnauth's determination became clear to the guards. Hemnauth had enlisted in another, shorter-lived strike three months earlier in solidarity with other inmates over the guards' brutality. He had also protested the food by refusing to eat it after a particularly vile spell. Apparently the jail authorities now viewed his refusal to eat as the genuine article, not a passing fancy. Far from a narrow grievance, the underpinnings of his current protest ran wide and deep, to the fundamental abuse and injustice that Passaic embodied. Under these circumstances, he would not be mollified by some minor measure of relief, such as switching his dorm. The sergeant must have realized as much in deciding to apply the formal protocol for hunger strikers.

Before moving to the "bullpen," Hemnauth made the round of his friends — "people who used to watch over me" — in the dorm and asserted the objectives of his hunger strike, which came down to a demand to be freed from Passaic or, at the very least, moved to a less barbaric place of custody. Three other inmates joined him, one of whom may have begun fasting a week earlier than Hemnauth, judging from a letter Hemnauth wrote to Rachel three days into his strike. At the time, of course, Hemnauth could not know how far he was going to take his protest, and he did not ask his early fellow strikers for a commitment to go the distance as he was bracing to do, although they shared his demand to be released or transferred from Passaic. Hemnauth believed that recruiting others to strike with him at the outset would draw the scrutiny of the INS. As Hemnauth knew, the detention standards did command that a detention facility report hunger strikes to the supervising INS field office. His logic was that several simultaneous strikes might be hard for the INS to ignore and inspire its agents to lend an attentive ear to inmates' grievances over conditions

207 "INS Detention Standard: Hunger Strikes."

at Passaic. A serious audit of those conditions might judge them to be irremediable. The reasoning possessed some logic, but logic could not guarantee the outcome Hemnauth sought.

The guards were supremely uninterested in the motives of Hemnauth's hunger strike, and more interested in punishing him for it. Isolation was step one. Step two was verbal intimidation, with guards arriving to yell and curse at Hemnauth every two to three hours.[208] The INS standards provide that "the [jail] staff shall make reasonable efforts to convince the detainee to accept treatment voluntarily."[209] There is no indication that intimidation could be considered "reasonable."

As retribution went, mere confinement to the "bullpen" in itself was hardly more painful than residency in the dorm block. For one thing, they put all four strikers in the same cell, which had four bunks and its own sink and toilet. On the minus side of the ledger, the men were under constant camera surveillance, including when they were attending to basic bodily functions and hygiene, a discomfort Hemnauth's sense of propriety would not allow him to overcome. The men were allowed to shower once or twice a week in the confinement area under escort. They passed their time "drinking a lot of water and reading a lot of books" in relative peace.[210]

Hemnauth's co-strikers gave up after about one week. They thought they had made their point and that possibly now they might be transferred to another facility. They had taken their best shot. However, for Hemnauth, this strike was not a mere statement that, once made, stood on its own. He was going to see his protest through to some kind of finality. With the three men gone, the guards moved Hemnauth to another cell, occupied solo by an Indian detainee named Nigel, also on a hunger strike, but independently from Hemnauth's call to one. In fact, his had commenced about two weeks prior to Hemnauth's. At least on the surface, his grievances were likely similar, judging from the mobilization of civil rights advocates jointly around the ordeal of both men.

---

208 Boulos, "Interview at Passaic with Hemnauth Mohabir."

209 "INS Detention Standard: Hunger Strikes."

210 I should note that in his testimony to me, Hemnauth places at this juncture a beating by a jail guard, possibly one with the rank of lieutenant, that I recounted earlier. Judging from Hemnauth's Passaic correspondence, the earlier date is more likely. While there is no material discrepancy between my sources in the nature and facts of the violence committed against him, there is one of chronology.

However, what is very apparent from Hemnauth's testimony to me is that his hunger strike was directed at the root of an existential problem that he was more apt to recognize than virtually anyone around him. The penal regimen was testing his spiritual attachment to harmony among all God's creatures and intent on turning everyone in its grips into the monsters caricaturized in the imaginations of all who would demonize them. Hemnauth, like the majority of immigrants caught in the detention system, had not entered it an angry, defensive survivalist communicating in curses and quick to clench his fists. But that is what he felt himself becoming. "I had had enough. This is not me. This is not what I wanted for myself." If starvation were the only way out of Passaic, so be it. He would take that exit and die his own pious man. When I asked him, apologetically but still quite directly, if he had been prepared to take his strike all the way to his own death, he deflects the question, out of modesty, an unwillingness to climb upon the pedestal of a would-be martyr. Regardless of his humility, the subsequent fact of a protracted hunger strike and the observations of others prove that he pushed his grit leagues beyond the boundaries of discomfort.

One of the guards, a conscientious one, whom Hemnauth describes as a "short Italian officer," caught on rather quickly to the nature of his protest, recognizing it as a serious and deliberate initiative that might end quite differently from the shorter-lived strikes to which Passaic was, by now, inured and rather indifferent. That is, end badly. While generally more affable than the average of the officers, he had never attempted to fraternize with Hemnauth in the past. Now he would come and chat with Hemnauth in the evenings. Off the record, he claimed, and Hemnauth, not one to impugn a person without evidence, was inclined to trust him. He seemed genuine. He styled himself a connoisseur of Asian cuisine and offered to bring Hemnauth Indian takeout food from the town, on his nickel, if Hemnauth would accept it. There is a rich patchwork of immigrant communities near Paterson, New Jersey, and good ethnic food would have been easy to procure. And, of course, very enticing even if Hemnauth were not as hungry as he had made himself. If this were a ruse, it was laughably unsubtle, so Hemnauth chose to consider the suggestion as heartfelt. The officer even told Hemnauth he would sneak the food in, so no one would have to know he had eaten. He was clearly worried and told Hemnauth that he was looking poorly and sickly thin. "I think it was a personal thing with him."

If the amicable guard had an ulterior motive, it was to find the knife Hemnauth had claimed was on the loose in the dorm. Many of the other guards had either dismissed the contention or did not care. This particular guard wanted to find it before someone got killed, an outcome he believed was distinctly possible. However, before he searched further, he was feeling Hemnauth out, both to determine if Hemnauth's claim were authentic and to gather clues as to where he might look. Nightly shakedowns that had been conducted after the brawl, and after the hunger strikers had been taken to isolation, had produced nothing. Hemnauth advised him it was futile "to tear the place apart." The shakedowns were more demonstrations of force than thorough searches, although in truth the detainees who had been living in fear at the thought of a knife in the hands of an embedded prison gang half-welcomed the displays as a deterrent against those who might use it, the lesser of the two evils. They had also been mounting vigils lest someone got stabbed in their sleep. Still, the guard, Hemnauth counseled, should concentrate his investigation — a personal one — on the bunks of the more pugilistic of the Cuban inmates, two in particular who had threatened violence, without the commotion of a full-bore raid on the dorm. Hemnauth did not have the mentality of an informer. He despises backbiting and would never have cooperated with any of the blatant abusers who reveled in shakedowns and beatings. This, to him — and to me — was less a matter of informing than preventing likely and imminent bloodshed.

The knife turned up within three days, a slender shank, fashioned from a strip of sheet metal, rubbed sharp on the rough concrete floor of the dorm and hidden along the spine of a magazine.

Two weeks into Hemnauth's hunger strike, the jail's monitoring standards triggered daily visits to its medical department, such as it was. The hunger pangs were not too bad, except in the morning when the guards showed up with trays in the hope the strikers would take them. The smells produced a sharp acidic reaction in Hemnauth's stomach. "It begins to burn, and create a desire for food." To quell the sensation of acidity, he drank water steadily and "began to get used to it."

He stopped passing waste and only urinated.

He did not have a bunk in the cell, just a mattress. He remembers waking up laying at the level of the floor and seeing the police boots go by. His head was by the bars toward the front of the cell, to avoid sleeping with his face by the toilet bowl. The indignity of having a toilet bowl and stomping jackboots as the sole decor options when his eyes greeted the day "made me feel like an animal." Once again, of all his memories of torment at the hands of the detention system, the humiliation is the most painful to him.

"On the morning of the seventeenth day, I remember that clearly . . . I felt normal" upon awakening. "I stood up to go to medical and felt a [wave of] weakness through my body. When I stood up straight, I swayed when I tried to move. I thought 'Hey, this doesn't feel right.' And I put my hand on the wall and I steadied myself. Then I walked slowly to the clinic." When he got to the infirmary, the nurse took a urine sample and immediately took it for analysis. Returning with the results, she told Hemnauth that she liked him, respected and supported what he was doing, that is, his protest. But, she told him, his organs were breaking down and passing through his urine. His body had begun to consume itself. The nurse's apprehensions do not surprise my acquaintances in the field of emergency medicine, who invoke the "rule of 3s" in assessing the odds of succumbing to hunger: three minutes without air, three days without water and three weeks without food.

"She said, 'Listen, you are doing this just to get out of this place, and I can understand because I, too, do not like this place.'" She implored him not to kill himself and persuaded him to take a half pint of milk and a half pint of juice to at least stay alive. She signed an order for the supervisory sergeant, on some kind of official medical form she felt confident would not be ignored. A copy went to the kitchen as well. The jail heeded the order. Hemnauth received the milk and juice once a day, in the afternoon, which he mixed and drank. "A kind of a milkshake." The potion, combined with his enfeebled constitution, made him sleepy. Mornings felt normal to him. He figured that with this minimal intake he could extend his protest comfortably for a long time, "a year or two," if he conserved his energy and gave himself to meditating. Quickly dying, as the nurse feared he might, would get tabulated as little more than another ICE statistic of suicides in custody, less impactful on a corrupt immigration detention system than the protracted grit of a stubborn striker who would not quite die.[211]

Meanwhile, the jail authorities were becoming increasingly irritated at Hemnauth and anxious for his strike to end, not out of concern for his life or health but rather, Hemnauth tells me, to avoid drawing the attention of ICE. His explanation is a deductive one, but quite plausible given Passaic's record of ducking scrutiny of its compliance to standards — not that ICE itself has an unblemished record of enforcing them. When Rachel Meeropol phoned the INS, recently reincarnated as ICE, to alert the agency to the hunger-striking at Passaic, the supervisor made it abundantly apparent that her call was not a welcome one and refused to commit to have staff visit the jail and speak to detainees. ICE was aware of Hemnauth's strike, but appeared disinclined to do anything about it or its roots.[212]

Immediately Hemnauth started drinking his juice and dairy potion, two officers, a captain and a sergeant, showed up in the afternoon at Hemnauth's and Nigel's Special Detention Unit cell. They unilaterally declared the strike over and had come to escort the inmates back to a jail dorm. They issued the Passaic standard "pack your shit" order, in keeping with their habitual disrespect for anything a detainee might prize. The order to pack in itself was nothing special. Guards had commanded Hemnauth and Nigel to prepare to leave on frequent occasions without actually moving them, in what appears to have been a tactic to unnerve them. In three instances, on successive days early in Hemnauth's strike, the guards moved them to a booking room and made them wait there for five hours without access to a bathroom as a disciplinary measure.

The notion that someone other than the hunger striker could pronounce that he had started to eat seems preposterous to the point of farce. It might have been precisely that if the officers had not arrived primed for violence. They had. Both men protested that their strike was not, in fact, over. Nevertheless, Hemnauth complied, gathered his few belongings and left with the guards. When they arrived at the dorm, the same one from which Hemnauth had wanted to be moved for fear of a knife attack, Hemnauth

---

211 The INS detention standards applicable when Hemnauth was in custody authorized an INS clinical director to prescribe the force-feeding of hunger strikers in imminent danger of death under certain procedural conditions. See: "INS Detention Standard: Hunger Strikes."
212 Meeropol, "Phone Call with INS."

resisted, reminding his escorts of his ongoing hunger strike. According to INS standards, "the medical officer alone may order a detainee's release from hunger strike treatment."[213]

In Hemnauth's experience, Passaic guards rarely let the wording of an INS or ICE rule stand in the way of their own creative interpretation. This day was no exception. "I was weak" from hunger, Hemnauth told me. An officer, a sergeant, grabbed Hemnauth by the neck and shoulder and slammed him toward a wall, face first. Hemnauth protected his face with his hands, which took the brunt of the collision. With the assault, the guards clearly overpowered Hemnauth, who was in no physical condition to defend himself — let alone that there would have been disciplinary action against him had he attempted, likely including further corporal punishment, what with the one-sided consequences of any altercation between detainees and guards. "They threw me inside physically. I wasn't walking in. I couldn't stand properly." Once they had installed Hemnauth inside the dorm, the jail could report the strike over, since, by INS definition, a hunger striker must reside in isolation. Hemnauth held onto a nearby bench to keep from falling. The guards were aware of how brutal the scene appeared to the other inmates who observed it. The sergeant decided to make the most of it. He stepped onto a table and harangued all the detainees: "See what happens when you go on a hunger strike?"[214] Indeed.

Hemnauth continued to refuse solid food.

The Legal Aid Society of New York, as its name implies and its mission states, provides legal assistance to underserved, low-income New Yorkers. The society was founded in 1836, making it the oldest such organization in the country. It is one of the most prominent advocates in the country for legal reforms and the advancement of civil rights in and through judicial proceedings. With 850 attorneys on staff, it also ranks among the largest law firms in the country, with an eye-popping caseload, some 300,000 matters every year. Whereas criminal defendants are entitled by law to legal representation, the Legal Aid Society also represents low-income — and,

213 "INS Detention Standard: Hunger Strikes."
214 Boulos, "Interview at Passaic with Hemnauth Mohabir."

consequently, vulnerable — individuals in civil cases, including immigration suits.[215] As Bryan Lonegan pointed out to me early in our discussions about Hemnauth, the Legal Aid Society shares a key attribute with other law firms guided by high professional standards: it scrutinizes the merits of the cases it takes. At the time of Hemnauth's ordeal, the society was fairly unique in its drive to send an immigration lawyer to the rescue of any immigrant detainee with ties to New York City, provided there was a basis for cancellation of removal or other form of relief. Other free and low-cost providers — the rules do not specify they specifically be pro bono law firms as is the society — tend to restrict their clientele to people presenting particular attributes, such as children or victims of torture.

Bryan took over Hemnauth's case on August 1, 2003, rescuing it from the limbo where Hemnauth's prior attorney, Mr. Allen, had left it to linger. Accepting to do so was not a simple decision for him. With immigration judges straight-jacketed by IIRIRA in their exercise of discretion, there is usually little room to maneuver. As Bryan told me, the vast majority of immigrants in detention have little chance of reprieve from deportation and, in his view, there are clearly some who should not. In advising immigrant detainees, he sugarcoated neither the aspects of IIRIRA he knew could not be circumvented under any conditions, nor the fact that IIRIRA was intended to be seal-proof in its goal to deport specific categories of aliens. Nevertheless, Bryan's sole criterion in accepting a client was the presence of a basis for relief. He did not rank potential cases for priority according to a preassessed likelihood of a favorable outcome. As result, he was often stretched to the edges of a Sophie's choice.

Bryan was familiar with Passaic for having conducted seminars for Passaic detainees on the application of immigration law, with an emphasis on IIRIRA. He distributed a guide for laypeople on the mechanics of the law to help them understand what they were up against, and perhaps dissuade the most hopeless cases from subjecting themselves to further hardship that inevitably accompanies fruitless efforts to dispute their removal. Bryan came to Passaic regularly. It was one of three jails in northern New Jersey assigned to him as the representative of the Legal Aid Society, along with those of Bergen and Hudson counties. Passaic presented a split personality

---

215 "The Legal Aid Society Annual Report 2010."

to Bryan, one side cooperative, its flip side brutal. On the one hand, Passaic officials never impeded Bryan's access to detainees, and made available the prison chapel for his "Know Your Rights" presentations and his meetings on individual cases. As caveat to the easy admission, Passaic did not allow access to the detainees' residential areas, where he knew brutality to be rampant. Ironically, his access to the inmates was so liberal that he knew from their consistent reports the extent of the abuse they suffered. Beyond the testimony of the detainees, Bryan had witnessed, firsthand, Passaic's trademark indecency: the dogs.

"The dogs were just too much," Bryan later told me, and inspired him to want to straddle, carefully, his role as attorney with privileged access he did not wish to jeopardize and that of concerned citizen disturbed by the repressive excesses of the Passaic regimen. The dogs were the detainees' single most persistent complaint and the source of genuine terror, which Bryan readily appreciated. He had seen a dog charge an inmate assigned to a cleaning duty, "a guy just mopping the floor," and had come within inches of having been badly bitten himself when a dog lunged at him near a counsel waiting area. He voiced his dismay in a liaison meeting between the jail, ICE and other constituencies held around a conference table at the federal building in Newark, with human rights advocates in the audience. No one of authority took his concern seriously, that federal detainees in administrative custody were being threatened by dogs bred for ferocity and quite possibly conditioned for hostility toward men in jumpsuits. Daniel Zwerdling at NPR did take the dogs seriously, once he learned of the abuse.

Jeannette Gabriel had introduced Bryan to Hemnauth and pressed him to take his case, with considerable persistence, Bryan tells me. "I would have taken the case just to get her off my back," he quips. Protests and demonstrations against Passaic were intensifying outside the jail, particularly on weekends, many organized by Jeannette, Flavia Alaya and the New Jersey Civil Rights Defense Committee. With IIRIRA's harsh strictures explicitly formulated to deter relief and cancellations of removal, Bryan would have normally deflected the urge to represent someone in Hemnauth's shoes, even under the pressure of Jeannette's passionate appeals. The facts of the case, given the impediments to judicial discretion contained in IIRIRA, shouted that the likelihood of prevailing was a long shot, and there are far more immigrant applicants for pro bono legal representation than there are attorneys available for it. Further, when one is as meticulous a lawyer as Bryan Lonegan, the time committed to each client is correspondingly extensive.

However, the circumstances of Hemnauth's case drew Bryan to accept it. One was the glaring, fundamental injustice of the deportation order — even in the view of the judge who had issued it — magnified by eighteen months' incarceration, including a year in the Passaic gulag, imposed on a lawful permanent resident whose offense was old, demonstrably frivolous and long expiated to the full satisfaction of a court of law. Mandatory immigration detention as an automated feature of the immigration code clearly shocked Bryan's conscience. As he later wrote, "the categorical detention of lawful permanent residents . . . is also antithetical to fundamental notions of liberty, which dictate individualized determinations of the necessity of detention."[216] Hemnauth's was not the only instance of imprisonment to which this view applied. Still, his treatment at Passaic qualified as the epitome of a system Bryan objected to as a matter of absolute right and wrong.

Second was Hemnauth himself. Bryan, as an immigration attorney working for the Legal Aid Society, was, and is, prone to empathy for many if not all the aliens caught in the jaws of the IIRIRA statutes. Still, Hemnauth stood out as particularly deserving by virtue of his human qualities — sincerity, guilelessness, devotion to his young son and charity to those around him — and despite, as Bryan puts it, "not having his hands entirely clean." In fact, Bryan dismisses the notion that Hemnauth is entirely above reproach for the predicament in which he found himself, regardless of its inherent injustice and the entrapment feature of the "buy-and-bust" sting that triggered it. Bryan certainly recognizes that Hemnauth's naïveté was the culprit, and that he was free of ill intent, yet the explanation does not unequivocally satisfy him as an excuse. A careful driver might still avoid an accident with another who is at fault. However, if anything, the solitary blemish on his police record made everything else about Hemnauth stand out, all of it honorable and sympathetic. And like Judge Riefkohl before him, Bryan was stung by the letter of a ten-year-old to the court, pleading that it see its way clear to giving him back his father. If there were one single thing that pushed him over the fence, Bryan told me, it was that letter.

---

216 Lonegan, "American Diaspora: The Deportation of Lawful Residents from the United States and the Destruction of Their Families."

The third attractant to Hemnauth's case was that Bryan saw a possible way to prevail, even if the chances were slim, and the immediate result might not be a wholesale cancellation of removal, but simply release from detention. A release would have allowed Hemnauth to fight deportation while reunited with his child, an infinitely more alluring prospect than allowing the government to whittle away his resolve as he rotted in jail. ICE had already made tremendous strides in that regard. Judge Riefkohl had told Mr. Allen in the plainest of terms that he should request of the court and the district attorney in Queens that Hemnauth's misdemeanor charge be vacated, more than intimating that he would then order Hemnauth released and cancel his removal. This is precisely the path Bryan Lonegan would travel, with all the due procedural and professional diligence his predecessor had been unable to muster.

Hemnauth remained on hunger strike until Bryan Lonegan, after having signed on as Hemnauth's immigration attorney, had completed his inquiry into Hemnauth's case and sketched out a strategy. Hemnauth "signed a form" appointing Bryan and officially separating from John Charles Allen. Hemnauth called off his strike after forty-three days, at Bryan's adamant insistence and as a condition of his counsel. Hemnauth was visibly sickened by the strike, and Bryan was "very disturbed" by what he saw. Like the nurse who had seen Hemnauth wasting away when his diet consisted of nothing but water, Bryan was afraid his client would die. He also knew from his dealings with jail officials that they could not fathom the notion of a hunger strike being anything but the byproduct of a mental disorder, the act of someone who was obviously crazy. So atop his worry that Hemnauth might starve himself to death was the rational apprehension the guards might attempt to force-feed him, an outcome with its own very damaging consequences. Bryan would have none of it. He also advised Hemnauth that the hunger strike would not help his legal case. Jeannette Gabriel was not pleased: Hemnauth's principled forbearance had given a powerful head of steam to the human rights protests against Passaic. Still, Bryan stood his ground.

For his part, Hemnauth made his despair plain. He wanted to get out. He told Bryan, early in their client-to-attorney relationship, that he was at the point that he would accept deportation, provided the removal was actually executed. His deportation order had sat dormant, with no information — let alone a resolution — provided him for so long that he was left with the impression of a life sentence to Passaic. A shortened life the way things were going, between the abuse, the tension among inmates living in deprivation, bare-bones health care and the dangerous hygienic conditions. The justice seeker in him wanted one more opportunity to find it, this time under the guidance of a conscientious attorney. But he was resigned to it being his last. "[Passaic] was turning me into some kind of a monstrous person. The same thing for everyone else in the jail. My friends were fighting among themselves . . . Friends who used to look after each other . . . now drawing blood from each other. It happens. One big demonic thing." A different jail, like Middlesex, nirvana by comparison, he could have withstood a short while longer. Not Passaic.

As Bryan Lonegan was leaping into action, Hemnauth's mother, Rawti, arrived for a surprise visit at the jail, just as he was coming to the end of his sanity's rope under the crush of Passaic's penal order. Hemnauth's voice takes a dejected tone as he recalls the sadness of it. "This is something I did not want to happen. She started to cry, it made me start to cry . . . It reminded me of the nice family times I had at home with my mom and with my son." I asked Hemnauth if, in hindsight, his mom's second visit had been at all helpful. He replied, unequivocally, "No. It made things worse for me. It was awful . . . for everybody." Rawti remained in New York for several weeks, with Rahoni and Kevin, but did not visit Hemnauth at Passaic again. She had spent a total of thirty minutes with her son. It was all the pain and sorrow either could tolerate.

An Indian prophet came into my dream, Sai Baba. He told me I had to go back to South America, back home.[217]

---

217 Shirdi Sai Baba (1836–1918), spiritual leader revered by both Hindus and Muslims throughout India and in diaspora communities, including the Caribbean. His teachings

I asked him, "Why must I return when I have my family out here, my son? And I am beginning to get back a relationship with my ex wife."

"America is going to divide itself."

"Still, why would I go back to Guyana when there are all these mass killings, people killing and robbing each other?"

He was sending me to a place where I would be required to chant mantras.

"I don't know Hindi mantras," I protest.

He said he would teach me what to say. He led me to an ashram. It resembled the Hare Krishna ashram I frequent here in Trinidad. He told me to enter. I objected: "I am not a holy man. I don't speak like holy people."

Sai Baba entered the temple, and beckoned to me. "I have prepared a place for you." We began to walk in a circle. He said: "All you must do is sing, play music and dance." I did as he commanded. I followed him, and began to sing and dance. I began to speak mantras I never knew.

Finally, in my dream, the prophet went to lie in some clear water. He assumed different forms. I did not understand what they meant. Then I woke up. One of the forms looked like Abraham Lincoln. I remember that.

The groundwork of Bryan's legal strategy lasted about a month. The concept was straightforward: removing the old misdemeanor as an obstacle to Hemnauth's release. Judge Riefkohl himself had suggested this approach to John Charles Allen, later confirming to Bryan Lonegan his favorable predisposition toward it, especially since he saw leniency on the part of any district attorney as eminently justifiable in cases such as Hemnauth's: a trivial offense had been caught in the tight stitching of IIRIRA's net. As simple as the approach was, building the edifice beneath it required careful legal steps and entailed formal appeals to two jurisdictions, one state and one federal.

---

often came in the form of parables rich with empathy for the poor and sick. He is also credited with miracles.

The Legal Aid Society assigned a criminal attorney from its staff to prepare a brief for the Supreme Court of the State of New York, County of Queens. The gist of the motion was that Hemnauth had waived the right to appeal his misdemeanor charge on the misinformed advice of his attorney at the time, Marvin Landou. There is no denying that Landou felt great empathy, even affection, for his client, and his "agency defense" at trial was fitting. In fact, as I have outlined earlier, it may have been the only defense technique available under the circumstances, and proved highly effective. Hemnauth was acquitted of two serious felony charges, carrying an enormous penalty, against the statistical odds. However, his assessment that Hemnauth's conviction would not affect his legal permanent resident status was rooted in the realities of the time, before the government, armed with IIRIRA, cranked up its deportation machinery. The choice of strategy was also deliberate: Landou had thought about the implications for Hemnauth's green card, at Hemnauth's repeated request, and had dismissed them out of hand, on the grounds that the court clerk had not mentioned any repercussions when Hemnauth went to pay his fine and close the case.

The result, as the motion argues, was that Hemnauth had been deprived of his right under state and federal law to effective counsel when "his attorney misrepresent[ed] the immigration consequences of his conviction." With the hindsight of the *Padilla v. Kentucky,* the motion needn't have said more: in a case eerily similar to Hemnauth's, the Supreme Court unequivocally affirmed the right of an accused immigrant to be apprised of the possibility of deportation pursuant to a guilty plea or conviction. However, *Padilla v. Kentucky* was not decided until 2010.

In 2003, the available precedents nodded in the same direction the Supreme Court would ultimately take, but were flimsier. The most contemporaneous of them — *United States v. Couto,* decided in a U.S. Court of Appeals for the Federal Circuit less than a year before Hemnauth's motion — contains language in the body of the opinion sympathetic to the notion that a defense attorney should apprise his or her client of all the consequences for an alien of an unappealed criminal conviction, including those affecting residency status: "An attorney's *affirmative misrepresentations* on the subject might well constitute ineffective assistance."[218] However, the justices in this case were less certain whether a failure to consider immigration consequences necessarily constituted an instance of delinquency on the part of a lawyer, and in their conclusion sidestepped the issue altogether by finding for the plaintive on separate grounds: "We need not decide the question of what effect, if any, recent changes to the Immigration and Nationality Act have on a court's obligation . . . to inform a defendant of the direct consequences of a guilty plea."[219] In sum, there was enough ambiguity in existing precedents to allow a criminal court to do what it wanted in Hemnauth's case regardless of his attorney's mistake. His lawyers would have to add to the argument if they were to sway a court to vacate the old misdemeanor sentence. Bryan was fully aware of this as he went about filling in the pieces. Indeed, the motion requests that the court in Queens "order a re-sentencing or, alternatively, grant a hearing to determine the merits of defendant's claim."[220]

Immediately after his colleague filed Hemnauth's motion in criminal court and obtained a prompt hearing date, Bryan filed a separate plea with Judge Riefkohl. There were two possible reasons for cancelling Hemnauth's deportation and ordering him released from detention. The first was the most compelling, but was conditioned on the misdemeanor charge being vacated or reopened: in the absence of a final criminal conviction, the grounds for removal from the United States no longer existed. This was also Judge Riefkohl's preferred approach, because, as he had made abundantly clear, it was an incontrovertible authorization to rule in Hemnauth's favor, as he genuinely desired. He could not go around the law.

The second point in Bryan's brief to the immigration court was that Riefkohl could reopen Hemnauth's case to allow him to apply for naturalization. On substance, granting Hemnauth the opportunity to become a U.S. citizen seems only fair. Not only the father, but as well the young son, would suffer immensely from the former's exile, as would Rahoni, who depended on Hemnauth for material and emotional support and had received it unconditionally. The suffering already inflicted on all parties, including

218 "United States v. Couto" (2002).
219 "United States v. Couto."
220 Johnson, "The People of the State of New York, Hemnauth Mohabir, Defendant: Notice of Motion to Vacate Judgment" (2003).

two U.S. citizens, was disproportionate to the crime triggering deportation by countless orders of magnitude. The testaments to Hemnauth's good moral character — from church and temple leaders, to his landlord, to Riefkohl himself — were spontaneous and more than sufficient in number to establish it.

Immigration law does, in fact, provide the immigration court some leeway for a judge to prescribe relief in order to allow a potential deportee to apply for citizenship. On its face — or *prima facie*, to use the legal phrase — the law accommodates persons in Hemnauth's situation seeking naturalization. He satisfied the conditions of being a lawful permanent resident with more than five years of residency. He had shown "good moral character" over the course of a separate five-year statutory period and demonstrated more than one extreme circumstance in his case. The one fragile claim concerned the statutory period of good conduct, since the government could argue that his time in jail did not count toward it. The larger caveat, however, was the view, expressed in the immigration code, that any hardship represent "exceptionally appealing humanitarian factors."[221] With the number of deportations increasing, along with IIRIRA's automated indifference to personal circumstances woven through its text and tone, distinguishing the exceptional from the exemplary is an arduous task.

In immediate response to Bryan's brief, Judge Riefkohl granted a stay of deportation to effectively block any sudden action ICE might take under a standing deportation order, even one that had lain dormant for the better part of a year. But he could go no further.

The motions filed in the criminal and immigration courts on Hemnauth's behalf were substantive, but also largely procedural, as precursors to the main thrust of Bryan's attempt to have Hemnauth released. The linchpin of the strategy was to petition the office of the Queens district attorney and to speak to the humanity of the prosecutors. The request was modest, circumspect and respectful of the district attorney's mission of protecting

---

221 Lonegan, "In the Matter of Hemnauth Mohabir: Memorandum of Law in Support of Respondent's Motion to Reopen and for a Stay of Removal," quoting Title 8 of the Code of Federal Regulations, section 239.2(f), since moved to 1239(f).

the public from crime. Bryan delivered it in person, in a meeting with a high-ranking prosecutor very familiar with Hemnauth's case. He did not go so far as to press the DA to simply vacate Hemnauth's misdemeanor, that is, consent to having the court erase it. No. He knew the DA held the cards and he, Bryan, was not in a position to throw down a gauntlet. Rather, he requested of the prosecutor that he join him in filing a late appeal of the conviction, nothing more, out of goodwill toward a man who had suffered in such great disproportion. With a formal appeal pending in criminal court, there would be no standing conviction against Hemnauth, and the immigration judge could order him released from mandatory detention under IIRIRA.

A release would not forever cancel Hemnauth's removal, but would render it unenforceable until a resolution of his appeal of the misdemeanor. Out of jail, and with deportation's sword of Damocles withdrawn, albeit temporarily, Bryan would be in a much better position to fight Hemnauth's removal and argue for the late dismissal of the misdemeanor. Even if the appeal failed, Hemnauth would at least be in a position to prepare for his departure from the United States, mitigate the separation from his family and perhaps avoid the ostracism heaped upon immigrants dispatched to exile directly from their place of detention. I would go so far as to speculate that a judge, hearing an appeal at the joint request of the prosecutor and a new defense attorney, might have been more prone to consider Hemnauth's previous attorney's failure to inform his client of the repercussions of his waiver of his rights. Hemnauth's moral character — including Judge Riefkohl's testament to it, written and on the record — and his punitive treatment during eighteen months in detention could have been entered into evidence.

Let alone that reunion with his son, and the lessening of the guilt over his mother's pain, would provide a more serene backdrop to his struggle than could Passaic.

We could identify any number of villains in Hemnauth's story: a sheriff and county freeholders who ranked profit, picayune media celebrity and political advantage over their custodial responsibilities, brutish guards whose behavior bordered on sadism, an ICE field officer who denied parole for a man presenting no public danger while declining to monitor horrible conditions in a detention center under his supervision, and others. I do not know the identity of the senior prosecutor in the Queens district attorney's office whom Bryan approached and was empowered to respond to Bryan's appeal to the DA. His name hardly matters. I *do* know that if I were compelled to select one protagonist of Hemnauth's ordeal as the most wicked of the cast, he would get the nod.

The prosecutor flatly rejected Bryan's request. His response might have been less damning of his person and that of the district attorney had he refused to give a reason for it or invoked some overarching bureaucratic imperative. Instead, he justified his denial by his and his colleagues' displeasure at the jury for having acquitted Hemnauth on the felony charges they had brought against him eight years earlier. Hemnauth's incarceration and pending exile under immigration law were the DA's way of exacting punishment against Hemnauth for crimes a jury said he did not commit after a trial conducted under all the rules of judicial due process. It is true that long were the odds of Hemnauth winning an appeal of his misdemeanor had Mr. Landou pursued it at the time. In fact, the very failure to appeal left the door open to Bryan's petition to the district attorney to allow a late one. But that is precisely the point: Bryan offered the DA an opportunity to align justice with minimal empathy. His office showed no interest in doing so.

In short, the prosecutor's motives were revenge for a verdict his office did not like and the satisfaction of offsetting it with punishment dispensed by the federal government in lieu of any imposed by the state of New York. The ethical argument against him is simple: confronted with a choice of vindictiveness over an uncomplicated act of basic humanity, the prosecutor chose the former. Uncomplicated because Bryan's plea did not entail mercy for a guilty man seeking to duck his penalty in part or in full: Hemnauth had paid the price imposed by his sentence. Basic, because what is more fundamental than a parent's desire for union with his child?

The prosecutor's response suggests misuse of the duty to uphold the law on the part of the Queens district attorney's office and points to a disturbing ramification of the immigration code that permits it.

Granted, the misuse I perceive exists on an ethical rather than a legal plane, since the law gave the district attorney the unconditional prerogative to either agree to a late appeal of Hemnauth's standing conviction or not. When I first discussed this point with Bryan, with his trademark penchant for honest debate, he objected that the district attorney might have been seeking to fulfill his mission of protecting the public from drug traffic. However, as I countered to Bryan, a DA's mission is to prosecute alleged traffickers to the full extent of the evidence, not convict them. That task is up to a jury, in a court, under the rules of due process. To the extent that the verdict of a jury is the law — and few would argue that it is not — it is as much the duty of law officers, including the district attorney, to uphold it as any other. In Hemnauth's case, by its own admission, the Queens DA's office saw in Hemnauth's imprisonment and exile a loophole for evading the decision of a jury, in effect corrupting it. Bryan conceded the point and later also ascribed the DA's position to spite.

It is symptomatic of the immigration and deportation system that the decision to deport Hemnauth ultimately landed in the hands of a local district attorney's office. By depriving Judge Riefkohl of the judicial discretion he needed to fully adjudicate the merits of Hemnauth's case, the immigration law, in effect, transferred that discretion from an impartial judge to prosecutors whose actions were driven by an ulterior motive: to mark their disapproval of Hemnauth's acquittal on felony charges and exact a penalty that a jury's verdict of "not guilty" had precluded.

According to Hemnauth, the prosecutors also told Bryan that they had other evidence of misbehavior, as if to justify the hard line they were taking. None related to either the felony for which they had taken him to court, or any other drug-related matter, and no other charges had ever been brought. Rather, they claimed, they knew of Hemnauth's involvement in instances of disorderly conduct. (They may have been referring to Hemnauth's being present when his juvenile-minded pal Phillip was stopped by the police for performing "doughnut" skids in an empty parking lot with his boss's limousine.) How disorderly conduct correlates with drug dealing is left to our imagination. By piling up the unsubstantiated accusations, the prosecutor further drowned reason in rancor.

Without the goodwill of the district attorney, Hemnauth's case before the immigration court lost most if not all leverage. Bryan had also invoked Hemnauth's application for U.S. citizenship, and had pointed to items in the immigration code that might have allowed a judge some latitude to terminate a deportation process in order to allow a detainee to pursue naturalization. The rub was that the applicant needed to plea extraordinary hardship — in Hemnauth's case the forced severance from his child — and demonstrate good moral character. Bryan addressed both requirements and any reasonable person would most likely concur that Hemnauth had satisfied them. However, the code explicitly notes that this particular provision must be used very sparingly. Hemnauth's circumstances might have been extraordinary by any absolute tally, that is, as compared to most people residing in the United States, but compared to that of other aliens in his situation his hardship was less than absolutely exceptional. There was ample precedent of the government deporting many an immigrant away from family, even his or her American children. Similarly, the condition of good moral character had to be met for an uninterrupted period of five years. Hemnauth also met that requirement, provided one count his time in detention toward it, or, alternatively include the year between being charged in 1996 and convicted of his misdemeanor one year later. The judge was not formally precluded from doing either, but the admonishment to use hardship relief stingily would certainly hinder a plea containing any ambiguity. Hemnauth recalls that Riefkohl had inquired about counting his time in detention toward the requisite five-year record of good moral character, but ICE told him that they did not consider time in detention U.S. residency. The inquiry and response reinforce the impression of a judge answerable to a prosecutor.

Absent the concurrence of the district attorney in Bryan's request for a late appeal, the judge in Queens denied it. A lawyer for the Office of Immigration Review immediately sent Riefkohl a submission opposing any reopening of Hemnauth's immigration case. It was four lines long and simply stated that since Hemnauth's misdemeanor had not been set aside, there were no grounds for reconsidering his removal.

The morning after Sai Baba appeared in Hemnauth's dream transubstanti-
ated as Abraham Lincoln, Bryan Lonegan arrived at Passaic to deliver the
news that he had been unsuccessful in his bid to enlist the district attorney's
cooperation. Consequently, the court in Queens would not grant a late appeal of the misdemeanor, and Riefkohl would feel bound by the rules to
deny the request to reconsider the deportation order. Hemnauth took the
news in stride and, respectful of what he assumed was his lawyer's busy
schedule, prepared to take leave of him.

"He wasn't in a hurry to leave . . . He kind of stayed a long time with
me. It was a little unusual." Or perhaps not, at least not for Bryan Lonegan.
True, Bryan is a lawyer's lawyer, meticulous, methodical and candid. Yet
atop his realism sits a rich layer of empathy for those he feels have been
deprived of justice with a capital J, notwithstanding the wording of the
legal code. IIRIRA is the law, a fact Bryan made plain to his clients and to
those whose cases he turned down as hopeless while working as an immigration attorney. That does not mean he likes it, nor does it mean that he
received the turndown of the Queens district attorney's office with clinical
detachment. His legal strategy was as sound as they come, of that there is
no dispute, and Bryan has never second-guessed himself. Still, he later told
me that he felt he had let Hemnauth down, that he had been unable to deliver justice to a man who represented an epitome of IIRIRA's failings. This
continued to haunt him for a very long time. So it was certainly in character
for Bryan to spend an extended moment with Hemnauth to help him sort
through the repercussions of the news he was bringing, as an attorney and
a fellow human being who had befriended him.

Bryan was willing to take the case further and explore other legal avenues. Such an effort would entail obtaining a federal court review under
the extremely tight rules governing judicial intercession in immigration appeals. IIRIRA is specifically designed to distance the judiciary system from
deportation decisions, severely narrowing the scope of intervention to formal constitutional issues, and to the strict exclusion of fact-finding or other
areas of scrutiny. Under these circumstances, the slog would be a long one
and success less than guaranteed. Bryan was willing to go the extra mile —
or, rather, the extra trip to hell and back — but had to make it clear that
Hemnauth would carry the bulk of a heavy burden.

"What will it cost me?" Hemnauth asked. Needless to say, the inquiry was not about money. "Bryan did the right things. He put the cards on the table."

Bryan told him petitioning the federal circuit court of appeals to hear the case and waiting for a ruling on it would take as much as three years. He had not even settled on what legal strategy he might adopt to push the case into the judicial system. Hemnauth would remain in jail for the entire period. "I told Bryan, I have had enough. To go through another three years . . . I might not last. Danger is all around you. Any second, something can go wrong. I would like to go home."

Not much earlier, "home" meant New York, with his young American son safely in his care. The deportation system had succeeded in forcing Hemnauth Mohabir to surrender to the hopelessness of its gulag, to the banishment of justice from its sphere, to its sentence of permanent exile.

Bryan completed the process of petitioning Judge Riefkohl for relief, without illusions. Still, in a final twist, telling of the tangle that our immigration code has created, Judge Riefkohl erroneously stated in his final decision that the section giving him the authority to suspend removal in order to allow Hemnauth to apply for citizenship had been deleted from the code. It had not been deleted, but rather moved; the wording remained the same. Bryan corrected him and entered a motion to reconsider. Without any expectation that he would prevail, Hemnauth instructed Bryan to withdraw it and to inform Riefkohl that he would no longer contest his removal.

His ordeal would come to an end, only not quite yet.

11

MR. MOHABIR, WAIT!

HEMNAUTH'S DECISION TO ABANDON THE BATTLE against his deportation co-incided with one last and particularly ugly threat on his person by the Passaic guards. It occurred a few days before his last conference with Bryan. The trigger was a random punishment by an officer who decided that Hemnauth be deprived his outdoor time one evening for having spoken on the way to the rooftop gym, in violation of a warden's or an officer's arbitrary "no talking" rule. In the jailhouse atmosphere of constant dispossession, the loss of the most meager entitlement made an enormous dent in an inmate's morale. With the quality of the detainees' existence pared to the bone — to the point where a guard could forbid inmates from talking at whim — any suggestion of further erosion was to be resisted. By then, Hemnauth admits, his survival instincts had been laid bare, as had his temper. When told he had lost his gym privilege for having shown the audacity to speak without permission — which he had not done — he accused the officer of lying. The officer voiced his exception to Hemnauth's disrespect by calling him a "brown piece of shit," an acceptable retort in the guard's tally despite the obvious dissymmetry. Hemnauth responded by telling the guard that he would file a formal complaint for the racial slur. The guard called a superior and they brought Hemnauth to isolation for a hearing. They took statements — including the guard's contention that Hemnauth had used "abusive language" — but there was no hearing.

The guard's animosity spread to his peers, already at odds with Hemnauth for his advocacy of detention reform, punctuated by a hunger strike deemed to have been serious enough to potentially awaken ICE from its oversight lethargy. At roll call two mornings later, Hemnauth rose to display his name band. The officer taking the roll smirked, "Are you eating now, you cocksucker?" Hemnauth cannot stomach references to his presumed promiscuity or sexual proclivities. There is nothing in the detention standards that says he must. Even allowing for an elevated degree of delicacy toward sex in Hemnauth's upbringing, the degrading intent of the verbal abuse could not have been clearer. A few minutes later, a sergeant walked by, and Hemnauth beckoned to him to complain about the guard's provocation. In response, the offending officer, still present, requested of his superior that he "open the gate and let me smack the shit out of him." He did not leave the impression that his proposal was a rhetorical flourish, but a menace he would carry out at his earliest opportunity. Four witnesses signed affidavits.

The incident explains, in part, the serenity with which Hemnauth received the disappointing news about his court case from Bryan Lonegan. His fear that "any second something can go wrong" was neither hypothetical musing nor hyperbole.

Just as Hemnauth's case was finally coming to a head, Rachel Meeropol secured the support of her organization, the Center for Constitutional Rights, for a class action against Passaic County Jail, challenging the conditions of detention there. She would need to be officially retained by Hemnauth and others in order to file a complaint and prepared to receive the final installment of his formal statement substantiating it. It is clear from Rachel's subsequent correspondence that Hemnauth's testimony would be instrumental. Not only was he methodical in gathering evidence inside the prison and journaling the abuse, but, since he had been in residence at Passaic for an extended period, he represented continuity in the observation of the jail's detention practices. Rachel knew something was brewing in Hemnauth's case when she came to see him at Passaic to review the class action filing with him. The ICE transit office had already assembled travel documents in anticipation of Hemnauth's deportation, even before the review requested by Bryan Lonegan on his behalf became dead letter, owing to the hard line adopted by the Queens district attorney's office. The stay ordered by Judge Riefkohl while Bryan attempted to have the misdemeanor vacated may have focused ICE's attention; a reinstatement of the order in the event of an adverse ruling would allow ICE to proceed with Hemnauth's deportation without impediment.

Hemnauth alerted Rachel as soon as he and Bryan concluded that he would accept removal and notify the immigration judge that he would enter no further pleas. Hemnauth's courage had deeply affected Rachel, and she felt relieved that he would be leaving the Passaic "hellhole" where he had suffered so much at the hands of the state and be "free in the huge, wide world."[222] At the same time, it was apparent to her that Hemnauth's departure from Passaic and the transfer of other plaintiffs would make progress on the class action against Passaic considerably more difficult, as she expressed in a subsequent letter.[223] Other circumstances would disrupt legal action against Passaic for its treatment of immigrant detainees, specifically Sheriff Speziale's later decision, in 2006, to terminate the jail's housing agreement with ICE merely weeks before CCR was to file its suit. Rachel and her colleagues continued their efforts in support of human and civil rights, including further legal action on behalf of immigrant detainees.[224]

Hemnauth chuckles as he recalls his last shakedown at Passaic County Jail at around 3 a.m. in the night prior to his transfer. The raid was particularly disruptive and, in Hemnauth's recollection, gratuitous. He has no doubt that it was staged for the guards' own entertainment. They found particular amusement in soiling inmates' bedding with toothpaste and grooming fluids purchased at the commissary, and throwing mattresses around, a mainstay of detainee repression. They made "a real mess . . . That's entertainment. That's their fun."

Hours later, at about 10 a.m., forty-five detainees, including Hemnauth, were ordered to pack up "their shit" for transfer to nearby Hudson County

222 Meeropol, in a letter to Hemnauth Mohabir, September 19, 2003.
223 Meeropol, in a letter to Hemnauth Mohabir, October 22, 2003.
224 Chang, Olshansky, and Meeropol et al., "Ibrahim Turkmen et al. Against John Ashcroft et al.: Third Amended Class Action Complaint and Demand for Jury Trial."

Correctional Center in Kearny, New Jersey, about fifteen miles away. There is no specific indication that Hemnauth's losing his legal battles triggered the transfer, especially as it involved a relatively large number of detainees. What seems more likely — albeit less than absolutely certain given the lack of documentary evidence — is that Passaic County authorities, including the freeholders, were feeling the heat of the protests against the conditions in the jail and may have wished to thin the ranks, at least temporarily, and rid itself of a few troublesome inmates, Hemnauth among them. News of the transfer made it into the local press, not an earth-shattering occurrence, but an unusual one, nevertheless.[225] Also, ICE officials were well aware of Hemnauth's and Nigel's concurrent hunger strikes, and as annoyed as they may have been at the strikers, it behooved the jail to calm any appetite the local ICE office may have had for anything more than a token investigation.

The men were shackled and cuffed by an ICE transit officer and loaded into vans for the short ride to Hudson. The inmates recovered whatever belongings Passaic had confiscated and held in storage. The Hudson guards greeting their new charges were "very nice. They treat us with respect." Respect qualified as a novelty, notwithstanding the strip search, which was "pretty quick." I continue to question the need to perform a strip search on nonviolent detainees — not prisoners — without specific grounds and when the opportunity was remote for shackled men to acquire contraband during a thirty-minute nonstop van ride. Still, the strip search at Hudson was, thankfully, conducted without the prurience that had infected the ritual at Passaic. Inmates were called for medical examinations individually over the course of a week.

Unlike the tortuous induction procedure at Passaic, which had lasted for many hours and brewed hostility among the inmates and contempt from the guards, Hudson's was rapid, with the apparent objective of getting inmates to their quarters without delay or incident.

Purgatory looks like Eden to one rising from hell, and such was Hemnauth's first impression of Hudson. The dorm was vast by comparison, and there were three working television sets. Sleeping quarters were arranged on two levels around a central space. They were unmistakably jailhouse

---

225 Travers, "Immigration Detainees Move from Passaic Jail to Hudson."

cells, but they were clean and the HVAC system functioned adequately. Each cell actually had a "light you to turn on and off as you liked," Hemnauth exclaims, another contrast to Passaic where the lights burned day and night without regard for possible sleep deprivation and disorientation — or, I cannot help but suspect, as a deliberate feature of the Passaic penal ambiance. Also, a table, stool and two stacked bunks, not three with the top one wedged just beneath the ceiling as at Passaic. A toilet as well, typical of prison design and a reminder to the inmates of where they were. The shower room, however, had a door that could be locked from the inside during use, allowing detainees to wash privately, another privilege denied them at Passaic.

There were fewer complaints about food, if for no other reason that electric pots for heating water were available and permitted, and the commissary stocked items such as instant noodles, as well as seasonings to cut the blandness of the prison fare. The diet trays were similar to Passaic's, minus the relentless filth.

Hemnauth could also see outside through a window in his cell. The pane was of the same long and narrow dimensions as at Passaic, but the transparency of the glass had not been scratched away. There was also a window to the common room — more for the guards to be able to see in than for the inmates to see out — and the cell door could be locked to bar entry not by the guards, but by anyone else. Since Hemnauth had acquired the habit of working by night and napping by day, this was an important feature, not to mention a deterrent to assault by another inmate who might wish him harm, a phenomenon with which he had some familiarity.

Unsurprisingly, the improved comforts at Hudson, modest as they were, had a soothing effect on the relationships among inmates, which had veered toward the animalistic at Passaic. The fighting among them stopped. Hemnauth reported that even the Cuban detainee who had literally wanted to kill him at Passaic turned amiable once at Hudson. Life without shakedowns and unprovoked retribution gave detainees something worth protecting, a reason to avoid trouble with the guards who, at first blush, seemed not to be looking for it.

Of all the perquisites offered by Hudson, the one Hemnauth valued perhaps most was the license to choose his own bunkmate. He eventually got to choose Farouk Abdel-Muhti, his friend and co-resistor from his earlier days at Passaic.

The government had it in for Farouk. As I outlined earlier, he did have a record of immigration violations and a checkered past, including a conviction for attempted assault in 1993[226], pursuant to a domestic dispute. Although Farouk had played a game of cat and mouse with immigration enforcement for many years and to the aggravated annoyance of the INS and ICE, his criminal file and immigration record were of less interest to the government than his pro-Palestinian militancy conducted over the airwaves. Had the government been able to enlist a host country, he would almost certainly have been deported. However, he was stateless, not a danger to the public, and under the *Zadvydas* ruling by the Supreme Court, ICE could not hold him indefinitely. However, ICE was not about to release him without a fight whose tactics included making his life extremely difficult.

From Passaic, he was transferred first to York County Prison in Pennsylvania — further from his support group — where he was held in 23-hour lockdown for almost 250 days, then to Bergen County Jail back in New Jersey, where he was beaten and kicked by guards.[227] He arrived at Hudson in December 2003, about two months after Hemnauth and in deteriorating health.

The pair resumed their writing, with Farouk supplying most of the thematic content and Hemnauth committing it to paper. The topics now usually addressed ICE and immigration policy in general, less often the conditions of detention that had preoccupied them at Passaic. The experience of Passaic was still raw in their memory and they were not about to either forget or forgive it. However, their immediate concerns had shifted, Hemnauth's to how long until he was to be removed, Farouk to his case for release in the United States. By the time he reunited with Hemnauth at Hudson, he must have known the law was on his side and had good reason to push for a prompt end to his imprisonment.

Hemnauth's initial impression of the Hudson County jail as a luxury resort in comparison to Passaic predictably wore off with time. Eventually, it showed its stripes as one more cog in the infernal machinery of immigra-

---

226 "Farouk Abdel-Muhti v. John D. Ashcroft."
227 "Government 'Disappears' NY Palestinian Activist to Atlanta."

tion enforcement as practiced by ICE, purposefully harsh and, when push came to shove, repressive.

"Farouk had a problem." At Hudson, breakfast would typically arrive at about 5 o'clock in the morning. While other inmates would accept their trays and return to their cots, Hemnauth left Farouk to the privacy of their cell, so he could use the toilet at his ease. The medical department had issued him blood pressure medication — "little red [unmarked] pills" — that produced severe constipation, so severe that it virtually blocked his ability to pass his waste altogether for weeks on end. "So one day, I tried one of these red pills . . . to see what was going on." The effect on Hemnauth was identical to what Farouk was suffering: bad cramps followed by hard, tiny, dark red and blackish stool fragments. "I got scared." Especially as Farouk's unresolved cramps increased in frequency.

It happened that Farouk had kept the labels from prescription bottles that had been confiscated as he was moved from jail to jail, so he could document a doctor's recommended dosage. Hemnauth took the pills and the labels to an older Egyptian detainee, who went by the name of George. He had trained as a chemist and apparently had lectured at the college level in Egypt. (Hemnauth describes him as a university professor.) He had a very difficult time coping with prison life, which affected him psychically, resulting in erratic behavior such as random, unintelligible shouting. He was too afraid to sleep in a shared cell. Other inmates believed him mentally disturbed and would avoid him. Hemnauth and Farouk, attuned to the man's emotional misery, made the effort to befriend him. "I realized this was not an ordinary man." His bouts of antisocial psychosis ebbed, and he was able to speak of his profession. Hemnauth brought him Farouk's red pills, and George estimated that they were about double the dosage a doctor had prescribed. I cannot know how George was able to determine the active ingredient in the pill or its identity, other than to speculate that it belonged to a class of medications called calcium channel blockers, with constipation as a common side effect.[228] Regardless, Farouk's health was in rapid decline, his vibrancy greatly diminished, his physical strength sapped, his movement ever slower. He protested to the medical department, demanding to see his own doctor. Hemnauth believes that the Hudson jail

---

228 "Medications for Treating Hypertension," *Harvard Women's Health Watch*.

authorities would have made some effort to accommodate him, since it would not work to ICE's favor for a judge to observe a party present at a hearing visibly diminished from being in the custody of the government. In the end, Farouk was released with his health irreversibly compromised.

Notwithstanding its outward appearance as a more civilized jailhouse, Hudson participated in a system that condoned a punitive outlook in its network of outsourced detention centers. Hudson may have eschewed the numbing, drumbeat oppression of Passaic. Like Middlesex County Jail, it had long adopted the direct-supervision model of behavior control by promoting human connections between officers and inmates. Still, Hudson was a patch of a leopard's skin that would not change all its spots. Two incidents at Hudson stand out in Hemnauth's memory, for different reasons.

The first once again revealed a detention regimen that catered to either the prurient interest of guards or their propensity to reduce detainees to the status of animals by treating their public nudity as an admissible display. Toward the end of Hemnauth's stay at Hudson, his block was strip-searched, anal probe included, on the command of a female police sergeant who claimed knowledge of a hidden weapon. (None was found.) Male officers escorted inmates, two by two, into the showers to undress and be searched, closing the door enough to shield their nakedness from the view of the woman. This would not do. She ordered the doors remain open, professing a need to watch, which she did, intently. In fairness, several of the male officers ordered to perform the shakedown were appalled, cushioning some of the sting of the humiliation. After nearly two years of cavalier regard for his humanity, including his right to a degree of modesty consistent with his culture and disposition, Hemnauth had become a little jaded, at least in his telling of the incident several years later. Still, the indignity of the frequent forced nudity sticks in his mind.

The second Hudson episode he recounted to me was a beating that ranked as the most savage he witnessed in his time in immigration detention. In fact, he later told Daniel Zwerdling of NPR that it was "the most disturbing act of violence he'[d] ever seen,"[229] despite it being far from the first.

---

229 Zwerdling, "Immigrant Detainees Claim Brutal Treatment at Passaic County Jail."

After yet another shakedown, the detainees were returning to their re-spective cells. One man, a very even-tempered Egyptian by the name of Sadek (pronounced sah-deek), was calmly proceeding toward the flight of steps to the dorm's second level of cells, where his was located. Hemnauth remembers him as so untroublesome as to have had a calming influence over those around him more prone to anger. Sadek had no criminal record and had been tortured in Egypt as a young man for having been a mem-ber of the Muslim Brotherhood, from which he had long strayed. He was picked up after being stopped for a traffic violation, charged with overstay-ing his visa, and spent fifteen months in detention without a hearing in immigration court.[230]

A guard by the name of Vargas[231] ordered Sadek to hurry, coaxing him toward a random cell. Hemnauth heard Sadek respond with "I have a right to . . ." He did not hear the end of his sentence, but assumed Sadek wished to continue back to his own cell at a normal walking pace. Yelling, "You have no rights!" — another recurring theme of abasement cultivated by immigrants' jailers — Vargas "ran at" Sadek. At this signal the other of-ficers piled on, joining the lopsided rumble. Once they had shoved their victim into a cell, they began to beat him mercilessly. He screamed in pain. The officers kept at it for about ninety seconds, according to Hemnauth. Sadek managed to force his way out of the cell into the common area, where now Hemnauth could witness the scene through the window of his cell door. The guards ran after Sadek, joined by others from across the main room. "When I looked through the glass of door, I saw Sadek lying on the floor. Now, I could see!" Vargas was kicking him in the face and head. Guards surrounded him, "kicking him like they were playing foot-ball." One kicked him repeatedly in the back, yet another in the stomach. They broke several teeth, and damaged his knees. "It was disgusting. I got real mad at that thing . . . They were kicking the shit out of the man. Then they bodily dragged him out of the dorm" by his legs. "That was the worst injury [from a beating] I have ever seen." And he had seen many. Hem-nauth told me he was crying with rage and frustration as he watched guards

---

230 Romero et al., "America's Disappeared."
231 The name was given me by Hemnauth and is confirmed in Daniel Zwerdling's interview of Sadek Awaed. See Zwerdling, "Immigrant Detainees Claim Brutal Treatment."

assault and torture a fellow detainee. His heartache was amplified only by the practical truth of Vargas's *cri de guerre:* "You have no rights!" It captured the entire spirit of a system that had seized control of his life with a mere parody of due process.

The Sadek incident led to Hemnauth's final resistance initiative prior to his deportation. With Farouk gone, he had once again assumed leadership of rights advocacy within the prison walls. Conditions at Hudson did not provide the steady flow of grievances that Passaic had, but what the jail lacked in the number of reportable instances of abuse it made up for in ferocity when its guards attacked Sadek. Also, the jail assigned Vargas, the officer who had started the police riot, to be the lead corrections officer of Hemnauth's pod, a decision Hemnauth specifically and vocally protested. (He was told that Vargas was needed in order to maintain discipline in the wake of a disturbance . . . that Vargas had fomented.)

Hemnauth also demanded that he be able to see Sadek and assure that he would be taken for medical care to a "civilian" hospital. Hemnauth simply did not trust the jail's infirmary or its independence from the correctional prerogatives of the guards. The response — a bluff — bordered on the farcical. The officers Hemnauth confronted, in the presence of a social worker, "consulted" the inmate list and professed not to find Sadek on it. They would, they said, attempt to locate him. "If Sadek had really gone missing, the place would have been locked down like a war zone." Hemnauth told the officials as much, referring to his two years of experience with the detention regimen and practices. "I told them they couldn't fool me. You would have seen helicopters flying around . . . it would have been all [over] the news. I told them, 'You think I'm stupid [enough] to believe this crap?'"

In reality, Sadek was interned in the prison infirmary, where Hemnauth saw him in passing. "The prison was hiding [him] there." Although Sadek had been injured by the guards, after emergency treatment and a short disability stay in the jail's clinic, he could have been allowed back to his cell between whatever therapy sessions he required. However, "they did not want Sadek to alert his lawyers" while he was covered in bruises and bandaged. The jail could not legally deny him visitors, certainly not from a lawyer, and his visible wounds might have been very damning of the jail's management.

Hemnauth would not be silenced and called the bluff. He confronted an

ICE field representative in charge of the oversight of immigration detention at Hudson — for what that oversight was worth. The agent visited
Sadek's cell and left without comment. Soon thereafter, a guard arrived and
asked his cellmate to pack Sadek's belongings. "They took it away."

Hemnauth alerted his civil rights contacts, by letter and telephone, about
the Sadek beating, and a steady stream of them arrived to take his testimony about it. He speaks fluidly of the event today, and he kept his turbulent
emotions in check when he challenged the prison officials, including the
ICE agent. He also confesses that he was so shaken up by the barbarity of
the assault against his co-inmate that he had trouble talking about it with
visitors until about two weeks had passed and he "had become normal,
again . . . I was very emotionally upset over this thing. I really couldn't talk
about it [without breaking down]." To this day, Hemnauth cannot get over
the idea of a man being cudgeled by public officials simply for having pronounced the four words, "I have a right."

Rain in drops the size of small fruit once again falls from the skies over
Trinidad and reverberates on the roof above us as Hemnauth recounts
his last day in an America that had turned on him like a hellcat and confined him to a stealthy gulag for two years. These included an almost six-
month coda at Hudson, after Hemnauth had formally abandoned any and
all actions against his removal.[232] I do not doubt that there is some sort of
procedural explanation for the additional jail time ICE imposed on Hemnauth. One possibility is that the government of Guyana dragged its heels
before issuing Hemnauth's travel documents. It had a history of resisting
the return of its expatriates, and ICE had to threaten Guyana periodically
with blocking its officials from visiting the United States unless it stepped
up its cooperation. Nevertheless, a moral question remains as to why ICE
kept a man behind bars who had never been sentenced to jail time for another almost six months once he had acquiesced to removal. He was not
a terror suspect, nor had he been charged with any other unlitigated crime
that might have prompted further investigation. ICE never furnished an

232 Lonegan, "Withdrawal of Motion to Reconsider."

explanation. It held Hemnauth longer because it could, regardless of the practical reason for doing so, or the absence of one.

I could not help but be reminded of an episode from my own past. Decades ago, I harbored in my home political refugees from South America, expelled from their respective countries during the continent's Dirty War, *la Guerra Sucia.* One was a woman named Iris. After serving two years without being charged, she had been cleared of any and all crimes, yet held another two years in a ghastly jail in Argentina before being expelled from the country.

Argentina, at the time, was run by an unrepentant dictatorship. How much better, really, was this? Our government had fought aggressively to cut off all avenues of relief and obtain a deportation order. ICE had had two years to prepare to carry it out. Its inability to do so, whether due to a failure of diligence or extraneous impediment, resulted in a surfeit of punishment without trial or due process. I wonder if such a concern even crossed the mind of anyone in ICE's employ. It crossed Bryan Lonegan's, and in March 2004 he wrote to ICE's Detention and Removal Branch to request that it move with greater urgency.[233]

Within a month it finally did. (I can also postulate with some confidence that had ICE kept Hemnauth in detention much longer, he could have moved to be released under the Supreme Court's *Zadvydas* decision limiting removal delays to six months.) A deportation officer appeared at Hudson to inform Hemnauth that his travel documents and plane ticket had been issued. The man took some ID pictures. Two weeks later, "a guard came and told me: 'Hey, Mohabir, pack up your shit.'" It was music to his ears, "shit" and all. He did not ask where they were taking him. By then he knew. "I was going home."

There was an exchange of clothing. Hemnauth recovered the civvies he had been wearing at the time of his arrest at Kennedy Airport two years earlier, and surrendered, gladly, his prison garb. He distributed most of his belongings from his cell to other inmates: T-shirts, pens, books, commissary food and the like. They were happy for it. They slapped his back, thrust phone numbers on him and wished him Godspeed. It was not the freedom he had fought for, and certainly not the justice, but it was freedom

---

233 Bryan Lonegan, in a letter to Robert Margist, March 10, 2004.

nonetheless. Along with the hand-me-downs, the release of a fellow detainee, even into exile, put the other inmates in a mood of celebration.

The process of leaving the Hudson County Correctional Center was
swift. Some papers to sign, certifying the return of his property, the ICE
transit officer acknowledging custody of the detainee; that was all. "When
I went out that door, I did not even want to turn around and look at [the
place I was leaving.]" When he had departed Passaic, he had shifted in his
seat and craned his neck to see whether the jail appeared as horrible from
the outside as it had proved to be from within. Not this time. His next
project, Hemnauth told me, was to forget. A project he quickly realized he
would have to abandon.

Hemnauth knew the ICE escort, Rodriguez, who had been assigned as
an ICE liaison to Passaic and Hudson. Rodriguez was powerless, but had
been consistently empathetic toward Hemnauth during his incarceration.
He cuffed Hemnauth as ordered by his procedures manual and put him
in the van for the drive to the airport. On the ride he chided Hemnauth
in jest for the "trouble I had caused him" for having been so outspoken a
detainee. It was clear to Hemnauth that Rodriguez believed many of the
grievances well founded, but any attempt at redress or reform was beyond
his pay grade.

They stopped at an ICE field office near Kennedy to collect $200 that
Rahoni had left for Hemnauth and that now represented his entire treasure.
Another officer joined the escort party.

When Hemnauth stepped from the vehicle, Rodriguez surrendered to
an urge to make a symbolic gesture toward the good man he was bringing to exile. He removed Hemnauth's cuffs, in violation of the prescribed
protocol, confident that Hemnauth would not "give him a hard time." He
wanted Hemnauth to take his last steps in America a free man, on principle.
Rodriguez walked ten feet to his left, his ICE colleague a few paces behind.
They kept Hemnauth in their line of sight, an alternative protocol to the
cuffs, although not an approved one. Still, it would have occurred to no one
that Hemnauth was under police escort. Rodriguez had spared him this last
humiliation on U.S. soil, and was pleased to have done so.

They walked up to the gate agent moments before departure. Near the
bottom of the jetway, Rodriguez instructed Hemnauth to stand back, as he
conferred with the flight's purser at the aircraft door, within easy earshot.

"Is he a dangerous one?" she asked as Rodriguez handed over Hemnauth's travel documents. "Do we have to take precautions?"

"No, he's okay," Rodriguez assured her. He beckoned Hemnauth forward, gestured him onto the plane and turned to leave. Just as Hemnauth was stepping aboard, Rodriguez called back to him: "'Mr. Mohabir, wait!'" Hemnauth went to him, thinking there might be a last-minute complication or overlooked process step that might send him back to detention. Nothing of the sort. Rodriguez embraced him as he would a friend or brother.

"He told me, 'When you get back to Guyana, run for president. You'll win.' He wished me luck. He said some nice things . . . He was apologizing for what the INS had done to me."

Sadek Awaed was deported to his native Egypt shortly after Hemnauth's return to Guyana. When Daniel Zwerdling interviewed Sadek several months later at his brother's home in Alexandria, a monster with the visage of the guard who beat him still visited in a recurring nightmare, trying to strangle him. "Sadek Awaed says — can you imagine? — he spent 13 years of his life trying to make his mark in the United States, and a few guards beat the hope out of him in a handful of minutes."[234]

By the time he was released — concurrently with Hemnauth, but from a different detention site — Farouk Abdel-Muhti had seen the inside of seven separate jails. The federal judge who ordered him freed pursuant to the Supreme Court's *Zadvydas* ruling called the government's prosecutorial tactics "Kafkaesque."[235] Farouk died of heart failure three months later.

Hemnauth was detained, again, immediately upon arrival in Guyana in the late afternoon of an illusory day of liberation. He was placed with a few other men in a police holding cell at the airport. The immigration police let them stew for a couple of hours and then returned to interrogate them.

234 Zwerdling, "Investigation of a Case Where Guards at Hudson County Jail Allegedly Assaulted Two Immigrant Detainees."
235 Fisher, "Stateless, Man Avoids Deportation from U.S."

As a deportee from the United States, Hemnauth was viewed dimly. If he was unworthy of U.S. residency, the logic went, he must be damaged goods, guilty of some vice. The Guyanese authorities piggybacked on the branding of deportees as criminals by the American immigration services. His persona non grata status traveled with him, including back to his homeland.

"I made up a story." Hemnauth knew from clippings he had received while in detention that several newspaper articles and newsletters in Guyana had featured the story of his imprisonment in the United States. None of them had mentioned drugs as its reason. With his background as a well-known Guyanese musician from his time at the Ministry of Culture and with bands popular around the country, his saga had presented human-interest appeal for the local press, for a period. The story he now told the police centered on his dissent toward U.S. immigration detention practices. It helped the narrative that the nature of his protests and dissent was factual. It would have been more difficult to explain the circumstances of his misdemeanor, and the Guyanese police upon hearing the word *drug* would treat him as a criminal, regardless of the context of his arrest and his acquittal on felony charges. Due process was not a concern of his handlers, even less an objective.

Hemnauth's answers to the interrogation fell on deaf ears. The police transported him to an infamous lockup at the Brickdam Police Station in Georgetown. The ostensible function of the lockup was pretrial police custody, but there have been reports of longer-term prisoners held at Brickdam. "This was a real filthy, stinking, nasty place," infested with swarms of mosquitoes. Men lay on a rough concrete floor cushioned, at best, by a layer of cardboard. There was no sanitation — none — and human waste was strewn throughout. There was just enough light for the police to see well enough to monitor the prisoners.

Hemnauth immediately made a point of introducing himself to the other Brickdam inmates, who appeared interested in his situation as a returning émigré who had enjoyed some stature before leaving for America. "There were all kinds of people in there," including foreigners. Hemnauth came across an Argentinian, a Sri Lankan and a Canadian, among others. Many if not all the inmates busied themselves creating some semblance of hygiene from the overwhelming contamination of the jail. It was a matter of survival.

Time and distance had eroded his familiarity with the social structure
and politics of Guyana, and he wished to learn what to expect. His immediate imprisonment upon landing did not bode well. He met a man by the
name of Ben — jailed on an alleged weapons violation and later ordered
released by a judge — who outlined not only the state of Guyanese politics,
but the crime situation as well. The latter topic was of immediate concern
to Hemnauth. As the outsider he had become, he was naturally wary of
becoming an unsuspecting target of street violence, which had increased in
Georgetown in his absence. He was also savvy enough to realize, without
much prodding, that lawlessness was likely to breed brutal and indiscriminate action on the part of the police in a country endowed with a relatively
primitive court system. The conditions at Brickdam were a testament to
the equation.

Within a day of his arrival, Hemnauth witnessed brutality to rival the
worst he had seen at Passaic and Hudson. The police pressed a newly arrived detainee into submission by beating him in the head with a padlock,
kicking him until he buckled and finally stomping him on the testicles. "A
real sick thing . . . A lot of people die in jail in Guyana. That was just a little
example."

Hemnauth's younger brother arrived at the prison the next morning,
bearing food — an amenity Brickdam did not provide and which Hemnauth shared with others. Hemnauth's brother "knew the drill" and told
him to expect a further interrogation from Guyana's Criminal Investigation Department. The CID had not participated in his arrest at the airport.
When they arrived to collect Hemnauth, they claimed that normally they
would have been present at customs and spared him the unpleasantness
of his detention among the piles of feces at Brickdam. However, they had
been short a vehicle. Hemnauth saw through the lameness of the excuse.
Still, they did not cuff him, but brought him unshackled to a CID office for
fingerprinting and repeat questioning.

A senior CID officer joined the proceedings to enjoin Hemnauth not to
turn to crime. For some reason, the officer felt duty-bound to warn Hemnauth that his picture would appear in the government-owned *Guyana Chronicle*, identifying him as a returning deportee from the United States and
summarizing the results of his interrogation. The source of the information could only be the CID. Hemnauth deployed his defenses instinctively.

The purpose of highlighting his removal to Guyana could only be to tag him as fair game and expose him to ostracism, or worse. Somehow he would need to persuade the police to refrain from adding him to a thinly veiled hit list. He submitted to the interrogation without hostility, underscoring his actions and reputation as a rights activist contesting the U.S. immigrant detention regime. These were not, of course, the proximate cause of his removal under U.S. immigration law, but the context of his detention and dissent were compelling enough for the CID officer to respect his plea not to disseminate his picture for publication. If nothing else, Hemnauth's testimony to the CID was complex and textured enough to defy an unmitigated portrayal of him as a common criminal expelled from the United States and, hence, as undesirable in Guyana as anywhere else. Hemnauth, by his own admission, had "played a game" with the CID, a successful one as far as he could tell. The police let him go. "They let everyone go." The difference was that Hemnauth was free without the customary appendage of a bull's eye on his back. For a man normally devoid of all guile, he had summoned the degree of cunning he needed to survive in a birthplace now foreign to him.

His reunion with his family was warm and unconditional. For the first evening in years he sat, ate and communed beyond the reach of those who might judge, humiliate or confine him.

He had not, however, ruled the case closed on the matter of the publication of pictures of returning deportees. It did not suffice, in his eyes, that he had won the empathy of a CID officer for himself. It troubled him that the Guyanese police would deliberately imperil anyone, and he set out to confront the issue. He went the next day to the Guyana Human Rights Association on Hadfield Street in Georgetown. A man he describes as a British attorney greeted him coolly and would not allow him past the reception window at the entry. "Guyana was a very dangerous place . . . He was scared." The association had a file comprised of documents and correspondence from various human rights organizations that had followed Hemnauth's immigration case, including copies of numerous items from the New Jersey Civil Rights Defense Committee files.

The cold shoulder did not deter Hemnauth. He took the association lawyer to task for not putting a halt to the newspaper pictures. He insisted that the local association use his writings from their file to stop the practice of tagging — in effect, denouncing — returning emigrants as criminals in the government-run media. "I don't know if he did anything, because it continued for a while." To be clear, Hemnauth firmly believed that exposure in the press encouraged vigilantes, or anyone who might bear a grudge against any individual returning emigrant. Any one of them could be killed with the tacit acquiescence of the police. Dead bodies turned up in Guyana regularly, and inexplicably. That, to Hemnauth, was precisely the point. He also postulated that ostracism against former ICE detainees would deny them a livelihood and lure them to crime. The newspaper photos continued for a while, and some of Hemnauth's acquaintances expressed surprise that his was not among them. He may have been off the hook personally, but he would not let the matter rest.

In fact, Bryan Lonegan contacted him and asked him to look into the case of a gay man, deported from the United States to Guyana, stigmatized by way of his picture in the *Guyana Chronicle* and later killed on the street. Bryan wanted any articles Hemnauth could find on the incident. The request dovetailed with Hemnauth's goal of demonstrating a link between the paper's printing deportees' pictures and unresolved crimes against them. It was not terribly difficult in the small world of Georgetown for Hemnauth to find a friendly acquaintance among the *Chronicle* writers. Hemnauth agreed to sit for an interview on his firsthand experience with human rights' issues in exchange for access to the *Chronicle*'s print archives kept in a seldom-visited storage room. He also discovered that the public free library kept a full set of back issues. The interview was never published. However, the newspaper's editors must have been impressed with Hemnauth's burgeoning mission and wary of his connections to potentially nosy American human rights advocates. They stopped printing the pictures once and for all.

Included in the abbreviated effort attorney John Charles Allen sustained to obtain relief for Hemnauth in immigration court was his cursory reference to the Convention Against Torture, simply stating in a court filing, with little argumentation, that Hemnauth rationally feared for his life in the event he was deported to Guyana. Judge Riefkohl, on his own initiative, dug a little deeper, but relied predominantly on published State Department findings outlining sociopolitical conditions in Guyana. Judge Riefkohl extracted from the State Department assessments that these conditions, while not perfect, did not lead him to presume Hemnauth in danger of probable persecution. State Department human rights reports published shortly after Judge Riefkohl's ruling against Hemnauth note an absence of systematic torture, killings and disappearances on political grounds, while recognizing that an ineffective and poorly supervised Guyanese police may have led to abuses.[236]

To the extent that the attorney decided to pursue relief for his client on the basis of the Convention Against Torture, he might have attempted to gather evidence to bolster the plea. Certainly the stakes for his client were high enough to inspire the extra effort. However, there is no indication that he exerted any.

True, Guyana did not have the record of abuse that has occurred in numbing abundance over the years under deliberately violent regimes around the world, and "political violence intentionally induced by the State in Guyana is relatively rare."[237] As a result, Guyana's rogue police force has not attracted the close scrutiny of international human rights observers with finite resources. (Not to mention that the country is very small, and the Jonestown massacre — an essentially American affair — dwarfed any other event or topic in Guyana's history.) Still, documentation of horrific detention conditions, particularly in police station lockups, disappearances and extrajudicial executions has surfaced and, while scant, such evidence might have made an impression on Judge Riefkohl had he been presented with it.[238]

True, it is a long-shot proposition that an American immigration court — even one presided by a sympathetic judge — might have been swayed by the fragments of evidence available at the time of an embedded human rights problem, to the point of granting relief from deportation. While immigration judges have some discretionary latitude to grant asylum in

236 Bureau of Democracy, "Guyana."
237 Guyana Human Rights Association, "Observations on Occasion of Consideration of Guyana's First Report to the Un Committee on the Convention Against Torture."
238 Guyana Human Rights Association, "Ambivalent About Violence: A Report on Fatal Shootings by the Police in Guyana, 1980 to 2001."

response to defined instances of persecution, the guidelines normally limit it to motions filed within a year of the petitioner's entry into the United States.

Nevertheless, immediately upon arriving in Guyana, Hemnauth uncovered the practice of officially condoned imperilment of returning deportees. It was only his particular charisma that kept him off a hit list. He directly witnessed vile mistreatment by unaccountable police and hideous standards of detention without warrant. All within twenty-four hours of landing.

Hemnauth struggled in Guyana to find stable employment. His mother gave him a roof over his head, and he played paying gigs with various bands for a few dollars in order to contribute whatever he could to the household expenses. Rahoni mailed him his electric guitar. Later in the year of his return, severe coastal flooding[239] disrupted indigenous food supplies. Again, Rahoni came through with a care package for Hemnauth's family. Hemnauth called her his angel. "She still is an angel."

His Apex diploma and various American certifications meant little in Guyana, other than to reinforce his outsider social status, a mark that ultimately did not go away. He still had friends from his youth and made more in the musical circles he infiltrated. Not enough to land a steady job in Georgetown. "Nobody wanted to hire me."

At long last, a friend among the musicians introduced him to the owner of a fishery. His deep freezer had a nagging problem with an esoteric hydraulic component called an inflation pump. No one had been able to solve it, including a mechanic flown in from Florida. The man hemmed and hawed for six months after interviewing Hemnauth, then relented and hired him as his one-man maintenance crew. Hemnauth somehow solved the problem with the hydraulic system. The job was soft servitude, requiring him to rent a house near the fishery and putting him on call twenty-four hours a day, seven days a week, with no reprieve. The boss was unhappy when Hemnauth left his post for two days to perform. "You have

---

239 Ghesquiere et al., "Guyana: Preliminary Damage and Needs Assessment Following the Intense Flooding of January 2005."

to choose between music and your job," he told Hemnauth. The dilemma was an easy one to resolve, and equated for Hemnauth as a choice between freedom and bondage. He had witnessed the latter, up close and personal, in more than one form and in more than one place. He had no desire to sample one more variety of it.

In time — and not much of it — he recognized his estrangement from the place of his birth, and that he had been repatriated to a land that might not reject one of its own out of hand, but that would forever keep him at arm's length.

So would Trinidad, for a time, but it offered a better chance for self-sufficiency. The largely Hindu settlement of Felicity south of the capital Port-of-Spain, where Hemnauth now lives, is endowed with the feel and benefits of a cohesive community. After a probation that has lasted more than five years, Hemnauth has now joined it for the long haul, married his roommate Sherry, and gradually built a new life around work, worship and his artistic aspirations.

The tumult of a violent world is still very much on display in Trinidad. Faced with a murder rate spiraling beyond its control, the government, in the summer of 2011, declared a crime-triggered state of emergency and imposed nighttime curfews.

The violence in Trinidad disturbs and saddens Hemnauth more than it actually scares him, although he has been its witness and victim. In April 2011, he called to tell me that, the week before, he and a friend had been seized at random by drive-by kidnappers at gun- and knifepoint. The kidnappers drove to an automated teller machine and ordered Hemnauth to empty his account. The amount it contained was small and Hemnauth complied. All might have ended without further trauma, but his companion panicked, causing the armed criminals to lose their own nerve as one of them tightened his finger around the trigger. Hemnauth, however, kept his composure and managed to convince the captors that trusting him to calm his terrified friend was preferable to committing the irreversible act of murder. He surrendered his identification as guarantee that he would not risk going to the police. The incident was more than a gauge of the

fragility of life in a developing country. For Hemnauth, it unmasked a supreme irony. Had it not been for the survival skills acquired at Passaic, he
told me, he would have been killed. "Everything happens for a reason," he
said. Even Passaic.

A last, brief tropical downpour pounds the roof as we complete the interview that has lasted five days. We have used every minute and I must leave
for the airport motel I had reserved. My plane to Miami was to depart
early the next morning, and Hemnauth objected to my traveling the crime-
ridden trunk road to the Port-of-Spain airport in the predawn dark, so I
could not remain in Chaguanas for the night. Still, he wanted to leave me
with a concluding thought, a moral to his story. While in prison, he told
me, "I spoke to God in my dreams." In the dream he swore always to heed
a self-imposed commandment: "Remember God at all times. Always chant
His name to escape the tribulations of this dark age."

EPILOGUE AND AFTERWORD

HEMNAUTH MOHABIR'S QUEST ENDED IN DEFEAT. He was deported, separated from his young son and left destitute, returning to start his life from scratch in a land that no longer looked upon him as quite one of its own. Imprisonment had eradicated the advancement he had achieved in his twin careers, as a skilled technician and ensemble musician. It had robbed him of two years of living.

True, there were patches of silver lining. The love between father and son never eroded by the slightest sliver, and in fact strengthened. Rahoni never questioned the fundamental goodness of the man to whom she had been married, never blamed him for the infectious suffering that had spread from Hemnauth to her and to Kevin. Hemnauth's dignity survived, intact and then some, the concerted assaults on his very humanity from prison guards and from the relentless gunnery of American immigration and deportation law. He had earned the abiding affection and respect of peers, advocates and even the judge who signed his deportation order. He emerged in better physical and spiritual health than many others in similar predicaments. He may even have acquired critical survival instincts, as his brush with violent assault in Trinidad arguably demonstrates. Despite these rays of light, there is no way to spin removal, exile and banishment for life as a victory. It is not. That the outcome could have been worse does not reverse it. We cannot sugarcoat the conclusion of his ordeal.

Nonetheless, if we shift the discussion away from the personal result, and toward the immigration detention and deportation regime, Hemnauth Mohabir's struggle appears less vain. Just ask the masters of Passaic.

The Passaic edifice began to scar immediately NPR's Daniel Zwerdling reported the abuses against its immigrant detainees, and in particular its deployment of attack dogs against inmates. Hemnauth was his primary source of information, duly fact-checked. Before the second installment of Zwerdling's story was even aired, the inspector general for the Department of Homeland Security committed to "a review focusing on the treatment of detained aliens."[240] Approximately two weeks after the NPR piece, an ICE spokesperson announced that the agency would no longer send immigration detainees to jails that employed canine units for prisoner control.[241] He claimed that the timing of the announcement in the wake of Zwerdling's reporting was a matter of coincidence, an assertion that strains credulity as much as reporting a visit from the Tooth Fairy.

The reaction of the Passaic County Jail brass to the attack-dog scandal was highly revelatory on several levels. Officials denied that the dogs were a systemic problem, deflecting blame for any incidents on the conduct of the inmates and — old habits die hard — extending the inflammatory "hardened criminal" stereotype that applied to some but far from all. They declined to commit to removing the dogs permanently from inmate-control duty, although Passaic in fact did exactly that. They insisted that any decision about the dogs was theirs alone to make and that they would accommodate ICE with some modifications in a spirit of cooperation, implying that Passaic was not answerable to the agency that hired the jail, a recurring theme of the sheriff. Finally — and quite astonishingly — they defended the use of the dogs because "the age and condition of the jail necessitated their presence."[242] The statement is curious and very damning. A facility contracted to detain aliens pursuant to a civil action, not a correctional sentence, was admitting to having augmented its punitive features to offset its deficiencies and inadequacies as a civil detention center. Such an admission raises a fundamental question: how could Passaic justify accepting federal detainees under contract when its deficiencies were so gaping as to require attack dogs to substitute for appropriate security measures? And, of course, how could the INS and ICE ever have justified awarding or renewing a contract to such a place?

---

240 Zwerdling, "Investigation of a Case."
241 Miller, "Calling Off the Dogs."
242 Miller, "Calling Off the Dogs."

The second ramification of Hemnauth's resistance involved the then–inspector general for the Department of Homeland Security and his field auditors. Passaic was added to a multistate audit after the NPR story was broadcast. The IG's team arrived at Passaic about nine months later and was promptly shown the door by the sheriff. "They're arrogant, they don't know what they are talking about, and they are a disgrace to the federal government," his spokesman harrumphed.[243] Apparently raising questions about documented abuse and violation of standards, clearly within the IG's job description, is an act of disgrace. The sheriff's dismissal of the ICE auditors is also akin to an office employee throwing the boss out of his office or, better yet, a shopkeeper chasing away a customer after pocketing his money. Hemnauth's friend and advocate Flavia Alaya witnessed the inspector general's irritation at Passaic in a meeting with him subsequent to the auditors' ouster from the jail. However, observers from human rights organizations were not invited to hear the later testimony of Passaic inmates.[244] Flavia believes, not unreasonably, that Passaic's sheriff tried to stipulate conditions for his jail's audit.

Nevertheless the audit took place, with findings promised within six months, a deadline that ultimately slipped. No matter how conciliatory ICE might have attempted to be toward Passaic, an audit is an audit, and even the most benign of inspectors could not paper over the entire mass of violations to ICE standards, from health and food to recreation and visitation. Auditors would hear an abundance of serious grievances, including allegations of violent abuse, and would be obligated to mention them in their report, even if they withheld judgment of their accuracy.

With no standing to block publication of an audit by the agency that hired his jail, Sheriff Speziale did the next best thing to head off its publication: he terminated Passaic's contract with ICE before the anticipated date of completion. He also embellished the grounds for doing so, to cloak the motive of evading the scrutiny of a federal inspector general. In his interview with CNN's Lou Dobbs, a news anchor notoriously sympathetic to immigration restrictionists, Speziale blamed human rights activists for his action. Their demonstrations, he alleged, had made the ICE contract disadvantageous. "It's definitely more trouble than it's worth. There are so many

243 Loder, "Sheriff Throws Feds Out of Passaic County Jail!"
244 Alaya, "Showdown at Sheriff's Plaza."

advocacy groups out there. There's demonstrations that cost overtime to the taxpayers of Passaic County, it's really not worth it."

There is no question that the demonstrators and other advocates were a sharp thorn in the sheriff's side, and they were not about to go away. They had persisted since the days when Hemnauth had helped inspire them. A class action lawsuit spearheaded by the Center for Constitutional Rights was imminent, shepherded by Rachel Meeropol, who had worked with Hemnauth in gathering evidence. Combined with the protests, an incriminating inspector general's report could prove costly, but not exactly in the way Speziale contended. It seems implausible that the net revenues to Passaic from ICE were in danger of being wiped out by the fact of marches outside the jail. On the other hand, the confluence of grievances against his treatment of administrative detainees, culminating in a negative report from a federal oversight authority, could be more than the sheriff's well-groomed reputation could withstand.

The remaining immigration detainees were transferred from Passaic within two months. The American Bar Association, apprehensive of violations of detainees' rights as they were being transferred, took it upon itself to write to ICE, insisting "that immigrants and asylum seekers in detention [at Passaic] are not disadvantaged by their transfer."[245] Although he never has, Hemnauth might claim some of the credit for the demise of Passaic's ICE contract.

The Homeland Security inspector general did, in fact, publish a report on immigration detention conditions, although not until December 2006, nine months after its original due date. It whittled the audit down to five detention facilities around the country from ten, but Passaic still figured among them, despite the end of the marriage between ICE and the county.

The report is not a whitewash: it details Passaic's noncompliance with most of ICE's own standards. Inadequate response to medical requests and negligent hunger-strike monitoring. Lax pest and vermin inspections, with no record of treatments. Unsafe stacked beds. Unhygienic food service. Grossly inadequate outdoor time. Missing disciplinary action reports. Missing medical files. No grievance log. No grievance committee. No privacy for phone calls made to legal counsel. Negligent inspections by ICE. Disciplinary segregation without hearing. The report also notes that Passaic

---

245 Robert D. Evans, in a letter to John B. Torres, Acting Director, Office of Detention and Removal Operations, U.S. Immigration and Customs Enforcement.

detainees in the period of Hemnauth's incarceration were not classified according to the standard levels representative of their propensity to unruly or physically aggressive behavior. The comingling of a minority of violent inmates with orderly ones translated into an infectious environment and jeopardy toward peaceable detainees like Hemnauth and, consequently, a significant violation of his rights. The jail's excuse, noted in the report, was that its officials were unaware of the requirement.[246]

The list goes on, largely corroborating Hemnauth's descriptions. The audit faults not only the individual detention facilities, Passaic included, but in one important instance, ICE itself: "The ICE Detention Standard on Detainee Grievance Procedures does not explicitly address detainee rights for the reporting of abuse and civil rights violations. All five detention facilities reviewed distributed handbooks that did not properly explain the process for reporting allegations of abuse and civil rights violations."[247] As for the Hudson County Correctional Center, the authors noted threats of retaliation against inmates with grievances and occurrences of photographing of naked inmates for the amusement of the guards. Again, Hemnauth was not making it up. Nor was the eminent law firm Latham & Watkins — acting on behalf of the American Bar Association — that reported its own findings to ICE the year before issuance of the inspector general's report, replete with details of Passaic's noncompliance with the standards governing its operation as an ICE contractor.[248]

As damning the inspector general's account of conditions at Passaic, Hudson and the three other subjects of its audit may be, as an assessment of ICE's detention system it is deeply unsatisfying. Certainly, it revealed such rampant deficits in the course of its audit of the five target jails to rouse the suspicion that the system as a whole was flawed. Yet, the report reads like a school report card admonishing the student to do better next time, while never recognizing that perhaps there should not be a next time. It even leaves open the opportunity for the student to appeal his grades.

---

246 Best et al. "Treatment of Immigrant Detainees Housed at Immigration and Customs Enforcement Facilities,"

247 Best et al. "Treatment of Immigrant Detainees."

248 American Bar Association Delegation to the Passaic County Jail, "Report Regarding Implementation of ICE Detention Standards at the Passaic County Jail." The identities of the individual attorneys contributing to the report are redacted.

The report acknowledges the distinction between administrative custody applicable to immigration detainees versus punitive correctional custody of criminal convicts serving a sentence imposed by a court under due process, as stipulated by the Fifth Amendment. However, it does not judge whether this distinction has been observed by the jails included in the audit, at least not in terms that could call into question their suitability for administrative detention as required by law. Nowhere does the inspector general's report pronounce what should be evident from its own findings: that the detention regimen it has audited is clearly, even harshly punitive. Computing the ratio of inmates to urinals, counting bunks without safety railings and the instances of undercooked chicken might yield useful performance indicators. However, checking boxes — or not checking them — is a far cry from censuring the penal ambiance and human rights fiasco of Passaic and its ilk. As a deconstruction of the immigration detention system, the inspector general's survey of conditions by way of a tally of discrete observations was a head fake. They do not, when reconstituted, depict the obvious: a universe of anxiety, deprivation, dehumanization and retribution. Detainees like Hemnauth Mohabir would have been well within their rights as administrative interns to ask the auditors whether *they* would eat Passaic's food. Would find Passaic's medical care adequate for themselves or a loved one. Could contemplate living under the gaze of guards mandated to beat them and with the constant threat of assault. Would enjoy the visit of a wife or child they were forbidden to hug. Would be satisfied with outdoor leisure measurable in minutes per day. Would tolerate forced nudity or being rechristened "motherfucker" at the whim of an officer. Could endure all of the above for weeks, months or years. Or simply ask them: is my detention punitive, or not? And expect an answer.

Hemnauth's experience at Passaic, once documented by Daniel Zwerdling, triggered an inspection that forced Passaic to, indeed, give an answer of sorts and draw a conclusion. Scrutiny by NPR should never have been necessary, of course, if ICE had adequately supervised its own contractors in the first place. Still, Passaic's forfeiture of its immigration detention deal counts as a small victory for Hemnauth and likely cost Passaic County a bundle of money, if not its very existence.

It did not have to be quite this bad.

Irma Becerra is a retired police captain who, over the course of a sixth-month commission, was the warden of the Mira Loma Detention Center in Lancaster, California, about sixty miles north of Los Angeles, owned and operated by the Los Angeles County Sheriff's Department. (She is currently pursuing a doctoral degree in policy, planning and development at the University of Southern California.) Mira Loma got "quite a bit of [Federal] money" to house about 1,000 immigrant detainees. The facility's intergovernmental service agreement (IGSA) contract was worth an annual $27 million during Irma's tenure, or about $75 per detainee per day. By the time the detention center closed in late 2012, the rate had doubled to $154.[249]

The Mira Loma I visited shortly before it closed differed radically from Passaic and from many other detention centers in terms of its basic living circumstances, specifically hygiene and safety. For openers, Mira Loma provided liberal access to officials wishing to inspect the facility and conditions of detention. Irma attributes this in part to the oversight prerogatives exerted by the state of California over municipal and county jails within its boundaries.[250] Mira Loma, during Captain Becerra's tenure, skimped neither on meals nor on medical care, the latter dispensed at a nearby hospital. The majority of the inmates, she told me, ate better "in terms of volume" in her facility than outside detention, and Mira Loma's cooks and dieticians (all direct employees of the sheriff's department) abided by nutritional standards set by the state, which cover "quantity, portion, size, color, flavor, and nutritional value, with particular attention to levels of fat and sodium."[251] A 2006 Latham & Watkins audit did note inadequate telephone access at Mira Loma, a fact the Los Angeles County Sheriff's Department notes on its own website and a problem endemic to the detention network

---

249 Chang, "Baca Shifts Course on Compliance with Deportation Program."
250 The authority of the state over Mira Loma is academic in so far as its wardens and deputies are on the payroll of the Los Angeles County Sheriff's Department: they presumably adhere to statewide standards and have been trained to them. Formally, the state of California is off the Mira Loma beat, since its ground rules have been supplanted by ICE's, along with governance.
251 California standards for jail food service are set forth in: California Department of Corrections and Rehabilitation, "Regulations, Chapter 5, Article 51: Food Service." I could find no such resource for New Jersey.

with its aggressive outsourcing practices. And despite the facility's peaceful record, contact visits between detainees and their families remained prohibited as elsewhere.

There were no incidents of violence on or among detainees on Captain Becerra's watch, despite overcrowding at the facility. None.[252] She likens the reigning ambiance to that of a peaceful school dormitory block. Fighting among inmates was averted by isolating any detainees with a violent past, particularly gang related, adhering to the stricture requiring segregation of physically aggressive detainees. While the deputies tended to be as dismissive and sometimes scornful of detainees as they would be to jailed criminals, they heeded orders to treat them according to the captain's guidelines: physical altercation as a last resort and none of the verbal belittlement that was the drumbeat norm at Passaic. The residential arrangements were in the style of barracks, with doors to the wider yard open at one end; detainees exited at will during the day and evening into the yard adjacent to their block.

Mira Loma as I observed it in 2012 remained much as Irma left it, although it has since closed as an ICE detention center. If all immigrant detention facilities emulated it, the system would seem less the gulag ICE and IIRIRA allowed it to become, just as Hemnauth had fewer grievances against Middlesex or even Hudson than he did about Passaic and the official permissiveness that engendered the latter's abuses. A thorough audit commissioned for the Los Angeles County Sheriff's Department in 2009 concluded: "Mira Loma, from our observations, is a well-run, well managed jail under a highly professional manager . . . and an able staff. It is not a grim or gruesome facility. Indeed, it is bright and sunny . . . with lots of open space."[253]

---

252 For purposes of full disclosure, Captain Becerra did mention one instance of an escape and recapture, one of a show of force — but no use of it — to a group of angered detainees whose visit to a consular office in Los Angeles had been aborted, and one accidental death by electrocution of a detainee performing volunteer maintenance work, which occurred after her assignment at Mira Loma. The local press also reported a disturbance in April 2008, which the sheriff's department ascribed to gang members among the detainee population and which the guards suppressed with tear gas. (See: Hernandez, "Mira Loma Riot.") On the day I visited Mira Loma in June 2012, part of the facility was in lockdown pursuant to a fight in a dormitory block.

253 Bobb et al., "Los Angeles County Sheriff's Department 28th Semiannual Report."

Such an assessment, from an unimpeachable source, might comfort proponents of the detention system into thinking of Passaic or the Tent Cities of Arizona and Texas as avoidable aberrations. Not so fast. The kudos cut two ways, and, for once, the hammer finds the head of its nail: "In many ways, [Mira Loma] is a model for a low to medium security jail. But that's the problem: it is a jail. The detainees follow a routine appropriate for convicts. Detainees, however, are not convicts."[254]

The departure from the inspector general's checklist-driven audit of Passaic is refreshing and rare. It underscores the conflict between the punitive mission of a prison and the limited custodial goals of administrative detention. As a jail, Mira Loma may have set high standards for itself, relative to others, and met them. Although uncontestedly a profit center for the county, it resisted the temptation to generate maximum monetary returns at any cost to its detainees in neglect and suffering, whereas Passaic clearly succumbed. However, the high marks earned by a single facility and its happy contrast with others further highlight an existential flaw in the immigration detention system: that the proper treatment of detainees hinges on the goodwill, professionalism and conscience of sheriffs and wardens assigned to the peculiar task of holding persons not serving a term under sentence. ICE, particularly as it built out the detention network, skimped on oversight and, in the process, relinquished its sway over it. Just as IIRIRA transferred discretion over the fate of Hemnauth Mohabir from a judge to a local prosecutor, ICE for years ceded its custodial authority to outsourced jailers. That authority landed with Mira Loma in the best of circumstances, with Passaic or Joe Arpaio in others.

ICE has stepped up the policing of its updated standards, and the detainees at Mira Loma had the comparatively good fortune to have fallen into the custody of a warden who negotiated with ICE with the understanding that detention standards have a legitimate reason for being. But negotiate she did, under a charter from the Los Angeles County Sheriff's Department, her boss, to operate the facility at a surplus. The pressures under that charter are intense. She deplored the cost of performing to ICE's standards on ICE's per diem allocation and, at the time of my visit, pointed out, less than approvingly, that ICE was taking compliance more seriously

254 Bobb et al., "L.A. Sheriff's Department 28th Semiannual Report."

under the Obama administration than it had under the previous one, to the jeopardy of the bottom line. So, to save money, detainees received a sack breakfast and lunch rather than daytime meals in the mess hall, as was the case earlier when Irma Becerra ran the facility. Los Angeles County does not house immigrant detainees as a civic duty — no county does — but to bring fiscal relief to the sheriff's budget through participation in a federal program. Mercifully, the profit motive did not completely quash a more humane outlook at Mira Loma than elsewhere: police deputies in California are accustomed to heeding standards from their experience with state oversight, and harshness toward immigrants is not as productive a political plank in California as it has shown to be elsewhere.

Still, some attitudes are deeply ingrained among the guards at detention centers, including the kinder and gentler Mira Loma. Having come through the police ranks, Irma was able to compare the mindset of deputies assigned to general criminal populations and to immigrant detainees. While none of the guards under her supervision would have defied protocol in her presence, she openly acknowledges their failure to distinguish convicted criminals from administrative detainees. As a principled law enforcement officer, she is troubled by that. When I visited the facility with Irma, all the deputies openly referred to the inmates as "bodies." The word was spoken without malice, but its dehumanizing thrust was as obvious to the ex-warden as it was to me.

As much as eschewing shabby characterizations of detainees might mitigate the immigration detention system's inhumanity, it is difficult to incriminate the guards alone. They are corrections officers, recruited and trained as such by the operators of a jail. The jail never denied its genesis as a correctional facility, so it is of little wonder that it bore the imprint of one. The ICE detention standards themselves retain much of their correctional trappings, despite some softening and improved oversight. Just as elsewhere, the Mira Loma detainees wore jumpsuits indistinguishable from those of convicted or indicted criminals. A glass barrier separated visiting wives and children from their husbands and fathers, and a glass ceiling over the visited inmates' heads, reinforced the impression of "a sort of cage."[255] The solitary confinement block with its barren eight-by-ten foot

---

255 Bobb et al., "L.A. Sheriff's Department 28th Semiannual Report."

cells is sinister and was routinely occupied during Mira Loma's tenure as an ICE detention center. Curls of barbed wire top the double rows of chain link fence around the facility. These features were all sanctioned by ICE. By largely respecting the detention standards penned by higher authority, Mira Loma, in exceptional contrast to Passaic, donned the cloak of the messenger one cannot blame. Title to the message belongs squarely to ICE and IIRIRA.

In the end, conflicting prerogatives led to Mira Loma's closure as an immigration detention center. ICE, having become more concerned with enforcing its standards of detention, such as they are, placed increasing demands on the outsourced facilities operated as profit centers. At $154 per detainee per night, one might think the reimbursement schedule adequate, given the scant amenities granted the residents. In Mira Loma's case, the Los Angeles County Sheriff's Department would not agree to ICE's financial terms. The sheriff also balked at allowing ICE to investigate use of force at the jail.[256] The detainees were moved out in late 2012.

The true magnitude of Hemnauth's and other protestors' ultimate victory over Passaic must be measured against the power of its ripple effects on other detention centers in the ICE network. An overview of the broad detention landscape can be disheartening. The sheer number of immigrants processed through the detention and deportation system has grown relentlessly, and correctional standards still inform conditions of immigrant custody. Sexual abuse has surfaced as a widespread, almost normalized phenomenon in detention centers.[257]

On the other hand, the Obama administration, while increasing the pace of deportations, finally stated the obvious, which the inspector general missed in its 2006 audit: that immigrant detainees are housed in jails operating as jails do, that is, as correctional institutions for felons. The administration also voiced its intention to reform the detention regimen, notwithstanding the continued increase in the number of detainees on its watch, and it has put a tooth or two into its audits of contract detention

256 "The Mira Loma Detention Center Mess."
257 Review of *Immigrant Detainees: The New Sex Abuse Crisis.*

facilities. The headwinds against detention reform remain many and powerful, blown by political interests and lobbyists for the prison industry.[258] Still, some light has been cast on the detention system as a whole, and there has been some effort at detention oversight even as contract jailers remain in the immigrant custody business. I cannot resist the temptation to credit Hemnauth as one of the sparks.

Another fallout of Passaic's exposure concerned one of Hemnauth's major grievances, a heavy weight on the morale among the detainees and that quite possibly fed discord among them by fueling the flames of individual survival reflexes: the food. Shortly after the rupture of its ICE contract, Passaic officials were shocked — shocked! — to discover that the food service on which they were spending all of one dollar per meal — including the provider's overhead and profit margin — was somehow lacking. The posturing of the sheriff and his spokesman would be almost comical had they not inflicted so much hardship for so long. Two years after Hemnauth first agitated against a starvation diet of ill-prepared, unvaried and contaminated rations, and was summarily rebuffed, the sheriff indignantly fired Aramark for serving measly, poor-quality meals on dirty trays, obligating the inmates to spend as much as $200 on packaged food from the commissary.[259] Since Hemnauth and the other immigrant detainees were no longer available to point out the irony, it was doubtless lost on the sheriff. At least the general population would benefit from an upgrade. (Before we get carried away, in 2011 Passaic County Jail contracted to pay $1.45 per meal, forty-five cents more than in Hemnauth's day, of which approximately twenty cents represents inflation in food prices over seven years. The unassuming name of the new provider is Gourmet Dining.[260])

By 2008, Passaic's growing notoriety had prompted a new class action against the jail alleging illegal conditions of incarceration. The action represented plaintiffs in the general population, since the immigrants held under administrative detention had departed. (The suit was brought by the

---

258 The 2011 removal by ICE of detainees from a county jail in Utah that the agency deemed deficient attracted a protest from Utah Senator Orrin Hatch. See: "Hatch Presses Homeland Security on Weber Jail ICE Audit."

259 Keller, "Citing Subpar Meals, Service, Sheriff Fires Jail's Food Provider."

260 County of Passaic Procurement Center (NJ), "RFP to Provide Food Services and Food Services Management for the Passaic County Jail." The inflation estimate is based on the Consumer Price Index tables published by the U.S. Bureau of Labor Statistics.

American Civil Liberties Union of New Jersey, the Seton Hall University School of Law Center for Social Justice, and Dechert, a prominent private law firm.) In fact, the complaint places in evidence the experience of the INS/ICE detainees, notwithstanding their relocation almost three years earlier, and references the ICE inspector general's audit.

There are two remarkable features about the complaint. One, the conditions and mistreatment detailed by the plaintiffs bear an eerie resemblance to those witnessed and experienced by Hemnauth, even though the complaint was filed contemporaneously with his oral account to me, and neither he nor I was aware of it: tensions leading to inmate-on-inmate violence, squalid living quarters, decrepit plumbing, contagion, infestation, unbreathable air, stingy and unsafe meals, excessive force by guards, and so on, all to extreme measure. Once again it would appear that Hemnauth, if anything, understated his grievances. For instance, the complaint cites evidence of acute fire danger, without so much as functioning alarms and detectors, let alone sprinklers and a workable evacuation plan. Hemnauth did not discuss the fire hazards in his testimony to me.

Second, the plaintiffs seeking relief were jailed by order of the criminal justice system and were therefore subject to correctional standards of incarceration. Hemnauth, by contrast, was an administrative detainee, although exposed to the same conditions as a criminal inmate despite the law's stipulation that he not be. Yet, even as correctional detainees, the plaintiffs had ample evidence of violation of their rights under the First, Eighth and Fourteenth Amendments.

Before we shrug off the suit against Passaic as merely the liberal advocacy of civil rights attorneys from the ACLU and elsewhere, I should note a fascinating prelude to their efforts — which continued for three and a half years. One year before the plaintiffs undertook their class action, a federal judge granted "a variance below the sentencing guideline range based on conditions in Passaic County Jail."[261] In effect, the judge ruled that a convicted inmate had suffered aggravated punishment beyond that to which he had been sentenced, simply by virtue of being in Passaic's custody — and that, consequently, his jail term should be shortened!

---

261 Hayden, "United States of America v. Franz Copeland Sutton, Defendant: Opinion on Defendant's Application for a Downward Variance as a Federal Detainee Housed in Passaic County Jail" (2007).

The proximate cause of the jeopardy cited by the judge was persistent overcrowding. Normally, overcrowding would have affected the general population more chronically than it did immigration inmates, who had to be segregated in separate areas of the prison, a regulation Passaic often overlooked. However, in deciding the case, the judge, in a lengthy, detailed ruling, looked beyond the numerical evidence of overcrowding to the human circumstances of imprisonment. She did so in stark, unmitigated terms. Once again, they mirror and extend Hemnauth's account: "Standing water plagu[ing] the jail," "sewage backup" flooding the showers, dining in proximity to exposed toilets, "ice crystallizing on the walls" in winter, defective ventilation, rodent and insect infestation, high "risk of loss of life" in the event of fire, "excruciating" noise, never a full night's rest, fights, assaults, prison management emphasizing "corrections for profit."[262] Again, Passaic did not come close to compliance with state and federal *punitive* standards of incarceration, let alone administrative detention.

Between a federal judge writing into a formal decision that "there is much to be shocked about in the number of years these conditions [at Passaic] have existed" and the power of the civil complaint, I entertained visions of a glorious Perry Mason moment when a court judge would order Passaic permanently shuttered with the exasperated crash of a gavel. The Seton Hall attorney working on the class action disabused me, as would have any able attorney. Her job was to extract the best possible outcome for her clients and to consider the practical realities of litigation in doing so. The list rarely includes Perry Mason moments of censure pronounced against law enforcement. Courts simply do not like to deviate in extremes from their standard deference toward institutions represented by men and women in police uniforms, notwithstanding the Supreme Court's five-to-four decision in *Brown v. Plata* (2011) ordering California to reduce its prison population.[263] What the attorney felt she could do successfully is obtain a series of court orders mandating radical improvements in conditions at Passaic that the county, politically, could not resist or circumvent. The results say she was right. A federal judge quickly granted class action status to the lawsuit against Passaic. The county and the plaintiffs reached

---

262 Hayden, "USA v. Sutton."
263 Kennedy, "Brown, Governor of California v. Plata" (2011).

an agreement in late 2011, and a federal judge signed it in April 2012.[264] The settlement tilts heavily in favor of the plaintiffs represented by the ACLU and Seton Hall. It imposes a sweeping overhaul of conditions and infrastructure at Passaic, as wells as submission to an independent monitor.

There have been other repercussions related, in some degree, to Hemnauth's experience and activism. Jerry Speziale, the blustery county sheriff, resigned in 2010 and took a high-profile security job with the Port Authority of New York and New Jersey. By then, Passaic had stopped accepting federal and state detainees under contract and had to trim its budget. By 2011, there was serious discussion among the Passaic County Freeholders of closing the jail altogether, particularly with the dimming prospects for generating renewed contract revenues and looming ones of a multimillion-dollar overhaul imposed by the legal settlement with the ACLU and Seton Hall. The proposed closing was dropped in the face of opposition from corrections officers, yet the fate of one of America's most ill-reputed jails remains in limbo. In the end, Passaic may well be headed for closure, gone to the dogs in more ways than one.

In an ideal world — a world most Americans aspire to inhabit — the rule of law and the attainment of justice manage to coincide. In his day, Chief Justice Earl Warren adopted the pursuit of such harmony as his mission, joined in key instances such as *Brown v. Board of Education*, by the other eight members of his court. The Warren Court conflated the union of law and justice with the notion that the U.S. Constitution and the Declaration of Independence should intersect as often and as extensively as possible in the Court's rulings, heeding Frederick Douglass' yearning for "a country which shall not brand the Declaration of Independence a lie."[265] Warren pursued this mission with greater alacrity than perhaps any other chief justice in recent memory. I will hazard to speculate that both Douglass and Warren would be appalled by the unapologetic separation of justice and law embodied in our immigration law and detention and deportation policies.

---

264 "Judge Approves Agreement to Overhaul Passaic County Jail's Inhumane Conditions," ACLU of New Jersey.
265 As quoted in: Blight, *Frederick Douglass' Civil War*.

Over the last two decades, an antiseptic view of the rule of the law and the role of the courts that enforce it has gained favor, resting on the axiom that justice is blind, and that attempts to reconcile the law and higher ideals risk violating the former. This view holds, at least implicitly, that if the law is at odds with justice, so be it, or, if redress is required, that it is a problem for the legislature, never the judicial system. The current chief justice, John Roberts, in his confirmation hearing before the Senate, famously likened the job of a judge to that of a baseball home plate umpire assigned to call balls and strikes, and nothing more. As seductive as the analogy may be, it omits a key feature of the actual role of an umpire, which is to set the strike zone for each batter. That is where the judging comes in, where fairness and rules intersect. A feature Justice Roberts ignored, lest it distort a view of the law as a robotic abstraction.

That the rule of law is the pillar of our national unity sounds like a threadbare cliché. Yet, too often the underlying observation is trumped by more blinkered forms of we're-number-one tribalism. Platitudes aside, that we are a nation of laws is what makes us a nation in the first place, not ethnic homogeneity, religion or the accident of geography that has contained us, more or less, between two oceans. True, nationalism, the collective expression of patriotic allegiance to the nation-state, is a hallmark of a century of recent world history, and we ignore the underlying emotions at our peril.

Equally perilous would be a failure to recognize nation-states as the fragile constructs and relatively recent experiments they are. They are rarely, if ever, ordained by nature. Results, as they say, may vary. The Civil War tested the fortitude of American unity not that long after the country's independence. Germany and Italy emerged as full-fledged nation-states but a century and a half ago. Countries like Kenya and Iraq sprang not from Adam's rib, but from the inevitable decline of the British Empire in the last century, and their boundaries, like so many others, are more a remnant of colonial ambitions than natural delineations drawn from human or physical geography. History dispatched one of its biggest conceits, the Soviet Union, to a special place in its dustbin within seventy-five years of its manufacture. In fact, the legitimacy and integrity of imperfect nation-states has been challenged continually throughout history, and those contests continue to this day, often, but fortunately not always, with spectacular violence. Congo comes to mind, a former colony of Belgium — a nation-state with its own wobbly national identity. Syrians who once identified with Syria "now say they are Alawites, Christians, Sunnis, Shias, Druze."[266] Ask a Catalan if he or she is a Spaniard or, better yet, a Tibetan if he is Chinese. Ask 95% of Guyanese how and when their forebears came to be South Americans contained within their own tiny nation-state.

Seen through the lens of history, the nation-state is often a contrivance, an engineered artifact. This is not all or always bad. The contrivance can serve its followers well, provided it is shaped around the rule of laws passed with the consent of the governed and subject to constitutional scrutiny under the watchful eye of an independent judiciary. Less so if it is merely the result of power plays, ideological allegiance, tribal reflex or colonial chicanery. We honor the rule of law, revere it even, as well we should. It alone preserves the nation as a union of citizens content to live within it, more than armies, the soil or God.

That said, the rule of law, even one anchored in a constitutional bedrock as hardened as ours, cannot run on autopilot, and attempts to erode or hamstring the authority of judges will run the nation off the tracks of its ideals, constitutional underpinnings and, ultimately, its unity. Immigration judges are the most hamstrung of them all.

Tensions will certainly arise, as they must, between appeals to absolute clinical dispassion that forbids judges from circumventing the letter of the law and the more sensitive quest for fairness in the absolute. Harmony between the two positions, commonly sought during the Warren years,[267] slips from reach when federal and state legislatures seek to strip the courts of their ability to adjudicate, using sentencing directives in criminal cases, restricted access to judicial review and, for immigrants, mandatory detention and deportation formulas, all in the name of preserving a dispassionate bench content to idly watch where the chips fall.

Court-stripping legislation strives to ensure that passions — fear, discontent, vindictiveness — codified as law are adjudicated without reference to individual circumstances or higher purpose, even higher purpose we claim to embrace, like human rights, equal protection or family values.

---

266 Giovanni, "Life During Wartime."
267 Newton, *Justice for All: Earl Warren and the Nation He Made.*

The erosion of judicial discretion[268] and review has proven especially lethal in the area of immigration. Hemnauth's ties to family and community were deemed utterly irrelevant to the disposition of his case and the decision to banish him, because the law specifically disallowed all consideration of them. The dispassion marketed as an admirable feature of automaton courts and a mark of their efficiency is a disguise. The emotions lurking behind ostensibly evenhanded immigration rulings are fear, frustration — over, for instance, perennially stagnant working- and middle-class incomes[269] — and, indeed, xenophobia, all joined at the hip to the ambitions of politicians seeking to turn such passions into electoral advantage by directing blame to the readiest of targets and the least likely to cost them votes.

Statutes such as IIRIRA that rob the courts, both the immigration and judicial varieties, of their ability to consider the full range of merits and circumstances of the respondent's case, and the interests of the state and society as a whole, do not strengthen the rule of law. They weaken it. In so doing, they imperil the foundation of the nation-state, whether those who drafted IIRIRA or who have championed its implementation realize it or not.

The passage of IIRIRA is of a piece with other initiatives to shorten the reach of certain classes of citizens and persons to constitutional protections. Is it really a complete coincidence that Congress also passed in 1996 the Prison Litigation Reform Act that hardens the barriers to redress of prisoners with grievances toward the conditions of their incarceration?[270] An oppressively common grievance is sexual abuse, affecting inmates by the hundreds of thousands.[271] The machinery of punishment will not be subject to scrutiny or accountability on the watch of politicians playing to voters' bumper-sticker sentiments. Many of the state governments that have ventured outside their jurisdiction to push restrictionist state immigration laws have also backed arbitrary voter suppression statutes targeting the young, the

---

268 The main areas of discretion afforded the immigration judge under the current statutes are grants of asylum upon satisfaction of specified preconditions, grant of the privilege of voluntary departure with deferred reentry if the deportee qualifies, acquiescence to bond for removal candidates eligible for relief under the statutes, and assessment of factual evidence presented by the parties in removal proceedings.

269 "Table H-3. Mean Household Income Received by Each Fifth and Top 5 Percent: 1967 to 2008," U.S. Census Bureau.

270 "Prison Litigation Reform Act: Legislative History," Ed. Margo Schlanger.

271 Kaiser and Stannow, "Prison Rape and the Government."

poor, African Americans and Hispanics, that is, groups most likely to question plutocracies or oppose them at the ballot box. Is this pure coincidence?

In the end, IIRIRA and the entire anti-immigrant ecosystem have engendered everything from penal standards of imprisonment for non-prisoners to Arizona's SB 1070 (along with the one-upmanship the bill spawned in other states)[272] to categorical disregard of international human rights standards. The law reflects a straight-jacketed outlook on the Constitution as much as, often, a violation of it. It is maddening to many Americans, myself included, to witness from members of Congress, a chief justice, Tea Party demonstrators and others, pious professions of fealty to the Constitution they claim as more devout than yours or mine by virtue of having removed it from the context of its higher ideals, including those explicit in the document's own Preamble. An antiseptic reading of the Constitution that blots out the spirit behind the words and phrases remolds it into a restrictive covenant, all law and no justice, to be wielded like a bludgeon.

Hemnauth Mohabir was struck by that bludgeon. He is far from alone to have been victimized, and as much as he has suffered, others have suffered even more. From the outset, alongside the deplorable injustice of indiscriminate condemnations to exile of people like Hemnauth, lies the utter waste generated by a ramrod-rigid detention and deportation system. Waste of resources, waste of money to be sure. Also waste of the real contributions a person like Hemnauth can and did make to his community. Waste of our human connection to people like him. Waste of his artistry gone mute. Waste of a precious bond between father and son. And waste of our country's ideological capital, one that undermines our cherished identity as the planet's beacon of individual rights and decency. Waste of our battles, many victorious and hard won, against bigotry and xenophobia.

---

272 Provisions of SB 1070, aka the "Support Our Law Enforcement and Safe Neighborhoods Act" (2010), criminalizing violation of federal immigration law at the state level, were overturned by the Supreme Court in June 2012. However, the "show me your papers" clause, allowing Arizona law enforcement to stop persons it suspected of being in the country illegally for the sole purpose of verifying their immigration status, was upheld. See: Kennedy, "Arizona et al. v. United States."

After I had completed the bulk of the legal research relevant to these pages, I again visited with Bryan Lonegan, Hemnauth's attorney who had gone to the mat to win his release and was prepared to go further.

Bryan returned to criminal law and the Legal Aid Society, and he still fights the good fight on behalf of those he believes are underrepresented in our courts. He is also the best critic one like I could wish for. On this latest occasion, apprehensive that I might be launching into a written diatribe against any and all restrictions on entry to the country, he cautioned me that he was not a proponent of wholesale open borders. Neither am I. The underlying principle remains that as long as a nation-state maintains its legitimacy through a body of law anchored in justice and informed by truth, it has a right to enact policies and set reasonable controls on who visits, inhabits or attains citizenship in it. "To be a sovereign nation, a people must have control over their territory. A nation of open borders runs the risk of not being able to govern itself because its sovereignty, to some extent, is in the hands of other nations of the world."[273] I assured Bryan that I agreed with this premise, and there is not a single word in this text that advocates unfettered entry and residency at will.

Nor would I dismiss out of hand the objections of middle- and working-class taxpayers who have seen their incomes stagnate and public investment deteriorate while they are asked to contribute a portion of their taxes to services — such as public schools and hospital emergency rooms — accessible by unauthorized aliens. These concerns must be addressed with all seriousness, as they raise a question of equity. What I shall dispute is mendaciously bloated and misleading assessments of the costs of immigration intended to place blame for our economic woes and social sorrows where it does not belong. It certainly does not belong with Hemnauth Mohabir, who paid income and payroll taxes over many years, and consumed little in public services, unless one counts his treatment at Passaic as a benefit. In the aggregate, the economic impact of illegal immigration — a category that does not formally include Hemnauth, but with which his designation as a "criminal alien" would tend to bundle him in the eyes of immigration restrictionists — is small to tiny according to academic research, certainly smaller than the anti-immigrant echo chamber would have us believe.[274]

---

273 Aleinikoff, Martin et al., *Immigration and Citizenship: Process and Policy* 6th ed.

274 Hanson, *The Economics and Policy of Illegal Immigration in the United States.*

Further, the remedies proposed by restrictionists, such as denying undocumented immigrants access to services, could easily result in social costs that far outweigh the burden on taxpayers of providing these services. In fact, according to researchers at Harvard Medical School, from 2002 to 2009, immigrants paid $115 *billion* more into Medicare than they received in benefits from the program,[275] the federal government's largest nondefense budget post after Social Security.

Hemnauth's story is a sad illustration of the effect of a body of immigration law enforced amid a policy vacuum. The Immigration and Nationality Act of 1965 was an expression of policy intended to promote orderly immigration practices, without a quota system that had run afoul of the emerging anti-discrimination ethos. The Immigration Reform and Control Act of 1986 did contain a limited amnesty provision, but much of the act focused on penalties over goals for the immigration system. Rather than evolve with economic and social realities that have surfaced over the last half-century, immigration policy has morphed into a litany of restrictions tethered to highly punitive formulas for retribution, soaked in a lethal potion of myth and hypocrisy and vacuum-sealed within a system of arbitration — the immigration courts — depleted of judicial discretion. I have a difficult time accepting as "policy" practices that led to Hemnauth's imprisonment and exile, that have tolerated Sheriff Arpaio's concentration camps in the Arizona desert or have inspired members of Congress to deny a path to citizenship to kids who are Americans in every way but their place of birth.[276]

For a good part of our history, beginning with the assumption by the federal government of immigration enforcement, we espoused immigration policies based upon preconceived notions of who would fit with a dominant white, Christian society. Shameful, without a doubt, but indicative of policy endowed with a consistent objective. The Chinese Exclusion Act, the National Origins Act's quota system implemented in the 1920s to dampen the influx of people deemed incapable of ready assimilation into an Anglo-Protestant universe (particularly if their skin was dark) and other manifestations of social control formed the backbone of an

275 Tavernese, "For Medicare, Immigrants Offer Surplus, Study Finds."
276 At the time of completion of this text, the outline of a bipartisan immigration reform proposal was close to introduction in the U.S. Senate. The bill includes the central themes of the unpassed DREAM Act.

immigration policy we ultimately and thankfully amended. One might say that older incarnations of nativism have yielded, in part, to we-got-here-first-ism.

While social control and economic interests have always inhabited the immigration landscape in one form or the other, the National Origins Act was also a milepost on the path that led official immigration policy away from predominantly labor-related legislating toward policing prerogatives. Early immigration authority was placed within the purview of the Treasury Department, which collected a head tax from arriving immigrants, casting immigration as an item of the federal budget. As immigration increasingly became a lever of labor policy, governance passed, in 1903, to the Department of Commerce and Labor, prior to that department splitting in two. Under Franklin Roosevelt, it shifted to the Justice Department, a harbinger of the emerging emphasis on enforcement.

> The downside to America's open heart and outstretched arms was public concern — indeed, alarm — that our too-open post-war policies were letting criminal aliens, communists, subversives, and organized crime figures enter or remain in the United States along with legitimate refugees. INS enforcement activities in the mid-1950s addressed those concerns. Public alarm over illegal aliens living and working in the United States resulted in stronger border controls and targeted deportation programs.[277]

The enforcement emphasis culminated in 2002 with the creation of the Department of Homeland Security, where the government has now lodged the administering of immigration and all related processes.

Past immigration policy promoting conformity with white, Protestant dominion was, of course, ultimately headed for bankruptcy for being out of step with the historical progression of the nation. And even as we liberalized immigration, and rid the statutes of their unvarnished appeals to ethnicity, the changes came as much as a response to economic imperatives as to compliance with modern notions of human rights codified in international conventions and treaties. Still, for whatever reason, one policy replaced another deemed deficient. With the

---

277 "U.S. Immigration and Naturalization Service — Populating a Nation: A History of Immigration and Naturalization," U.S. Department of Homeland Security.

ascendance of IIRIRA and the enforcement zealotry that inspired it, we have created a vacuum where policy used to reside, guided by broad national objectives.

It is comforting to think that human rights considerations triggered the 1965 transition from a quota-based immigration policy to one more partial to family unification. Congress certainly acknowledged the racist dimension of the National Origins Act of the 1920s enshrined in the immigration code and the need to reverse it. It is also true, however, that the United States has powered its economic engine, led by consumer demand, in no small measure with demographic expansion, bolstered by our ability to attract arrivals from overseas. This dynamic stands in stark contrast with the constant challenges to their growth hovering over countries in Europe with stagnant populations. Not to mention our ability to harvest the bounty of our farms thanks to the immigrant labor that for years has come through the big back door on the Rio Grande, which no one will ever completely shut, fence or no fence. Not as long as it remains in our interest to leave it ajar and swing it open when it is time to bring in the crops.

It takes little in the way of partisan editorializing to tag Alabama House Bill 56 as holding a record for sheer ugliness: it was designed to stigmatize virtually every form of interchange with an undocumented person, and criminalize many of them. While the language of the bill ostensibly singles out unauthorized immigration, its tone erodes the distinction. The state's new immigration law is also stunningly self-defeating. Consider what the Alabama state legislature achieved in its battle against the imaginary blight of excessive immigration. As one business publication observed,

The post-tornado reconstruction of Tuscaloosa[278] has been hindered by a lack of skilled labor, partly because, after the law was passed, Hispanic tradesmen began leaving the state. Meantime, during the recent harvest, tomatoes and other crops were left rotting in north Alabama's fields. There are other economic costs. Rental properties

278 In April 2011, a devastating tornado wreaked death and widespread destruction in Tuscaloosa, Alabama.

are going empty; stores and restaurants catering to immigrants have lost customers.[279]

Some of the bill's prominent sponsors had second thoughts, which occurred to them with unsurprising swiftness. As did some officials in Arizona and conservatives on the national scene otherwise sympathetic to that state's SB 1070: they promptly awakened to the backlash from having alienating Hispanic voters, from business lost to boycotts. Or perhaps the spectacle was simply too crude, of seeing Sheriff Arpaio, the anti-immigrant zealot they loudly applauded and courted, face legal scrutiny for "fostering a pervasive culture of discriminatory bias," including racial profiling.[280] (The United States *District Court* for the District of *Arizona* ruled against Arpaio in May 2013 and ordered that his department's racial profiling practices cease under injunction.[281]) Two years after the enactment of Alabama's immigration bill and a year after a federal appeals court blocked implementation of much of the law, the state of Alabama agreed to reverse its most egregiously unconstitutional provisions, including, among other gems, criminalization of benign assistance to undocumented immigrants.[282]

That said, many if not most conservative officeholders and seekers remain wedded to a restrictionist ideology, foreclosing any shift of immigration law and policy away from its enforcement-heavy drift any time soon, even if the push for eventual legalization of a broad swath of the undocumented succeeds. It is simply too gratifying a political tool to abandon, whether or not all conservatives actually believe in the underlying tenets. Sheriff Arpaio was reelected in 2012, even if Governor Mitt Romney, the presidential candidate who sought — and received — the sheriff's endorsement, failed in his own bid.

The commanding premise of the current body of immigration law, reinforced by the unconstitutional overreach of individual state legislatures, and of the policing of its enforcement, appears to be that immigration is a supreme privilege with benefits accruing solely to the immigrant and

279 Wilkinson and Shipley, "Alabama Immigration Law Robs Citizens of Their Own Future."
280 Lacey, "U.S. Finds Pervasive Bias Against Latinos by Arizona Sheriff";
Adam Nagourney, "Across Arizona, Immigration Ire on Back Burner."
281 Snow, "Manuel De Jesus Ortega v. Joseph M. Arpaio" (2013).
282 Chappell, "Alabama Agrees to Permanently Gut Immigration Law."

costs to the rest of us. In this light, the granting of permission to enter, reside or work in the United States is an act of selfless magnanimity for which we are owed boundless gratitude, while we owe nothing in return. It follows that we can hold those we bless with such privilege to whatever standards we want, including many to which we do not hold ourselves or our own leaders, extract any retribution we see fit to impose for any transgression we deem a violation of those standards and deny Constitutional protections at will by blithely changing the definition of what constitutes punishment — just as the Chinese Exclusion Act, upheld by a nineteenth-century Supreme Court, said we could. It is as sad as it is ironic that the ability of the government to declare detention something other than the imprisonment it is, or to classify immigration violations as civil offenses while imposing criminal penalties without adjudication by the judicial system, is grounded in one of the most overtly racist texts in post–Civil War legislative history.

The vacuum of immigration policy exacerbates the peremptory quality of our immigration law. True, keeping genuinely harmful individuals at bay is a worthwhile objective, and in many cases the compelling interest of the State in doing so may indeed trump other considerations, such as family integrity. However, the credibility of this prerogative as a guiding principle of our current IIRIRA statutes fades in the face of the law's provisions stripping judges of the discretion they need to determine whether a candidate for exile presents an actual threat to society. Let alone that IIRIRA is so draconian that it ensnares decidedly unthreatening immigrants and deprives judges of the latitude they need to weigh other professed interests of the State — protecting children, for instance.

So, besides rigorous enforcement tucked behind a thin veil of security prerogatives, what have we had for an immigration policy? What objectives has it met? Is it tailored to labor needs? Is it intended to optimize economic growth by perpetuating moderate demographic expansion? Does it preserve our identity as the world's beacon of human and individual rights? Does it strengthen communities? Or does its design imply that immigration comes at such great cost to our society that the privilege of entry is to be bestowed with extreme parsimony upon better applicants for sainthood than any of us, and, seasonally, upon those who pick our fruit?

The policy void of the last fifteen years has left in its wake a body of

law sanctioning enforcement for its own sake, and with scant higher purpose other than maintaining a network of detention wards operated to
the monetary benefit of county jails and private contractors, and for the
gratification of politicians feeding at the trough of the nation's fears, notably of downward economic and social mobility. To be sure, the results
of the general election in 2012 highlighted the displeasure of Hispanic
and Asian American voters with the restrictionist immigration platform
of the Republican Party and its emphasis on enforcement, including that
embodied in IIRIRA. The outcome of the presidential contest, in particular, inspired fears of forfeiture of a growing segment of the electorate
and triggered an astonishingly rapid shift of congressional Republicans
toward accepting the need for immigration reform. However, there has
been little to no impetus for an overhaul of IIRIRA and its demands,
under pain of removal, that noncitizen residents display a degree of immaculate rectitude that we would never require of ourselves. Indeed, new
proposed legislation, while undeniably a victory for immigration reformists, retains an undertone of vindictiveness in its insistence on stiff enforcement, penalties and long delays, lest members of Congress be suspected of promoting "amnesty," a novel addition to the political lexicon
of dirty words.

Even before the recent momentum for reform, a measure seeking to
tweak the code of the Immigration and Nationality Act might have gar-
nered broad congressional approval in response to demands from the
business community, attune to the realities that affect its prosperity. For
instance, in late 2011 the House of Representatives overwhelmingly passed
the Fairness for High-Skilled Immigrants Act that eliminates per-country
immigration quotas for employment-related visas. (The per-country-of-
origin restrictions on technology workers have been unpopular among
businesses dependent on them, and the reform legislation introduced in
April 2013 raises the admission caps for high-skilled workers.) However,
isolated alterations of the existing code stand a far cry from the thoughtful
review of our immigration *and* deportation system. One that might survey,
for instance, the impact on the supply of labor in the United States of the
impending stagnation and decline of the Mexican youth population.[283] Or

---

283 Terrazas, Papademetriou, and Rosenblum, *Evolving Demographic and Human-Capital
Trends in Mexico and Central America and Their Implications for Regional Migration.*

another that might consider the waning influence of our Constitution as the preferred model for other countries.[284]

For the past ten years, as it did during other extended periods of our history, the enforcement-only ethos has smothered most discussion of policy goals other than retribution against immigrants. The laws on the books ostensibly target illegal aliens and those who, like Hemnauth, have seen their legal-immigrant status confiscated pursuant to brushes with the criminal justice system. While the contemplation of updated electoral maps might alter the discussion, by all indications the government's commitment to enforcement is unlikely to recede anytime soon. Restrictionists will require a quid pro quo in exchange for their acquiescence to any measures granting legal status, let alone citizenship, to those benefiting from "amnesty." Reformists seem willing to make that deal.

Arizona's and Alabama's claims of jurisdiction over immigration enforcement are still very recent and demonstrate hostility toward all immigrants — particularly those of color — by creating a climate of ostracism and, certainly in the case of Alabama's new law, denunciation. (Survivors and students of Jim Crow, the Fugitive Slave Act or, for that matter, the Holocaust, might find disturbing parallels as they read the Alabama statutes.) In the end, the Supreme Court did not — could not — uphold a state's claim of the right to legislate its own immigration policy, in effect defanging, if not completely gutting, SB 1070 and, by extension, copycat laws in other states. Nevertheless, states did, very recently, attempt to usurp authority over immigration in response to anti-immigrant passions, and may try again if new winds fan those passions anew. Antonin Scalia, in his breathtaking dissent[285] from the Supreme Court majority, asserted a states' right of sovereignty extending to immigration law. (We wonder what the justice now thinks of the "plenary powers" doctrine, since it posits that immigration must be adjudicated by the political branches of the federal government, exclusively.)

Justice Scalia's position dovetails with an anti-immigration impulse still prevalent in conservative legislative circles, notwithstanding the recent awakening of Republican strategists to the shunning of their party by a growing political constituency comprised of Latino and Asian voters with

---

284 Liptak, "'We the People' Loses Appeal with People Around the World."
285 Scalia, "Arizona et al. v. United States, No. 11-182, Opinion of Scalia, J." (2012).

immigrant affinities. In July 2011, Representative Lamar Smith (Republican of Texas), chair of the Judiciary Committee's Subcommittee on Immigration Policy and Enforcement, introduced a bill to deny ICE, under President Obama, the authority to exercise discretion in deportation cases and focus on those of individuals whose presence in the country is most dangerous to American communities. Setting aside the practical impossibility of pursuing every possible immigration violation that comes before ICE, the role of prosecutorial discretion in serving the ranked priorities of any law enforcement agency, and Smith's mischaracterization of prosecutorial discretion as "amnesty,"[286] his bill revealed the penury of any policy project on the part of anti-immigrant legislators other than unmitigated enforcement. Smith, not coincidentally, was an architect of IIRIRA.[287] He continues to emphasize enforcement and resist comprehensive reform beyond it.

In the immigration policy void of the last decade, the cruelty resulting from IIRIRA — or, worse, its very basis — became the policy. President Obama has made clear that he opposes the current norms, notwithstanding the zeal with which his administration has carried out removals to demonstrate a compliance with existing law. His anger over Congress's indecent refusal at the end of 2010 to pass a measure as basic and benign as the DREAM Act was genuine, as he demonstrated by implementing a policy under his executive authority sparing from removal many of those who would have benefited from the act.[288] However, the president cannot institute fundamental changes to IIRIRA on his own, even less reverse the retributive mindset that inspired it and endures, too often with a stridency that reflects a hostile plane of "the ambivalence with which we have always confronted immigration policy in this country."[289]

---

286 "Hearing on: H.R. 2497, the 'Hinder the Administration's Legalization Temptation Act'," U.S. House of Representatives Judiciary Committee, Subcommittee on Immigration Policy and Enforcement.

287 Hing, *Deporting Our Souls*.

288 On June 15, 2012, President Obama announced that the government would exempt from deportation persons younger than thirty who arrived prior to their sixteenth birthday and with no criminal convictions. See: Obama, "Transcript of Speech on Immigration Policy"; Cushman, "Obama Says New Federal Policy Limiting Deportations Is 'More Just'."

289 Guttentag, "Immigrants' Rights in the Courts and Congress: Constitutional Protections and the Rule of Law After 9/11."

Even within ICE, the changes in prosecutorial guidelines set forth by the president and the agency's own director have encountered resistance typical of entrenched bureaucracies. For instance, four months into the revised policy on prosecutorial discretion, ICE still deported an alien with absolutely no criminal record about to marry a U.S. citizen and rectify his immigration status.[290] ICE's bureaucratic resistance to prosecutorial guidelines — embodied in the leader of its union, the National ICE Council — has prompted a full review of deportation cases to ensure that priority rankings among deportation candidates are respected, that is, violent convicts are removed first, undocumented immigrants with no criminal record last, if at all.[291] Importantly, cases that up until now have been brought directly to the docket of the immigration courts by non-attorney ICE officers may receive some prior examination by the attorneys charged with prosecuting, whereas previously they were restricted in their ability to deflect low-priority prosecutions.[292] With a caseload approaching 500,000 per year and a shortage of immigration judges, prosecutorial discretion is eminently sensible in a system where the judges' discretion is narrowly constricted, short of changes in the law, which, of course is what is most needed.

In partial defense of the ICE union's position, it is arguably ill conceived to require of line officers that they perform a triage as part of their police duties in order to align arrests with the prosecutors' priorities. That is not a job they are trained for and could potentially lead to abuse. The union's position loses its charm when it exploits valid concerns of line officers to denounce the soundness of priority setting by immigration prosecutors or to press for ideological orthodoxy. The union leaders speaking for ICE and the U.S. Citizenship and Immigration Services (USCIS) officers have come out boisterously against the comprehensive immigration reform and allied themselves with vocal immigration restrictionists in Congress and the media.

With the passage of IIRIRA and in the aftermath of September 11, the distinction between enforcement and policy all but evaporated. Militarization of the southern border is the signal immigration policy achievement

---

290 Preston, "Obama Policy on Deporting Used Unevenly."
291 Preston, "U.S. to Review Cases Seeking Deportations."
292 Shusterman, "New Deportation Priorities Will Bring Focus to ICE Enforcement Efforts."

of the federal government in recent years and one its promoters, many of whom are still in Congress, will most likely defend vigorously in any new legislation. True, immigration reform has built momentum, with emphasis on elements of policy beyond enforcement, particularly conditional legalization of undocumented residents. Still, leading up to the 2012 election, attempts to extend enforcement — and its attendant cruelty — multiplied in quarters with, at best, tenuous legal jurisdiction over immigration, cheered on by officials such as Governor Jan Brewer of Arizona, as well as by presidential nominee Mitt Romney, an advocate of "self-deportation." We should not expect anti-immigration restrictionism to simply vanish as Congress considers new federal immigration legislation.[293]

In retrospect, abuses at Passaic in Hemnauth's day seem less like aberrations, and more like place-setters, for Sheriff Joe Arpaio's Tent City and the vindictive state laws in Arizona, Alabama, Georgia and elsewhere. After all, if enforcement is the predominant federal objective, who could have objected to any given state taking matters a step further? The Obama Department of Justice has vigorously pursued federal court action against constitutional violations and jurisdictional overreach by individual anti-immigrant state legislatures. The attempted usurpation of federal authority was simply too blatant for the government to even hint at accommodating. ICE is also gradually eliminating the 287(g) collaborative programs that gave cover to the claims of some states that their internal immigration measures had implicit federal sanction, although 287(g) remains available to future administrations as part of IIRIRA. Despite its resistance to vindictive state-level immigration legislation, the crush of deportations under Secure Communities is evidence that the Obama administration, as a practical matter, has sanctioned the emphasis on enforcement while awaiting an overhaul of immigration law and the enactment of an actual national policy that, until Obama won his second term, seemed desperately elusive.

---

293 An amendment to S.744 restricts reimbursements by the federal government for prosecution and detention of immigrants illegally detained according to federal statutes. The amendment — if it and the underlying reform legislation bill are adopted by the full Congress — might inhibit individual states from practicing unsanctioned arrests. (See: "Comprehensive Immigration Reform," U.S. Senate Committee on the Judiciary.)

It is tempting to think that even in the absence of congressional action on immigration reform, Hemnauth might have been spared his ordeal under later circumstances, thanks to the 2010 Supreme Court order in *Padilla v. Kentucky*, the Obama administration's scrutiny and intended reform of detention conditions, the president's application of prosecutorial discretion to counter Congress's jettisoning of the DREAM Act in 2010, and former New York Governor Paterson's decision to vacate petty misdemeanor charges that triggered unreasonable deportation orders. Except for the Paterson measure, which benefited only persons with convictions in New York State for a brief time at the end of the governor's term, I have my doubts. Had any one of these avenues of relief opened to Hemnauth, it would have sanctioned Judge Riefkohl's assessment of Hemnauth's case as a rarity.

Padilla might have offered hope had the Supreme Court been asked to act on the underlying issue earlier. The ruling ordered that defense attorneys in criminal cases must advise their clients of the deportation consequences of a conviction or guilty plea. In his drug case, which occurred years prior to *Padilla*, Marvin Landou, Hemnauth's defense attorney at the time, clearly failed to do so. He encouraged Hemnauth to strategically accept a misdemeanor charge because the $250 penalty and a brief driver's license suspension were a negligible price to pay for putting the episode behind him. Had Hemnauth been a citizen, this would have been unquestionably reasonable advice, the epitome of the legal "no brainer." Under then-prevalent deportation practices, there was also reason to discount damaging repercussions on Hemnauth's future beyond those a small misdemeanor might have on, say, employment applications. In fact, however, the ultimate price for Hemnauth was far, far higher: two years of prison, exile and forced separation from his child.

At the time of Hemnauth's criminal court trial, IIRIRA was recent legislation and the record of enforcement short and shallow, so Mr. Landou's error, if that is what it was, became detectable, in practice, only with the 20/20 vision of hindsight. However, from a strictly legal standpoint, the advice he gave Hemnauth was incompletely informed, and Landou was sufficiently aware of the existence of the deportation statutes to ask Hemnauth whether residency consequences had been mentioned when he went to the court clerk to pay his fine. Landou then assumed that in the absence of any explicit, immediately issued threat to Hemnauth's residency, Hemnauth was in the clear. At the same time, to conclude that Hemnauth would have benefited from *Padilla* to the point of cancellation of his removal is a bit speculative.

The misdemeanor conviction was part and parcel of Landou's "agency defense." Absent this approach, we simply cannot know beyond all doubt that the trial would have ended in an acquittal on all counts. It is possible it would have, since the jury clearly did not believe Hemnauth was a felon. But we cannot know with certainty what result might have transpired in the end, had Landou not taken the misdemeanor tack to acquittal on the prosecution's felony charge. Criminal court practice does not generally abide concocted lines of defense, and Landou chose the most effective one from the short menu of standard strategies at his disposal. The consequences of a felony conviction were so dire — many years in state prison and a crippling criminal record — that Hemnauth was best advised to take the surest avenue to acquittal on the felonies his lawyer could conceivably map.

In the final analysis, *Padilla*, as welcome as it was to immigrant advocates, like the executive initiatives championed by the president, only skirts the issue of fairness in our immigration code. It does not confront the prospective inequity of what Justice John Paul Stevens, author of the *Padilla* decision, calls the "drastic measure of deportation" and "an integral part of the penalty" for prosecuted immigrants.[294] A part of the penalty to which no judicial court ever sentenced Hemnauth Mohabir.

When I first embarked on the project I am now completing, I imagined that an unencumbered narration of Hemnauth Mohabir's encounter with U.S. immigration and deportation practices would elucidate the relevant issues of history, equity, constitutionality and human rights on its own power. One could, as it were, draw one's own conclusion, without intrusive explanations or commentary. Not only did this turn out to be too tall an order, but the policy ramifications, historical context and legal complexities that Hemnauth's story summoned led me, personally, up a steep path of discovery.

294 Stevens, "Jose Padilla, Petitioner v. Kentucky." In adopting the phrase "drastic measure," Justice Stevens quoted a Court precedent, *Fong Haw Tan v. Phelan* (1948).

353

Under those circumstances, I could hardly exclude from this text the exegeses I myself required to grasp the full sweep of implications of Hemnauth's passage through our immigration, detention and deportation system.

By the same token, it would only be fair if the reader asked what it is I am advocating in these pages, now that we have navigated the broad expanse of Hemnauth's story, from his roots to the present, and now that a larger segment of the political spectrum has warmed to the prospect of immigration reform. My fondest hope would be that such reform would encompass an overhaul of detention and deportation practices reuniting justice and law, which have drifted into separate orbits with a big shove from IIRIRA. Short of a utopian brass ring, I think there are attainable aspirations for our immigration enforcement code, modest in scope, but helpful for those who, like Hemnauth was in his day, are deserving of relief. Some of these aspirations find voice in S.744, the bill passed in the U.S. Senate in June 2013 and that embodies the first legislative stab at comprehensive reform. [295]

As I have noted, President Obama has also instituted over the course of his tenure in office a certain number of executive initiatives intended to modulate immigration enforcement within the confines of the law as it stands today: prosecutorial discretion in deportation cases, attempts — with mixed success — to refashion the immigration detention apparatus, and his implementation of key elements of the unenacted DREAM Act under executive authority[296] over the howls of protest from restrictionists and political foes.

Executive initiatives, as we know, are eminently reversible and subject to administrative foot-dragging or undermining by the federal budgetary process. With a Congress as pugnacious on immigration issues as that seated in 2011, such resistance to President Obama's exercise of his authority would have seemed likely. However, the 2012 presidential contest has awoken the defeated party to the sensitivities of Hispanic voters, in addition to having lifted the threat of imminent reversal by virtue of Obama's reelection.

---

295 "S.744: Border Security, Economic Opportunity, and Immigration Modernization Act."

296 The presidential initiative was not an executive order, but rather a "reprieve program, officially known as deferred action for childhood arrivals." See: Preston, "Young Immigrants Say It's Obama's Time to Act."

Indeed, the central themes of the DREAM Act have been included in the immigration reform bill introduced in the Senate. In addition, with regard to enforcement, shortly after the election, ICE further honed its priorities for issuing "detainers." (An immigration detainer is a notice to another law enforcement agency of ICE's intention to assume custody of an individual in its custody.[297]) The current list of priority offenses, disclosed by ICE in December 2012,[298] includes drug trafficking but not simple possession, the charge leveled against Hemnauth.[299] However, detainers concern persons held by the criminal justice system; Hemnauth was apprehended directly by ICE at a port of entry, and it is uncertain by what mechanism detainer discretion would have prevented his deportation or allowed him to retain his green card residency papers.

There are many individual reforms to our immigration codes I could suggest, inspired by Hemnauth's story. Some are incremental, others further-reaching. The current landscape of immigration law and politics, even with Congress contemplating comprehensive reform, might argue for a stepwise reshaping of enforcement practices over the pursuit of a sweeping decision in the Supreme Court, where the plenary powers dogma lives undisturbed, let alone a *Mr. Smith Goes to Washington* moment in Congress that radically recasts the architecture of immigration enforcement. The same general congressional temperament that not long ago found fault with the DREAM Act's minimal appeal to civility is not poised to repudiate IIRIRA, notwithstanding recent election results and the growing appetite for new legislation. Immediately prior to passage of immigration reform in the Senate, the House passed an enforcement-only measure that, among other things, authorizes states to write their own immigration laws in defiance of jurisdictional boundaries affirmed by the Supreme Court, and prohibits the use of prosecutorial discretion by ICE,[300] an absurdly impractical notion. The House bill stands no chance of becoming law, but stands as a measure of the persistent sway of anti-immigrant sentiment in Congress.

---

297 See: "ICE Detainers: Frequently Asked Questions," U.S. Department of Homeland Security.

298 Morton, "Civil Immigration Enforcement: Guidance on the Use of Detainers."

299 Of 409,849 deportees in 2012, 40,448 had been previously convicted of a drug offense in court. See: "FY 2012: ICE Announces Year-End Removal Numbers."

300 "H.R. 2278: Strengthen and Fortify Enforcement (SAFE) Act."

In the current, mainstream discussion of immigration reform, perpetuation of muscular rules of enforcement has been positioned as a necessary condition to the achievement of legalization for the undocumented, a bargaining chip that will doubtless be expended. In fact, it is already offered in the Senate bill, before legislation of any kind is introduced in the more restrictionist House of Representatives. The Senate bill prescribes financial penalties emblematic of residual opprobrium toward candidates for legalization, a snail's-pace path to citizenship intended to thwart accusations of amnesty and extensive militarization of the southern border.[301] Even in the event immigration reform generally deemed comprehensive passes the full Congress, enforcement will doubtless retain the disciplinarian tenor of IIRIRA. Despite the glaring conflict between our modes of immigration control and the substantive rights of individuals, the enforcement imperative has acquired the sheen of settled law — *stare decisis* in judicial jargon — by force of reaffirmation of doctrine over more than a century.

In the current legal and institutional setting, the most progress we have been conditioned to expect in recognition of immigrants' substantive rights is the occasional crack in the steely edifice of retributive enforcement. We have witnessed a few. An administration that recognizes the stern punitive nature of immigration detention, for instance, or that modulates its prosecutorial priorities in deportation hearings to a more elevated sense of justice and proportion. A Supreme Court decision mindful enough of due process to require a criminal defense attorney to alert his client to the immigration consequences of a plea bargain. New laws in some states to accredit resistance by state and local police to indiscriminate compliance with Secure Communities. A proposal that new federal immigration legislation allow deportees with clean police records or only minor offenses to return to their spouses and children.

In the spirit of restraint and realism, I shall confine myself here to a single motion for enforcement reform, one that would have spared Hemnauth from imprisonment and exile: the reinstitution of pre-IIRIRA standards of judicial discretion for immigration judges. Call it a modest down payment on conformity with the minimal standards of civil liberty most Americans embrace.

---

301 "S. 744: Border Security."

The proposed legislation contained in S.744 as passed by the U.S. Senate is, in many of its aspects, quite expansive, despite its concessions to restrictionists: it adopts the substance of the DREAM Act and proposes to legalize, in one form or the other, millions of immigrants living in the shadows into which we have herded them. We do not know at this juncture whether the legislation will survive opposition to it or to what extent it will be trimmed or altered to secure its passage by the full Congress. Still, it would be ungracious towards its framers to brand it incremental.

The sections of the new bill that soften the terms of immigration enforcement are of modest reach and eminently vulnerable to amendment in the House of Representatives, on the whole more accommodating of restrictionist opposition to reform than the Senate. They do not dismantle IIRIRA or the machinery of detention. However, they do include new language commanding oversight of detention facilities, including their use of solitary confinement, and recommending alternatives to detention.[302] Notably, the term "judicial discretion" does appear, albeit only once, in a section heading: for the first time since IIRIRA's passage in 1996, Congress has been asked to restore limited judicial discretion to grant relief in hardship cases where a minor crime would have previously resulted in mandatory removal.[303] Hemnauth's case would have qualified had IIRIRA encompassed the new bill's elementary appeal to humanity.

A bolder loosening of IIRIRA's tightfisted constraints on judicial discretion would again allow immigration courts, within reasonable guidelines of the law, to weigh various, and sometimes divergent, interests of the state and society: interest in public safety, to be sure, and in the protection of national sovereignty, but also economic interests, an interest in protecting our reputation as champions of human rights, in remaining true to our national ideals, in the diplomatic benefits of complying with international treaties and conventions; an interest in family integrity and fostering cohesive communities.

In some instances, the law-and-order prerogative will clearly trump the state's other objectives, for example when considering the removal of a violent criminal. A judge endowed with the latitude of judicial discretion over petitions for relief can still make that determination. Article III judges — that is, officers of the judiciary branch — make analogous sentencing

302 "S. 744: Border Security," Sections 3715, 3716 and 3717.
303 "S. 744: Border Security," Section 2314.

and bond decisions all the time. The obvious byproduct of judicial discretion is that it can cut both ways, erring on the side of leniency in some instances, harshness in others, although IIRIRA's strictures are so unforgiving that it is difficult to imagine the latter in immigration hearings. In a normal adjudicative setting, misuse of discretion can be rectified by a process of judicial review, which IIRIRA also severely inhibits.

Consider Hemnauth Mohabir one last time in closing. Our intransigent immigration code obligated a judge — against his sense of fairness — to order this good man torn from his child, stripped of his livelihood, thrown into a gulag and banished. It commanded him to vindicate a single interest of the state to the exclusion of all others, mindlessly and under the spurious pretense that society would benefit. Was this necessary, or even useful? Was this just? Will this change?

Draw your own conclusion.

ACKNOWLEDGMENTS

THE EXERCISE IN INDEPENDENT INQUIRY that is Passaic would have been an impossible quest without the goodwill and assistance of a veritable legion of men and women whose outlook on the issue of the immigrant experience resonated so tightly with this project. Their ranks included journalists, professors, attorneys, human rights advocates, friends, family and, of course, my subject himself.

It is a great gift to be called "brother" by someone of such a contrasting background to mine as Hemnauth Mohabir. All the more so that he meant it. His enthusiasm for what began as a figment of my literary aspirations was palpable from the first moment I contacted him in Trinidad via a scratchy phone connection, and it never wavered. Neither did his patience, since the more didactic segments of my text took so many moons to research and fact check. He was extraordinarily forthcoming in telling his story, even in those moments when some of his recollections were painful to him. He hesitated only when he felt that disclosure might harm someone else or violate their privacy, and usually, as my probing ultimately revealed, his discretion concerned details with relatively little bearing on the arc of my argument. In only one instance did I need to insist that Hemnauth confirm a suspicion I developed on my own: that his friend Phillip's calculated dissembling on the witness stand had placed him in lethal jeopardy. Hemnauth's loyalty trumped any resentment he might rightly feel toward someone who did not reciprocate. The days and nights I spent taking Hemnauth's testimony in his humble lodgings under the equatorial heat of Trinidad were memorable for both their context and their content.

His recollections, honesty and humanity are the backbone of these pages. They also benefited from the openness of Hemnauth's former wife Rahoni Sharma and their delightful son Rajendra Kevin Mohabir.

Several of the protagonists in the Passaic chronicle contributed generously to my work, and more. Daniel Zwerdling of National Public Radio, the investigative journalist who first broadcast the detainee abuses at Passaic County Jail, kindly acquiesced to my extending the story he had broken, including Hemnauth's connection to it. Without Daniel's reporting, this project would never have come to being.

Daniel also introduced me to Bryan Lonegan of the Legal Aid Society of New York, among the most remarkable and compassionate attorneys I have ever met, and I have known many. With the cynicism of my advancing years, I had begun to associate courtroom virtue more with classic movie actors than with the contemporary realities of the American legal profession: Gregory Peck in *To Kill a Mockingbird*, Fredric March in *Inherit the Wind*. Not so. Bryan is not only a committed servant of justice, he is also a punctilious practitioner and does not traffic in delusions. He was no more complacent with me than with his clients, which is to say not at all. I cannot begin to thank him enough for the many hours he spent coaching me on the intricacies of criminal and immigration law and for reviewing my work with candor and care.

When I began work on *Passaic*, Bryan had taken a temporary leave from the Legal Aid Society, which I petitioned for the files Bryan had made on Hemnauth's case. The Society responded completely and diligently once it had secured Hemnauth's formal permission.

Rachel Meeropol also reviewed my draft in full, but her comments on the text were but icing on the cake. Rachel has extensive files on Hemnauth's case, which she shared with me willingly, again in compliance with the rules of consent. Rachel was instrumental in helping Hemnauth chronicle the abuses at Passaic County Jail and collect the testimony of fellow detainees. In the process, Rachel and Hemnauth became friends. She visited Passaic often enough to develop a deep, accurate and unvarnished sense of his experience and suffering, and her impressions constitute a valuable and in some ways intimate record of the detainee experience. Rachel as well I cannot thank enough, not just for helping me in this project, but for her dedication to aligning law and justice every day at the Center for Constitutional Rights.

Several other immigration scholars helped my along the way and were more than generous with their time. In addition to Bryan Lonegan, Professor Bill Ong Hing of the University of San Francisco School of Law and the University of California at Davis, as well as Professor Polly J. Price of Emory University School of Law reviewed my work in its entirety. Dean Nora V. Demleitner of Washington and Lee University School of Law, and Deborah Weinberg, a law graduate of the University of Brussels, instructed me on the distinctions between European and American immigration enforcement legislation. Lucas Guttentag, professor at Yale Law School and former national director of the ACLU Immigrants' Rights Project, assisted in my understanding of recent Supreme Court rulings, in particular *INS v. St. Cyr,* which he successfully argued. My friend Maria Blanco of the California Community Foundation and former executive director of the Earl Warren Institute on Law & Social Policy at the UC Berkeley School of Law has been my constant soundboard on all matters of immigration law as they have evolved since I began work on *Passaic.* Carl Shusterman, an eminent immigration attorney, provided his valuable insight from many years of practice. Julia Preston of the *New York Times* kindly shared the perspective of the field's most prominent journalist.

While I was denied entry to Passaic County Jail, which has ceased operating as an immigration detention center, Captain Irma Becerra (Los Angeles County Sheriff's Department, retired) generously arranged for me to tour the Mira Loma detention facility in Lancaster, California before it closed as well. Admittedly, Mira Loma had a lot less to hide than Passaic.

Several additional attentive readers kindly trained their keen eyes on my text: my son, Josh Kunstler, and my dear friends of many years Ann Lombard, Lawrie Mott and Sandy Zimmerman. Natasha Singh brought to her reading of *Passaic* her own writer's acuity and deep empathy with its subject. I was very fortunate to find in Mali Apple an enthusiastic, inspired and meticulous editor. My old buddy Matthew Naythons steered me toward the many journalists he knows whose interests resonate with my project.

And as trying as it can be to put up with my obsessive behavior even under normal circumstances, my darling wife, Bonnie, daughter Naomi and son Josh pulled out all the stops in supporting me during the long birthing of *Passaic.*

BIBLIOGRAPHY

"Adults Corrections." Ed. Middlesex County, NJ. www.co.middlesex.nj.us.

Alaya, Flavia. "Showdown at Sheriff's Plaza." Bill of Rights Defense Committee newsletter, September 18, 2005.

Aleinikoff, Thomas Alexander, David A. Martin et al. *Immigration and Citizenship: Process and Policy* 6th ed. St. Paul, MN: Thomson/West, 2008.

Allen, Matthew Harp. "Rewriting the Script for South Indian Dance." *The Drama Review* 41, no. 3 (1997).

American Bar Association Delegation to the Passaic County Jail. "Report Regarding Implementation of ICE Detention Standards at the Passaic County Jail," 2005.

American Civil Liberties Association of Arizona. "In Their Own Words: Enduring Abuse in Arizona Immigration Detention Centers," 2011.

American Immigration Lawyers Association, "Application Process, Eligibility," April 28, 2011. www.aila.org.

Amnesty International. "Jailed Without Justice: Immigration Detention in the USA," 2009.

"Aramark Corporation Form 10-K." Securities and Exchange Commission, 2002. www.getfilings.com.

Ash, Kristina. "U.S. Reservations to the International Covenant on Civil and Political Rights: Credibility Maximization and Global Influence." *Northwestern University Journal of International Human Rights* 3 (2005).

"Asylum Denial Rates by Immigration Judge: FY 2000–FY 2005." Eds. Susan Long and David Burnham. Transactional Records Access Clearinghouse, Syracuse University, 2010. trac.syr.edu.

"Asylum Law, Asylum Seekers and Refugees: A Primer." Transactional Records Access Clearinghouse, Syracuse University, 2006. trac.syr.edu.

Barnes, Robert. "Immigrant's Survivors Cannot Sue Federal Health Officials, Supreme Court Rules." *Washington Post,* May 4, 2010.

Barry, Tom. "A Death in Texas." *Boston Review*, November/December 2009.

"Beharry v. Ashcroft" (2003). United States Court of Appeals for the Second Circuit (New York). caselaw.findlaw.com.

Bernstein, Nina. "Few Details on Immigrants Who Died in Custody." *New York Times*, May 5, 2008.

Bernstein, Nina. "Hurdles Shown in Detention Reform." *New York Times*, August 20, 2009.

Bernstein, Nina. "Ill and in Pain, Detainee Dies in U.S. Hands." *New York Times*, August 12, 2008.

Bernstein, Nina. "9/11 Detainees in New Jersey Say They Were Abused with Dogs." *New York Times*, April 3, 2006.

Bernstein, Nina. "The Making of an Outlaw Generation." In Suárez-Orozco et al., eds., *Writing Immigration: Scholars and Journalists in Dialogue*.

Bernstein, Nina. "Officials Hid Truth of Immigrant Deaths in Jail." *New York Times*, January 9, 2010.

Best, Alexander, et al. "Treatment of Immigrant Detainees Housed at Immigration and Customs Enforcement Facilities" (December 2006). Office of Inspector General, Department of Homeland Security.

Bhagwati, Prafullachandra N. "A (Name Deleted) v. Australia, Communication No. 560/1993," U.N. Doc. CCPR/C/59/D/560/1993 (1997). Office of the United Nations High Commissioner for Human Rights, United Nations Human Rights Committee.

"Bharat Sevashram Sangha," January 7, 2010. www.bssmumbai.com.

Bilger, Burkhard. "Beware of the Dogs: Can New York's Canine Units Keep the City Safe from Terrorism?" *The New Yorker* LXXXVIII, no. 2 (2012).

Blight, David W. *Frederick Douglass' Civil War: Keeping Faith in Jubilee*. Baton Rouge, LA: Louisiana State University Press, 1989.

Bobb, Merrick J., and Police Assessment Resource Center. "Los Angeles County Sheriff's Department 28th Semiannual Report," October 2009.

Boulos, Maissa. "Interview at Passaic with Hemnauth Mohabir" (memo to files at the Center for Constitutional Rights), 2003.

Brendon, Piers. *The Decline and Fall of the British Empire, 1781–1997*. New York: Alfred A. Knopf, 2008.

Brennan, William J. "Weinberger v. Wiesenfed, 420 U.S. 636" (1975). Supreme Court of the United States.

Bureau of Democracy, Human Rights and Labor. "Guyana," 2005. U.S. Department of State. www.state.gov.

California Department of Corrections and Rehabilitation. "Regulations, Chapter 5, Article 51: Food Service," 2010. www.cdcr.ca.gov/regulations.

Campbell, Trevor A. "The Making of an Organic Intellectual: Walter Rodney (1942–1980)."

Latin American Perspectives: The Caribbean and Africa 8, no. 1 (1981).

Chang, Cindy. "Baca Shifts Course on Compliance with Deportation Program." *Los Angeles Times,* December 6, 2012.

Chang, Nancy, Barbara J. Olshansky, and Rachel Meeropol et al. "Ibrahim Turkmen et al. Against John Ashcroft et al.: Third Amended Class Action Complaint and Demand for Jury Trial" (2004). Center for Constitutional Rights. www.ccrjustice.org.

Chappell, Bill. "Alabama Agrees to Permanently Gut Immigration Law." National Public Radio, October 29, 2013. www.npr.org/blogs.

Checkland, S. G. "John Gladstone as Trader and Planter." *Economic History Review* 7, part 2 (1954).

"The Chinese Exclusion Case, 130 U.S. 581" (1889). Supreme Court of the United States, Justia U.S. Supreme Court Center. supreme.justia.com.

Clark, Tom C. "Shaughnessy v. Mezei, 345 U.S. 206" (1953). Supreme Court of the United States.

"Comprehensive Immigration Reform." United States Senate Committee on the Judiciary, May 22, 2013. www.judiciary.senate.gov.

County of Passaic Procurement Center (NJ). "RFP to Provide Food Services and Food Services Management for the Passaic County Jail." service.govdelivery.com.

Cowen, Richard. "Conditions at Passaic County Still Crowded, Shabby as Improvements Proceed." *The Record* (Bergen County, NJ), 2010.

Cushman, Jr., John H. "Obama Says New Federal Policy Limiting Deportations is 'More Just'." *New York Times,* June 15, 2012.

Danticat, Edwidge. *Brother, I'm Dying.* New York: Alfred A. Knopf, 2007.

Davis, Peggy Cooper. *Neglected Stories: The Constitution and Family Values.* New York: Hill and Wang, 1997.

"Deaths and Mortality." Centers for Disease Control and Prevention, 2011. www.cdc.gov.

DeVivo, Dan, and Valeria Fernandez. *Two Americans* (film), 2011. www.twoamericans.com.

Dolnick, Sam. "Removal of Priest's Cases Exposes Deep Hole in Immigration Courts." *New York Times,* July 7, 2011.

Donohue, Pete. "Road-Rage Slay Suspect: Mom 'Deserved' to Die." *New York Daily News,* June 6, 1998.

Dow, Mark. *American Gulag: Inside U.S. Immigration Prisons.* Berkeley, CA: University of California Press, 2004.

Evans, Robert D. Letter to John B. Torres, Acting Director, Office of Detention and Removal Operations, U.S. Immigration and Customs Enforcement, Re: Detainee Transfers from Passaic County Jail, New Jersey, 2006.

"Farouk Abdel-Muhti v. John D. Ashcroft," Civil Action No. 1: Cv-03-0927 (2004). Administrative Office of the U.S. Courts. www.pamd.uscourts.gov.

Finnegan, William. "Sheriff Joe." *The New Yorker* LXXXV, no. 21 (2009).

Fisher, Janon. "Stateless, Man Avoids Deportation from U.S." *New York Times,* April 14, 2004.

Fuentes, Julio M. "Auguste v. Ridge No. 04-1739" (2005). Third Circuit United States Court of Appeals. caselaw.findlaw.com

"FY 2012: ICE Announces Year-End Removal Numbers, Highlights Focus on Key Priorities and Issues New National Detainer Guidance to Further Focus Resources," 2012. U.S. Department of Homeland Security, Immigration and Customs Enforcement. www.ice.gov.

"FY 2013: ICE Immigration Removals," 2013. U.S. Department of Homeland Security, Immigration and Customs Enforcement. www.ice.gov.

Ghesquiere, Francis, et al. "Guyana: Preliminary Damage and Needs Assessment Following the Intense Flooding of January 2005" (February 14, 2005). The World Bank. www.siteresources.worldbank.org

Giovanni, Janine di. "Life During Wartime." *New York Times,* July 21, 2012.

Glaberson, William. "Are Lawyers for the Poor Inadequate?" *New York Times,* March 16, 2010.

Goldberg, Emily B., Christopher J. Mitchie, et al. "Angel Colon, et al., Plaintiffs, v. Passaic County Jail, et al." (2008).

Golub, Andrew Lang, and Bruce D. Johnson. "Crack's Decline: Some Surprises Across U.S. Cities." *National Institute of Justice, Research in Brief,* 1997.

Gopnik, Adam. "The Caging of America: Why Do We Lock Up So Many People?" *The New Yorker* LXXXVII, no. 46 (January 30, 2012).

Gorlin, David C. "Evaluating Punishment in Purgatory: The Need to Separate Pretrial Detainees' Conditions-of-Confinement Claims from Inadequate Eighth Amendment Analysis." *Michigan Law Review* 108 (2009).

"Government 'Disappears' NY Palestinian Activist to Atlanta." Philadelphia Independent Media Center, April 10, 2004.

Gray, Horace. "Fong Yue Ting v. United States, 149 U.S. 698, 707" (1893). Supreme Court of the United States.

Guttentag, Lucas. "Immigrants' Rights in the Courts and Congress: Constitutional Protections and the Rule of Law After 9/11." *Washington University Journal of Law and Policy* 25, no. 11 (2007).

Guyana Human Rights Association. "Ambivalent About Violence: A Report on Fatal Shootings by the Police in Guyana, 1980 to 2001" (2002). United Nations High Commissioner for Human Rights. www2.ohchr.org.

Guyana Human Rights Association. "Observations on Occasion of Consideration of Guyana's First Report to the Un Committee on the Convention Against Torture," November 2006. United Nations High Commissioner for Human Rights. www2.ohchr.org.

"Guyana's Economic Decline During 1985–1991," October 21, 2009. www.guyana.org.

Hakim, Danny, and Nina Bernstein. "New Paterson Policy May Reduce Deportations." *New York Times,* May 3, 2010.

Hancock, J. "The People &C., Respondent, v. Carlos Andujas, Appellant" (1992). Cornell University Law School Legal Information Institute. www.law.cornell.edu.

Hanson, Gordon H. *The Economics and Policy of Illegal Immigration in the United States.* Washington, DC: Migration Policy Institute, 2009.

"Hatch Presses Homeland Security on Weber Jail ICE Audit," October 20, 2011. Orrin Hatch, United States Senator for Utah. www.hatch.senate.gov.

Hayden, Katharine S. (United States District Judge). "United States of America v. Franz Copeland Sutton, Defendant: Opinion on Defendant's Application for a Downward Variance as a Federal Detainee Housed in Passaic County Jail," Case 2:07-cr-00426-KSH Document 17 (October 25, 2007).

"Hearing on: H.R. 2497, the 'Hinder the Administration's Legalization Temptation Act'" (July 26, 2011). United States House of Representatives Judiciary Committee, Subcommittee on Immigration Policy and Enforcement. www.judiciary.house.gov/hearings.

Henry, Samantha. "Terror Claims Against NJ Muslim Leader Rejected." *USA Today,* September 4, 2008.

Hernandez, Sarah. "Mira Loma Riot." *LA Daily Journal,* April 23, 2008.

Hing, Bill Ong. *Deporting Our Souls: Values, Morality and Immigration Policy.* New York: Cambridge University Press, 2006.

Holbrook, Ames. *The Deporter: One Agent's Struggle Against the U.S. Government's Refusal to Expel Criminal Aliens.* New York: Sentinel, 2007.

Hollett, David. *Passage from India to El Dorado: Guyana and the Great Migration.* Teaneck, NJ: Fairleigh Dickinson University Press, 1999.

"House Vote on Passage: H.R. 3012: Fairness for High-Skilled Immigrants Act." www.govtrack.us.

"H.R. 2278: Strengthen and Fortify Enforcement (Safe) Act," 2013. U.S. House of Representatives Government Printing Office. www.gpo.gov.

"Human Development Report 2000; Trends in Human Development and Per Capita Income," October 21, 2009. United Nations. www.nationsencyclopedia.com.

"Human Rights Violations in the Immigrant Detention System," 2010. Ninth Session of the Working Group on the UPR Human Rights Council. Ed. United Nations Universal Periodic Review.

"ICE Detainers: Frequently Asked Questions." U.S. Department of Homeland Security, Immigration and Customs Enforcement. www.ice.gov.

"ICE/DRO Detention Standard: Medical Care," December 2, 2008. Immigration and Naturalization Service, U.S. Department of Homeland Security, Bureau of Immigration and Customs Enforcement. www.ice.gov.

"In Re C-V-T, Respondent" (1998). U.S. Department of Justice, Executive Office for Immigration Review, Board of Immigration Appeals. www.justice.gov.

"In Re Jesus Collado-Munoz, Respondent," File A31 021 716 (1998). U.S. Department of Justice, Executive Office for Immigration Review, Board of Immigration Appeals.

"INS Detention Standard: Admission and Release," 2000. Immigration and Naturalization Service, U.S. Department of Homeland Security, Bureau of Immigration and Customs Enforcement. www.ice.gov.

"INS Detention Standard: Hunger Strikes," November 1, 2011. Immigration and Naturalization Service, U.S. Department of Homeland Security, Bureau of Immigration and Customs Enforcement. www.ice.gov.

"INS Detention Standard: Medical Care," September 20, 2000. Immigration and Naturalization Service, U.S. Department of Homeland Security, Bureau of Immigration and Customs Enforcement. www.ice.gov.

"INS Detention Standard: Recreation," 2000. Immigration and Naturalization Service, U.S. Department of Homeland Security, Bureau of Immigration and Customs Enforcement. www.ice.gov.

"International Fellowship of Bible Churches, Inc.," January 7, 2010. www.ifbc.org.

Johnson, Laura R. "The People of the State of New York, Hemnauth Mohabir, Defendant: Notice of Motion to Vacate Judgment," 2003.

"Judge Alberto J. Riefkohl," 2008. Eds. Susan Long and David Burnham. Transactional Records Access Clearing House, Syracuse University. trac.syr.edu.

"Judge Approves Agreement to Overhaul Passaic County Jail's Inhumane Conditions," 2012. ACLU of New Jersey. www.aclu-nj.org.

Kaiser, David, and Lovisa Stannow. "Prison Rape and the Government." New York Review of Books, March 24, 2011.

Kalhan, Anil. "Rethinking Immigration Detention." Columbia Law Review Sidebar 110 (2010).

Kanstroom, Daniel. Deportation Nation: Outsiders in American History. Cambridge, MA: Harvard University Press, 2007.

Keller, Karen. "Citing Subpar Meals, Sheriff Fires Jail's Food Provider." NJ Herald News, February 22, 2006.

Kennedy, Anthony. "Arizona et al. v. United States, No. 11-182" (2012). Supreme Court of the United States. www.supremecourt.gov/opinions.

Kennedy, Anthony. "Brown, Governor of California, et al. v. Plata et al.," No. 09-1233 (2011).

Kerwin, Donald, and Serena Yi-Ying Lin. "Immigration Detention: Can ICE Meet Its Legal Imperatives and Case Management Responsibilities?" Washington, DC: Migration Policy Institute, 2009.

Kohli, Aarti, Peter L. Markowitz, and Lisa Chavez. "Research Report—Secure Communities by the Numbers: An Analysis of Demographics and Due Process." University of California, Berkeley, 2011.

Kurzban, Ira J. Kurzban's Immigration Law Sourcebook, 12th ed. Washington, DC: American Immigration Council, 2010.

Lacey, Marc. "U.S. Finds Pervasive Bias Against Latinos by Arizona Sheriff." *New York Times,* December 15, 2011.

Lai, Walton Look. *Indentured Labor, Caribbean Sugar: Chinese and Indian Migrants to the British West Indies, 1838–1918.* Baltimore: Johns Hopkins University Press, 1993.

Latham & Watkins LLP. "Review of ICE Detention Standards at Middlesex County Jail in New Jersey," 2003.

Lee, Margaret Mikyung. *Legal Ethics in Immigration Matters: Legal Representation and Unauthorized Practice of Law* (CRS Report for Congress). Washington, DC: Congressional Research Service, 2009.

"The Legal Aid Society Annual Report 2010." Legal Aid Society of New York. www.legal-aid.org.

Legomsky, Stephen H. "Immigration Law and the Principle of Plenary Congressional Power." *Supreme Court Review* 1984 (1985).

Legomsky, Stephen H. *Immigration and the Judiciary: Law and Politics in Britain and America.* New York: Oxford University Press, 1987.

Legomsky, Stephen H. "Fear and Loathing in Congress and the Courts: Immigration and Judicial Review." *Texas Law Review* 78 No. 7 (2000).

Legomsky, Stephen H. "The New Path of Immigration Law: Asymmetric Incorporation of Criminal Justice Norms." *Washington and Lee Law Review* 64:2 (2007).

Lelyveld, Joseph. *Great Soul: Mahatma Gandhi and His Struggle with India.* New York: Alfred A. Knopf, 2011.

Levine, Harry G. "Testimony Regarding Pending and Proposed Legislation to Collect DNA from All People Convicted of a Misdemeanor in New York State and Also Regarding New York City's Epidemic of Marijuana Possession Arrests," May 31, 2007. www.drugpolicy.org.

Levine, Mark. "Holy Smoke," May 8, 2007. www.beliefnet.com.

Lippman, Matthew. *Contemporary Criminal Law: Cases, Concepts and Controversies.* Thousand Oaks, CA: Sage, 2008.

Liptak, Adam. "'We the People' Loses Appeal with People Around the World." *New York Times,* February 6, 2012.

"List of Deaths in ICE Custody, October 2003–July 28, 2011." ICE Health Services Corps. www.ice.gov.

Loder, Asjylyn. "Sheriff Throws Feds Out of Passaic County Jail!" *NJ Herald News,* August 17, 2005.

Lonegan, Bryan. "American Diaspora: The Deportation of Lawful Residents from the United States and the Destruction of Their Families." *New York University Review of Law & Social Change* 32.1 (2007).

Lonegan, Bryan. "In the Matter of Hemnauth Mohabir: Memorandum of Law in Support of Respondents' Motion to Reopen and for a Stay of Removal," 2003.

Lonegan, Bryan. Letter to Mr. Robert Margist at the Bureau of Immigration and Customs Enforcement, March 10, 2004.

Lonegan, Bryan. "Withdrawal of Motion to Reconsider," October 31, 2003.

Lute, Jane Holl, Deputy Secretary of Homeland Security. Letter to Michael J. Wishnie, Esq., Clinical Professor of Law, Yale University and Paromita Shah, Esq., Associate Director, National Immigration Project of the National Lawyers Guild, 2009.

Mangru, Basdeo. *Indians in Guyana: A Concise History from Their Arrival to the Present.* Chicago: Adams Press, 2000.

Markowitz, Peter L., Jojo Annobil, et al. "Accessing Justice: The Availability and Adequacy of Counsel in Immigration Proceedings." *Cardozo Law Review* 357 (2011).

McWhirter, Robert James. *The Criminal Lawyer's Guide to Immigration Law: Questions and Answers.* Chicago: ABA Publishing, 2006.

"Medications for Treating Hypertension." *Harvard Women's Health Watch,* August 2009.

Meeropol, Rachel. Letter to Hemnauth Mohabir, September 19, 2003.

Meeropol, Rachel. Letter to Hemnauth Mohabir, October 22, 2003.

Meeropol, Rachel. "Phone Call with INS" (memo to files at the Center for Constitutional Rights), 2003.

Meeropol, Rachel. "Visit with Passaic Detainees" (memo to files at the Center for Constitutional Rights), 2003.

Miller, Jonathan. "Calling Off the Dogs." *New York Times,* December 5, 2004.

Miller, Teresa A. "Citizenship and Severity: Recent Immigration Reforms and the New Penology." *Georgetown Immigration Law Review* 17 (2003). Cited in Legomsky, "The New Path of Immigration Law."

Milne, R. S. "Bicommunal Systems: Guyana, Malaysia, Fiji." *Publius* 18, no. 2 (1988).

"The Mira Loma Detention Center Mess." *Los Angeles Times,* October 17, 2012.

Morawetz, Nancy. "Understanding the Impact of the 1996 Deportation Laws and the Limited Scope of Proposed Reforms." *Harvard Law Review* 113 (2000).

Morton, John. "Civil Immigration Enforcement: Guidance on the Use of Detainers in the Federal, State, Local, and Tribal Criminal Justice Systems" (memo), December 21, 2012.

Motomura, Hiroshi. *Americans in Waiting: The Lost Story of Immigration and Citizenship in the United States.* New York: Oxford University Press, 2006.

Motomura, Hiroshi. Testimony in "Shortfalls of the 1996 Immigration Reform Legislation." Hearing Before the Subcommittee on Immigration, Citizenship, Refugees, Border Security, and International Law, U.S. House of Representatives Committee on the Judiciary. Washington, DC: U.S. Government Printing Office, 2007.

Nagourney, Adam. "Across Arizona, Immigration Ire on Back Burner." *New York Times,* February 26, 2012.

Newton, Jim. *Justice for All: Earl Warren and the Nation He Made.* New York: Riverhead Books, 2006.

"New York City Department of City Planning Jamaica Presentation," August 31, 2007. New York City. www.nyc.gov.

Nollkaemper, André. *Domestic Courts and the Rule of International Law.* New York: Oxford University Press, 2011.

Obama, Barack. "Transcript of Speech on Immigration Policy." *New York Times,* 2012.

Office of Inspector General. "Conditions of Confinement at Passaic County Jail in Paterson, New Jersey," Chapter 8 in *A Review of the Treatment of Aliens Held on Immigration Charges in Connection with the Investigation of the September 11 Attacks.* United States Department of Justice, 2003.

Office of the United Nations High Commissioner for Refugees. "Revised Guidelines on Applicable Criteria and Standards Relating to the Detention of Asylum-Seekers," 1999.

Onishi, Norimitsu. "Neighborhood Report: Glendale; Finally, That's All He Wrote." *New York Times,* November 20, 1994.

Outten-Mills, Deborah, et al. "The Performance of 287(g) Agreements." Office of the Inspector General, U.S. Department of Homeland Security, OIG-10-63, 2010.

Outten-Mills, Deborah, M. Faizul Islam, and Wynne Kelch. "Removals Involving Illegal Alien Parents of United States Citizen Children." Office of Inspector General, U.S. Department of Homeland Security, OIG-09-15, 2009.

Parker, Alison. "Forced Apart: Families Separated and Immigrants Harmed by United States Deportation Policy." New York: Human Rights Watch, 2007. www.hrw.org.

"Parole of Aliens into the United States," October 5, 2011. Washington, DC: National Archives and Records Administration.

"People v. Colon" (1997), Supreme Court of the United States, Appellate Division, First Department, New York. caselaw.findlaw.com.

Powell, Lewis F. "Fiallo v. Bell, 430 U.S. 787" No. 75-6297 (1977), Supreme Court of the United States.

Preston, Julia. "Beside a Path to Citizenship, a New Course for Immigration." *New York Times,* April 17, 2013.

Preston, Julia. "Illegal Immigrants in U.S. Face Increased Deportations." *New York Times,* May 1, 2007.

Preston, Julia. "Obama Policy on Deporting Used Unevenly." *New York Times,* November 13, 2011.

Preston, Julia. "U.S. to Review Cases Seeking Deportations." *New York Times,* November 17, 2011.

Preston, Julia. "Young Immigrants Say It's Obama's Time to Act." *New York Times,* November 30, 2012.

Priest, Dana, Amy Goldstein, and Scott Pelley. *Detention in America. 60 Minutes* video, 2008.

Priest, Dana, Amy Goldstein, and Washington Post Staff Writers. "System of Neglect: As Tighter Immigration Policies Strain Federal Agencies, the Detainees in Their Care Often Pay a Heavy Cost." *Washington Post,* May 11, 2008.

"Prison Litigation Reform Act: Legislative History." Ed. Margo Schlanger, University of Michigan Law School. www.law.umich.edu.

Ramnarine, Tina Karina. "'Indian' Music in the Diaspora: Case Studies of 'Chutney' in Trinidad and in London." *British Journal of Ethnomusicology* 5 (1996).

"Reckless NJ Police Convoy Escapes VA Justice," 2006. www.vatrafficlaw.com.

Rehnquist, William. "Bell v. Wolfish, 441 U.S. 520" (1979). Supreme Court of the United States. caselaw.lp.findlaw.com.

Review of *Immigrant Detainees: The New Sex Abuse Crisis* by David Kaiser and Lovisa Stannow. New York Review of Books, November 23, 2011. www.nybooks.com.

Richsbourg, John S. "Liberty and Security: The Yin and Yang of Immigration Law." *University of Memphis Law Review* 33 (2003).

Riefkohl, Alberto H. "In Removal Proceedings of: Mohabir, Hennauth [sic], Decision of the Immigration Judge" (2002). Executive Office for Immigration Review, U.S. Department of Justice.

Rodriguez, Cristina M. "The Integrated Regime of Immigration Regulation." In Suárez-Orozco et al., eds., *Writing Immigration: Scholars and Journalists in Dialogue.*

Rodway, James. *History of British Guiana from the Year 1668 to the Present Time* Vol. III, 1833–1893. Georgetown, Demerara: J. Thomson, 1894.

Romero, Anthony D., et al. "America's Disappeared: Seeking International Justice for Immigrants Detained After September 11," January 2004. American Civil Liberties Union.

"Rules of Professional Conduct," 1984. New Jersey Courts. www.judiciary.state.nj.

"S. 744: Border Security, Economic Opportunity, and Immigration Modernization Act," 2013. U.S. Government Printing Office. www.govtrack.us.

Savage, Charles. "Vetted Judges More Likely to Reject Asylum Bids." *New York Times,* August 23, 2008.

Scalia, Antonin. "Arizona et al. v. United States, No. 11-182, Opinion of Scalia, J." (2012). Supreme Court of the United States. www.supremecourt.gov.

Schriro, Dora. "Immigration Detention Overview and Recommendations," 2009. U.S. Department of Homeland Security, Immigration and Customs Enforcement.

"Secure Communities and ICE Deportation: A Failed System?" Transactional Records Access Clearinghouse, Syracuse University, 2014. trac.syr.edu.

"Secure Communities: IDENT/IAFIS Interoperability, Monthly Statistics Through August 31, 2011," 2011. U.S. Immigration and Customs Enforcement. www.ice.gov.

Seghetti, Lisa M., Karma Ester, and Michael John Garcia. "Enforcing Immigration Law: The Role of State and Local Law Enforcement." Washington, DC: Congressional Research Service, 2009. www.au.af.mil.

Semple, Kirk, and Tim Eaton. "Detention for Immigrants That Looks Less Like Prison." *New York Times,* March 13, 2012.

Shea, Thomas J. "CBP Inspections at JFK." *Immigration Daily,* 2004.

Shusterman, Carl. "New Deportation Priorities Will Bring Focus to ICE Enforcement Efforts." Shusterman's Immigration Update December 2011 newsletter.

Simanski, John, and Lesley M. Sapp. "Immigration Enforcement Actions: 2011." *Homeland Security Annual Report* (2012).

Simchi-Levi, Yuval. "The Agency Defense: Can the Legislature Help?" *Buffalo Law Review* 59 (2011).

Siskin, Alison. *Immigration-Related Detention: Current Legislative Issues* (CRS Report for Congress). Washington, DC: Congressional Research Service, 2012.

Smith, Aaron. "Madoff Arrives at N.C. Prison," July 14, 2009. CNNMoney. money.cnn.com.

Smith, Huston. *The World's Religions.* 50th Anniversary ed. New York: Harper One, 1991.

Smith, Marian L. "Overview of INS History to 1998," 2009. U.S. Citizenship and Immigration Services. www.uscis.gov.

Snow, G. Murray, United States District Judge. "Manuel De Jesus Ortega, on Behalf of Himself and All Others Similarly Situated; et al. Plaintiffs, v. Joseph M. Arpaio, in His Individual and Official Capacity as Sheriff of Maricopa County, AZ; et al., Defendants" (May 24, 2013). United States District Court for the State of Arizona. www.aclu.org.

"Sodexho Spotlights Dock3," 2002. Eds. AllBusiness.com, Dun & Bradstreet, Nielsen Business Media, Inc. www.allbusiness.com.

Sotomayor, Sonia. "329 F.3d: Don Beharry, Also Known as Donald Beharry, Petitioner-Appellee, v. John Ashcroft, Attorney General of the United States" (2003). Second Circuit United States Court of Appeals. law.justia.com.

Souter, Justice David. "Jose Antonio Lopez, Petitioner v. Alberto R. Gonzales, Attorney General No. 05-547" (2006). Supreme Court of the United States. www.supremecourt.gov.

Spencer, Stephen. *A Dream Deferred: Guyana, Identities Under the Colonial Shadow.* London: Hansib, 2007.

Stevens, Jacqueline. "Lawless Courts." *The Nation,* November 8, 2010.

Stevens, John Paul. "Immigration and Naturalization Service v. St. Cyr, 533 U.S. 289" (2001). Supreme Court of the United States.

Stevens, John Paul. "Jose Padilla, Petitioner v. Kentucky" (2010). Supreme Court of the United States. www.supremecourt.gov/opinions.

Stevens, John Paul. "Mathews, Secretary of Health, Education and Welfare V. Diaz et al., 426 U.S. 67" No. 73-1046 (1976). Supreme Court of the United States.

Suárez-Orozco, Marcelo M., Vivian Louie, and Roberto Suro, eds. *Writing Immigration: Scholars and Journalists in Dialogue.* Berkeley and Los Angeles: University of California Press, 2011.

Supreme Court of the United States. "Immigration and Naturalization Service v. St. Cyr, 533 U.S. 289" (2001). Legal Information Institute, Cornell University Law School. www.law.cornell.edu.

Supreme Court of the United States, "Moore v. City of East Cleveland 431 U.S. 494" (1977). caselaw.lp.findlaw.com.

Supreme Court of the United States, "Santosky v. Kramer (Syllabus)" (1982). Legal Information Institute, Cornell University Law School. www.law.cornell.edu.

"Table H-3. Mean Household Income Received by Each Fifth and Top 5 Percent: 1967 to 2008." U.S. Census Bureau. www.census.gov.

Tangeman, Anthony S. "Strip Search Guidelines for Admissions to Detention Facility" (memo), April 15, 2003.

Tassel, Fabrice. "Sarkozy Désintègre L'Immigration." *Libération,* March 8, 2012.

Tavernese, Sabrina. "For Medicare, Immigrants Offer Surplus, Study Finds." *New York Times,* May 29, 2013.

"Tent City Jail." Phoenix, AZ: Maricopa County Sheriff's Office, November 11, 2010. www.mcso.org.

Terrazas, Aaron, Demetrios G. Papademetriou, and Marc R. Rosenblum. *Evolving Demographic and Human-Capital Trends in Mexico and Central America and Their Implications for Regional Migration.* Washington, DC: Migration Policy Institute and Woodrow Wilson International Center for Scholars, 2011.

Thomas, Roger, Deputy Warden, York County Prison. "Division of Immigration Health Services (DIHS)" (memo), November 28, 2005.

Thronson, David B. "Choiceless Choices: Deportation and the Parent-Child Relationship." *Nevada Law Journal* 6:1165 (2006).

"TRAC Immigration: Huge Increase in Transfers of ICE Detainees," 2009. TRAC Reports, Inc., Syracuse University. www.trac.syr.edu.

"Transcripts: Lou Dobbs Tonight January 3, 2006," 2006. www.cnn.com.

Travers, Suzanne. "Immigration Detainees Move from Passaic Jail to Hudson." *The Record* (Bergen County, NJ), September 24, 2003.

Tumlin, Karen, Linton Joaquin, and Ranjana Natarajan. "A Broken System: Confidential Reports Reveal Failures in U.S. Immigrant Detention Centers." National Immigration Law Center, 2009.

"212 Crimes Involving Moral Turpitude." U.S. Department of Justice. www.justice.gov.

"United States v. Couto" (2002). United States Court of Appeals for the Second Circuit (New York). www.openjurist.org.

Urofsky, Melvin I. *Louis D. Brandeis: A Life.* New York: Pantheon Books, 2009.

U.S. Department of Justice, Executive Office for Immigration Review. "The Executive Office for Immigration Review Swears in 23 New Immigration Judges (News Release)," 2010.

U.S. Department of Justice, Executive Office for Immigration Review. "Observing Immigration Court Hearings (Fact Sheet)," 2010.

U.S. Department of Justice, Executive Office for Immigration Review. "Representation of Aliens in Immigration Proceedings: Attorneys, Recognized Organizations, and Accredited Representatives; Qualified Representatives; Free Legal Service Providers (Fact Sheet)," 2010.

U.S. Immigration and Customs Enforcement. "2008 Operations Manual: Performance-Based National Detention Standards (PBNDS)," November 26, 2010. U.S. Department of Homeland Security. www.ice.gov.

"U.S. Immigration and Naturalization Service — Populating a Nation: A History of Immigration and Naturalization." U.S. Department of Homeland Security, Customs and Border Control. www.cbp.gov.

Virtue, Paul W. Testimony in "Shortfalls of the 1996 Immigration Reform Legislation." Hearing Before the Subcommittee on Immigration, Citizenship, Refugees, Border Security, and International Law, U.S. House of Representatives Committee on the Judiciary. Washington, DC: U.S. Government Printing Office, 2007.

Wheeler, William, and Ayman Oghanna. "After Liberation, Nowhere to Run." *New York Times,* October 29, 2011.

Wilkinson, Francis, and David Shipley, eds. "Alabama Immigration Law Robs Citizens of Their Own Future: View." Bloomberg View, October 20, 2011. www.bloombergview.com.

"Wong Wing v. United States" 163 U.S. 228 (1896). Supreme Court of the United States. www.caselaw.lp.findlaw.com.

Yogananda, Paramahansa. *Autobiography of a Yogi.* New York: The Philosophical Library, 1946.

Yoshikawa, Hirokazu, and Carola Suárez-Orozco. "Deporting Parents Hurts Kids." *New York Times,* April 20, 2012.

Young, Rick. "Lost in Detention, Reported by Maria Hinojosa." *Frontline,* WGBH Boston, ed. Leslie Atkins, October 19, 2011. www.pbs.org/wgbh/pages/frontline.

Zheng, Eddy, ed. *Other: An Asian and Pacific Islander Prisoners' Anthology.* Oakland, CA: Asian Prisoner Support Committee, 2007.

Zupan, Linda L. *Encyclopedia of Crime and Punishment,* Vol. 4. Ed. David Levinson. Thousand Oaks, CA: Sage Publications, 2002.

Zwerdling, Daniel. "Profile: Immigrant Detainees Claim Brutal Treatment and Abuse by Guards and Dogs at the Passaic County Jail in New Jersey." *All Things Considered,* PBS, hosts Robert Seigel and Melissa Block, November 17, 2004.

Zwerdling, Daniel. "Profile: Investigation of a Case Where Guards at the Hudson County Jail in New Jersey Allegedly Assaulted Two Immigrant Detainees, Part Two." *All Things Considered,* PBS, hosts Robert Seigel and Melissa Block, November 18, 2004.

Zwerdling, Daniel, and Tom Casciato. "Investigating Abuse." *The Leonard Lopate Show,* WNYC New York, September 14, 2006. www.wnyc.org.

Zwerdling, Daniel, et al., *Exposé: An Inside Job* (excerpt). PBS video, 2007.

INDEX

www.ingramcontent.com/pod-product-compliance
Lightning Source LLC
Chambersburg PA
CBHW022132020426
42334CB00015B/854